THE GERMAN TRADITION
IN LITERATURE
1871-1945

BY THE SAME AUTHOR

Goethe the Alchemist
(Cambridge, 1952)

Kafka's Castle
(Cambridge, 1956)

The Twentieth Century Views Kafka
an anthology (Prentice-Hall, 1963)

Brecht
(Oliver and Boyd, 1961)

An Introduction to German Poetry
(Cambridge, 1965)

THE GERMAN TRADITION
IN LITERATURE
1871-1945

BY

RONALD GRAY

*Fellow of Emmanuel College and
Lecturer in German in the
University of Cambridge*

CAMBRIDGE
AT THE UNIVERSITY PRESS
1965

PUBLISHED BY
THE SYNDICS OF THE CAMBRIDGE UNIVERSITY PRESS

Bentley House, 200 Euston Road, London, N.W. 1
American Branch: 32 East 57th Street, New York, N.Y. 10022
West African Office: P.O. Box 33, Ibadan, Nigeria

©

CAMBRIDGE UNIVERSITY PRESS

1965

Printed in Great Britain at the University Printing House, Cambridge
(Brooke Crutchley, University Printer)

LIBRARY OF CONGRESS CATALOGUE
CARD NUMBER: 65–17206

CONTENTS

CONTENTS

PART IV RESHAPING THE TRADITION

PREFACE

I have tried to keep in mind the words of Dr F. R. Leavis that 'no "sociology of literature" and no attempt to relate literary studies with sociological will yield much profit unless informed and controlled by a real and intelligent interest—a first-hand critical interest—in literature', and that 'a real literary interest is an interest in man, society and civilization, and its boundaries cannot be drawn...'. This accounts for the structure of the present book, which begins with a broad survey of German literature against the political background of the twentieth century, and goes on to close analysis of 'words on the page', to turn in the final chapter to the inquiry: what course is best suited to German literature now, to what extent can it rely on the tradition to which most of its renowned achievements belong, and to what extent must that tradition be reshaped or reformulated?

Some of the ideas in this book were suggested by Professor E. M. Butler's inaugural lecture, referred to on p. 369; others developed in parallel with the investigations by Professor W. H. Bruford, mentioned on the same page. However, the particular formulations I have reached are my own, and I would not wish to imply that either of these former occupants of Cambridge chairs necessarily shared any of my views. Humphry Trevelyan read the manuscript and gave me comments which I was glad to have; as did the staff of the Cambridge University Press, to whom I should like to offer my thanks. I would also thank the many friends and pupils who have by discussion helped me to see more clearly what it was that I wanted to say.

R. D. G.

Cambridge
June 1965

ACKNOWLEDGEMENTS

For permission to reproduce copyright material, acknowledgement is made to the following: S. Fischer Verlag (passages from works by Thomas Mann and Hugo von Hofmannsthal); Martin Secker and Warburg Ltd, and Alfred A. Knopf, Inc. (translations of passages from works by Thomas Mann); Routledge, Kegan Paul Ltd, and Bollinger Verlag (translations of passages from *Der Schwierige* by Hugo von Hofmannsthal); Insel-Verlag (passages of prose and poetry by Rainer Maria Rilke); The Hogarth Press and New Directions Inc. of New York (translations of Rilke by J. B. Leishman (*The Sonnets to Orpheus*) and by J. B. Leishman and Stephen Spender (*The Duino Elegies*)).

THE GERMAN TRADITION

So they loved, as love in twain
Had the essence but in one;
Two distincts, division none:
Number there in love was slain.

The Phoenix and Turtle affords the simplest indication of the present theme. Nowhere in English literature is there any closer approach to the mystical strain in German thought which makes itself felt throughout the centuries. 'Mystical' is not quite the word—it is a strain which has to do with the mystic's absorbed identity with the godhead, and yet often finds expression in quite unmystical and even unreligious fields. The 'coincidentia oppositorum' of the fifteenth-century Nicholas of Cusa, Plotinus's 'flight of the alone to the alone', Luther's belief in a God who 'works by contraries', all these have to do with it, but so does the belief of the German Romantics in 'polarity', the Hegelian contrasts of thesis and antithesis, and the dialectical pattern of Marxism, adapted from this feature of Hegel's philosophy. And so does the combination of 'male and female' world-principles found in the Tao of Chinese religion.

One cannot help noticing how frequently these opposites, or often merely so-called opposites, recur in German thought and literature. They are found in the works of the seventeenth-century Silesian mystic, Jacob Boehme, in the form of the 'philosophic Sulphur and Mercury', which he borrowed from the alchemists and transformed into symbols of the Wrath and the Mercy of God, the Father and the Son, the Bridegroom and his Bride; and again half a century later in his compatriot Angelus Silesius. They come again in the Romantics, especially in Schelling, for whom the mysterious force of electricity, with its 'positive' and 'negative' poles seemed to be the very manifestation of the World-Soul. From this usage comes the name, 'polarity', by which these systematizations are often characterized. It is not until the Romantic age, however, or to be precise the age of Goethe which begins a few decades earlier, that the notion of polarity becomes really widespread. It is very familiar to Goethe himself, who had it from both the alchemists and from neo-Platonists like Giordano Bruno and perhaps Plotinus; it is most familiar to us in the 'Zwei Seelen' speech of Faust, in which he contrasts the working of the one soul within him, clutching at earthly life in all its poverty, and that of the other soul which soars aloft to reach Elysium. It is equally prominent in the Second Part of Goethe's masterpiece, where the marriage of Faust and Helen is a symbolical representation of the union between these two souls: the Northern with the Southern, the Gothic striving for the infinite with the Classical acceptance of earthliness, intellect with perfect bodily beauty, Germany with Greece. But it is also very noticeable in the play *Torquato Tasso*, where almost every speech seems designed to underline the contrast between the poet and the practical man of affairs, between heaven and earth, inspirational ecstasy and the daily round, doubt and certainty, and where once again the desired ideal is some fusion of all these, such as, it has often been felt, Goethe experienced in his own life.

From Goethe onwards the flood begins. Schiller, similarly attracted to neo-Platonist and theosophical speculation in his youth, continually employs a mode of thought in which all things are divided among two categories (and no more). Not only did he contrast himself as the 'sentimentalisch' poet—the poet constantly in search of Nature, constantly dissatisfied, constantly struggling—with Goethe as the 'naiv' poet, at one with Nature, serenely above all conflicts and quests, at home in an unquestioned world. He extended these two opposites to embrace all poets whatsoever in two universal, 'polar' categories, and he developed something very similar in his ethical theory, which rests on the contrast between 'Duty' and its opposite, 'Inclination'. Once again, there are for Schiller two types of ethical perfection, that of the 'Beautiful Soul' whose Duty always coincides with Inclination, and that of the 'Sublime Soul' in which such coincidence is the result of struggle and effort.

The similarities can be simplified down to the one similarity, that both Goethe and Schiller work with a duality which they seek to bring to a singularity or unity. Such a simplification is too simple, yet it will serve for the moment to indicate how many more German poets and thinkers of the late eighteenth and the nineteenth century thought on parallel lines. In Hölderlin's poetry there is the contrasted symbolism of Christ and Dionysus and the attempt at their fusion, a symbolism comparable to that of Heine, in the concepts of the life-denying 'Nazarene' and the life-affirming 'Hellene', as well as to the 'Apolline' and the 'Dionysian' in Nietzsche, and the combination of 'Ecstasy' and 'Clarity' which Stefan George sought to embody. (Another division of the same kind, outside the field of German literature, is in Ibsen's *Emperor and Galilean*.) Schopenhauer sees the whole world as both the Will, brutal, blind and beyond all morality, and as the Imagination, reflecting and criticizing the Will in the name of morality. Thomas Mann sees the Germany of his day in terms of an unreflective (and hence in a way amoral), active, practical society of burghers, opposed to a highly reflective, morally critical but impractical group of artists and intellectuals, whose comments are incapable of doing more than make society aware of its own nature. Through all these there runs the notion of an untrammelled enjoyment of earthly existence, opposed to an ineffectual, passive, even negative denial of the worthiness of such existence. And almost everywhere the polar opposites return.

Coupled with the notion of 'polarity', however, there is very often the notion known to Goethe and some others as 'Steigerung', meaning 'intensification' or 'heightening', but perhaps better known in the Hegelian form as 'synthesis'. It refers of course to the fusion of the opposites, or the process by which such a fusion is reached, an ideal derived perhaps from the general sense that to be only other-worldly or only this-worldly, only believing and never doubting, is to be less than wholly human:

3

the complete man subsumes the opposites within himself. Thus Schiller speaks of Inclination coinciding with Duty, the poet Tasso ends by at least momentarily embracing his opposite, the diplomat Antonio; Stefan George evolves the ideal of 'der Christ im Tanz'. The fullest sense of the notion may be illustrated more vividly by means of an example drawn from Goethe's scientific work.

It is a feature of Goethe's 'Colour-Theory' (of which he once said that he rated it more highly than his literary work) that, while it appears superficially to deal solely with matters of optics and chromatics, almost every detail is capable of carrying a symbolical meaning. The colours of the spectrum are divided, for this purpose, into two contrasting groups, the one according to its affinity with Yellow, symbolizing the positive, the male, the active and so forth, the other according to its affinity with Blue, symbolizing the negative, the female, and the passive. (These are, as I have argued elsewhere, the exact counterparts of Jacob Boehme's Sulphur and Mercury, ostensibly in a more scientific dress.) Goethe speaks of them in this way, it seems, because he sees in colours one manifestation of the system or pattern of polarity and synthesis which in his view informs the universe: colours are a microcosmic and identical repetition of the patterns of the macrocosm. Seeking to trace the analogies further, however, Goethe encounters some difficulties. His intention is to show that the cycle of colours (such as interior decorators use) can be expressed also in the form of a triangle of which Yellow and Blue are the points on the base, while Red is the apex above them. Red, he maintains, can be seen to develop both from Yellow and from Blue *via* what he calls Yellow-Red and Blue-Red—the midway points on the respective sides of the triangle—and this development occurs when there is a heightening or intensification ('Steigerung') of either Yellow or Blue.

The practical aspect of this is not convincing (Goethe argues for instance that a yellow liquid in a vessel, viewed from above, takes on a tinge of red as more yellow liquid is poured in, as it were intensifying the quantity of yellowness present. Even if this

4

should happen in some circumstances, it clearly would not result at length in complete redness). The figurative aspects are more revealing, especially when one sees what the colour Red symbolizes in Goethe's scheme. It is, for reasons which he does not give, the 'highest colour' (perhaps because in the parallel systems of alchemy, Red is the colour of the Philosophers' Stone). It is an 'ideal satisfaction' to the beholder, whereas Green, formed merely by the mixture of Yellow and Blue without heightening, is no more than a 'real satisfaction'. Red is the colour of the Day of Judgment, and, most strangely of all, for no evidence of this is offered, Red 'contains in itself all other colours'. It is, then, so to speak, the acme of colour, the supreme form subsuming in itself all other forms, the fusion of the opposites within the particular sphere in which it exists, but no doubt also a reflection of the same fusion in the sphere of all spheres. What is true of the world of colours is true of the universe.

Goethe's inability to demonstrate any of this in practical terms is significant in itself. The world of colour simply does not answer to this explanation. All the same, the triangular diagram Yellow–Blue–Red is useful to keep in mind as a guide to some of the complexities of later writers. What is not quite clear from Goethe's account is to what extent he thought of the opposites in this case as representing amongst other things good and evil. It is evident that, if these are indeed included, the supreme form may be thought of as actually being a fusion of even these opposites— a view which has some theological backing, but which is evidently fraught with possibilities of disastrous error.

Here a new aspect of my general theme emerges. The preoccupation with polarity and synthesis in the German tradition is a certain fact. Less certain is what the precise implications of these words may be in any particular circumstances. For the very reason that the so-called opposites are differently conceived by different authors, and that in general the idea of describing them as opposites (rather than mere contrasts, or gradually differentiated groups) is somewhat vague, a variety of meanings can be supposed, all within the overall pattern. *Corruptio optimi pessima.*

What may be noble in its best form may become hideously deformed if misused. And it is my argument that on the whole the tradition which flowered in Goethe's day, whether or not it was already undermined at that stage, had gone disastrously wrong by the early decades of the twentieth century.

The marriage of the phoenix and the turtle was not the only way in which Shakespeare envisaged the wedding of opposites. 'Two distincts, division none'—his wording calls for careful attention, and I shall try to show in a final chapter how that particular conception is revived in a work by D. H. Lawrence. Such a union in love, each partner remaining distinct, sounds moving and admirable. A not dissimilar union, like the one in the imagination of Troilus as he strives to retain in his mind the picture of the perfect, faithful Cressida, and that of the woman he has just seen, yielding herself to another man, is only sickening:

> If souls guide vows, if vows be sanctimonies,
> If sanctimony be the gods' delight,
> If there be rule in unity itself,
> This is not she. O madness of discourse,
> That cause sets up with and against itself!
> Bifold authority! where reason can revolt
> Without perdition, and loss assume all reason
> Without revolt. This is, and is not Cressid!
> *Within my soul there doth conduce a fight*
> *Of this strange nature, that a thing inseparate*
> *Divides more wider than the sky and earth;*
> *And yet the spacious breadth of this division*
> *Admits no orifex for a point as subtle*
> *As Ariachne's broken woof to enter.*

What Shakespeare describes here is not the true matrimony but the thought that haunts his hero in *Othello*, that perfection may be maggoty through and through, the thought in *Macbeth* that fair is foul and foul fair, or in *Hamlet*, that one may smile and smile and be a villain. This is not bliss but torment, yet there may be times when the two forms are outwardly indistinguishable. Where is the true form to be found and how is it to be recognized?

Corruption within this tradition in Germany begins with the willingness to accept what Troilus finds distractingly unacceptable. Thus Heinrich von Kleist, writing in the first decade of the nineteenth century, seems to employ the same concept of synthesis as his contemporaries, and yet produces at times results far more like the vision of Troilus. More significant, he occasionally allows one to suspect that such a vision is to his way of thinking and feeling not a tragic horror but a cosmic revelation of the way things are, and therefore to be accepted. It is then not a question of two separates with one essence, but rather of one inseparate unity which appears at the same time wholly good and wholly wicked, as Cressida appears to Troilus. And then there really is madness of discourse. Kleist's story *Michael Kohlhaas* is a case in point. This is the account of a horse-dealer who is so outraged by his mistreatment at the hands of a local Junker that he swears to do everything in his power to obtain justice. Finding none, he holds society up to ransom, ravaging and pillaging across an entire countryside. The point about the story to be made here is that Kleist as narrator introduces us to Kohlhaas as 'one of the most honest (rechtschaffen) and at the same time one of the most horrifying (entsetzlich) men of his times'. The meaning of this is evidently that in his demand for justice Kohlhaas was honest, in the means he used, a horror. The reader may well be uncertain, however, at some moments in the story, whether Kleist does not mean that Kohlhaas continued in some sense to be an honest man even when he was setting whole cities on fire, as though his initial motive were still in some sense operating, and as though the combination of opposite qualities in him were in some way evidence of a superhuman stature. The intensification of both sides in him is reminiscent of the process outlined in the symbolism of Goethe's Colour-Theory, and while it is true that Kleist brings his hero ultimately to execution, the confused ending of the story allows the suspicion to form itself, that there were moments in the telling when Kleist was inclined to end it differently. The story *Die Marquise von O.* tends to confirm that suspicion. Here a woman discovers that the officer who saved her life during

7

a battle also took the opportunity, while she was still lying unconscious, to get her with child. She marries him out of love, declaring that he would not seem such a devil to her when she discovered it was he who raped her if he had not appeared such an angel when she first caught sight of him. It is difficult to believe that this fantastic ending was not, in Kleist's distorted mind, a reflection of the complementary opposites which are our present theme.

Something similar, though not this time perverse, seems to be contained in the structure of Kleist's best-known work, the play *Prinz Friedrich von Homburg*. In this the plot concerns a young officer who, by disobeying orders during a battle, covers himself momentarily with glory but enables the enemy to escape with less than the total defeat which seemed imminent. His uncle, the Elector of Brandenburg, gives orders that whoever was responsible is to be punished with death, and does not rescind these orders even when he learns that his own nephew is involved. The young prince, however, after at first assuming that the sentence of death is a formality, comes to see that it is a necessity and actually demands that it be carried out. Meanwhile the Elector has decided on leniency—although nothing is known of this till the last possible moment—and the play ends as the prince, blindfolded and expecting to be shot immediately, learns that he is not only pardoned but is expected to join in the command of an army preparing the final assault on all the foes of Brandenburg. There could be no clearer instance than this of the coming together of opposites, the individual and the State, condemnation and pardon, justice and mercy, self-denial and self-assertion, total unworthiness and supreme worthiness. Moreover, both sides have been driven to extremes, 'gesteigert', in the Goethean sense. The Elector has been driven to realize to the full what his demand for justice and discipline involved, and the Prince, refusing the opportunity granted him to sign his own release, has been driven to recognize the unpardonable nature of his offence. With all this, there are overtones lending to the Elector a kind of godlike status, so that it also seems at times that Kleist is influenced by the

Christian, or more particularly the Lutheran teaching, that a man must know himself damned before he can be saved. That is, after all, the situation of the prince. By recognizing that his fault is worthy of no less punishment than death, or rather, as he feels it, total annihilation, the prince makes himself worthy of the pardon which is meanwhile being prepared in the mind of the Elector. It is very close to the repentance of the sinner, especially as it has been regarded in the Lutheran Church. But there is this important difference, that the self-condemnation of the prince includes no element of love, nor, so far as one can see, does the Elector's pardon. What takes place is rather a secularization of the religious concepts in which the repentance of the sinner becomes the self-abnegation of the military subordinate or the subject of the State, and where a loving embrace becomes the self-alignment of the individual with the State in which he exists. What is at stake is never love or redemption.

In this play, therefore, there lies one of the chief turning-points in the history of the German tradition—a turning-point whose significance was not realized for many decades to come, for it was in Hitler's time that Kleist's reputation reached a climax. By transferring the idea of polarity and synthesis from the religious to the secular sphere, Kleist was accomplishing something similar to what Hegel was doing at the same time, for Hegel's philosophy in one aspect is an application of Christian theology to the world of history and politics. In those early years of the nineteenth century, years in which, under the stimulus of the Napoleonic conquests, the realization of German unity was beginning to become a possibility, the mystical and religious forms began to lose their transcendental sanction (or better, transcendental sanctions ceasing to be credible, only the systematic patterns remained, to be filled in with the analogies that came to hand).

From now on one distinguishing mark of German literature in relation to all other literatures is the consistency with which its major figures concern themselves directly or indirectly with political issues in their literary works. Kleist remains forgotten for a good long while, but as the years progress towards the

Bismarckian era and the foundation of the Reich, others take his place. The cosmopolitanism of Goethe and Herder recedes into the background. The dramatist Grabbe sings the praise of Frederick Barbarossa and the Hohenzollerns; the Austrian Grillparzer, in a much more accomplished way, comments pessimistically on the contemporary scene through motifs drawn from Austrian history. Yet another dramatist, the North German Hebbel, writes a play in defence of the tragic necessity to destroy subjects of the State, however morally innocent, who cause trouble. Heine, compelled to leave the country, delivers satirical broadsides against all its institutions, while his contemporary Büchner draws a grim picture of the impossibility of all political progress. Freytag writes a series of novels entitled *The Ancestors*, in which the whole course of German history from its beginnings to the significant period of the 'War of Liberation' is portrayed— the sense of belonging to that particular section of the past is promoted. Fichte preaches the autarkic state, which Germany was temporarily to become within not much more than a hundred years; Friedrich List follows in his wake with practical proposals.

To some extent, this very natural concern with the most pressing issues of the day (it must be clear that these writers were by no means all nationalists or reactionaries) goes hand in hand with further developments in the philosophy of polarity. The association does not become really important, however, until the closing years of the nineteenth century. Then, as I have tried to show in the early chapters of the present work, it becomes very close indeed, and the vital questions begin to impose themselves: what is happening to the tradition, what distortion is it undergoing, to what extent do these distortions assist the development towards the catastrophe of 1933–45, and, most important of all, are there any works of literature in which something sane and wholesome is retained or discovered?

These questions lead, then, first to a survey of the whole field of German literature from 1871 until 1945, the period of the Second and Third Reichs and of the intervening Weimar Republic. This is not a history of literature; it is rather a study of the literary writers of the time in their relationship both to the tradition I have just outlined, and of which I have cited a few well-known figures by way of illustration, and to the political movements which, whether causally or not, led towards the catastrophe. I think it will appear from this that there was a close linkage between the tradition of 'polarity and synthesis' in its distorted form, and the political events, that an atmosphere of thought came into being which was favourable to, though not directly responsible for, the growth of Nazism. That part of the book is panoramic and inevitably less detailed than the later part in which individual works are treated at length. It is nevertheless essential to place this survey before the reader, if only in order for him to see the fuller implications of the later chapters in which the binoculars are replaced by the microscope, particularly those chapters treating of the work of Thomas Mann.

No other German novelist has been so persistently concerned with the state of Germany in his own day, no other has kept abreast of contemporary developments as Mann did. It has several times been said that no other has been so representative,[1] but this needs some qualification. It is true that Mann was very conscious of his position as an heir to the thought of Goethe, Schopenhauer, Wagner and Nietzsche, and that these four were among the dominant influences in the Germany of his day. With Goethe he claimed the ability to enter into a kind of mystic union, and he promoted in public the idea that his own life was in some sense a recapitulation of that of the earlier genius.[2] Schopenhauer deeply influenced Mann's youthful work, especially *Buddenbrooks*. Wagner and Nietzsche stimulated him to assent, dissent, and reconsideration all through his life. Moreover, despite their differences, these four do form part of the main tradition.

It is worth noting, however, that not all German thinkers and writers in the last two centuries have operated with these concepts of 'Polarität' and 'Steigerung' or 'Synthese' in mind. Kant, despite his insistence on the 'antinomies', that is on the contradictory conclusions produced by the use of reason, was not inclined to synthesize, fuse, or resolve the contradictions in some 'higher' unity. Nor were Büchner and Kafka, Keller and Stifter, Fontane and the young Hauptmann, at all prone to range people and phenomena into no more than two groups of contrasted classes. As a result, they produced little or nothing in the way of an all-embracing system, a 'Weltanschauung', and therefore could not create the sense of a traditional development or school which is created by those who did write in terms of polarity. Their worlds are disparate, individual, whereas when Mann writes of the 'Bürger' and the artist, or of 'Spirit and Life', we can see at once that he is thinking in terms of a very powerful tradition, perhaps the only philosophical tradition of any consequence for German literature in recent times.

Mann's work is 'representative', then, as one variant in a particular traditional system. In addition, its field of view is limited. The world of Mann's fiction, so far as it is not historical or mythical, is almost entirely that of the 'Bürgertum'. It includes nothing of the proletariat which rapidly became prominent in his own lifetime, nothing of life on the land, nothing of the 'Junkertum'. One does not become aware, through Mann's novels, of the industrialization of Germany, the conflict of democrats with Communists and Nazis and of these with each other, the change in the position of the 'Bürger' *after* Bismarck, in relation to the new organizations of society. And this is of course unexceptionable, worth mentioning only in so far as Mann's representativeness needs defining.

The fact remains that Mann is often acclaimed as the novelist of the twentieth century most worthy to be placed alongside Goethe as the champion of a liberal humanism on which post-Nazi Germany can build intellectually with confidence. This acclaim is heard on both sides of the line dividing East and West: from the Marxist Georg Lukács as well as from Erich Heller, who sees in Mann 'a great artist, one of the few writers who, by giving valid form to the chaotic mind of this century, will have helped it to be remembered with at least a measure of friendliness and respect'.[3] There was in fact a time when at least some intellectuals envisaged Mann as the President of a German Republic to be set up after the Second World War,[4] a suggestion which, whether it could ever have been practical or not, he deprecated, but which indicates the kind of esteem in which he was held. One could not imagine such a suggestion being made on behalf of Rilke, Kafka, Brecht, George or Hofmannsthal. It is also true that Mann has been strongly and even violently attacked, for example by Hans-Egon Holthusen and Walter Muschg.[5] Such attacks, however, have been almost entirely directed against Mann's ideas; they have not been primarily concerned with his achievements as a novelist.

In view of their political and social importance, these achievements are of more than purely aesthetic interest. This is why I propose to outline the results of an inquiry which has proved to be unfavourable to Mann's work. There would be no profit in that if it were merely a question of demonstrating dissent: one would rather, in that case, try to communicate the enlightenment or pleasure received from some author one admired. But since the claims made on behalf of Mann as a writer have been so ambitious, not merely in terms of German culture but of the twentieth century as a whole, and since these claims have won considerable respect, it is useful to look at his literary work closely, and first and foremost from a literary point of view.

There remains the question, to be regarded as primarily a literary one although one with political implications, whether any strand of tradition still visible in the twentieth century is of more value for the future than that represented in Mann's work. My answer to this is also less positive than I would have liked it to be. The poetry of Rilke undoubtedly belongs to the same main tradition of thought as the novels of Mann, but while there are traces in it of a tendency which to my mind is more fruitful, there is still a great deal of confusion not only in thinking but even in ways which affect its poetic value. Kafka, on the other hand, is one of those for whom the tradition means very little, although he was tempted at times to feel the deathlike state in which he lived as a kind of guarantee, a keel supporting both himself and society by the very paradox of its being heavy enough to sink to the bottom. Although there is not much inspiration to be had from Kafka, and his devotion to the darkness is only rarely enlightening, he did occasionally make poetic wholes of his stories, and these seem more valuable than all the wisdom of the syntheses, when these remain only synthetic. Kafka's complete frankness, though it made his work as a writer almost impossibly difficult, makes his achievements all the more remarkable when they do succeed.[6]

Kafka, however, is one of the few authors in German, writing in his day, in whom there is no explicit handling of the 'polarity-and-synthesis' theme at all. We must look elsewhere for signs of any valuable restatement in traditional terms—not that these terms carry any guarantee of truth with them, more than those of some other tradition, but because piety towards the German past must look for the excellences achievable within the conditions imposed by that past.

It was Hofmannsthal who said[7] that whereas one could profit from reading Goethe, so long as one was not confused by him, it was impossible to profit from German literature, but only to be confused. The remark, rather more sweeping than Hofmannsthal would have wanted it to be outside the pages of the diary in which it was written, does reveal something of his mistrust of the synthesizing tradition. He was not wholly free from it himself: especially his early work reveals the Narcissism, the awareness of duality, and the yearning for unity which are so often met in the century before his birth. And as he said at another place in the diary: 'German men of intellect have a difficult, late birth into life true and proper; it is indeed a kind of second birth, and many die of it.'[8] Hofmannsthal was one of the fortunate ones in this respect. His own second birth was signalled by the appearance of a work which rings true in its language as well as in its structure, and at the same time in the balanced critique of tradition it contains. To this play, then, *Der Schwierige*, special attention is due, even though, by contrast with the works by others which came out at the same time, it tends to enforce assent to yet another diary-entry: 'We have no modern literature. We have Goethe and a few beginnings.'[9]

These are harsh words to come from a mature writer of Hofmannsthal's standing. Yet even Goethe, in pessimistic mood, may have foreseen something like them when he confided to Eckermann his feeling that German literature was, so far as modern times were concerned, only beginning to emerge, and that it would be 'several hundred years' before a stable, civilized tradition could be established.[10] We have witnessed over the last two centuries the most astounding display of vigour, creative power, and self-assertion of German interests against longer-established nations. Most middle-aged Germans alive today have experienced two national disasters either of which might have crushed a less resilient people. It is as though some volcanic energy had been stirred into life and could not be extinguished. Yet one cannot avoid the impression, despite all the achievements of German music and architecture, that the potentialities of this dynamic force have not been fully realized. On the contrary, so far as literature is concerned there has been all too often a trend towards assimilation in that flood of ideas which led ultimately to disaster. What is worse, the corpus of German literature since 1750, the literature to which young men and women today look for guidance and for some kind of forming influence, has yet to be critically sifted by critics neither neutral (as all 'Literaturwissenschaftler' are) nor anti-German in their outlook. It is an oppressive thing to hear, for instance, that one of the most popular authors among sixth-formers in German schools today is Kleist. There is a very great need to awaken a lively, critical interest which, without tarring all with one brush, will distinguish the particular qualities of German writers and be prepared if necessary to reject some aspects decisively. The present study is meant to contribute to that end. If it serves ultimately towards diverting the immense vitality of recent years away from new catastrophes it will have served its turn.

PART I

WRITERS AND POLITICS

Evolutionism, fatalism, pessimism, nihilism—how strange it is to see this desolate and terrible doctrine growing and expanding at the very moment when the German nation is celebrating its greatness and its triumphs! The contrast is so startling that it sets one thinking. . . .

Self-mockery, starting from a horror of stupidity and hypocrisy, and standing in the way of all wholeness of mind and all true seriousness—this is the goal to which the intellect brings us at last, unless conscience cries out. The mind must have for ballast the clear conception of duty, if it is not to fluctuate between levity and despair.

HENRI-FRÉDÉRIC AMIEL,
Journal Intime, 29 Dec. 1871 (transl.
Mrs Humphry Ward)

CHAPTER I

WRITERS AND POLITICS: 1871–1918

In 1871, four years before the births of Thomas Mann and Rilke, three years before that of Hofmannsthal and three years after that of Stefan George, the political unity of the German people was achieved; after twenty years of manœuvring the King of Prussia was crowned by Bismarck Emperor of Germany. This was the culmination of a movement that had begun at least a century before, and which fulfilled even older aspirations. For six hundred years the area in which German was the chief language had consisted of independent states, more than four hundred at times, owing at most a nominal allegiance to Holy Roman Emperors who did not always rule over even their personal domains. Before that, it had never been more than part of a larger whole whose very structure weakened its coherence. Yet it had always been ruled by kings of German origin, and the memory of it as a great German political power was still alive. Bismarck's manœuvres, cutting out the non-German elements which Austria-Hungary might have brought in, now gave hopes of realizing a unity not Holy or Roman, but an Empire. As if in confirmation of the new strength accruing from the achievement, the economy developed by leaps and bounds. The industrial revolution, long under way in Britain, had hung fire in Germany until this moment: now, with the railway net already complete, the new factories and mines enjoyed unparalleled facilities. The population grew from 41 millions in 1871 to 65 millions in 1913, industry and foreign trade boomed, for almost the first time German colonies were established abroad, while at home the first 'welfare state' provided workers' insurance, subsidies for opera and drama, compulsory further education. Such rapid and widespread developments, affecting every class, had not been experienced in the whole course of German history.

The success was not only in the political and economic sphere but also in that of the arts. It is true that for some twenty years no new names of international reputation appeared. In opera, however, there was one great work to crown almost immediately the political victory. The production at Bayreuth in 1876 of Wagner's tetralogy *Der Ring des Nibelungen* has properly been called the first national achievement of the united German nation; Bayreuth showed signs of becoming the shrine of German culture, a place of pilgrimage symbolizing the great rebirth. 'Im Vertrauen auf den deutschen Geist entworfen' were the first words in Wagner's dedication of *The Ring* to Ludwig II of Bavaria: 'Composed out of confidence in the German Spirit.' Yet it is also significant that the concluding music of *Götterdämmerung*, the end of the tetralogy, was intended to express a mood of deliverance from all rebirth. The gods perish, Brünnhilde rides exultantly into the flames of Siegfried's funeral pyre, to enter the 'wunsch- und wahnlos / Heiligstes Wahlland'.[1] She is 'redeemed from rebirth',[2] her desires and illusions forsaken, and yet she is now in a 'realm of choice': it is she who will choose her destiny henceforward, in harmony with the pure gold of the ring which has now returned to its true home in the depths of the Rhine. Whereas the gold had been formerly used in the selfish interests of both Wotan and Alberich, it gleams now in an eternal present, perfect in its sheer existence, subject to no man's claims on it. In this symbolism there is a good deal to be learned about the spirit of the new Germany. How far it was consciously understood nobody can say. Certainly the ideal of identification with an undivided, unappropriated Being in a synthesis beyond all individuation, was to be prominent in German literature as well as in politics from this time on, as was also the belief in total annihilation as a path to this end. Wagner's work had a prophetic quality.

The new literature, however, distinct in mood, presuppositions and preoccupations from that of the mid-century, did not emerge until the generation which had grown up within the Wilhelmine Empire reached maturity. When it came, in the 1890's, it bore witness to the perplexity in which the younger men now found themselves. From now onwards, for the next fifty years and more, German literature was to be concerned above all with the overcoming of the blackest pessimism. The Naturalist authors, Hauptmann, Sudermann, Arno Holz and Johannes Schlaf, portrayed the misery of life in the industrial regions and cities now developing; the neo-Romantics, Rilke, George, and Hofmannsthal, turning their backs on this,[3] looked for the spiritual comforts of total isolation. In the 1900's the forebodings of catastrophe, heralded by the armaments race and the crises of Algeciras and Agadir, are reflected more and more: they can be felt in Rilke's poem 'Spätherbst in Venedig', in George's cycle of prophetic poems *Der Stern des Bundes*, as also in Mann's *Der Tod in Venedig*, where the passages dealing with the outbreak of cholera often read like an account of an even greater evil. Indeed, when the war came, it was greeted by all three of these writers as an end to the pretence of civilization with which they had been living for the past thirty or forty years.

There had been a certain falsity, a certain self-conscious and self-doubting assertiveness, about the Wilhelmine Empire from its beginning, to judge by the novels of its severe though still tolerant critic, Theodor Fontane. One thinks of the husband of Effi Briest, in the novel of that name, who insists on the rigid observance of a duel to the death in defence of his wife's honour, but who in his heart no longer believes in the traditional code, so that his adherence to it is both coolly formal and ruthlessly exacting; or one thinks of the comical family pride of the industrialist in *Frau Jenny Treibel*: 'Wir sind die Treibels: Blutlaugensalz und Eisenvitriol!' But the most stringent criticisms were those of Nietzsche, whose first *Unzeitgemäße Betrachtungen* appeared in 1873. Nietzsche castigated the illusion that by means of the recent victory over France there had come about a victory for German culture. It was rather, he affirmed, a victory for military discipline, courage, leadership and obedience, qualities valuable in themselves which had, however, merely established the 'culture-philistine', a smug product of pedantic schoolmastering who was completely without true German-ness and creative power.

There was also opposition from a different quarter. For while the parliamentary voting system heavily favoured the propertied classes, and while the Reichstag itself was constitutionally powerless to overthrow any government, the Social Democrat (Marxist) vote increased in forty years from 124,000 to over 4,000,000 in 1912, and the Catholic 'Zentrum', conservative in tendency but jealous of its confessional interests, polled in the same year nearly 2,000,000 out of 12,000,000 votes cast. The potential opposition was thus, by that time, about half of the active vote. The literary record leaves little trace of this, for with very few exceptions men of letters paid no regard to the political and religious doctrines which, given the opportunity, could have radically changed German society. The study of the literature and philosophy in these years thus gives a one-sided emphasis to neutrality or acceptance. All the same, the results are revealing, if only of the fundamental beliefs shared by those in power and some at least of their most influential critics. Doctrines apart, no literature was ever more concerned with national, political and religious themes than this one, not even the literature of the ancient Hebrews.

At first sight, there appears to be little in common between those who opposed the new Empire. Nietzsche had no interest in the schemes for social welfare introduced by Bismarck, and would have attacked the portrayal of industrial life given by Naturalist authors as an intolerable yielding to the sense of pity. His ideal of German-ness, the criterion by which he found the new culture wanting, was aristocratic and pagan, anti-democratic and anti-Christian; its contrasts were not 'good' and 'evil' but 'noble' and 'mean'. He had no criticism to offer of the way in which Bismarck had brought the Empire into being or of the way in which it was maintained; he was not concerned with the 'Kultur-kampf' between Catholics and Government, or with the colonial question. As his ideas developed after *Unzeitgemäße Betrachtungen* they dealt rather with the individual, and with society only in so far as it restricted or promoted the individual's growth towards the supreme form, the Superman. For Nietzsche, traditional morality was merely the means by which the weak and powerless sought to hamper the natural energy of the strong, it was the expression of a slave-mentality. His mood was optimistic, 'saying yea' to all manifestations of life, whether cruel or kindly, savage or civilized; it was pessimistic, in so far as it perceived the present 'all-too-human' nature of mankind; ultimately it was beyond either pessimism or optimism, seeking to transcend humanity in living a life of sheer instantaneous, unreflective action.

At the heart of Nietzsche's thought is a desire to live what would otherwise have been called, in Christian terms, the life of the lilies of the field, although he would have added to this the life of the beasts of the jungle. The fascination of his work lies in the flashes of insight it provides into the possibilities of such existence. In fact it sometimes appears that his real intention is to transform human nature once and for all by an almost Christ-like insistence both on its hypocritical evil and on a generous toleration, in attendance on the promptings of the spirit. In this connection, one may quote the passage in which he speaks of wars as a curative means ('eine Brutalitäts-Cur') for decadent nations only, whereas more healthy nations have no need of them.4 Here his meaning might seem to be that war, like the unjust anger of one's neighbour, is an evil to be understood and endured, if not actually forgiven, as an essential as well as an inevitable consequence of men being what they are. On the other hand, another passage from the same work gives an entirely different colour to the thought. Here Nietzsche declares that such a highly civilized and therefore decadent humanity as that of contemporary Europe needs not only wars, but the greatest and most terrible wars, if it is to restore itself to eminence and health; it needs 'that deep impersonal hatred, that cold-blooded murderousness coupled with a good conscience, that communal, organizing zest in the destruction of the enemy',5 without which it must cease to exist. From sayings like these it becomes clear that whatever Nietzsche's ultimate aim may have been—and he does speak of it elsewhere, however ambiguously, as the innocence of a child—so far as the immediate practical task was concerned, he incited to war. Germany, in his eyes, was decadent: the way to health led through a deliberate cultivation of cold-blooded murderousness. By some process of homeopathy, perhaps, the decadence would be overcome.

Nietzsche's criticism of the Empire thus became an attack on hypocritical attachment to outdated, Christian standards, which were for him the very source of hypocrisy. At the same time, his conception of health was so much a matter of accepting human nature in its totality that his main object became self-awareness— or, more accurately, self-oblivion after self-awareness had been achieved. Thus his observations on human nature, penetrating as they often are, are made in order to affirm that nature in the long run, indeed to accept it with joyful abandonment, to achieve a kind of synthesis of affirmation and negation. His doctrine of the Eternal Recurrence, in which he offered a kind of test whereby the quality of affirmation might be judged, reveals this paradox. It asks the question whether, confronted with the prospect of living the same life over again an infinite number of times to all eternity, men would be ready to do so not resignedly, in the consciousness of the inadequacies it contained, but with delight in every moment of it. The genuinely affirmative answer is given only by the Superman, and what distinguishes him from the Christian or Jewish saint who might also answer affirmatively is that for the saint there must always remain some duality; the saint will delight in the work of a loving and good Creator, and thus not escape grief at the world's defection, whereas for the Superman God is dead, and there remains only the dynamic creativity of living beings. Or, to put the point in another way, it may seem to the saint as much as to the Superman that God does not exist— the Psalms are full of laments which almost amount to such a realization—but while the one continues to praise the divine love and justice, the other concludes that they are never to be thought of again.

To give a proper account of Nietzsche's thought, which is thus constantly running so close to Judaeo-Christian ideas as to require the most scrupulous distinctions, is impossible within a few pages. He was, as he felt, driven to his conclusions not by any mere Machiavellianism, not by arguments of expediency, but by the deepest of religious concerns, and by the desire to have life more abundantly. He demanded courage, endurance, self-sacrifice, as well as barbarism, cruelty and parasitic self-preservation, and the core of his teaching is really as ineffable as the force that moves lions and butterflies, if there is one. However, certain conclusions can fairly be drawn even without full definition. In the light of the doctrine of the Eternal Recurrence, the criticisms of Bismarck's Reich, made in Nietzsche's earlier days, would have to end in an affirmation of the very conditions he had criticized. It would always remain, it is true, an affirmation tempered with knowledge, a 'knowing' optimism rather than the blind and smug one he had attacked. But his aim was an unhypocritical assertion of the life of the pirate and the *condottiere*, by those who had it in them to live such a life, and an unenvying submission to such men on the part of those unwilling to use their Will to Power. That this aim was qualified at times by other considerations is largely irrelevant to the practical effects his teaching was bound to have. Certainly, there is nothing in his teaching which seriously detracts from such an aim. And thus, for the majority of his sympathetic readers, rightly or wrongly, the conclusion most readily to be drawn was one which would promote the militarism and expansionism of the German state as it already existed. It was merely necessary to clear the mind of cant, the kind of cant which Wilhelm II displayed when he imagined himself at the time of the Chinese campaigns as a Crusader against Asiatic paganism. For the Emperor to have attacked China in the full knowledge of his Will to Power would, in Nietzschean terms, have been no sin.

It is a strange paradox that Nietzsche's doctrines, so interpreted (and I am concerned here solely with their propensity for practical interpretation), look like a rationale for the actual conduct of the state in which he lived, the conduct of Bismarck rather than of Wilhelm II. Bismarck was highly aware, more so than any other statesman of his time, of the complexities of human nature; he had a more clear-sighted view both of his own purposes and of the situations by which they might be fulfilled. While his whole aim was to promote the strength of Prussia, he had no illusions about the qualities of the Prussians, so that his unsentimental patriotism seems at times wholly pointless. For liberals and socialists he had a shrewd contempt, together with a surprising ability to detect serviceable qualities in an adversary. His attitude towards the Polish insurrections in 1861 seems to have all that Nietzsche could have required in the way of awareness and ruthlessness. 'Strike the Poles', he wrote in a private letter, 'in such a way that they will despair of their lives; I have every sympathy with their situation, but if we want to exist we cannot do anything else but *exterminate* them. The wolf, too, is not responsible for being what God has made it, but we kill it nevertheless, if we can.'[6] It is difficult to see on what grounds Nietzsche might have faulted such frankness. The situation is clearly seen, the rights of the enemy acknowledged; there is no spurious appeal to justice, and the religious reference has just the same implications as Nietzsche's atheism had: the claims of self-assertion are overriding. Since it was on the basis of such an attitude that the Empire had been founded, Nietzsche's objections must often imply that Germany's real weakness was the lack of more Bismarcks. Nietzsche was ambiguous, it is true, and could speak of the Superman at times as of some ideal far beyond the reach of contemporary humanity; in so far as this was, on the other hand, an ideal to be inculcated in the present, it could only promote the Bismarckian spirit.

Moreover, Nietzsche's writings came to be widely known— from the 1890's onwards—at a time when historians and politicians were beginning to become more and more strongly aware of Germany's dynamic power and of her claim to a place among the Great Powers. Men of great influence held the view that world history, by virtue of some trend immanent in it, was lifting

26

Germany to dominance as though on the topmost shoot of a newly flourishing tree.[7] Nietzsche's 'Will to Power' could be readily interpreted as yet another aspect of this immanent driving force, and his teaching on the subject was easily understood (or misunderstood?—one can never be quite sure) to mean that frank acceptance rather than hypocritical virtue was the one thing needful.

Nietzsche's influence was dominant on almost all the major writers of the ensuing decades, up to and beyond the 1930's, although it naturally altered in emphasis with each individual. Closest to him in spirit was Stefan George, whose poetry, beginning with evocations of pagan splendour, ended in 1926 with prophecies of a new Empire led by a core of dedicated Supermen. In the period before 1914 George was above all concerned, in his poetry, to combine the Dionysian qualities of the German with the Apolline calm and clarity of the Roman and Italian, a fusion which is deeply indebted to Nietzsche's thought. What he at length achieved, despite the great poetic sensitivity of many of his lyrics, was an obtrusive formalism together with an ecstatic call to battle which could easily be taken as an incitement to war on behalf of Wilhelm II's Empire.[8] Equally close to Nietzsche was the Swiss Carl Spitteler, whose lengthy epic poem *Olympischer Frühling*, refurbishing the Greek myths with Nietzschean meaning, appeared between 1900 and 1910. (Although Switzerland was politically independent, German-speaking Swiss were already beginning to feel the tug of their racial affinity with a nation whose recent achievements were so impressive.) Others more or less in the same tradition were Thomas Mann, Rilke and Hofmannsthal, of whom there will be more to say later.

Even the Naturalist authors were not so far removed from this kind of thought as might be imagined, for while European Naturalism was generally positivistic, the German form had features linking it rather with the main currents of mysticism or quasi-mysticism in the nineteenth century. Thus, while the theoretical ideal of the movement was a photographic realism, this had certain connotations not found elsewhere. Arno Holz, the leading theoretician, attempted the most complete reproduction of Nature in the so-called 'Sekundenstil', whereby actions were described as they happened, second by second, and even the most insignificant events such as the tapping of a tree-branch against a window, or the shrivelling of a fly in the wax surrounding a candle-wick, were given as much prominence as events essential to the narrative. The relevance of such incidents was immaterial: they happened at the same time, and were therefore included. In addition, all Naturalist authors reproduced exactly local dialects and tricks of speech; they gave precise instructions for the furnishing of indoor scenes in stage plays, and tended to write plots which had no clear beginning or end, but 'ran off into the sand' with the inconsequentiality and lack of pattern of life itself as they saw it. The theory—so far as that goes, for it was not rigidly observed by all authors—was summed up by Holz in a phrase which has had some currency, despite its apparent absurdity. 'Art', he wrote, 'has a tendency to become Nature again. It does so in proportion to the means at its disposal, and the way they are used.'[9] The point to be observed here is not the broad generalization, which cannot apply to such forms of art as music, architecture, or ceramics, and only in a limited sense to painting or literature, but rather the notion that Art tends to become Nature *again*. There is no doubt that Holz thought of the best art as actually being Nature, much as Schiller thought that the best artists 'were' Nature, while inferior art was for him restricted by its media, and by the lack of skill of the artist, from achieving such an identification. The ideal was thus not so much a reproduction of Nature as the creation of a work so identical with Nature (whatever that might be) that it stood as a natural object in its own right. In addition, however—if we take Holz literally—this was evidently in some way a return to Nature: at some time, presumably, Art and Nature had been one, and the present tendency of Art was to revert to this unity. It is plain enough, from the assumptions it makes, that this way of thinking has the same kind of pattern as that of the general tradition

28

already outlined. An initial unity is broken up by some process of individuation, there is an ensuing period of dividedness, and an ultimate return to the first state. Holz's theory, for all its pretensions to scientific exactness, owes its form to what we may call, in the widest sense, a neo-Platonist tradition. It implies, as much as ever Mann or Rilke's work did, an acceptance of the given situation, and differs from them only in its freedom from speculation or doubt.

Indeed, while Naturalists in other countries were often reformists imbued with a deep sense of the need to put right injustices—Zola's defence of Dreyfus is a case in point—there is no such sense in the German school. It is true that M. G. Conrad demanded, in his manifesto published in *Die Gesellschaft*, that writers should seek out and expose the ills of society with ruthless frankness. Yet Conrad's novels, imitative of Zola's, have the reputation now of being written very much in the spirit of the contemporary 'Prachtkerl'. On the other hand, there was an appeal to Bismarck for a state subsidy to writers which seems scarcely compatible with freedom to criticize, and a suggestion that Naturalist authors should not concern themselves with the sick and decadent, but with the promotion of the simple virtues of the average citizen.[10] Even Gerhart Hauptmann, the leading dramatist of the movement, might be thought to have sympathized with this attitude, at least in his earliest play. Whether *Vor Sonnenaufgang* is a *pièce à thèse* may be open to doubt. It is difficult to interpret as a tragedy since the hero is endowed with such high-minded callousness as to destroy all sympathy for him. Certainly, a young man who abandons a woman with whom he is deeply in love on the eugenic grounds that, were she to bear children, they might inherit the dipsomania of her relatives, and who leaves her so abruptly as to cause her to take her life, shows too little human feeling to be accounted a tragic protagonist. And if the play is not taken as tragedy, it must appear rather as advocating the course taken by the hero, unpalatable though it is, in the interests of that healthier society which usually seems to be his real concern: the circumstances of the play do then take place, as the title puts it, 'before the dawn', the dawn of a disinfected world in which loving will present no problems. It is easier to believe that this was Hauptmann's intention—that he shared the hero's eugenic principles and therefore regarded his decision as a 'tragic' necessity—than that he thought it possible to make a mean-spirited action into the crux of his play. The contemporary emphasis on 'health', to the disregard of all forms of 'sickness', lends weight to the former interpretation.

A much more mature work of Hauptmann's, though written only a few years later, is his play *Die Weber*. There is no possibility of interpreting this as a *pièce à thèse*; rather, the play impresses by the generosity displayed towards all the characters, industrialists and workers alike, and the sense it conveys of a relentless fate overcoming all efforts at amelioration of the weavers' poverty. Neither the employer nor the weavers themselves are responsible: he is hamstrung by foreign competition, they revolt because their conditions of work are beyond endurance; and yet the suppression of the revolt by the militia at the end of the play seems to be equally a part of the workings of Fate. *Die Weber* is, for all its vivid characterization, its powerful tempo, and its skilful presentation of a mass-movement, a quietistic work, helplessly recording a disaster from which no political escape is envisaged. In this perhaps it reflects its author's other preoccupations, for Hauptmann was already writing at this time in a symbolical vein and on supernatural themes. Within thirty years, Naturalism itself having remained powerful for a decade and a half, Hauptmann had shed most of his concern with social issues and had turned to the sexual mysticism of his short story, *Der Ketzer von Soana*, in which a priest abandons his Christian religion for a Dionysian vitalism.

Hauptmann in his youth had least in common, of all the major writers of his time, with Nietzschean doctrine; far less than the poet Richard Dehmel, whose welcome to 'our human beast-divineness'[11] plainly echoes Nietzsche's ambiguities. In his trend towards eroticism, however, Hauptmann was moving with the times which were shortly to see the frenzies of Expressionist drama, and were already in the first decade of the twentieth century witnessing the naked portrayal of sexual appetites in the plays of Frank Wedekind.

The bridge between Naturalism and Expressionism is made in Reinhold Sorge's play *Der Bettler*, written in 1911. In this the acts alternate between Ibsenesque realism and stylized scenes in which spotlights stab fiercely on a darkened stage at choruses of airmen and prostitutes, chanting in staccato rhythms. Sorge's hero, an 'autobiographical' one, feels intensely the desire to work for humanity at large, and thus far shares the social concern of the Naturalists, but envisages his ideal in terms of an inexpressible revelation which he is called on to announce, and so comes closer to the Expressionist school. The play is also the culmination of Sorge's efforts to come to terms with Nietzschean thought, bringing momentarily into blurred identity the two streams which had been in progress since the early 1890's.[12] From now on, it is more difficult than hitherto to make any clear distinctions of category. The more rationalistic spirit of Naturalism, scientific in its pretensions, gives way to dynamic ecstatic philosophies of intoxication; the 'Heldenlosigkeit' of the Naturalist plays gives way to the presentation of orgiastic masses in which the individual disappears from view.

However, despite the increasing emphasis on zestful living and Dionysian self-identification, many writers of the Wilhelmine Empire felt a sense of shame in their profession. A flood of 'Künstlerromane' was published around the turn of the century, novels in which the 'artist', whether painter, musician, or poet, is presented as effete, sexually impotent, crippled with doubts of his own capacities, unproductive in contrast with a robust society that has no place for him. Although the roots of this genre go back at least as far as Goethe's *Torquato Tasso*, it has never formed so large a part of German literature as it did between 1890 and 1920. Thomas Mann's Tonio Kröger was not alone in thinking that no banker, or any other respectable member of society, could properly demean himself by indulging in creative literature. The inferiority of the artist to the man of action is one of the major themes of these years. It is the theme of Arno Holz's and Johannes Schlaf's sardonic picture, in *Papa Hamlet*, of a down-at-heels, out-of-work actor, written in a spirit of smug Philistinism, as it is also of the more generous though sentimental novel, *Das Gänsemännchen*, by Jakob Wassermann. Heinrich Mann's story *Pippo Spano* treats of the same subject, which recurs in scores of others, including the early works of Hermann Hesse, *Peter Camenzind* (1904), *Gertrud* (1910), and *Roßhalde* (1914). The artists in these works are relatively helpless, able only to accept with an ironical reserve, to withdraw into self-centred isolation, or to succumb to a crushing defeat at the hands of 'Life'. Thoroughgoing protest or confident satire does not exist except in such works as the witty, prolix tragedy of the Austrian Karl Kraus (written between 1915 and 1917), *Die letzten Tage der Menschheit*, the comedies of Carl Sternheim, and the novel by Heinrich Mann (Thomas Mann's brother), *Der Untertan*, censured on the outbreak of war for its attack both on the person of the Emperor and the society he led.

With the widespread sense of inferiority goes also a sense that the artist is a pretender to feelings he does not truly have, or an actor playing a part required of him by society rather than a man speaking in his own person. The most conscious manifestation of this sense is Thomas Mann's novel *Felix Krull*, begun in 1911, the autobiography of a character (an artist only in Mann's very broad usage) who adapts himself with astonishing ease to every situation, and who displays, with rare exceptions, just those feelings which people most expect of him. It appears also in painting, especially in the portrait by Lovis Corinth of himself as a Bacchanalian, a work painted in 1905 which is of some significance for the times. The heavily jowled face, crowned with ivy, seems about to express triumphant laughter, but the wide-open mouth is awry, the eyes have a pained look, and the whole expression is equally close to hysterical tears: the masquerade is frankly portrayed as a desperate pretence. In a not dissimilar way, the rather earlier paintings by the Swiss Arnold Böcklin, mostly taking myth or heroic legend for their subject-matter, are rendered with a derisive mockery. One thinks of his 'Venus Anadyomene' in which a pallid society lady, undressed rather than naked, rises from the sea on the back of a squid-like monster with goggling headlamp eyes; or of his 'Ruggiero liberating Angelica', where a black-mustachioed hero in armour puts a protecting arm round a flabby heroine clutching her fingers between her teeth, while the severed head of a dragon leers up at her as though ironically commiserating with her at her new peril. Böcklin seems as aware as Corinth of the impulse to make the grand gesture, and yet is unable to do so, in his artistic integrity, without at the same time deriding his own highly finished achievement. Like many of the men of letters, both these artists felt the need of some dynamic to replace the dreariness of mechanical routine in a newly industrialized society, and yet remained conscious of the spurious quality of self-conscious striving after such a goal. It is just such a consciousness as Felix Krull has in mind when he explicitly asks the reader to accept the operetta-hero he himself represents, and to forget the ageing actor behind the cosmetic mask. There are also, however, stories in which degradation is more nakedly and viciously portrayed. Gustav von Aschenbach's cosmetic rejuvenation in *Der Tod in Venedig*, his pretence at youthful vigour, is degrading; we are not explicitly asked to forget the mask in his case. Heinrich Mann's story, *Professor Unrat*, treats the theme of a respectable citizen's fall from grace in decidedly unambiguous fashion. Here the parallel to Aschenbach is a worthy elderly schoolmaster who becomes infatuated not with a beautiful boy but a cabaret artist ('die *Künstlerin* Rosa Fröhlich' as she is always called); his equivalent of Aschenbach's journey to Venice is the attempt to live in her sphere of Bohemian generosity and easy-going unconventionality; his degradation is the moment when, having debauched the whole town in which he lives, he is arrested for theft and deluged with filthy water. Where Thomas Mann is, however, always aware of a dual possibility, of condemnation and approval running hand in hand, Heinrich portrays his hero with a pitiless fury whose only purpose seems to be to wreak vengeance on some image of authority. *Professor Unrat* loses interest as a novel, not because it pretends black is white, but rather because it presents a world so completely black that none of its features can be distinguished.

By 1914 the dilemma of men of letters had become apparent. There was, on the one hand, the feeling of inadequacy expressed in Hofmannsthal's famous 'Chandos' letter (entitled 'Ein Brief'), in which he confessed his inability to use any of the traditional concepts of religion and metaphysics or to come to any settled conclusion about any topic whatsoever: a kind of paralysis or 'ligature', to use the jargon of the eighteenth-century quietists, in which awareness of the ineffable made all attempt at expression seem indecent. Related to this was the dilemma of Aschenbach and Tonio Kröger, both of whom saw in the phrase 'tout comprendre, c'est tout pardonner' an inducement to unbearable laxity, an antinomianism which they both desired and abhorred. The same difficulty confronts Arthur Schnitzler in his stories and plays, particularly in *Professor Bernhardi*, in which an attempt at decisive moral protest peters out in a series of justifications of all the parties involved. Frequently, as here and in Hauptmann's *Die Weber*, the indecisiveness is due to a scrupulous care in avoiding prejudiced condemnation. There is also, however, as in Thomas Mann, a tendency to conclude that since nothing is justified everything is justified, or, as in Nietzsche, that the concepts of good and evil are nullified and need to be replaced by new values of daring assertiveness. This too brings its dilemmas, for Rilke the dilemma of confronting death as a part of life, for Mann that of mocking his own creations. The attempt is therefore made to merge the contraries in one, to welcome contradictions as inherent in all intenser forms of living and thus to escape their inhibiting influence. Stefan George, living among a group of poets whose stress lay all on irrationalism, 'Rausch', intoxication, opposed them with the demand for clarity, formal excellence, 'Helle': his poetry was to be the fusion of both, and the boy-god Maximin whom he discovered and revered was said to display the living embodiment of these contraries. Rilke sought, in the 'Dinggedichte', to combine a subjective perception with complete objectivity; he sought contact with others through a love which should also be intransitive, to live and write in a replete isolation which should also, paradoxically, be all-embracing. Thomas Mann oscillates between Schopenhauer's denial and Nietzsche's affirmation of the Will, and yet stands outside both. Yet the dilemmas are not felt to be solved, nor is there, among the writers in the Nietzschean tradition, any intention of solving them: it is rather a matter of accepting the dilemma as an integral part of existence.

Occasionally, it is true, some reference is made to the traditional Christian standards, which despite the general decline in religious belief had by no means lost their grip on the population at large. Thomas Mann frequently ended his novels with some form of quasi-Christian statement; several of Rilke's poems, and a few of George's, at least treat of Christ, as does the novel by Gerhart Hauptmann, *Emanuel Quint*. On the whole, however, it was to some form of Buddhistic belief that writers felt an affinity. Schopenhauer had ended the main exposition of his philosophy with an explicit comparison with the Buddhists' Nirvana; Nietzsche had seen in Buddhism at least a more acceptable religion than Christianity. Rilke, while he wrote a poem in denigration of Christ, wrote another in praise of the Buddha; Hermann Hesse's post-war novel *Siddhartha* was an interpretation of Buddhist teaching, and Franz Werfel's dramatic trilogy *Spiegelmensch* had as its theme the Buddhist conception of selfhood. In the years before 1914 no writer or poet of note within the German Empire held any Christian convictions or was sympathetically inclined to any, and even in 'Catholic Austria', where Kralik's 'Society of the Grail' (Gralbund) represented a movement unknown in Germany, the only outstanding poet of Christian persuasion was the Protestant poet Georg Trakl. In Trakl's poetry the forebodings of war are expressed with sombre intensity. There is no ambiguity about his work, nor any form of irony; the dark landscapes of his poems, like his moods, are unassuaged by any philosophical reflections. His constructions are for the most part a seemingly fortuitous assemblage of unconnected

3-2

passages, and when a peaceful mood emerges from them, as it does surprisingly often, it is the result of a particular mood which may be broken again as a new poem begins to form. Trakl is distinguished by his complete lack of any systematic 'Weltanschauung', and was thus less well equipped, in one sense, to meet the horror of the war when it came. The spectacle of slaughter on the Eastern Front, which he was one of the few pre-war writers to witness in person, was overwhelming; his inability to give any help, as a member of an ill-equipped medical detachment, to the wounded men he had expected to tend, drove him within a short while to take his own life. His defencelessness against experience, the frankness with which he sets down his lyrical moods, his simplicity and directness and the almost inarticulate grief in many of his poems make him a kind of Woyzeck in the society of his own day. By comparison, and despite Trakl's ultimate despair, the turning towards Christian belief in Hofmannsthal's version of the morality-play *Everyman* looks facile.

The outbreak of war in August 1914 was greeted in Germany as in England with tumultuous enthusiasm, much of it naïvely patriotic or chauvinistic.[13] The Social Democrat party alone was divided, its Marxist wing under Karl Liebknecht opposing the vote for war-expenditure; but of 110 members of the party in the Reichstag, only fourteen were thus opposed, and none opposed the majority in the House itself. German workers went to war to meet the threat of Russian autocracy, as their English counterparts did to defeat German imperialism. The middle-class man was likely to see in the foreign opposition to Germany's belated rise to power a hypocritical refusal to allow what other nations had already achieved through war. There was also the unashamedly militarist view that Germany was entitled to assert herself as a world-power; what the Netherlands and Sweden had temporarily achieved by force of arms in the seventeenth century, and what England and France enjoyed at this day, was not to be denied to the most populous nation in Central Europe. The new

Empire was now to win its spurs as others had done. The long process since the Reformation, which had had such startlingly rapid results for the Dutch and the Swedes, was now felt to be reaching its culmination. As the great sociologist Max Weber wrote in a letter of April 1915, 'we have proved that we are a people of great culture (großes Kulturvolk): human beings who live amidst a refined culture, yet who can even stand up to the horrors of war (which is no achievement for a Senegalese!) and then, in spite of it, return basically decent like the majority of our soldiers—this is genuinely humane...'.[14] The war, seen in such a spirit, was a sign of Germany's awakening from decadence; the insistent self-consciousness of the awakening hid the doubtfulness which it might have revealed.

For Rilke, a citizen of the Austro-Hungarian Empire by birth, although German by inclination, the war was a revelation. In a way quite untypical of his normal mood, he proclaimed that at last, out of the lifeless sham of the preceding years, a god had arisen, men were truly in the grip of emotion, no longer mild and reasonable but giving vent to the terrible impulses within them. A few days later the reports of bloodshed and destruction, together with his own gentle nature, made him pause in doubt whether this could truly be the fearful god himself: there appeared to be no awareness in him, but only savage destructiveness:

> Ist er ein Wissender? *Kann*
> er ein Wissender sein, dieser reißende Gott?*[15]

This fury seemed purely barbaric, not that deliberate murderousness in the knowledge of the necessity for barbarism, which Nietzsche would have welcomed. It was a manifestation of the Will in its primal integrity, not in its conscious self-affirmation. Rilke turned therefore to the task of bringing about this self-knowledge. The war must be lamented, in order that it might be more duly praised. His own hesitation must be swallowed

---

* Is he one of those who know? *Can*
He be such a one, this tempestuous god?

up ultimately in abandonment to the driving impulse of the times:

> Sei euch die Klage nicht schmählich. Wahr erst
> wird das unkenntliche, das
> keinem begreifliche Schicksal,
> wenn ihr es maßlos beklagt und dennoch das maßlos,
> dieses beklagteste, seht: wie ersehntes begeht.*

Rilke's desire is not that the war should end or the destruction cease. It is rather that the war should 'become true', that it should arouse both the fullest acceptance and the fullest rejection. The lament should be entered upon as though what was lamented were at the same time what was most desired. Without this, the existential experience of war would not attain complete truth, for war needed this dual response in order to come into its fullest range of being. In this way Rilke came to make his own affirmation of existence, fully in the Nietzschean sense. Yet his desire for truth of experience was curiously diminished by his deliberate welcome to illusion. The culture he defended still did not exist, but it must be asserted as though it did exist and as though it had cosmic significance; the beliefs he held were not authoritative and yet must be held to be so:

> Nun seid ihr aufs Eigne wieder beschränkt. Doch größer
> ist es geworden. Wenns auch nicht Welt ist, bei weitem, —
> nehmt es wie Welt!†

Rilke's achievement as a poet is a matter to which more thought will be devoted later. His political views, with their paradoxicalness, have a peculiar significance in the present context. This determination to affirm what was recognized as inadequate has an unexpected echo in the words of the forerunner of National Socialism, Moeller van den Bruck, when he declared that Germany

---

* Let not lament seem disgraceful. This faceless, incomprehensible destiny cannot come true till you have lamented it measurelessly, and yet, lo, have engaged on this measureless, most lamentable thing as though it were dearly desired.

† Now you are restricted again to what's yours. But it has grown larger. Even though it is not a whole world, by far, take it as a whole world.

was 'strong as a state, and consequently strong in military matters, in everything that had to do with defence, but extremely weak in possessing anything to defend'.[16] The deliberate cultivation of what Rilke called a sham is one of the strangest aspects of German thought in these years.

Thomas Mann's attitude to the war—his achievement as a novelist is of course another matter—did not differ essentially from Rilke's, and was expressed first in his essay *Friedrich und die große Koalition*, dated December 1914 and published in 1915 together with his letter to a Swedish newspaper in defence of German policy. In effect, it is at once a criticism and a justification of Frederick the Great's Prussia and of the Wilhelmine Empire. Mann does not give the sentimental picture of 'der olle Fritz', the good-hearted old pirate, that many of his readers might have liked. He emphasizes the king's brutal cynicism towards his subjects, his flouting of common decencies, the savagery of his instructions to his troops. He suggests that Frederick was probably the father of bastards as well as a homosexual, and makes no pretence that he had any moral justification for the invasion of Silesia and the partition of Poland. But at the same time he portrays the almost incredibly tenacious willpower in Frederick, the faith in his own ability to encounter the greatest odds, his immense industriousness, his social reforms and financial successes. 'Germany today', he concluded, '*is* Frederick the Great. It is his struggle that we have now to carry through to the end, that we must fight again.'[17] Mann felt for Frederick an admiration which his frankness did not diminish. Indeed such frankness was in itself a justification. The Germans, he asserted, were more deep-sighted than other nations, and more manly in their endurance of what they were able to see: they knew the evil in themselves and despised civilization because it hid that evil under hypocritical pretences, preventing its true expression. For them war meant an end to the corrupting ease of peaceful times, and thus their conduct had a moral justification lacking in the conduct of other nations; it was a deliberate expression of the totality of human nature: 'this is a matter of brutality for intellectual reasons (eine

Brutalität aus Gedanklichkeit), an intellectually based will to become worthy of the world, to qualify in the world.'[18] 'Germany's whole virtue and beauty...is unfolded only in war.' 'The German soul is too deep for civilization to be for her a high value, let alone the highest value.'

All this sounds reminiscent of Nietzsche's 'Brutalitäts-Cur', and there are times at which, in this essay, Mann seems to see the brutality he now advocates as a step towards a 'Third Reich' in which the liberal ideals of 1848 will be realized in a fusion of might and right.[19] This notion of war as a cure for decadence, rather than as a healthy activity in itself, plays a part in the collection of occasional pieces written by Mann in the next few years and published under the title *Betrachtungen eines Unpolitischen*. Indeed, Mann does not seem to have been over-proud of what had been, perhaps, an ill-considered outburst, or at least of some of the more fanatical passages it contained. In the *Betrachtungen* he lays frequent emphasis on the civilized qualities he had recently disdained. 'Good breeding', he wrote, 'is the sphere in which I live and breathe; I love, indeed at bottom I respect only what is kindly—crudity offends me, personal hatred I fear, and suffer from that which I deal out as much as from that which I bear, although I know very well that in order to live out humanity to the full one must experience hatred both actively and passively.'[20] There are many passages to a similar effect—to much the same effect, indeed, as Hans Castorp's dream of the 'Grail' in *Der Zauberberg*, insisting on courtesy, reverence and love as essential human qualities. But, again as in the dream, there is also a recognition of the cruelty inherent in human nature and in life itself, finding expression here in racial hatred, jingoism, wild and dark accusations against the enemy coupled with a persistent affirmation of the homeland's moral right to be brutal and a denial that it could possibly be so. Mann's attitude is ultimately detached and quietistic: 'The horrors of war may set your hair on end—well, my hair stood on end at a birth which lasted thirty-six hours. That was not human, it was *hellish*, and so long as that continues to exist, war can continue to exist, for all I

40

care.'[21] Birth, like war and death, was part of life; far from attempting to assuage the pangs of either, Mann preferred to accept both, seeing in each a 'mystical element' common to all fundamental feeling, whether of religion or of love. Or rather, Mann seems to have had such a preference, for in the preface later added to the rest he both associates and dissociates himself from the views he had expressed, claiming that they were no more than a daily record of his varying opinions. The contradictions they contain are thus paradoxically regarded both as worthy and as unworthy of attention. But this is characteristic also of Mann's fictional work at least up to this date: it has the same ambiguous affirmations and denials. And as in Nietzsche, the practical results are notable for the support they give to society as it exists at the moment.

During the war-years, those who had been most influenced by Nietzsche published almost nothing of a literary kind. Rilke and Mann restricted themselves (as far as publication is concerned) to the political utterances just described, George was silent, Hofmannsthal was principally occupied with the definition of a Christian, conservative tendency in Austrian history from which he hoped for some unification of the rapidly disintegrating, multinational Empire of Franz Josef.[22] Hermann Hesse published only the tales of *Knulp* (1915), a figure in the Romantic tradition of Eichendorff's *Taugenichts* who provided an escape from the present reality rather than a confrontation with it. Sorge, whose play *Der Bettler* had been followed almost at once by his conversion to Catholicism, wrote only two more plays, both of them now almost forgotten, before his death at the front in 1916. The Expressionists, all of them young men, and often serving soldiers, published poems of agonized horror whose impact was not fully felt until after 1918. The one writer of international reputation who continued both to write and publish throughout the war was a man remarkably different from most of his predecessors, Franz Kafka.

Kafka did not become widely known until the late 1920's, after the posthumous publication by his friend Max Brod of his three unfinished novels, and suffered an almost complete eclipse in Germany from 1933 till 1945. The greater part of the works he himself was prepared to publish did appear, however, between 1912 and 1919. They are distinguished from most of the works so far discussed in that they have no explicit political concern whatsoever. Apart from Zionism, Kafka had no political interests, and in so far as he was concerned with society, it was the bureaucracy of the Austro-Hungarian Empire, of which he himself was an official, which claimed his attention and formed the subject-matter of his two major works, *Der Proʒeß* and *Das Schloß*. In each of these novels the central character is confronted with a mysterious organization which both makes the most exacting demands on him and preserves to the end an inscrutable superiority; K. and Josef K. alike are left exhausted by their efforts at penetrating the mystery. On this account, Kafka's detractors have been prone to see in his work a lack-lustre acquiescence in the society of his day.[23] To hold this view, however, is to see in the two K.'s a kind of Tonio Kröger, whereas in fact neither of them makes any such acknowledgment of the 'Bürger's' superiority as he does. Where Tonio concludes with the expression of 'Bürgerliebe' and with contempt for the greatest works of art and philosophy, Kafka's heroes continue throughout to assert their inability to solve their riddles. They are frustrated men, sometimes desperately anxious to be accepted by society, sometimes wishing to stand completely apart, but constantly persuaded of the impossibility of either. That they are also neurotically prone to see this as their own guilt rather than that of society is a mark of Kafka's own situation, not of any desire for easy accommodation. There is never—this is a further mark of distinction—any philosophy of synthesis informing Kafka's work. Nor does he in his short stories set out to illustrate the workings of a system of beliefs, already held, but, as a rule, to explore the situation of his characters in an ignorance as complete as the reader's of what the outcome will be.[24] His usual method relies too much on the inspiration of the moment to allow of any such appearance of form as Mann's work has. By the same token, although Kafka's fictional *alter ego* desperately

42

seeks some sense of community, he is never willing to accept such a sense at the cost of his conscience.

This scrupulousness of Kafka's makes generalized interpretation misleading: his stories and novels do not bear out one common solution of a problem, but have a wide variety of moods, each regulated by the particular context. (It is absolutely clear, for example, that *Das Schloß* was never meant to end like *Der Prozeß*.[25]) The task of interpretation is even further complicated by the suggestion that Kafka's work is of allegorical and religious significance. For Kafka himself was certainly occupied for most of his life with Jewish and Christian theology, particularly that of Kierkegaard, and this is reflected even in his purely literary writing. In much the same way as K. and Josef K. struggle against a mysterious authority, Kafka struggled with his convictions, both that there must be a point of view from which it was possible to see the world as good, and that to express such a view in human language was an intolerable act of *hubris*. He could not escape from this dilemma through self-affirmation, or through such affirmations of meaninglessness as his recent admirers have made.[26] To him the Absurd remained absurd, never to become acceptable and never to be accounted for in philosophical terms. So far as complete ignorance of God's existence was concerned, he was in the Nietzschean situation, but not of it, and would never make that change of front which sought to make an intolerable world tolerable or even welcome. Dreams of punishment, meaninglessness, the Absurd, dread, retain their full import to the bitter end, not paradoxically turning into praiseworthy values or 'gratuitous' facts of existence.

Despite his unorthodoxy as a Jew, Kafka has seemed to some writers[27] to typify the faith of Judaism, at least in the respect that no amount of awareness of God's absence and of present misery weakens his belief in God's faithfulness. Kafka wrote as he did in the conviction that the worst could be said and experienced by men without stain to the divine perfection. (What orthodox Jew today, in the light of the concentration camps, to say nothing of Jewish history since the Dispersion, could believe otherwise?)

His religious aphorisms, never published although apparently prepared for publication, are full of this conviction, and if his stories do not reveal it, that is probably because he saw his task primarily as that of a modern novelist, recording experience rather than conquering it, remaining open to every facet of his own moods. In this, he is a man of his times: Tolstoy, Dostoevsky, Dante, the English Metaphysicals did not feel the need to exclude their religious beliefs from their artistic work. The same determination to remain firm by the inspiration of the moment, with all its quietistic implications, must account for that tendency of Kafka's to lengthy developments of minutiae, which interrupts the fascination his grim narratives often exert. Yet in his insistence on living out his tragic life as a writer to the full, without recourse to irony and without laying claim to a belief he could not wholeheartedly affirm, Kafka stands opposed to every German writer of his time, with the sole exception of Georg Trakl.

K. never reaches the Castle; Josef K. never learns the nature of the guilt with which the Court charges him. The one is executed by officials of the Court, the other, we are told by Max Brod, was to have received permission to stay in the village, outside the Castle's walls, only on his deathbed. It may seem from this as though the alternative to the tradition of acceptance and affirmation were despair to the point of annihilation, and it is true that there are stories of Kafka's which suggest such terms of choice. The man fantastically transformed into an insect in *Die Verwandlung* is swept away with the rubbish after his death, leaving his unreflective family to enjoy a happier existence. The 'Hungerartist', in the story of that name, is a man of the past whose hungering, apparently symbolical of the hunger after righteousness, is no longer appreciated by the world at large: he too is swept away with the refuse, to be replaced by a wild beast who takes the public's fancy rather better. It is as though Kafka were allegorizing here with some prescience the tendency of his times, in which such a preference was already showing itself. The gruesome story *In der Strafkolonie* might be interpreted in a similar way. The machine of torture described here, by means of which

44

men formerly gained enlightenment, evidently stands for the traditional conception of redemption through conviction of guilt. The explorer who flees from the scene after the machine has broken in pieces could well be taken to represent that contemporary attitude which shuns all suffering as an obscenity. Yet to make such interpretations into a message from the author, as though he himself sought to shun suffering and to inculcate such an attitude in his readers, is to make Kafka less of an artist than he is. He makes these endings to his stories in his awareness of his own times: 'hungering' and the endurance of torment are outmoded, and the public would rather live in ignorance of them. However—'You can shut your eyes to the suffering of the world', he wrote in his notebook, 'that is the one suffering you might be able to avoid'. In each of these stories there is at least a moment, fleetingly glimpsed, when the sufferer shows signs of a purity of spirit which passes unnoticed by the world around him. These are very faint gleams, barely recognizable and perhaps not even consciously felt by Kafka to exist. In times of extreme self-consciousness, however, when messages were being proclaimed by writers on every side, such tentativeness and such unwillingness to make any parade of insights were one way in which a writer of scrupulous integrity could continue to write without a completely overwhelming sense of shame. They were perhaps not the only way; Kafka's neurotic imbalance partly accounts for them. But they were at least not corrupted by willing self-contradiction. They had no political implications: the drift towards the concentration camps could not have been halted by such a mode of writing, even had it become widely known before the Nazis seized power. But at least those for whom release from the camps was as unforeseeable as was Kafka's release from his own, mental torment could have faced their extermination with a similar composure—as some did.

CHAPTER II

WRITERS AND POLITICS: 1918–1933

Opposition to the war had grown yearly. With starvation and other hardships, there had been an increasing number of strikes, demonstrations and desertions from the armed forces. But there was no certainty of direction among the Social Democrats from whom leadership of this opposition was to be expected. The party was divided between its 'Fabian', Reformist wing under Bernstein and its Marxist-revolutionary wing under Karl Liebknecht and Rosa Luxemburg. The Russian Revolution served to accentuate this division, presenting the extreme Left with a model of what might be accomplished in Germany, and increasing the fear of 'Bolshevization' in the supporters of the Right. In the autumn of 1918, however, a decisive rejection of the Wilhelmine Empire seemed about to be made. The German front having been broken, the majority parties accepted as chancellor Prince Max of Baden, the Emperor left the country, the Republic was proclaimed, and the armistice signed. Yet despite the apparent finality of these events, they were markedly ambiguous. It was by no means certain, up to the very last, that the Emperor would be called upon to abdicate. Friedrich Ebert, chairman of the Social Democrats in the Reichstag and a member of the triumvirate which formed the first post-revolutionary government, nursed half a wish that the new regime might still continue to exist as a monarchy: the desire to preserve the traditional form, even that of an Empire which his party had opposed, was still strong. From the outset of the revolution he was also in contact with the General Staff in the attempt, ultimately a successful one, to retain the militarists even though it might be at the expense of establishing socialism. Under Ebert's leadership the new Republic allowed former Imperial officials and Army officers to hold much the same power as they had held hitherto.[1] The high regard in

46

which the Imperial family continued to be held in many quarters is shown by the deference paid to an impostor who successfully impersonated the son of the Crown Prince.[2]

The body of the politically conscious working class meanwhile remained bewildered. Believing it to be the intention of the Social Democrats to introduce socialism, they had given their support to Ebert and his colleagues, and remained aloof from the 'Spartacist' uprising of the Communists in late 1918 and early 1919. The government's main concern, however, was rather to prevent the sovietization of Germany, which it feared more than the retention of capitalism and of military predominance. The brief revolution in Bavaria in 1919, proclaiming a Bavarian Soviet Republic, was put down by regular troops of the Reich, together with Right-wing volunteers from East Prussia. The Bavarian radical Kurt Eisner had been assassinated a little earlier; his murderer escaped with a comparatively light sentence. The officers who clubbed down and shot Liebknecht and Luxemburg received trivial sentences from a military court, while those involved in an attempt at overthrowing the government itself in 1920 went unmolested save for their leader Kapp. Such events lent some colour to Rilke's observation, made in 1923, that Germany 'wanted to persist and not to alter'.[3] There was at least some willingness in the leaders of the Republic to maintain the old rather than risk the new, and their reluctance to envisage change must seem remarkably like the acquiescence, both philosophical and political, of many of the leading men of literature.

There was also, however, widespread determination to reassert civil liberties in the spirit of the revolution of 1848. The choice of Weimar, the home of Goethe and Schiller, as the seat of the national Assembly, was meant to be one indication of more humane ideals. The Weimar Constitution itself was regarded as a model democratic document, and erred rather by excess than by lack of liberalism. The voters in the election of 1920, after the Constitution had been adopted, showed decisively the direction they expected from the Republic. In a Reichstag of 459 members, now for the first time elected on a universal suffrage, 102 Social

Democrats were returned, 84 Independent Socialists, and 4 Communists, giving a Socialist wing of 190. The Catholic 'Zentrum', now more liberal than it had been under Bismarck, counted 64 members; the Democrats, an alliance of progressive Liberals with all but the right wing of the National Liberals, and standing left of centre—though this was still right-wing in terms of the politics of other nations—mustered 39. On the conservative side the German People's party and the German National People's party had 65 and 71 members, making a comparatively small right-wing block. Judging by the figures alone, and ignoring the difficulties of forming alliances—no party having an overall majority—the former opposition parties seemed to have established themselves.

The hundreds of plays and poems, largely written in or inspired by the war years, which flooded out after 1918 give a different picture of the general trend. These are the works of such writers as Ernst Toller, Georg Kaiser, Fritz von Unruh, Walter Hasenclever, Hanns Johst and Arnolt Bronnen, to mention only a few of the leading figures. Some of them record, as does Toller's play *Die Wandlung*, the transformation brought about by the war from patriotic rejoicing to desperate rejection of the national cause. Others acclaim the war as an Armageddon whose end must mean a rebirth into a better world. The Expressionist works are full of expectations of 'the New Man' who will now arise in Europe and spread the message of loving brotherhood and a more intense existence. The age of Mammon and its machines is over; new suns rise, the night is past. Few writers of any nation can have been so intimately concerned with the situation of the day as those of Germany at this time. Yet there is a disturbing quality about their plays, something melodramatic about the ghastlinesses they portray, and an excess of emotional language. Skeletons go on parade as soldiers and roll skulls by numbers; a severed head in a sack converses with its former owner; a woman bleats her Dionysiac love to a billy-goat; a father horsewhips his son, a son chases lustfully round the table after his mother, a society is formed for the Brutalization of the Ego. A man earns his living by eating live mice; a crowd of spectators exults pitilessly over the exhausted riders in a seven-day cycle race; the shades of Shakespeare and Kleist stalk over the battlefields; the German navy sinks in ecstatic and apocalyptic splendour in Scapa Flow. Too often there emerges from such scenes a radiant sun flooding the landscape with light while bands of pilgrims rejoice in a new-found freedom, or some similar note of boundless optimism is struck. A crowd of dancers press orgiastically together, groaning their self-discovered divinity—this time, no doubt, as objects of satire, although one may ask what kind of society called for such satirizing. A bank-cashier stands with arms outstretched in front of a crucifix, his dying gasps accidentally suggesting the words 'Ecce Homo'. An atmosphere of painful contrivance is felt everywhere, a hysterical abandonment to the wildest hopes and the unlikeliest despair.

It is usual to divide the Expressionist poets and dramatists into two groups, the religious or metaphysical, and the Activist or Communist, the one advocating spiritual remedies, the other political ones. From their works alone, however, it is hard to see where the distinction lies. Toller, who had been a Minister in the short-lived Bavarian Soviet Republic, was the most politically active. But his first play, published in 1918, has decidedly religious preoccupations, and so long as he remained a writer in the Expressionist vein he was undecided in his allegiances. Only in his later, realistically documentary plays, *Feuer aus den Kesseln* and *Die Maschinenstürmer*, does he treat of strictly political themes, and even here a measure of religious symbolism is apparent. Johannes Becher, later to be a Minister in the East German Democratic Republic, was in his earlier days similarly half-inclined to the supernatural. It is not until the end of the twenties that an exclusively political theatre makes itself felt.

The real bond between all Expressionist writers is seen in the catchword 'Rausch'. Ecstasy, intoxication in one form or another is the common theme, whether in the realization of the New Man, or the union with all mankind, or the acceptance of defeat and destruction, or the satisfying of sexual desires, or the mystical union with the cosmos. Even where ecstasy is opposed,

4   49

and a cool determination advocated in its place, as it is in Kaiser's *Die Bürger von Calais*, the opposition is expressed with a magniloquent emotion that fails to distinguish itself from what it criticizes. The new generation found its spokesman in the theoretician Kasimir Edschmid, whose manifesto of 1919 drew a picture of the poet-man now about to emerge:

His heart breathes, his lungs roar, he yields himself to creation, not being a part of it, but cradling it in himself, mirroring it. His life is regulated not by trivial logic, without any rationalistic or shame-producing morality, but only in accordance with the tremendous calibration of his heart....He does not think about himself, he experiences himself.[4]

A lingering memory of Nietzsche's Dionysianism can be perceived here. This is a bathetic version of the Superman, living exultantly and amorally as the inspiration of the moment carries him along. To a greater or lesser degree, all the Expressionists sympathized with such ideals, and the effusiveness of their protestations portended nothing good. Indeed, as Edmond Vermeil has said, 'stage by stage, through this distracted lyrical poetry [of Expressionism] we see in preparation the themes, the state of mind, the intoxication, fervent and sincere, which was the intoxication of a youth that escaped from a decaying social structure and found itself ready to plunge into the great adventure of the Third Reich'.[5] A historian of the cinema has reached a similar conclusion from his study of the Expressionist film: after 1933, writes Siegfried Kracauer, 'Germany carried out what had been anticipated by her cinema from its very beginning'.[6] It was not the case by any means that these poets, playwrights, and film-producers were themselves inclined towards National Socialism. Johst and Bronnen, it is true, became leading dramatists in the Third Reich; the works of Toller, von Unruh, Becher and Kaiser were, after 1933, banned along with many others; the Left-wing film-producer Pabst was both driven into exile and allowed by the Nazis to return to exercise his former profession on their behalf.[7] No generalization can do justice to the variety of individual beliefs and circumstances. All the same the vagueness and frequent emotionalism, the often ludicrous immoderation of Expressionism as a whole, reflects an intellectual mood that was still indeterminate. Such a chaotic ferment might readily be poured into one mould by a skilful operator.

The ambiguity of direction was already signalled by the title of an anthology of verse published in 1919. At a time when the New Man was all the rage, this volume of Expressionist lyrics had the title, *Menschheitsdämmerung*, in allusive contrast to that of Wagner's opera. Similarly, an avant-garde literary periodical of the war-years had been called *Der jüngste Tag*, or 'Doomsday'. The titles were significant marks of the 'Untergangsstimmung', the mood of downfall or decay which was as strongly represented as the mood of exultant expectation. Just as Nietzsche had seen the Superman both as a rejection of human nature and a transition to a new nature which strangely resembled the first, so the Expressionist Man was conscious of his impending end as much as of his new beginning. A welcome is offered to extinction, whether with nonchalance, as in the early lyrics of Bertolt Brecht:

> Bei den Erdbeben, die kommen werden, werde ich hoffentlich
> Meine Virginia nicht ausgehen lassen durch Bitterkeit*[8]

or with the nostalgia of Gottfried Benn:

> . . . tagen
> sieh diese letzte Glück-Lügenstunde
> unserer Südlichkeit
> hochgewölbt.†[9]

The most comprehensive statement of all, however, was that of Oswald Spengler, the first instalment of whose *Der Untergang des Abendlandes* appeared in 1918, some years after it had first been written. Here a whole philosophy of history was erected to demonstrate the inevitability of a coming doom. The great

---

*   During the earthquakes that are going to come, I hope
         I shall not let my cigar go out, out of bitterness.
†   See dawning the last happy-mendacious hour
         of our Mediterranean selves, high-vaulted.

         4-2

civilizations of the past had arisen like plants, flowered and withered away in accordance with a common pattern of growth which Spengler claimed to have detected. The fourth and most recent, the 'Western', or European, or more accurately the Germanic, for Spengler identified the two, had now reached its own final stage, and must be succeeded by a new civilization rising in the East. The importance of this theory was not in its pessimism, for most ages have their jeremiads, but rather in its reflection of a widespread determination to welcome such a downfall as Spengler predicted. (Though there were also many who opposed him vigorously.) Thus the apocalyptic ending of Georg Kaiser's play *Gas* requires not merely that a victorious army should reduce everything in sight to rubble, but that having done so, it should be heard offstage, firing its own artillery 'evidently in self-destruction', as the stage-direction puts it with little regard for the problems of the stage-manager. But such a desire for disaster was equally represented in other quarters. 'For all peoples', wrote Moeller van den Bruck, 'comes the hour when they must die by murder or suicide, and no grander ending can be imagined for a people than destruction (Untergang) in a world-war in which the whole earth had to rise and suppress a single country.'[10] This was intended to refer to the First World War, recently lost; van den Bruck derived some comfort from the sheer magnitude of Germany's enemies. Yet Thomas Mann had written in very similar terms while that war was still continuing. The German poets, he had written in his essay on Frederick II, had greeted the war with enthusiasm: 'they sang the praises of war as though in rivalry, rejoicing, with deep-throated triumph—as though they and the nation whose voice they are could meet with nothing better, more beautiful, more fortunate, than that a desperately overwhelming enmity should rise against that nation'.[11] The great events in the history of Germany at this time were dogged by this sense of futility and inevitable disaster, as though self-assertion could only be proclaimed in the foreknowledge of punitive counter-action. The same sense is present in a writer far apart from Mann, Alfred Rosenberg, whose work, *Der Mythos des*

20. Jahrhunderts, expressed the so-called philosophy of Nazism with a confused appeal to almost every aspect of the German past. A striking feature of this book is the images of doom with which it concludes. What was meant as a challenge to display true German qualities ends with two portrayals: that of the sailor who stood on the keel of the sinking battleship *Nürnberg*, refusing to save himself, and that of the naval officer who drowned himself to prevent a secret code from falling into enemy hands. It may be significant that the final pages of *Mein Kampf* are similarly devoted to accounts of those who gave their lives for the Movement; not that these sacrifices were thought to have been in vain, but that such emphasis should have been placed on them. As the post-war years proceed, it becomes more and more apparent that Hitler's slogan 'World Power or Ruin' is meant as a deliberate welcome to either of these two possibilities, and the attacks on nation after nation look masochistic in their seeming determination to arouse an enmity truly overwhelming.

These were events still twenty years distant. In the years immediately following the peace-treaty of Versailles the strength of those who looked for a resurgence of militarism was still comparatively small. It gained with the growth of the legend that the German armies had surrendered not because they were defeated but because the Left-wing had deliberately made a cowardly peace, a legend which reached a climax in the 'Stab-in-the-Back' trial at Magdeburg in 1924, when President Ebert himself was virtually accused of treason. Assassinations of Socialist and liberal-minded representatives continued. The first attempt of the National Socialist party to overthrow the government came in 1923, when the Munich 'Putsch' of Ludendorff and Hitler was suppressed. These were all signs of an almost chaotic disunity. There were also signs, however, of a latent unity. The amazed resentment in Germany at the terms of the Treaty of Versailles bound the most disparate elements in a sense of un-deserved injury. The continuation of the Allied blockade after the war had ended, and the occupation of the Ruhr by French troops in 1923, fostered more indignation. There was, further, the unity arising from all suffering borne in community. Widespread unemployment and severe financial inflation were seen as obstacles which national pride could overcome; the success of the German film-industry, the only one in the world at that time to devote itself to films of artistic purpose, and the international acclaim accorded to German architecture under the leadership of Walter Gropius and the 'Bauhaus' movement, were greeted as signs of a capacity to live creatively even under adverse conditions. Nevertheless, the constant threat of upheavals was hard to bear with equanimity. The first consolidated German Empire in all history had lasted for not quite fifty years; it had met with a disaster of unimagined severity, and its future—for the Republic continued to style itself 'Deutsches Reich'—was wholly uncertain. Intellectual ideas were equally chaotic. There was a need felt for some new faith or system of belief, which received proffered answers from the anthroposophy of Rudolf Steiner's Goethean cult, founded in the pre-war years, and in Hermann Graf Keyserling's School of Wisdom at Darmstadt. The similarly mystical works of the Bengali poet Rabindranath Tagore were widely read. The spread of Marxist doctrine, to which all Socialist parties adhered, was indicated by the increased representation of the extreme Left in the elections of 1924. The first volume of *Mein Kampf* was published in 1925.

It was in these circumstances that the greater works of literature, all of them with some message for the times, began to appear. Rilke, silent for many years, had since 1919 sought solitude in Switzerland in attendance on the time when poetry would again become a possibility. He had not been inactive: as recent editions of his works have shown, he was writing both prose and poetry throughout the years of war. But the public had seen very little of his work, and he was dissatisfied both with its quality and with his inability to achieve a genuine realization of his spiritual goal. In February 1922 the moment came. Within a few weeks he wrote in a flood of inspiration not only about half of the *Duineser Elegien*, begun in 1912, but the whole of the *Sonette an Orpheus*, fifty-five in all. The two volumes, published in the following year, were like twin poles of an immensely difficult revelation, the *Elegies* sombrely tormented, struggling towards an unattainable unity of purpose, the *Sonnets* delicate and tender, harmoniously rejoicing in the transforming power of Orpheus the supreme poet. At the same time there was a sense of affinity between them. The terrifying and splendid Angel of the *Elegies*, remote from human consciousness, all-enveloping in his serene unawareness of any distinction between life and death, was reflected in a kindlier form in Orpheus, the god who took human shape, whose singing endured in every age by virtue of his knowledge both of the underworld of the dead and of the world of living beings. While the *Elegies* denied the possibility of attaining angelic stature, the *Sonnets* affirmed that something equally valid was attainable here and now through the mediation of the god; the true poet, clothed in the god's nature, always assumed if only momentarily the totality of being which the Angel enjoyed. The poems became in Rilke's eyes a fulfilment of all he had striven for. There was no possibility of critical revision of these inspired works, which demanded only submissiveness from the reader. For the few remaining years of his life Rilke spent a great part of his time in elucidating the poems, writing scores of letters explaining his interpretation of them to friends and unknown inquirers. In the public at large, there was an equally great sense of promised revelation. Scholars and critics set to work in the spirit of theologians expounding the prophet of a new religion. No other lyric poet was to have an influence on literature or ways of living comparable to that of Rilke in these two cycles.

The quality of Rilke's poetry is undefinable in such a study as this. Like his earlier work, the *Elegies* and *Sonnets* are full of verbal felicities, striking phrases, fascinating rhythms and alliterations. They are also frequently so baffling in their syntax, in their simultaneous contradictions, and in their sometimes inapplicable imagery, that to read them is a severe task, even with the aid of voluminous commentaries.[12] Some have felt, after long study, that the task is unrewarding. To defend such a view would, however, require a further-reaching survey[13] and deeper consideration of the nature of poetry. Within the present context it is enough to suggest that Rilke's revelation was still essentially in the tradition of 'synthesis'. Rilke lays little stress, it is true, on the warrior-like qualities which were admired by Nietzsche and George, though he makes passing acknowledgment to the cultivation of ruthlessness. He does, however, continue to see in intensity of experience a justification of existence, and accepts contradiction as its necessary form. He would both be completely detached from the world and at the same time include the whole of externality in a world within himself: the poet in his eyes is the joyful singer as well as the horrified witness of all that is. As for the practical concerns of the day, the import of the *Elegies* and *Sonnets* does not seem to be inconsistent with Rilke's words in a letter already quoted.[14] 'What can we do?' he asked in 1923. 'Let us, each one of us, remain on our own little island of life— still peaceful, still safe—going about our own business, alone with our feelings and our suffering.' His resignedness was not a recognition of defeated hopes, but rather a momentarily pessimistic welcome to the existing state of things. It could at any instant become a more positive welcome, for as a critic has said of Rilke's poetry, 'It is as though someone were writing with two hands at once, speaking with two mouths, and each time one hand, one mouth is making invisible and inaudible what the other said or wrote'.[15] The effect of such double-language in rendering acquiescent a generation for whom the existing state of things was, as we know after the event, leading to catastrophe, remains to be seen in a later chapter. And it should be seen; it should be recognized for what it was. For Rilke was not a poet who sang his songs in seclusion; he was by his own wish a prophet, and his message, unlike other forms of poetry, may be taken to task for the influence it had on the society of his time.

The same year in which Rilke's poems were published, 1923, saw also the appearance of a play by an author whose development had been entirely different. A striking feature of both Rilke and Thomas Mann is the absence of any essential change in their thought from their earliest important work onwards: both extend their range within the same framework of ideas. Hugo von Hofmannsthal, by contrast, had begun with poems and short plays very much in the neo-Romantic spirit of the nineties, languorous, richly evocative of vanished splendours, mystically inclined. In 1922 came his adaptation from Calderón, *Das Salzburger Große Welttheater*, a work of great simplicity and directness in which his friend Richard Strauss noted with good cause a certain 'dogmatic rigidity'.[16] It was, however, one of the few works of any consequence to appear in the post-war years with a clearly Christian bias, and revealed a Hofmannsthal who rejected the Nietzschean trend of the past four decades with the clarity and conviction displayed three centuries or so earlier by the artists of the Counter-Reformation. The same trend continued in his most ambitious work *The Tower* (*Der Turm*), published in 1925 and revised in 1927.

The apparently less ambitious comedy *Der Schwierige* (1922) is of a completely different stamp, reminiscent of the work of Oscar Wilde, which Hofmannsthal knew well, and yet also marking a culmination in a long Austrian tradition. Its theme is a balanced and sympathetic critique of a whole trend of German thought, made from an assured sense of social values. In the person of Count Hanskarl Bühl, the 'difficult' or fastidious man about whom the whole play circles, Hofmannsthal drew a portrait not only of himself, in one aspect, but also of that almost mystical self-awareness which had either crippled or distracted many writers of his own and preceding generations. That Hanskarl is brought out of his isolation by the tactful sanity of his cousin Helene Altenwyl, and that this is achieved with such psychological verisimilitude, is not merely a happy ending in the traditional sense, but a genuine liberation from an impasse of much more representative significance. In writing what was one of the few great comedies in the German language, Hofmannsthal also succeeded in creating a moral touchstone. It was an unhappy irony that he did so at the very time when the Empire for which he wrote was reduced to one of the smallest nations in Europe, barely capable of economic survival. What he said in the last year of his life of Lessing was fit to prove his own epitaph: 'He was of another race than they; he revealed a possible development in German character that had no success; he mastered his materials, instead of letting them master him. His importance for the nation resides in the contrast he affords.'[17]

Der Schwierige had nothing like the popular success of Mann's *Der Zauberberg*,[18] which was shortly to earn for its author the award of the Nobel Prize, nor did Hofmannsthal show any of Mann's capacity for adapting himself to new situations. The year in which the play appeared was also that in which Mann, hitherto a spokesman of conservative Imperialism, made his speech at the Beethovensaal in Berlin, 'Von deutscher Republik'. This was, as to superficial appearance, a remarkable *volte-face*, in which Mann declared his adherence to the State newly constituted at Weimar. Closer attention, however, revealed that there was less contradiction in this than might have been supposed. Mann's main concern was to show that 'republican democracy', defined in his own sense, was not un-German as many claimed it to be, but rather the true expression of the highest ideals of German Romanticism, usually associated with royalism and Catholic reaction. To this end, he used the term synonymously with not the actual Republic of his day, but with the State; it was not the achievement of the 'cunning Jew-boys' (die scharfen Judenjungen) he set out to praise, but a nation in which these should have been removed from control, in which all should join in a mass-movement, fused by the ecstasy of erotic love and sharing in the mighty power of the whole: a 'democratic fanaticism', and an 'intoxicated philosophy of Socialism', and 'erotically all-embracing democracy'. The terms were vague enough, for all that they were defined in terms of an 'obscene root-symbol' and rejected any idea of love 'in a diluted, anaemic, ascetically pitying sense'. It was sufficient for Mann that the State was the 'res publica', and the 'res publica' was the republic: on these terms he could welcome even the republic of Weimar. Yet the fact that he could use such phrases at so crucial a moment in German history is a sign of the irresponsible *amor fati* in which he still trusted. Within a few years, he was to recoil in horror from the movement which gave a practical interpretation to such language as he had employed. His opposition, still in a sense ambiguous as will appear, dated from the time when his vagueness had been ousted by the Movement's more specific doctrine.

Three major writers had thus contributed their message to the post-war generation. A fourth, Stefan George, waited until 1928 before publishing his own, a volume of poems with the now ominous title *Das neue Reich*, whose contents, though austere, were sufficiently in accord with the aims of the National Socialists for them to offer him high honour on their accession to power. But even as these contributions were made, the chaotic state of Germany was already beginning to shape itself. The inflation came to an end in 1925, with the stabilization of the mark brought about by the economic policies of Hjalmar Schacht, who later performed a similar service under the Nazi rule. The humiliations to which Germany had been subjected began to be removed when in December of that year the Treaty of Locarno, in which Germany participated on an equal footing, was signed. In the following year came tokens of the recovery not only of prosperity but also of international prestige. In January the evacuation of the First Occupation Zone was completed; in April the German–Soviet non-aggression pact was signed, in May the Preparatory Disarmament Commission opened at Geneva with the implied promise that Germany would no longer remain the one unarmed nation among the major Powers. In September Germany was admitted at last to the League of Nations, and the astute diplomacy of Gustav Stresemann began to show results. In addition, although the Presidency had passed, on the death of Ebert, in 1925, to Field-Marshal von Hindenburg, the representative of the militarist Right-wing, elections showed an increasingly strong tendency to the Left. By 1928 the Social Democrats were twice as strong as any other single party, and the possibility of a stable majority, replacing the coalitions of the past, was not too remote. As happened after the Second World War, it did not take more than a few years for Germany to find her feet again.

The changed circumstances were immediately reflected in works of literature. By one of those swings typical of German literary history, Expressionism came to a sudden halt. From 1925 onwards, though Expressionist plays had continued to pour out during the inflation, scarcely any dramatic work characteristic of the movement appeared, as though the increased prosperity had all at once rendered it pointless. In its place came the movement vaguely held together for the literary historian by the name 'Neue Sachlichkeit', which had been gathering way for two or three years.[19] It had no special features except, as the German implies, a matter-of-fact realism in contrast to the heady ecstasies of the earlier movement. There was no programme, no manifesto, no theory, no representative author, rather a reversion, in many cases, to the methods of the Naturalists against whom the Expressionists in their turn had been in revolt. There were novels not much different from reportage, like Remarque's *Im Westen nichts Neues* and Ludwig Renn's *Krieg*, and more ambitious ones like Alfred Döblin's portrayal of working-class life, *Berlin Alexanderplatz*. There was a flood of semi-documentary plays largely written for Left-wing theatres, propagandistic in intention and dealing with political and social issues of the moment. The term can perhaps be stretched to include the children's story by Erich Kästner, *Emil und die Detektive*, one of the few internationally famous works of the time, which with all its fantasy displays a decent humanity, a sense of humour, and a determined insistence that justice be done. It may also be applied to the novel by Franz Werfel, *Verdi*, and his play *Juarez und Maximilian*, both published in 1924. The former, based on a close study of the composer's works, life, and letters, is significant not only for its adherence to documents. It also presents a deliberate contrast between the Italian and his German contemporary and rival, Wagner, and is thus implicitly a sympathetic critique of the still dominant tradition in Werfel's own day, with which matter-of-factness assorted ill. The play, similarly, has contemporary relevance. Based on the history of Mexico, it portrays the efforts of the Emperor Maximilian to introduce liberal reforms in a land threatened by revolution, and is clearly intended to reflect on the German situation of the day. Maximilian's failure, sentimentally presented though it is, seems to be a warning to Werfel's generation against allowing more hard-headed opponents to carry the day in their own country.

Although 'Die neue Sachlichkeit' had no great achievements to its name, it was a movement tending away from the perilous mysticism of the writers within the main tradition, and akin in some ways to the post-war literature of both East and West Germany after 1945. The 'matter-of-fact' writers were the least likely of all to be attracted by the promises of an emotional mass-movement. Yet matter-of-factness in itself was no guarantee of a defence of liberal and humane standards. In a somewhat different form it had been showing itself in a writer of completely different persuasions, the soldier Ernst Jünger.

Jünger had first become known to the public not through his writings but by his conduct in battle, which had earned for him the highest distinction for valour, the 'Pour le Mérite'. His early works, of which *In Stahlgewittern* had been published in 1920, were entirely concerned with accounts of his participation in the war, couched in a language of calculated detachment and calm analysis. There is nothing in them of the Expressionists' horror, or of exultation either, but rather what Jünger was later to call a 'höhere Lebensgesundheit' that recognized bloodshed and warfare as necessary to existence. Relating the execution of captured prisoners, Jünger observes that men who have just been in the thick of battle can expect no mercy; of his own capture of a machine-gun nest he remarks that the effort had resulted in a cure of his recent chill; throughout, every event is reported in a mood of cold-blooded inquiry which plays down all emotional reaction. The general impression is one of activity pure and simple, a series of happenings on which almost no reflection is made and which seems to have no purpose or pattern: shells explode, men are wounded or killed, the enemy advances or retreats, there are days of rest and days of battle, moments of fear and moments of victory, but nothing to suggest that these have any remarkable significance, no expressions of patriotism or belief in a cause.

This detachment was to remain Jünger's chief characteristic until after 1945. Even in the twenties, he remained on the whole aloof from the militarist group who sought his support, and he never became attached in any way to the National Socialist party. Nevertheless, his ideas began to shape themselves into a form very similar to theirs. The ideal he has in mind, in his sociological study *Der Arbeiter*, published in 1932, is a kind of Superman, the 'echte Gestalt', who differs from other individuals in that he is not subordinated to a whole greater than himself—this 'genuine man' is himself 'the whole', living in harmony with its amoral sequence of events, unprotesting and uncomplaining as Jünger himself had been in battle. His philosophy is a kind of *active* quietism, participating to the full, and unquestioningly, in all that falls to his lot. It is not merely concerned with destruction: significantly, Jünger was decorated in the Second World War for saving life, not taking it; but it is equally at home in all fields of action. What mattered to Jünger, in his own imagery, was to be exposed in a forward reconnaissance position well out beyond the front line. Against the smug comfortableness of the 'Bürger' he set the romantically 'adventurous heart' which recognized the elemental forces in man and sought not to ignore them but to ride with them. In the same way, the working class, related to the State as the unconscious mind was to the individual, was to be not ignored but ridden like a stallion. 'Our task is not to be the opponents of the age, but to back our last penny on it.'[20] The primitive urges must be liberated not only in the individual but in the masses, and for this the constitutional form of the German state was useless. 'There is a need for actions of a brutality such as can be engaged in "in the name of the people", never in the name of the King.'[21] Those men should gain power who were in themselves the whole of the people, distinguished by their racial characteristics from its effete components. Yet when such men did gain power, Jünger was not with them; on the contrary, he was the sole author permitted to publish a work under the dictatorship which could be construed as an attack on the regime.[22] It is true, on the other hand, that he declined to join the conspirators during the war of 1939–45. But this is characteristic of many of his contemporaries whose ideas seemed to tally closely with those being put into practice from 1933 onwards and who yet would commit themselves neither to support nor to opposition. The simultaneous, paradoxical detachment from and self-identification with the events of the age could perhaps have no other result. Jünger's attitude of calm registration, on the battlefield, was still in evidence during the period of Nazi rule, and only gradually gave way to one of rejection.

Hermann Hesse, later to receive, like Thomas Mann, the award of the Nobel Prize, was of an older generation. He differed from Jünger also in that he remained abroad from the end of the First World War onward, in that he was a pacifist and a much more popular author, and in that the quality of his writing was inferior.[23] His great reputation, continuing today and reflected in numerous popular editions, would be hard to account for, were it not for the unsure basis of so many reputations in this century, and not only in the German-speaking world. It is certainly due in part to the fact that his philosophical outlook, taken in the abstract, bears a resemblance to a good deal of the speculation that was going on in his time, and is presented in an easily assimilable form. Hesse is the outstanding popularizer among the neo-Nietzscheans, a novelist whose effect was to make more palatable the agonized affirmation of a Nietzsche and a Rilke, and who did so by creating an imaginary world in which their doctrines were comfortably realized. In Hesse's world there are never any serious obstacles to affirmation; where any obstacles are introduced it is as though for form's sake, and the reader no more expects them to provide real difficulties than he would in a boy's adventure-story. The works are illustrations of a philosophy which has been fairly summarized by a sympathetic critic: 'All ways lead to God'[24]—the life of the senses, sexual fulfilment as much as asceticism, orgies of love-making as much as dreams of mass-murder, all are realizations of the many-faceted whole, and all are justified in their several ways.

It is a philosophy with some kinship to that of the 'great Soul' in Mann's *Zauberberg*, dreaming of its lovers and of its blood-feast,[25] and yet more crudely stated, for whereas Mann sometimes reveals just what pains his beliefs have caused him, Hesse as a rule allows his characters to sail serenely through, convinced from the outset of their natural rightness. This, together with his often negligent manner of writing, would rule him out of consideration in a purely literary study, were it not that both his style and his treatment of his subject-matter gained him a large public. The influence of the popularizer is probably more powerful than that of the genuine man of letters, and Hesse's ideas may well have gained more currency in his time than those of any of his contemporaries in art.

The extent to which the public was open to such ideas is shown by their appearance even in the work of Bertolt Brecht, later to become the best known of the Communist dramatists. The main character of Brecht's earliest play, *Baal* (1922), is a man very similar to the protagonists of Hesse's novels in his all-embracing acceptance, though he differs in that he has very little of Hesse's sentimentality. Nor did Brecht ever take leave of the idea that a life lived intensely, regardless of moral claims, was in some way desirable and in some way the most natural form of existence, although the later embodiments of this ideal were increasingly subjected by him to criticism. But Brecht's development in the twenties was directed towards the rejection of such purely individual fulfilment and towards the subjection of the self to communal life. Always at least concerned with, if not committed to the doctrines of Marxism, he came to assert for a time, in the propagandist plays of the early thirties, their overriding authority. On the way, however, his plays showed a curious trend. Over and over again he portrayed figures who seemed to be meant as exemplars of the capitalist way of life to which he was opposed, and yet who seemed so close to his own ideals as to make his satirical intention quite ambiguous. Thus in *Die Dreigroschenoper*, the play which brought him fame in 1927, the gang-leader Macheath is at once the representative of 'bourgeois capitalism' and at the same time a gay bohemian for whom Brecht seems to invite much sympathy. Brecht's intention had been, as he wrote later, to write a report on the kind of entertainment preferred by bourgeois audiences: the result, at all events, was a work so closely adapted to those preferences that it scored a great success with many who can have had no notion of the author's subtle reservations. Similarly, in the libretto for *Mahagonny* (1929), Brecht seemed to portray licentiousness both as the concomitant of capitalism and as a desirable thing in itself. In fact one of the chief characteristics of his work up till about 1930 was a strange chameleon-like adaptation to circumstances which joined opposition with approval in a way peculiar to him and yet oddly reminiscent of the ambiguousness of the traditional writers.

It was not until 1929 that Brecht threw in his lot decisively, in his plays at least, with the cause of the Communist party. Here for the first time a clean break appeared, away from the earlier uncertainty of purpose. His dramatic work underwent a complete change. From the racy, confused and contradictory, but impetuous and satirical form and style of his earlier plays he turned to a rational, straightforward simplicity in which the moral is rammed home without a trace of hesitation. This was, of course, the time at which the Nazis were beginning to make their strength felt; there was street-fighting, and the daily newspapers carried advertisements for repeating pistols. Brecht's reaction was to suppress all thought of self-fulfilment. With the enthusiasm of a neophyte he preached, in such plays as *Der Jasager*, the necessity to give up life itself for the sake of the party. The Communist, learning from the Russian Revolution, must apply all his talents to the cause of the proletariat: this was the implied moral of *Die Mutter*, the best of the propagandist works, several of which were adopted by the Left-wing organizations of working class actors. He must even be prepared, in a given situation, to take the life of a comrade who deviates from the official party-line: this was the message of *Die Maßnahme*. Yet for all their decisiveness, and for all Brecht's new insistence on a mood of calm rational appraisal in his spectators, these plays were for a large part scornful of argument and imperiously didactic towards their audiences. The conclusion of *Die Maß-nahme*, reached with an ostentatious display of reasoned consideration, was, in the first version, affirmed without trace of argument,[26] and when the amended version appeared, the reasons advanced for killing the errant comrade were perfunctory. Again, in *Die heilige Johanna der Schlachthöfe* (1932), the Communist message is blurred by an hysterical appeal, not to destroy the capitalist system but to wreak violence on the priests who implicitly support it. The general impression gained from these propagandist works, despite the humorous and shrewd cunning displayed in *Die Mutter*, is of a desperate attempt at self-subdual in a common cause, with more emphasis on the unfortunate need for brutal discipline within the party ranks than on ways and means of combating the opponent. The Nazis themselves scarcely appear in the works written with the object of preventing their success, and when they do appear, as in the allegorical *Die Rundköpfe und die Spitzköpfe* (1932–4), they are underestimated and misunderstood. Until 1933—although the plays written in Brecht's exile are in some ways a different matter—the development of his work is on the whole the tragic account of a talent which could find no satisfying outlet. Attaching himself to the Communists as the most active opponents of the movement he detested, Brecht felt constrained to make so ruthless a curtailment of his claims as an individual that his propaganda appears negative rather than positive, inhuman rather than a defence of the values he saw threatened. And the all-embracing attitude of his earlier plays, which seemed to envisage such inhumanity as part of the total meaning of being human, was perhaps one of the factors contributing to the ineptitude of his new declarations of doctrine. Having so ambiguous a definition of humanity, he was the less able to assert his claims, and postponed the attempt at realizing them to some future age of proletarian unity.

Brecht's career until the time of his exile presents the obverse of that of many of his contemporaries. To go willingly with the tide of events in a kind of Hegelian self-identification with the processes of world-history was Thomas Mann's guiding purpose. To make such events become truly real by meeting them not in any critical or discriminating mood, but in all other respects with the fullest range of human responsiveness, was Rilke's ideal. Hesse's development of all facets of human personality was based on a similar belief that to shun or oppose any emotion or any experience was to be less than a whole self, while to embrace and affirm all events was to be at one with the spirit of the cosmos. Jünger's matter-of-fact portrayal of war and his insistence on 'backing the age' were yet another manifestation, in terms of his personality, of the same fundamental attitude. Brecht, as early as the time when he wrote *Mann ist Mann* (1926), was becoming aware of the dangers inherent in such more or less pantheistic self-immersion in the All. In that play he set out to show how a man who moved with the times was likely to turn into a savage and brutal warrior, defending a purely national ideal which had ceased to have any meaning for him. Yet in turning away from the easy-going acceptance displayed in his character Baal to the incorporation of Marxist ideas in his plays he did not win clear. For the Marxist dialectic was based on the Hegelian one, and in some aspects remained remarkably similar. Where the Hegelian looked to the fullest recognition of the contradictions of present existence as a means to 'overcoming' them: that is, to continue to affirm them in the knowledge of their contradictoriness, and thereby to enter a new phase of innocence, the Marxist could believe—though other beliefs were open to him within the system—that the contradictions of capitalism, were they allowed to develop themselves to their fullest extent, would bring about their own destruction and thus pave the way to a new and innocent society. What the Hegelian and the neo-Nietzschean saw as happening within the individual who recognized his own contra- dictory nature, the Marxist saw as happening in society as a whole: at length a 'qualitative leap' was made, which for the individualist was a leap into the world of Spirit—a parallel to the religious man's 'leap into the dark'—while for the Communist it was a leap into the world of a classless society. In both cases the final goal was without distinctions, whether between good and evil on the one hand or between class and class, man and man on the other; it was a seamless unity reached either on a spiritual or on a material plane. The Marxist was thus as prone to speak of the inevitable processes of world-history, and of the necessity to work in harmony with these, as the writer within the tradition extending from Hegel to Nietzsche and beyond. Brecht, assimilating the Marxist tradition, was still not making a complete break with his own past. He was still able to hold to the belief that the fullest portrayal of present contradictions was in itself enough to make the necessity for Communism apparent, if not indeed to bring about the classless society. This must account in part for the well-known theory of 'alienation' or 'estrangement' which he announced at just about the time when his propagandist plays began to appear. His intention seems to have been to display the circumstances of his time, full of contradictions as they appeared to him, in the belief that this would evoke in any fair-minded spectator an immediate apprehension of the unity, the future Communist society, which must replace and transcend them. And although his plays of the early thirties, far from achieving the calm analysis he promised, supplied the spectator with a ready-made answer, the plays of his exile increasingly withdrew from didacticism, increasingly called on the spectator to make that leap into recognition which Brecht believed he must make. Meanwhile, in the years up to 1933, he continued to show a certain quietism on the one hand, and a fanatical insistence on the correctness of party doctrine on the other.

When the Nazis seized power, however, not one of the major writers still living was content to remain in Germany, with the sole exception of the ageing Gerhart Hauptmann, the last years of whose life, until his death in 1946, were spent in black pessimism. (Although perhaps one should mention here Gottfried Benn, at that time comparatively unknown, but to become a leading literary figure after 1945.) Thomas Mann had already made his own position clear, both in his short story *Mario und der Zauberer*, which was partly a satirical allegory of Fascist rule in Italy, and in public speeches in which he denounced the Nazis by name. Brecht's opposition was equally manifest. Stefan George, offered the honour of presiding over the new regime's Academy, rejected it and retired to Switzerland to die. Hesse remained in Switzerland, where he had been living for some years. For few of the other German writers was there any prospect of staying at home. Among those who found their works banned or who were driven into exile or imprisoned were not only Thomas Mann and Brecht but also Johannes Becher, Alfred Döblin, Georg Kaiser, Heinrich Mann, Erich Maria Remarque, Ludwig Renn, René Schickele, Carl Sternheim, Ernst Toller, Fritz von Unruh, Jakob Wassermann and Franz Werfel, to name only men already mentioned in these pages. To these may be added, from scores of others, Arnold and Stefan Zweig, Ferdinand Bruckner, Carl Zuckmayer, whose satire on Prussian militarism *Der Hauptmann von Köpenick* had scored a great popular success, and Ricarda Huch, a writer with a reputation of some thirty years' standing, who voluntarily resigned from the Prussian 'Dichterakademie' in 1933. All these had in one way or another voiced their humanity in such terms as to mark them out as opponents of the new movement. Those who remained were almost all writers of smaller reputation, with the exception of the popular neo-Goethean, Hans Carossa, and the equally popular Wilhelm Schäfer, and Rudolf Binding, whose death in 1938 brought drapes of purple mourning to bookshop windows. Active propagators of Nazi ideals in literature were extremely few: they included the pan-Germanist Hans Grimm (whose pan-Germanism was his sole link), and the dramatist Hanns Johst, but few others who had achieved much fame.[27] The philosopher Martin Heidegger, whose ideas owed much to Rilke, gained notoriety by his rectorial address welcoming the regime. Ernst Jünger remained aloof as he had always done, despite the trend of his recent work, although he continued to live in Germany and enjoyed the respect due to his valour in war. On the whole, however, by far the greater number of writers were either driven out or chose to go.

The impression that has probably been given so far, of literary movements often unwittingly and perilously near to creating an atmosphere in which Nazism could exist, thus needs modifying. Such a peril did exist, and yet there was a quality in all these writers, Communists, liberals, Christians and neo-Nietzscheans alike, which either abhorred Nazism or was abhorred by it. To define that quality is a delicate undertaking, but perhaps one point can reasonably be made here: it is that all the opponents of Nazism were in some way 'deniers', in some way adversely critical of the state of affairs, even though their denial might be, in certain instances, the prelude to affirmation. Thomas Mann has confessed that, while as a rule he had always been prone to see some right on both sides of an argument, there was one occasion and one only when he had no such feeling. 'Hitler', he wrote, 'had the great merit of producing a simplification of the emotions, of calling forth a wholly unequivocal No, a clear and deadly hatred.'[28] And perhaps it was precisely such forthright denial that most galled Hitler in his struggle for power. It is difficult enough to find any common feature in the vagueness and contradictoriness of Hitler's utterances, but this at least can be said, that he was consistent in his attacks on those 'destructive elements', as he called them, 'or simple fools whose sole common profession of faith is their "No" launched against the community of the nation and against constructive work.'[29] Time and time again he accused his opponents of what he called nihilism, a term which includes all forms of resistance, so that it is as nihilistic to have the self-criticism of a Christian or a Jew as it is to seek the overthrow of the existing order in the name of Communism. Anything that smacked of doubt or disillusionment, recognition of inadequacy or 'defeatism of the will' was a mark of un-German qualities, whether or not the occasion justified it. 'I held it to be my first and most important task (*scil.* in 1933) to restore the self-respect of the German people, in every sphere and whenever I had a chance. I wished to drive from the minds of the people their fatal doubt of their own ability and to make them once more a proud and self-conscious people.'[30] Bolshevism hindered the achievement of this aim because it promoted internationalism instead of nationalism, religions because they taught the virtue of humility. Nietzsche, though the Nazis were apt to claim him as their prophet, was unfitted for such a role in so far as he attacked the virtues shown hitherto by the German nation, and engaged in keen-sighted psychological inquiry. Thomas Mann, for all that his works had constantly treated the theme of unreflective self-assertion, had evidently disqualified himself both by his attacks on the party and by his preoccupation with disease and death. True, his ideal had repeatedly shown itself as an affirmation of life in all its aspects, to be attained after the fullest knowledge of disease and death had been reached. But his subtle equivocation was unlikely to be appreciated by the Nazi leaders: the mere nature of his preoccupations was enough to stamp him a Bolshevist. George, on the other hand, had never given voice to doubt or equivocated as Mann had done; from the early days when he had proclaimed the gospel of the boy-god Maximin he had been sure of himself, and the masochistic traits in some of his poems probably passed unnoticed. This certainty, together with George's insistence on Germanic traditions, was probably the characteristic which led to the offer of high honour. By comparison, Mann's vision of the indifferent World-soul in *Der Zauberberg* would have appeared effete. It would have had too much of the pale cast of thought, the affirmation would have seemed too painfully won and too self-conscious to appeal to Hitler's quite genuine unreflectiveness, had he ever come across it. Hitler's aim was rather an assertion of national supremacy which would not permit even the faintest flicker of a doubt, a reassertion of the Will in its primal integrity, and for this the traditional doctrines were all unsuited, for they all were based on the notion of a progressive self-awareness that was only transcended in the ultimate instance.

Nevertheless, the ground had, however unwittingly, been prepared for Hitler's advent. There had been very little inculcation of brutality and savage violence in literary works—Thomas Mann, for one, had almost always expressed a reluctant recognition of the need for it, rather than a direct incitement. The Expressionists had sought some way of liberating men from the prim correctness of polite civilization; their ecstatic manifestoes were meant to arouse a new dynamism in a world of bureaucratic machinery, and while they failed in literature, much as the 'Sturm und Drang' had failed in the eighteenth century, by virtue of their complete reliance on emotional fervour and their rejection of disciplined objectivity, they had their success in painting. The work of Oskar Kokoschka shows what great insight could be achieved through technical precision in the 'expression' of the inward man, the inward landscape, in close correlation with the observed face and the observed scene. But the vague incoherence of so much literary work, together with the quasi-mystical self-immersion in the flood of events, the insistence on a realization of all aspects of human nature, and above all the lack of any exploration of reality in relation to these doctrines, the use of fiction to preach them rather than to discover what they would look like in imagined circumstances, must have created, in a large section of the public that concerned itself with literature, a mood that was half inclined to go with the Nazis when they came to power. Or, if such doctrines did not actually create the mood, they were surely a reflection of it, of a frame of mind which by no means actively willed the new regime and yet might be disposed to recognize its claims. For Thomas Mann and many others like him that was sheerly impossible: conscience cried out, no matter what the 'Weltanschauung' might suggest. For others, still uncommitted and not faced with personal hostility towards themselves, acquiescence was easier.

The political scene was not very dissimilar from the literary one, in that here also a large proportion of the population was in opposition to the ideals of the Nazi party, while yet in some sense remaining half-hearted. The rise of the party was meteoric: reconstituted in 1925, it had 12 deputies in the Reichstag by 1928, and 107 by 1930, by which time it was the second strongest party after the Social Democrats. Yet in that same year, out of 35 million Germans who voted there were as yet less than 7 million votes cast for the National Socialists, and 20 million for parties representing Left-wing and Christian opinion. Even in March 1933, after Hitler had succeeded to power, he had still only 288 deputies to support him, in a Reichstag of 647 members. He had been helped by the world economic depression of 1929, by the resultant unemployment, and by the failure of the Republic to fulfil its promise of a national recovery, but he still had no majority. Despite the size of the opposition to Hitler, however, it went to the wall as though determined not to fight. Just as on the outbreak of war in 1914 those who were most opposed to the Imperial regime found themselves aligned with it nevertheless, so now the Left wing and the Catholic 'Zentrum' were brought to heel at once. The Social Democrats trusted in Hitler's promise never to go outside the constitution; when the trade unions were taken over by the Labour Front on 1 May 1933 the former syndicalist organization gave in without a show of resistance, without even a strike. In July of the same year a Concordat with the Holy See was signed, debarring the clergy from all political activity; it filled even Hitler with astonishment. 'Who would have believed', he asked a meeting of Brownshirts in Dortmund, 'that within five months of our assumption of power the Zentrum would capitulate?'[31] In the November plebiscite of 1933, 93·6 per cent, or over 40 million of the voters, were declared to have been in favour of Hitler's action in leaving the League of Nations, and in the following August almost as many, it appeared, upheld the action of the Cabinet in appointing him Führer and Reich-Chancellor. It had taken less than ten years since the reconstitution of the party to swing over almost the entire nation, and less than two to bring the apparent opposition into line.

This was not merely a matter of quietism, and cannot be explained simply in terms of ideas held. Despite the alleged 'bloodless seizure of power', of which so much was made in later years, terrorism had played a large part in it and accounts for the popular swing at least as much as any traditional atmosphere of ideas. In the first few months of 1933 thousands of opponents had been deprived of office, sent to concentration camps, publicly degraded. Workers' homes had been ransacked, Jewish shops defaced and entrance to them barred. A Socialist Prime Minister had been dragged through the streets in an open cart. Hundreds had been shot down in the street, beaten to death, hanged by the heels, drowned in sacks, thrown out of windows, tortured in prison.³² For those who knew of these events, they could be intimidating. The historian F. Meinecke relates how he spoke to a 'Zentrum' deputy shortly before the passing of the Enabling Act of 23 March 1933, whereby Hitler became all-powerful. 'I asked... "You will certainly vote against it?" He shrugged his shoulders and replied, "Then things would get even worse".'³³ Yet it seems certain that many people did not even know of happenings which neither press nor radio reported except to belittle their importance. For them, the deliberately gigantic lies of Josef Goebbels did not seem incredible. National Socialism usually claimed, in the early days, to be based on Christian beliefs, to be peaceful in its aims and to demand no more than a just reversal of the conditions of the Versailles Treaty. It was also successful in representing itself as the true inheritor of the best in German tradition. Anyone who has seen the film of the Nuremberg rally in 1934, *The Triumph of the Will*, will recall how the massive broad gables of the ancient city, the parade of peasants in the dignified splendour of their traditional costumes, the shots of manly Germanic profiles and muscular bodies are subtly used to suggest the welcome of the entire nation, past and present, to a leader who descends by aeroplane from towering cumulus clouds as though from Valhalla itself. The claim that the Third Reich would endure for a thousand years was implicitly a claim that it would equal its predecessor, the Holy Roman Empire, and achieve the same eminence, this time in an unambiguously German realm. Hitler made it known that he resided at Berchtesgaden where, according to one version of an old legend, the spirit of the medieval Emperor Frederick Barbarossa waited to save Germany in the hour of need. Every-

74

thing was done to support the myth of these deep roots in the past. The mysticism of Meister Eckhart, treating of the ultimate fusion of Man and God, was adapted by Alfred Rosenberg into a doctrine of mystical identity with the State. The German classics, particularly Goethe, Kleist and Hölderlin, were pressed into service. And everywhere the suggestion of absolute unity was implanted. Hitler rarely spoke of his opponents by name; it often seemed doubtful whether he thought he had any. He implied rather that the support he had gained came from the mature reflection of the whole nation. He was all things to all men, more or less; a democrat, duly elected by the people, on some occasions, and on others an embodiment of the people's will, intolerant of opposition. He was a socialist who left the major industries in the hands of capitalists, a pagan to some, and a political Christ to others. To say no to such an undivided unity of purpose as his appeared to be, so the propaganda suggested, was to declare oneself opposed to almost every form of political and religious allegiance that had ever been thought of. 'The doctrine of the Totalitarian State as expounded by the Nazis at the beginning of 1933', writes a French historian, 'satisfied the traditionalist bourgeoisie, the big industrialists, the great land-owners of plebeian origins, the bureaucrats, Army officers, and university professors'.34 It satisfied also, with its emphasis on public works and housing programmes, a large part of the working class. There was something for everybody.

All this could not have achieved success, however, if there had not been a tradition in thought which was at least amenable to the Nazi doctrines. It was easy to see in Hitler what Hegel had called the 'world-historical man', the figure so completely identified with the trends of his times that opposition to him was tanta-mount to sinning against the Holy Ghost—easy, that is, when the paradoxical idea had once taken root. The ideal of restoring the Holy Roman Empire as a German and national one went back to the Romantics, to Friedrich Schlegel and Novalis; the notion of an autarkic state, with complete authority over its members, had been first proclaimed by Fichte. It was Fichte also who maintained that only the German truly had a 'folk', which could demand every sacrifice from the individual and was entitled to assimilate foreign nations into itself. The dramatist Kleist, at the same time, had counselled the use of every atrocity, every deliberate lie, to save the Fatherland from foreign domination. Mystical writers like Schelling and Görres had developed the idea of the state as an all-embracing organism, and many others had claimed to find in Germany alone the proper foundations for such a unity. With the passing of Romanticism, there had been some regression from nationalism expressed in these terms: the Young Hegelians had revolted from the doctrine that what exists must be rational and justifiable, and the liberal movement which succumbed in 1848 was comparatively free from such ideas. Yet by the latter half of the century they were beginning to emerge again in force: the dramatist Hebbel preached Germanic virtues and the tragic necessity of suppressing the individual, the doctrines of Fichte were revived by the socialist Lassalle, Richard Wagner took up the ideas of the superiority of 'the genuinely noble breeds of Germanic descent', of a purified and germanized Christianity, and of the un-German nature of democracy. Treitschke extolled the sublimity of the state and glorified war as good in itself; Nietzsche taught that the magnificent blond beast was the prime mover of all distinguished races. Anti-semitism, which Nietzsche rejected, had been preached by Arnim and was preached again by Wagner, Houston Stewart Chamberlain, Dühring, Spengler and Keyserling. The reflection of such ideas, with or without explicit political implications, is constantly met with in the purely literary works of the Wilhelmine Empire and the Weimar Republic. Yet as the historian of these developments has said, 'It is certainly true that numbers of Germans would be horrified at the propositions thus attributed to the German spirit and outlook, and that of the German thinkers whose theories have been examined a fair proportion would be shocked at the extremer instances'.35 Some would have gone into exile or died in opposition to the reality brought to life out of their teachings. We have seen that some of those who witnessed the events of 1933 were either confirmed in their hostility to pan-Germanism, egoism, and anti-semitism, or shocked out of their earlier devotion to similar ideals. Nevertheless, the neo-Nietzschean, neo-Hegelian, neo-Romantic trend did not yield its attachment to ambiguity so very readily, but continued to wield its power up to the last, until the state it had helped into existence fell in ruins, and even until later.

CHAPTER III

WRITERS AND POLITICS: 1933–1945

Echter als er
Schwur keiner Eide;
Treuer als er
Hielt keiner Verträge;
Lautrer als er
Liebte kein andrer!
Und doch alle Eide,
Alle Verträge,
Die treueste Liebe —
Trog keiner wie er!

Götterdämmerung.

The most telling symbol of the early twentieth century in Europe ever to be created was the one in Dostoevsky's tale of the Grand Inquisitor. Interpretations of the story's meaning have been exhaustingly varied, and there is no need to offer another here. Perhaps it will be conceded, though, that there is an uncanny resemblance between the figure of the Inquisitor himself and that of the man who appears to be a Christ returned to earth some fifteen centuries after his death. The apparently inhuman upholder of doctrinal assertions, bereft of faith himself, an atheist by all observational tests that might be thought of, and yet determined to live with the knowledge of his own unbelief in order to spare other men the same overwhelming burden, seems at times in the story almost to change places with the Christ he condemns. The Inquisitor is also, it is true, a ruthless tyrant who will not allow men the freedom Christ intended for them: he prefer their happiness to his own. It is a deliberate deceit that he practises, involving him ultimately in a contemptuous disregard for men. All the same, the strange effect of the story is to leave the reader almost sympathizing with the

78

Inquisitor: as in the case of Mann's Leverkühn, the features of Christ seem to flit across his face in a disturbing way, and it is not until the last moment, delayed until after Ivan Karamazov has apparently finished his narration, that the distinction between the two becomes clear. Ivan's story, he says, had been meant to end not with the consignment of the new Christ to the flames of the *auto da fé*, as it had seemed to do, but with Christ's kiss on the Inquisitor's lips, and his release by the intransigent yet afflicted captor. With this, Dostoevsky manages to convey both the sense so common in the nineteenth and twentieth centuries, of the close parallelism between seemingly divergent beliefs, and the essential difference between them. He creates a parable which helps to explain how Nietzsche could call himself both 'the Antichrist' and 'the Crucified', how Marx could appear to many as an Old Testament prophet, how Lenin could be venerated like a saint, Hitler be represented on picture-postcards as the modern Joan of Arc, and in general how an age in which faith was supposed to be crumbling (though it was also the age in which Christianity was carried into every quarter of the globe) could be so full of all the superficial manifestations of faith.

The oscillations between extremes, changing pattern like the surface of shot silk, are the significant feature of the story for the present topic. In fact the notion has gained such currency in Germany that the word 'schillern', meaning to iridesce, is commonly taken to mean not a flashing of every colour in the rainbow, but a rapid flitting between two colours only, with metaphorical allusion to the idea of polarity. It is, of course, one way of hinting at the synthesis, the duality-in-unity, to say that the contrasts rapidly displace one another, and it is also a way of suggesting an identity of opposites. Thus Schiller, in *Don Carlos*, the play from which Dostoevsky seems to have derived his Inquisitor figure, allows his Marquis of Posa to say that the atheist is as true a performer of God's will (since God intentionally hides himself from human view in order that his presence may be denied) as is the most fervent of believers—a forthright statement of a paradox which often seems to be more indirectly stated in the work of Schiller's contemporary, the theologian Schleiermacher. Similarly Kierkegaard, in his attempt at defining a quality of heart and mind to which the Christian should aspire, is at pains to give a definition which shall make that quality as objectively indistinguishable as possible from the quality of other, non-Christian men. In his conception of 'the knight of infinite faith', Kierkegaard sets out the picture of a kind of man so completely dedicated to the acceptance of life as he finds it, within the wise purposes of Providence, that he appears identical with the ordinary, everyday, man-in-the-street. 'I examine his figure from tip to toe to see if there might not be a cranny through which the infinite was peeping. No! He is solid through and through.... When one looks at him one might suppose that he was a clerk who had lost his soul in an intricate system of book-keeping, so precise is he.'[1] Kierkegaard evidently did not mean that the true quality of Christianity was not to be differentiated from any other quality. Like Dostoevsky he must have had in mind, in writing this passage, the ultimate distinctiveness of a charity that ignores distinctions. Still, his conception, together with the novelist's, provides an invaluable starting-point for studying Germany during its twelve years of tyranny and war.

For one of the strangest features of that period, at least in its first half, was the appearance of ordinariness that it contrived to convey. Of course there were mass demonstrations, concentration camps, secret menaces, subtle compulsions as well as crude ones. But they did not make up the atmosphere of day-to-day living, any more than reported murders and riots do at the present time. For a large part, the Nazis were content to speak of their bloodless revolution, to point to their extensive housing programme and low unemployment figures. 'Any idiot can rule with a rubber truncheon', read an official placard exhibited in Frankfurt in 1938, '—a far better and more successful way is to draw every comrade into co-operating with us.' It was effrontery, but not ineffective. In a way, people believed it, and wanted to believe it: if nothing else, it looked like evidence of good will.

And this was so even with shrewd observers who had had every opportunity to ascertain the facts.

It was probably so in the case of a poet who in 1933 was comparatively unknown except in 'highbrow' circles: Gottfried Benn, who became the controversial grand old man of German literature in the era after 1945. His audience in the 1920's was drawn mainly from humanistic, Jewish, and liberal groups. His name, as he was reminded by Thomas Mann's son Klaus shortly after the Nazi seizure of power, was 'a byword for high standards and an all but fanatic purity'.[2] He had seemed to his admirers, by virtue of his outspoken condemnation of Marxist literary tyrannies, to be equally opposed to tyranny in any shape. Yet he too, when the moment of choice came, made an almost inexplicable *volte-face*. He did not, it is true, join the party then, and never did. Yet he made it clear that for him history was leading to these events in Germany, and that he was unwilling to stand aside. 'A masterly race', he quoted Nietzsche as saying, 'can grow only from terrible and violent beginnings. Problem: where are the barbarians of the twentieth century?' For Benn, it was a matter of consciously choosing the barbarians as he saw them—'everyone, the man of letters included, must stand up and choose: private hobby, or direction towards the state. I choose the latter....'[3] And he chose as he did because he saw the whole movement of his day as elemental and impulsive, 'an inescapable phenomenon', not something to be discussed and reasoned about, but 'the emergence of a new biological type, a mutation of history and a people's wish to breed itself'.[4] Thus he too swung over in a way that astonished all who had known him.

Why, though, should Benn ever have come to feel that this particular movement in history deserved his allegiance rather than another? Why did he see the new biological type as a blond beast rather than as a liberal defender of human rights? The question may be a little absurd, leaning over backwards to look for reasons where there probably are none, but it will lead us a little further towards understanding. For many Germans of this time, Hitler was right because Hitler had happened.[5] If he had not been 'meant' to achieve power he would never have done so: now that he had, it was the duty of every German to support him. There was a crude echo here—and perhaps not so crude at that— of Hegel's doctrine that the real must be the rational: that whatever took place in reality must have some rational justification, must be in accordance with the Spirit underlying history, and should therefore not be opposed. At the same time, there was a sense that opposition to the dynamic uprising of the German people, to which the whole nineteenth century bore witness, was the most obvious of misreadings of the course of recent events. There was what historians had called an 'immanent trend in world history', which was bringing the German nation to the fore and could only end in its final victory and hegemony.[6] As the philosopher Martin Heidegger said in his rectorial address at Freiburg University—the first academic welcome to the Nazis after they took power—the moment had come when the German people must choose itself. Whether or not Germany crashed into insane chaos depended solely on this choice, 'whether we as a historical and cultured people will to be ourselves—or not to be ourselves.... But we want our people to fulfil its historical task. We want to be ourselves. For the younger and the youngest generation of our people, reaching out beyond us, has already decided the matter.'[7]

This was a roundabout way of saying that Hitler had happened, and so Hitler was right. The young people (not young in years, presumably: Hitler was a ripe forty-four by now) had decided, and thus Germany had decided: it did intend to be itself, and in the context this could only mean that it intended to assert itself ruthlessly in the historical role for which it fancied itself cast. What seemed on the one hand to be a fatalistic acquiescence in the inevitable course of history was thus at one and the same time an extremely subjective interpretation of that course in terms of aggressiveness. It was right for Germans to be aggressive because in that way they would be acquiescent, and *vice versa* It was right, as Heidegger said, for university professors to occupy posts of extreme spiritual danger, maintaining a 'permanent uncertainty about the world',[8] and yet they had no just claim to academic freedom and must conform in their views to the views of the popular mass. Total doubt and total certainty must go hand in hand.

'Choosing oneself', and acquiescing in one's destiny (*choosing one's destiny*, as some paradoxically and synthetically put it) were thus different ways of saying one and the same thing: that Germany was ebulliently rising, and that there was to be no brooking of opposition. People were as unclear as they usually are, everywhere, about where their deepest convictions lay, so that it must sometimes have been a matter almost of chance, or of comparatively petty motives, for a man to go with or against the tide. One would be glad of a good deal more enlightenment on the problem whether men such as, say, Paul Ernst, the dramatist, novelist and critic, would really have been attuned to the Nazi state or not. As a recent commentator has pointed out, his work was beginning to enjoy more recognition in Germany in 1932, 'largely due to the fact that many of his ideas seemed consistent with the attitude of the National Socialists then coming to power'.[9] Would he, but for his death a few months later, have accepted this success or not? Was his 'rugged individualism', and his 'insistence on the primacy of moral integrity', irreconcilable with Nazi practice, as has been claimed, or would the anti-democratic insistence on the primacy of the state, which his writings certainly show, have carried him away with the rest? His case is similar to that of Stefan George who, as we know, retired to die in Switzerland rather than accept the eminence offered him by the party. For it has been very truly though enigmatically said of George that 'he saw his ideals put into practice by Hitler, and it was more than he could stand'.[10] There was a sense in which the selfhood, the identity which Hitler chose for Germany was the identity which George had helped to fashion, and thus the one did offer the other at least a close resemblance to his true self, as he had conceived it. That George turned away in disgust may have been a matter of contempt for vulgarity, or of jealousy at a better-organized and thereby vulgar rival, more than of any genuine

6-2

regard for humane values. Certainly we have no reason to think that he was opposed to the Nazis as some others were.

This difficulty arises again and again. It arises even in the case of Thomas Mann himself, whose opposition to the dictators has sometimes been thought unequivocal and who was certainly tireless in his denunciations, even before the Nazis came to power. It is not that Mann ever retracted his condemnation, but that he was capable of a strange oscillation. As a by no means hostile contemporary critic said, at times during the 1920's his voice 'might almost be that of a Nazi ideologue of today'.[11] Indeed, despite the undoubted fact of his opposition, which nothing said here is intended to discount, there was something disturbing about its form. He was attacked within a few months of the Nazis coming to power, and although not at first officially banished, he remained in voluntary exile which very soon became morally compulsory. Critics serving the regime quickly took up the attack on him, using just such epithets as he had used formerly against his own opponents: he was a 'Zivilisations-literat', he had too much 'sympathy with death', no roots in native soil and national life—the precise features which, in his dualistically ironic way he had earlier denounced.[12] It was a curious case of his own self confronting him and offering itself to him for his choice.

During his exile, Mann continued to be outspoken: after less than four years of Nazi rule, he said, Germany was ruined, 'loved by none, watched with dread and cold dislike by all';[13] the annexations of Austria and Czechoslovakia were the crimes of 'animals and inferior beings' whom at length he wearied of explicitly denouncing. Even here, however, Mann's voice remained as self-contradictory and confused as it had ever been. Not that on any occasion he was in doubt about the nature of Nazi inhumanity: this, as he rightly said later, always produced in him an unequivocal 'No'. But as late as the Munich crisis of 1938 he was as two-faced in his attitude to real events as ever he was in his novels. First, he was inclined to see the 'peace with honour' achieved by Chamberlain at Munich and Godesberg as

84

the sign of a 'redundant love of peace', of a general will at work in Europe ('ein europäischer Gesamtwille') which was bent on giving in to the Nazis (much as the Italian audience in Mann's story *Mario und der Zauberer* was fundamentally if unconsciously determined to give in to the hypnotist Cipolla).[14] Running alongside this interpretation, however, Mann saw the Munich pact as part of a deliberate policy on the part of the British Government to strengthen the Nazis as a bulwark against Communism: Chamberlain was aiming at 'die Fascisierung des Kontinents', and therefore had deceived the British public into shunning resistance to Hitler. The incompatibility of these two interpretations, which require on the one hand a general will to yield, and on the other a deceit practised on a public whose will is to resist, is not explained or referred to in Mann's essay. But then it is doubtful whether he took seriously any of his statements, except at the instant of making them, for despite the assertion of a general will, he goes on to assert on behalf of the German nation, although not of any other, a fundamentally anti-Nazi spirit. Chamberlain's crime, Mann asserts, was that he did not make even that gesture of defiance to Hitler which would have instantly roused the German people and the German army against the dictator.

All this is confusing enough. It certainly appears from part of what Mann says that at least the British and the German public, by and large, were opposed to Hitler, and that they were being hoodwinked by political leaders of almost equal depravity. And since Mann is writing within a month of the Munich crisis, it would seem as though he might count on this latent opposition and attempt to arouse it by his writing. But he is riding two horses at once. Having put forward the idea of a general will, by the end of the essay he is completely taken up with it, and, faced with the question what should be done now, talks as though that alone had been his theme. The rest of Europe (which at that time meant at least Britain, France, the Benelux and Scandinavian countries, and Poland) must, he believes, be abandoned to the course that the general will is taking.

The nazification (Fascisierung) of the continent which will now, as a planned result of English policy, be quickly accomplished, is in the last analysis not to be rated merely negatively, not simply as the triumph of a hated enemy. It is, after all, at one and the same time a counter-measure and an adaptation; it meets the necessity to annul some extremely illicit advantages of the opposition,[15] and to place ourselves on an equal footing with it. From an objective point of view, this means grave moral and intellectual sacrifices, sacrifices of freedom, civilisation, and human dignity, yet it is not only a matter of compliance but also of defence. Who can reveal the paths of Destiny? The victory of Fascism—it may very well be its self-annulment. . . . .

This is not the pathetic attempt of an *émigré* to discern some hope yet for his native country, it is the conclusion of an argument whose main purpose has been to denounce the very attitude Mann now adopts. Where at first he had denounced a 'redundant love of peace', as though the British and French diplomats at Munich had wanted peace at any price, rather than deliberate nazification, he now declares, within the same essay, that war 'has become something to be avoided under all circumstances'. Although resistance a month ago would have aroused the entire German nation against its leaders, now the policy must be to yield all along the line, as though by giving way one ensured ultimate success. (Mann had in mind that a United States of Europe might somehow emerge from the Nazi hegemony.) It is in part the philosophy of *Der Zauberberg* and of *Doktor Faustus* that inspires these thoughts: by yielding to sin and 'death' in the case of Hans Castorp, and to one's own damnation in the case of Leverkühn, one hopes to be on the path to salvation all the same. But it is also the philosophy of Hegel, as is clear from Mann's use of the word 'Selbstaufhebung', self-annulment. In Hegelian thought the intensification of a principle or state leads to an ambiguous condition which is both the defeat of the earlier stage (its annulment or termination, using that sense of 'aufheben') and the raising of it to a higher sphere (its 'lifting-up', using another sense of the same word). The word also means to 'preserve'. Evidently, Mann had in mind that by allowing the Nazis to have

their way one would be giving them enough rope to hang themselves, a view which might be more impressive had he held it
consistently. As it is, one is impressed more by the ultimate
veering of his thought to take up this attitude after all his denunciations of those who would not resist Hitler. Mann ends up, for the
time being, by taking just the attitude of many of his compatriots
who stayed in Germany, hostile to the regime and yet unwilling
to express that hostility, but rather awaiting passively the turn of
events brought about by others (or, as they would have said, by
destiny). It is close to the attitude of those ex-soldiers of today,
who comfort themselves with the thought that though they never
opposed Hitler they were against him from the beginning.[16]
Mann was against him from the beginning, and yet there was a
sense in which he was prepared never to oppose him again.

There was something in Germany, both in those who stayed
and in those who went into exile, corresponding to the condition
of Austria described by Robert Musil.

For there it was not merely the case that dislike of one's neighbours
was felt to such a degree as to qualify as community spirit, but even
that distrust of one's self and of one's whole destiny assumed the
character of profound self-assurance. In that country people always
performed—sometimes indeed at the utmost pitch of fervour, with all
its consequences, the exact opposite of what they were thinking, and
thought the exact opposite of what they were performing.[17]

This was not a matter of the usual discrepancy between deed and
intention, as Musil's context makes clear. It was rather that
people thought of themselves, say, as extremely self-distrustful
and by that very fact became extremely self-confident, that they
disliked their neighbours and therefore felt a great sense of
community spirit. Similarly, it may be, by virtue of their support
for the Nazis they felt themselves to be among the Nazis' most
bitter opponents. At the same time, since this ambivalent attitude resulted in nothing very definite by way of actions, both
Austrians and Germans had the curious sense of merely playing
a part in a play of which they themselves were the spectators.
Austria, Musil goes on to say, 'war der Staat, der sich selbst

irgendwie nur noch mitmachte'; it was the country which some-how merely 'joined in its own activities', a country in which people were 'negatively free', to use Musil's words again, and in which mere facts were tossed about as lightly as feathers.

Of those writers who remained in Germany and Austria, none were allowed full expression. Werner Bergengruen gave an allegory of dictatorship in his novel *Der Großtyrann und das Gericht,* and circulated clandestine poems during the war, since published in the volume *Dies Irae;* Gertrud von le Fort and Elisabeth Langgässer wrote novels and poems that were prized after the regime had fallen. The Austrian poet Josef Weinheber, strongly influenced by Rilke, was more inclined to go with the times; Rudolf Alexander Schröder on the other hand, the trans-lator of some of T. S. Eliot's plays, and a poet in his own right, maintained a greater reserve. Authors whose works were actively supported by well-wishers of the Nazi regime were first and fore-most Hans Grimm, author of *Volk ohne Raum* and celebrator of German life in South Africa, and Erwin Guido Kolbenheyer, the exponent through novels such as *Paracelsus* of a mystical concep-tion of humanity. Others frequently mentioned favourably by the same well-wishers of the regime were Paul Ernst, Hermann Stehr, Emil Strauss, Hans Carossa, Will Vesper and F. Griese.

The case of Gerhart Hauptmann was somewhat different. Known in the years before 1914 as a pacifist, at variance with the Imperialist regime, there was nevertheless a resigned passivity about his literary work, together with a heavy sentimentality which permeated even some of his earlier and best plays. By comparison with Ibsen, he lacked spirit, despite the technical ability which made him internationally known. Even so, the First World War found him writing patriotic verse and defending the Imperialist cause in an open letter to Romain Rolland. And during the Weimar Republic he suddenly and a little unaccount-ably became the grand old man of German letters. On the occasion of his sixtieth birthday in 1922, his plays were performed throughout Germany. Thomas Mann, heir-elect to him at the time, greeted him with a characteristic paradox as King of the

Republic. He was awarded all manner of official recognition: the freedom of the city of Breslau, the Goethe Prize (the Nobel Prize he had had already, in 1912), the Peace Medal 'Pour le Mérite'. But by this time his vital forces were spent, though he still had some twenty years of life to endure. Nothing that Hauptmann wrote for the stage after the age of 45 has survived so far. At the centenary celebrations in 1962, the German theatres put on *Die Weber*, *Der Biberpelz*, *Rose Bernd*, and other works published in the 1890's and early 1900's. They scarcely touched the later work, although Hauptmann continued to write at prodigious length almost until his death in 1946. In his old age he had become a helpless reed, at first out of favour with the Nazis for his passivity, for his 'enlightened' ideas and his reputation as a democrat and a socialist during the Republic, then suddenly welcomed back to the same kind of prominence as he had enjoyed in 1922. On the occasion of his seventy-fifth birthday in 1937, a gala performance of *Michael Kramer* was given at Berlin; whereas he had earlier been honoured by the presence of President Ebert, it was now Josef Goebbels who came to the theatre. His plays were performed again, and his books, having at first been banned, appeared once more in the bookshops. Why, nobody explained. It was a freak of fortune which the old man could scarcely appreciate. He was left to write on in blacker and blacker pessimism which reached its peak at the total destruction of Dresden, where he was living, in the bombing raids of February 1945. 'When that happened, I would gladly have died', he said later to a friend, and wrote shortly after, 'I stand at the exit of life, and envy all my dead comrades in the spirit who have been spared this experience.'[18] It was a savage blow to a man who had always believed that the true spirit of Germany was shown in works of charity, and who could not understand how Englishmen and Americans who had had so much from Dresden's art and music could have turned the city into a sea of flames. His feelings were shared by many Germans at the time, especially those who, like him, had been turned away, picked up again, and thrust aside with very little comprehension of what was happening to them.

This was not the case, however, with a writer who stood almost at the opposite pole to Hauptmann. Ernst Jünger was one of those writers who had come perilously close to Nazism: not only were the ideas in his book *Der Arbeiter* reminiscent of those the Nazis put into practice,[19] he had even sent to Hitler signed and inscribed copies of his own works. On the other hand, he explicitly dissociated himself from the party as early as June 1934, in a letter to the *Völkischer Beobachter* newspaper, an action he could afford to take, since he had military friends in high places. As time went on, moreover, he became increasingly dissatisfied, as did many other soldiers both active and retired. In 1939, just as the war began, he published his strange allegorical novel *Auf den Marmorklippen*, which could certainly be construed as an attack on the Nazi State in general and on Hitler in particular, and yet, surprisingly, was not suppressed. Recalled to the Army, he served on the staff of the Military Governor of Paris, where he prepared a document entitled 'Peace', which had some clandestine circulation, and where he was in touch with some of the officers who plotted the assassination of Hitler on 20 July 1944. In February of that year, his son Ernst was arrested and condemned to serve in a penal battalion for listening to foreign broadcasts, for forming a resistance group among his classmates, and for declaring that Hitler deserved hanging. Yet with all this, Jünger seemed curiously reluctant to commit himself whether in literature or in action. In his novel, the figure of the Senior Forester may well be taken to stand for Hitler, while the two brothers who oppose him can easily be interpreted as Jünger and his brother Friedrich Georg, the poet. But it is hard to say what values they feel themselves to be defending. There are signs of a vague trend towards, or at any rate respect for, Roman Catholicism. A serene love of order and of the contemplative life, coupled with an interest in botany and natural history such as the author himself had, seems a fair account of the fictional brothers' tendencies. They oppose the Senior Forester because of his domineering brutality, but there is a zest in describing the murderous battle between his pack of dogs and those belonging to the brothers which is hardly consistent with this opposition. And, although a positive symbol emerges from the destruction at the end of the novel, the final scene shows the departure of the brothers from their native soil to a place that appears to be meant for neutral Switzerland. Jünger abdicates allegorically here from any desire to provide further opposition. He states his objection, acknowledges defeat, and passes on to the next stage in his life.

Similarly, in refusing to join the conspirators in 1944, Jünger was not vacillating and yet strangely inactive. As a member of the staff of General Stülpnagel, who was later hanged for his complicity, and as a friend of Field-Marshal Rommel, he had the opportunity of taking part in the plot had he wanted to, and nobody need suppose that it was lack of physical courage that held him back. By his own account, published in *Strahlungen* in 1949, it was rather a feeling that the conspirators were men trying needlessly to hasten an inevitable end, and thereby putting themselves in the wrong to some extent. They were attempting 'to bring down the colossus before he, together with his numberless following, found his ultimate goal in the depths of the abyss': in short, they were historically mistaken, though morally right. Jünger does not say what action he would have thought appropriate, beyond that Rommel would have played a part had he lived. At no time, in fact, has he ever acknowledged that any action of his own was mistaken: 'he has never "recanted"', his biographer says, and he himself has asked his readers to regard all his work as one single whole, in which there are various epochs, but no contradictions. 'I should not like to be one of those who do not want to be reminded today of what they were like yesterday.'[20] This is much the same spirit as that of Thomas Mann in the *Betrachtungen*, refusing to admit any contradiction between his support for the Imperial regime and that for the Republic. There might, Mann had admitted, be a contradiction between the thoughts he had uttered at that time and this, but this was a contradiction between the thoughts only, not a contradiction of himself by himself. And similarly Gottfried Benn, in the years after 1945, reiterated the thought 'To be mistaken and yet be compelled to go on believing what one's innermost being tells one—that is man, and his glory begins yonder, beyond victory and defeat'.[21] In all these authors there is a determination to continue unabashed whatever happens: really to admit error would be disastrous folly. They have lived through their times, and that is their justification, if one is needed. As Rilke said of his contemporaries after 1918, they have preferred to persist rather than to change.[22] Identified with the times, they are identified with the Spirit of the time, and no better warrant is required.

There remains, then, only one other representative form of opposition to Nazism, that of the Communists, whose chief literary representative, it became increasingly clear after 1933, was Bert Brecht; and Brecht's opposition, as has been seen, was downright and outspoken. Yet to see even his work in its proper light, it is necessary to use a word of caution about what Communism implied. Being in origin partly Hegelian (so far as it was Marxist), it was also partly committed to ideas about the supremacy of the state over the individual. In the days of Lassalle, its tendency was most unclear: Lassalle, it has been said, 'should be counted among the founders not only of European socialism, but equally of the doctrine of personal dictatorship and fascism';[23] and indeed, but for his early death in 1864, Communism in Germany might have run to tyranny far sooner than 1945. As it was, Marx and Engels won the day, and it was their doctrine rather than Lassalle's which gained the allegiance both of the Social Democrats in Germany and of the revolutionaries in Russia. Even so, the form actually taken by Russian Communism, despite its hostility to National Socialism, was sufficiently close to that of its adversary to arouse comment. The personal dictatorship of Stalin, the songs, uniforms and slogans of the political organizations, the secret police, terroristic suppression, the attempted extermination of a whole class of opponents, the prison camps for political and social enemies, though they may have had little enough to do with Marx,[24] were not remarkably different from the methods of the Nazi regime, nor was the Soviet–German pact of 1939 a contradiction in terms.[25] Stalin's policy, in contrast to Trotsky's, was certainly 'national socialism', in that it was 'socialism in one country': there was a strange parallelism between the two states, although it should not be exaggerated. And Brecht was not unaffected by this. His play *Furcht und Elend im dritten Reich* is the clearest documentation and denunciation of the Nazi tyranny ever to have appeared in theatrical form. On the other hand, his allegorical representation of the same events, *Die Rundköpfe und die Spitzköpfe*, is absurdly and even dangerously wide of the mark it tries to hit. The conclusion of this play is quite nakedly that the Nazis are wrong to persecute the Jews, not because Jews are men like themselves, but because they ought to be persecuting the capitalists instead. The parallelism between a Communist and a Nazi interpretation of society's ills, with victim and villain varied to taste, could scarcely be clearer.

Against this, there has to be remembered Brecht's determination to prevent his audiences from falling into acquiescent torpor. *Der aufhaltsame Aufstieg des Arturo Ui* is the title of his allegory on the life of Hitler: the dictator's success, it implies, was something that could have been stopped. Brecht's plays were meant to insist on that thought: it was the 'bourgeois' theatre, he believed, that encouraged acceptance. 'The theatre as we find it shows the structure of society (reflected on the stage) as incapable of being influenced by society (in the auditorium).'[26] The stage-tragedies of the past encouraged men to believe that disasters were inevitable, or something that one could learn to accommodate. Brecht wanted to stimulate revolt against all such commodiousness: the slogan was 'change the world, it can do with it'.

And yet with all this, it is surprising how ambiguous many of Brecht's plays have been, and not merely by virtue of the spectators' wilfulness, as has been the case with *Mutter Courage*. In this, one of his best plays, Brecht was determined to show war as folly and wickedness, to force his audiences into recognizing that it was due not to inexplicable fate, but to their own intention to profit by war. In the process, he made the character of Mother Courage herself so full of his own vitality, wry humour, and laconic sympathy as to attract rather more liking for her than he intended, and in later versions he introduced more and more ruthless actions in order to frustrate this liking. The character remains as fundamentally sympathetic as ever, and the conclusion has been drawn that Brecht therefore failed in his purpose. But to argue thus is to argue too rigidly. Mother Courage may remain sympathetic—in fact she should do so, if the audience is to see how applicable her case is to their own—and yet her share of responsibility for events may be acknowledged. There need be no ambiguity about that. With some of Brecht's other plays, however, there is a genuine doubt about what is intended—and unlike most Shakespearean plays these plays of Brecht's are supposed to convey a meaning, a message: they are supposed to help in 'changing the world'. *Galileo* is a case in point. Here Brecht chose to write about one of the most famous recantations in history: Galileo's confession, at the moment when he was faced with the threat or the hint of torture by the Inquisition, that the earth did not as he had claimed move round the sun. When Brecht took up the theme in 1938–9, it was of great actuality; men in Germany were being faced with the equivalent of Galileo's dilemma almost daily. Yet he seems at first to have been more concerned to demonstrate the value of Galileo's shrewd refusal to play the hero, his cunning devotion to his scientific task, even at the expense of moral integrity, than with the impropriety of any scientist defecting from his knowledge of truth. In the final version of the play, both sides of the question receive about equal emphasis. Galileo's recantation is clearly condemned, and yet, in the last scene of all, the fruits of his continued persistence are decidedly brought to the spectator's notice, so that in the end one has the impression of a moral protest akin to those already noticed in this chapter. The fault is condemned, there is no doubt about that, and yet it seems to be condoned at the same time, so that the total effect is somewhat blurred.

Similarly in *Der gute Mensch von Sezuan*, while Brecht's sympathy with the charitable impulses of the heroine, Shen Te, is very apparent, the purport of the whole is less clear. Did he mean to imply, as he had certainly done in earlier plays, that such impulses must be disregarded so long as the communistic utopia had not been achieved—that it was necessary to adopt the harsh measures of Shen Te's counterpart and 'other self', Shui Ta? He has been taken to imply that by Communist critics, though 'Western' critics have tended to suppose that he saw the choice between charity for all and ruthless disregard of many, in the interests of efficiency, as a tragic dilemma. It is very difficult to speak with confidence on this point, and that is itself a mark of Brecht's failure to do what he set out to do. Perhaps, however, he would really have preferred a fusion of attitudes such as is seen in his best play, *Der Kaukasische Kreidekreis*. In this, the two sides of his personality which had always preoccupied him—the amoral, zestful, all-accepting side that is seen in his earliest work *Baal* and again in the central character of play after play, and the charitable, deeply sympathizing side which led him into Communism and for a time, paradoxically, to the inhumanity of his propagandist works—these two are juxtaposed, and ultimately they come together for an instant which may reveal Brecht's deepest intentions. In the first half of the play there is Grusha, the good woman, faithful wife and lover, and brave rescuer of a child who ought to mean nothing to her at all; in the second half there is Azdak, the thief, time-server and coward, corrupt, licentious and contemptuous of law and order, a lickspittle who nevertheless, given a free hand in time of anarchy, does manage to deal out a sizeable quantity of rough-handed justice. It is precisely because Azdak rather than a conventional judge is in power in the final scene of the play that Grusha, appearing before him, is awarded custody of the child that is not hers, for, as the one person who has treated it as a mother should, she has every right to continue cherishing it. By this ending Brecht apparently meant to show that the spontaneity and amorality of Azdak, although in some ways despicable, was able finally to provide justice for Grusha when nobody else could or would. (The rather irrelevant political moral in favour of Communism, explicitly drawn in the final lines, can be disregarded.) Her moral uprightness is given its due by Azdak's undetermined, unpremeditated surrender to impulse, as though by some paradox the one attitude were in need of the other. And theatrically this can be effective. It is as though Grusha's unblemished though not at all priggish honesty could only exist, dramatically, in association with so outrageous a flouter of respectability as Azdak, as though she were a kind of Prince Hal to his Falstaff. Put the two together, and you have satisfying theatre, where one alone might be repugnant. Yet in so far as Brecht tries for more than theatrical effectiveness, hesitations crop up again. Azdak awards custody of the child to Grusha, after all, only because he happens to be safe from retribution at the time. A few moments earlier, when he believed his own life in danger, he was cringing with promises to have her executed at once, and we are not given the opportunity to discover whether he would have kept his word or not. Perhaps, like Galileo, whom he resembles in some ways, Azdak would have caved in under serious pressure, as Falstaff certainly would have. It takes a powerful actor—someone like Ernst Busch for instance—to persuade an audience that Azdak is despite some of his appearances a rather wise 'judge'. And there is, these days, always the disturbing thought at the back of a spectator's mind that the chameleon-like adaptation of Azdak, like that of so many Brechtian characters before him, is a replica of Brecht's own behaviour in the last years of his life when he returned to live in the German Democratic Republic. He did not approve of all that happened there, least of all the suppression of the popular demonstrations in Berlin by the Soviet authorities on 17 June 1953, and he made an ineffective attempt at saying so. He discovered then that he simply was not allowed to speak his mind: his letter of protest was mutilated so as to appear to be a letter of support, and he was reduced in his last two years to the position familiar to so many Germans for at least two decades: he could be against the government as much as he pleased, in private. In public, the dictum of Frederick the Great still operated: 'Complain about what you like and as much as you like, but obey!' There was not much an Azdak could do about that. At most he might, like the 'good soldier Schweik' in another of Brecht's plays, maintain a humorous, quizzical reserve, mocking the power that was too strong to be more openly resisted. But many Germans had been doing that for some time past; there was nothing inspiring in it.

The fanatically pure aesthete, the 'Bürger' and the liberal humanist, the soldier, the well-intentioned lover of peace, the Communist—so far as literature was concerned they might make their protest or not, in any event they were swallowed up, and even despite themselves tended towards a conformity which they might also denounce. It was unheroic, and yet the best that could be said for it was that it showed a kind of Chinese serenity (Confucius, for instance, was much admired by Brecht), a confidence that genuine human concerns would continue despite anything the war-lords might do. That may have been present: it is a difficult thing to define adequately, and this is not the place to inquire deeply how right it was, or who showed it at its best. The possibility is worth bearing in mind. What is probably most difficult of all to understand is the frame of mind not of the poets and men of genius, but of the young intellectuals who admired them and yet were obliged by circumstance to remain in Germany and to fight in Hitler's army. These must concern us last, because those of them who survived are now middle-aged men, with sons of their own of military age and able to vote. What they believed in the years from 1933 to 1945 must still be potent today, despite the immense changes that have occurred at least in Western Germany, and despite the really refreshing signs of independence of judgment in the last few years. They felt themselves heirs to a tradition of thought and literature which is still insufficiently questioned, and which is still propagated without awareness of all it implies. Many letters of such men survive and have been published: the handful it is possible to quote is less than fully representative and yet profoundly disturbing. For with a good deal that is moving, with all the sympathy expressed in such letters for the Russian enemy, the longing for home and peace, messages of love to children and wives, and even, despite military censorship, the denunciations of the ruling power, there are also in them signs of an attitude very close indeed to that of the men of letters. These are the letters of students, more articulate than those of the average soldier and yet not necessarily different in spirit from his; and they reveal repeatedly the same combination of opposition and acquiescence already observed.

There were some who saw the fighting much as Rilke had seen it in the First World War, as a means to realizing existence more intensely, of 'living out the deepest law of our being, in a quite primitive sense',27 as one of them put it. Or as another said, writing to a friend at the front, 'you soldiers out there, beyond, you are standing in truly philosophical *existence*. Anything I might say would be only a shadow of what you *are*.'28 This thought, recurring often in writer after writer, sees no moral issue as yet, only a determination akin to that of Rilke's Malte, to reject nothing in the form of experience, to savour it all, bitter and sweet, without regard to the cause that is being defended. One young man explicitly relates his ideas to those of the poet:

...those words from Rilke's *Requiem*...'Wer spricht von Siegen? Überstehn ist alles'—'who speaks of victory? to endure is all'. These are really *the* words for us, for me here. Tense to breaking-point, I sometimes don't know *whether* I am enduring, and yet I know that the meaning of this testing-time, of the whole existence of these years, can only lie in endurance [Überstehen].29

It is hard to realize that these words come from a letter full of bitter denunciations of the war, by a writer who asks 'Is it my fault that I am compelled to be wrongly orientated?' The issues of the war do not concern him, though he is aware of them; he is not even concerned whether Germany is victorious: the main issue is whether he can persist in living through it all. For others who shared this view, the point of the war was even more strangely stated, although in terms reminiscent of Mann's Adrian Leverkühn:

Let us have no fear of this struggle, whose meaning lies in its meaninglessness, whose value is the devaluation of the human spirit or at all events of the present forms of the human mind and its constructive abilities.... *Even terrible disaster, perhaps that above all,* will bring us closer to knowledge and truth.[30]

Similarly, but with a new and revealing emphasis:

The situation of having to fight for something in which you don't believe, and to feel this obligation not as an external compulsion but as a reasoned deduction, the alternative being to renounce Germany as a first-class power or as a realm of the spirit; to do one's duty in this dilemma not merely for good or ill, but with impeccable alacrity down to the last detail—this is the most terrible situation imaginable.[31]

In this last extract, something deserving long reflection is conveyed—the quite religious devotion to a national cause, like the devotion of a son to a criminal father. Where was the line to be drawn between mercy and condemnation of one's fatherland? For some it was not to be drawn at all: Germany was committed to this course of action, repulsively wrong though it was, and thereby all her 'children' were committed.

I have a great yearning for non-uniformed people, for non-militarised parlours, even if they are the middle-class, friendly, humdrum parlours of these Dutch. It's all so attractive and pleasant, and when I see the contented people pouring out of church on a Sunday I sometimes have a straightforward feeling that this is all good and proper and I look for nothing else. Later of course I realise that this will all be destroyed, for the sake of something new. We Germans have already gone on further, we have chaos in us and realise it and have an inward disposition to seek new things in the very depths.[32]

This was widespread, this feeling that the entry into chaos was an essential for Germany, as for European civilization. ('You have not enough chaos in you', Nietzsche had said, and Wagner had shown Siegfried the hero reducing his sword to chaotic fragments before forging it again into the invincible 'Nothung'.) Men were committed to it, though they could see the pleasures of ordinary existence. Like Adrian Leverkühn, really representative here, they consciously chose the path to destruction in the belief that there was no other way to health, or even, paradoxically, that to choose so was in itself the mark of health. They felt this as part of their tradition, as something essential to Germany despite its meaninglessness:

After this war, the Führer has said, there will be no victors and van-quished, but only survivors and destroyed. But survival will not be a matter of vegetating along on the ruins of the world, but of surviving freely, that is of 'sur-viving', living on beyond oneself ['sondern nur in der Weise der Freiheit des Überlebens, das heißt Über-sich-hinaus-lebens']. That is the meaning of history as it has revealed itself to the all-seeing eye of the seer for a hundred and fifty years. That is what is prophesied by the work of Hölderlin as it is by that of Nietzsche, George and Rilke. If history—and that is the meaning of their work—is to go on essentially happening, then it can only be in the 'sur-vivors' or it will exist no more.33

The strange language with its esoteric vocabulary seems to mean something of this kind: that German prophetic writers and poets have long since foretold the necessity to accept all the most destructive and barbaric impulses in human nature, to realize them as a part of that nature, not in order that they may be subli-mated or overcome, but simply that they may become real: that thereby men will themselves become more real, and history will take place more essentially, because none of its horrors will be glossed over just as none of its ecstasies will be lost.

The thing is to maintain yourself. That is why the will to live unfolds itself with power. At times it urges us to outbreaks of wild delight. You live for the moment. You give yourself to it completely. To live at all is happiness. But even in grave times you feel the full content of life. It is bitter and sweet, all and one, because we savour it down to the dregs, because we learn to see the essential, and this perception rewards us a second time with all its riches.34

In this self-realization the effect on the rest of the world was not considered. Committed to the realization of the moment, these soldiers fought as savagely for a cause in which they did not believe as they might have done for any other, till the Rhine and the Elbe were crossed, and all the cities in Germany were rubble. Occasionally one wonders what has really replaced that nihilistic acceptance, whether the sudden cessation of almost all admiration for the Nazis, once the war ended, was really a recognition of what had happened, or whether people were continuing to exist in the same centre-less will-less way as before. Was the dynamo merely running idle, waiting for the next drive-belt, or was there to be a conscious redirection of purpose? As late as 1954 Gottfried Benn was publishing the words already quoted: 'To be mistaken and yet be compelled to go on believing what one's own innermost being tells one—that is man, and his glory begins yonder, beyond victory and defeat.' Was this still evidence of the determination to 'sur-vive', to persist and never to change? And were the old values (or whatever one calls them: 'trans-valued values') going to be reviewed or not? So far, by 1965, there has been not much sign of a review. Certain figures have become controversial; but 'official' labels of one kind or another are already beginning to make their importance felt. The portrait of Thomas Mann, appearing on a postage-stamp, probably has more influence on popular estimates of his quality as a writer than any number of critical assessments. The publishing of the Complete Works of Hermann Hesse establishes him as a subject for research theses more securely than anything else could. Space given in literary histories is yet another substitute for a proper reputation. And so long as a large *œuvre*, a well-known name, and a preferably obscure philosophical content are taken as the main pretexts for concerning ourselves with a writer, the living quality of literature will continue to be ignored.

The main stream of modern German literature is impressive in its unity, and sometimes deeply disturbing in its closeness to the stream which ended in apparent national insanity. Of course it is not identical with that other stream, and only lack of caution makes it seem so. It is really part of a much larger European current which has now and again left strange flotsam behind. Yeats, Lawrence, Pound, Gide, d'Annunzio, Unamuno have all left recorded utterances which look so much the worse when the country in which they lived or were born has turned to fascism for the solution of its urgent problems. A certain amount of what was said in Germany would have sounded much less repulsive had it not coincided with a period of fervid nationalism, although the opportunism of some writers, both in literature and in real life, can scarcely find any excuse at all. Allowing for that, though, there remains a coherence within the main German stream which does not exist in other modern literatures. The liberal voices are ineffective, weak or equivocal, and the major figures are nearly all more inclined to float with the tide than seriously to swim against it. A tradition has become well established, and while it is absurd to speak of a national character, in any racial sense, it is true that a tradition creates an atmosphere of thought in which certain assumptions are generally taken for granted, and thus certain kinds of action follow. The German tradition treated here can be described as Hegelian, Marxist, Nietzschean, dualistic, synthesizing; it has a considerable ancestry, extending back through Plotinus to Plato and beyond, and if only on that account should not be disregarded or lightly thrown aside. More important than any frontal and would-be demolishing assault, therefore, is an attempt at seeing what can best be made from that tradition, in what its excellences consist, as well as where its pitfalls lie. From the point of view of German literature (which influences in some ways German life and society) nothing matters more than that the best possible definition is given of its best tradition, and that the works of outstanding greatness are singled out from those which merely affect greatness. Since literary criticism in any proper sense scarcely exists in Germany, this is laborious, and a great many accepted masterpieces will have to be rejected before the issue can even be properly seen. The task is even more difficult when the critic must so often walk on a razor-edge, distinguishing the false synthesis from the true one (or the one that at all events rings true), the Inquisitor from the Christ, and when writers are so often bent on confusing these issues. It will be surprising if in the process the critics do not themselves fall into overstatements and false emphases, wrong rejections and over-eager affirmations. But the attempt will have to be made by everybody who counts himself enough of a German to feel Germany's disaster as his own.

PART II

THOMAS MANN

Sondern die Hellen, die Wackeren, die Durchsichtigen —
das sind mir die klügsten Schweiger: denen so tief ihr
Grund ist, daß auch das hellste Wasser ihn nicht — verrät. —

Also sprach Zarathustra

Blickte man hinein in diese erzählte Welt, sah man: die
elegante Selbstbeherrschung, die bis zum letzten Augenblick
eine innere Unterhöhlung, den biologischen Verfall vor
den Augen der Welt verbirgt. . . ..

Der Tod in Venedig

CHAPTER IV

BUDDENBROOKS (1)

A paradox? A paradox!
A most ingenious paradox!

Mann's style in his first novel already shows the frame of mind which continued, essentially unchanged, till the end of his life. The curious irony, so unlike that of anyone else, except perhaps *irony* Goethe in some of the works of his old age, is already apparent, and although the scope of his ideas increases greatly with advancing years, and their implications become more intricate and hard to grasp, the foundations of his attitude are laid in *Buddenbrooks*. A few examples will illustrate and define my point. Here is a passage about a character who has only a small importance in the novel as a whole, the unfortunate Christian Buddenbrook, the artist *manqué* who has married a former prostitute, and whose lack of success in any undertaking has scandalized the prosperous 'Bürger' family to which he belongs. It will be remembered that, towards the end of the novel, Christian becomes mentally ill:

Über Christian lagen betrübende Nachrichten vor. Die Ehe schien sein Befinden nicht günstig beeinflußt zu haben. Unheimliche Wahnideen und Zwangsvorstellungen hatten sich bei ihm in verstärktem Maße wiederholt, und auf Veranlassung seiner Gattin und eines Arztes hatte er sich in eine Anstalt begeben. Er war nicht gern dort, schrieb lamentierende Briefe an die Seinen und gab dem heftigen Wunsche Ausdruck, aus dieser Anstalt, in der man ihn sehr streng zu behandeln schien, wieder befreit zu werden. Aber man hielt ihn fest, und das war wohl das Beste für ihn. Jedenfalls setzte es seine Gemahlin in den Stand, unbeschadet der praktischen und ideellen Vorteile, die sie der Heirat verdankte, ihr früheres unabhängiges Leben ohne Rücksicht und Behinderung fortzuführen.[1]*

---

* Theie weie sad tidings to hand of Christian. Marriage seemed to have had no very favourable influence on his state of health. Uncanny delusions and

This seems a straightforwardly satirical passage. The mincing tone in some of these phrases, and the dryly official terms, suggest an ironical rendering of the conventional show of sympathy for the afflicted. The news about Christian did not simply arrive, it 'was to hand', as though on somebody's desk. There is something sardonic about saying that Christian's health, or rather his state of health, had been 'not favourably influenced' by marriage, and the 'Fremdwort' in *lamentierende* Briefe', so much less sympathetic than 'klagend' would have been, strikes a slightly comic note as though the sufferer were being mocked. 'He gave vent to the ardent desire' is the expression of someone who has refused to have any personal concern; 'ohne Rücksicht und Behinderung' suggests 'without let or hindrance', with its legalistic ring, just as the reference to the delusions 'recurring in aggravated measure' sounds professional in another way. Take all these features together, and the sentiments seem to be those of some supercilious relation or friend who is rather irritated by or gloating over Christian's misfortunes than grieved by them. They seem the sentiments of the Buddenbrooks at their most brusque and business-like, and Mann's own role is easily seen as that of an ironical masquerader, adopting this language in order to reveal its hypocrisy.

Reading the passage in that sense, however, we find cause for hesitation. In the earlier sentences such a reading works well enough, but at the end there is a remark which none of the Buddenbrooks or anyone like them would have made. The last sentence, referring to Christian's wife, expresses a morality quite opposed to the conventional. The euphemistic mention of her 'former independent life' can only mean that she returns to her

hallucinations had recurred in aggravated measure, and at the instigation of his wife and of a doctor he had entered an institution. He disliked it there and wrote lamentatious letters to his kith and kin, expressive of a fervent desire to be released from this institution, where, it appeared, he was very strictly treated. But they kept him shut up, and that was no doubt the best thing for him. At all events it put his wife in a position to continue her former independent mode of living, without let or hindrance, and without prejudice to the practical and notional advantages accruing to her from her marriage. [I have kept very closely to Mann's style, which in the standard translation is more freely rendered.]

life as a prostitute, and the remainder of the sentence, on reflection, must say that she can now use her married status as a cloak of respectability, with the 'practical' advantages of, presumably, her husband's money and his name for any children unexpectedly born.[2] If Christian suffers, at least his wife benefits. This thought, although couched in the same indirect style, is too cynical or too sophisticated to be part of the train of ideas of a Buddenbrook. Mann cannot be parodying a conventional attitude here, for surely none such exists. Hypocrisy pretends to be moral, not to be amoral.

Another reading may then be tried. By the time *Buddenbrooks* was published (1900), the traditional ideal of sympathy and pity for suffering had been sharply criticized and even ridiculed in the work of Nietzsche, whose influence is readily apparent in other passages in this novel.[3] It may be that Christian—the name itself is suggestive—is not presented here as an object of pity, but as a failure deserving contempt, and treated much as Nietzsche suggested that physicians should treat their patients, 'with a dose of disgust'. On this reading, the language which appeared to be that of a mind merely pretending to itself that it was expressing charity, while revealing to us its lack of charity, is not hypocritical but intentional. The 'saddening' news saddens only the conventional sympathizers; the 'lamentatious' letters are meant to be found amusing, and the over-formal reference to Christian's relatives as 'die Seinen' is a jibe at family love. The final sentence about Christian's wife now fits readily into place, suggesting that she is a woman who can live with zest, quite unaffected by her husband's troubles; that she has a ruthlessness matched, if this interpretation be correct, by that of the author himself. What is admired is a healthy self-assertion; what is ridiculed is weakness, sickness, and dependence on others.

Should this reading be substituted for the first? To do so would seem not to accord with the author's whole intention, as distinct from his effect. One has the impression that what Mann sought to do here was to write in such a way that both readings would be possible. Much later in his life, we find him writing of such a double vision, involving both charity and scorn, as though it were essential to art (although, being a remark made by a character, it cannot strictly be attributed to the author). 'Whether they lie close together or far apart, it is two eyes that make up one gaze', he makes the secretary Riemer say of Goethe, in *Lotte in Weimar*. 'So now I ask you: what sort of gaze is that wherein the horrifying contradiction of the eyes is annulled? It is the gaze of Art, of absolute Art, which is at once absolute love and absolute destructiveness or indifference, and implies that horrifying approach to the godlike-diabolic which we call genius.'4 In the light of what Mann called his *unio mystica* with Goethe, it cannot be doubted that he himself admired and cultivated such a combination of incompatibles, and of course the synthesis of opposites in general is a major feature of his way of thinking and of the tradition from which he descends. Perhaps, then, we should read the 'Christian' passage in a similarly dual fashion, if that is at all possible, keeping in mind both the interpretation in which a loving and pitying mood seems inherent, and that in which the controlling factor is mockery of Christian's inaptitude for life. However, quite apart from the impossibility of maintaining these two interpretations *simultaneously* ('zugleich' is the word used in the passage about Goethe, and the whole idea of synthesis implies it), we must recognize that, whatever else may be said, the attitudes we are trying to define are not attitudes of love on the one hand and malice or hatred on the other. In other words, the author does not convey by his style either love for Christian or hatred for him, whether simultaneously or not.

What is conveyed is, on our 'first' reading, satirical mockery of *hypocritical* pity. This does not necessarily imply admiration for or condemnation of pity in any other form. The target of the satire is hypocrisy, and the norm to which the satire implicitly appeals is some kind of genuineness of emotional response. Such a norm may be admirable (much depends on the word 'genuineness'), but it implies no particular attitude towards loving or pitying. On our 'first' reading we noticed the hypocritical turns of phrase and perhaps drew the conclusion that the author made use of them out of a sense of compassion. This, however, was an inference, as must always be the case with irony, and an inference which the passage as a whole does not support. On the contrary, the 'second' reading—and this is the reading which makes consistent sense throughout, whereas the 'first' had a sense-destroying break at the last sentence—implies a viewpoint which finds compassion absurd or life-denying. On the whole, then, we are driven to a third reading in which we hear, not love or pity together with indifference, but mockery both of hypocrisy and of compassion.

Yet even this is not really satisfactory. For the last sentence, with what certainly seems to be its approval of the wife's infidelity and prostitution, is couched in just the same formal, euphemistic, and, occasionally, mealy-mouthed terms as the rest of the passage. 'Without prejudice to the practical and notional advantages accruing to her from her marriage'—'her former independent mode of life'—these are curiously indirect references, requiring some reflection on the background of the passage before they are properly understood. If Mann really intended to welcome this 'affirmation of life', he is inappositely coy. Indeed, seeing that the 'second' reading was the one which made coherent sense, it seems that he was coy throughout. If the amoral, anti-compassionate reading is the correct one, there is no reason to suppose that hypocrisy was the target at all. Pedantry and euphemism characterize the whole passage, being applied both to the comments on Christian and to those on his wife. A strong impression is given that Mann was ill-at-ease with the Nietzschean ideas he was striving to adopt or adapt, and masked his discomfort with a persiflage that both implied amorality and teasingly disavowed it.

Such a charge could not be sustained cogently on the basis of a single passage. Before turning to another, however, there is one more observation to make, one which cannot carry much weight at this point, but whose significance should appear more clearly later. It is that we are told so very little in the novel about Christian's wife. Broadly speaking, there is no reason for saying that her returning to prostitution was certainly either for better or for worse—it is conceivable that under certain circumstances a woman might do better to be a prostitute than to remain faithfully married, if for example the marriage itself had become in spirit a 'licensed form of prostitution'. The frank acknowledgment might be preferable to the pretence. All depends on the circumstances, which it is usually a novelist's desire to portray. Mann, however, tells us in the novel almost nothing about Christian's wife. The fact of her having been a prostitute is the only point about her to which this passage refers. And while she is of course only a very minor character indeed, the easy assumption made about her, and the absence of any detail, will be seen to be characteristic of a great deal of Mann's writing.

A passage about Hugo Weinschenk, husband of Toni Buddenbrook's daughter, indicates a similar easy-goingness, and a similar apparent ambiguity. Weinschenk too is a minor character, and the comments on him after his return from prison closely resemble those on Christian:

Das Gefängnisleben hatte seiner körperlichen Gesundheit nichts anhaben können, denn Hugo Weinschenk war stets von durabler Konstitution gewesen; aber es stand doch äußerst traurig um ihn. Es war entsetzlich zu sehen, wie dieser Mann, der höchstwahrscheinlich nichts Anderes begangen hatte, als was die meisten seiner Kollegen ringsum mit gutem Mut alle Tage begingen, und der, wäre er nicht ertappt worden, ohne Zweifel erhobenen Hauptes und unberührt heiteren Gewissens seinen Pfad gewandert wäre — durch seinen bürgerlichen Fall, durch die Tatsache der gerichtlichen Verurteilung und diese drei Gefängnisjahre nun moralisch so vollkommen gebrochen war. Er hatte vor Gericht aus tiefster Überzeugung beteuert, und von Sachverständigen war es ihm bestätigt worden, daß das kecke Manöver, welches er seiner Gesellschaft und sich selbst zu Ehr' und Vorteil unternommen, in der Geschäftswelt als Usance gelte. Die Juristen aber, Herren, die nach seiner eigenen Meinung von diesen Dingen gar nichts verstanden, die unter ganz anderen Begriffen und in einer ganz anderen Weltanschauung lebten, hatten ihn wegen Betruges verurteilt, und dieser Spruch, dem die staatliche Macht zur Seite stand, hatte seine Selbstschätzung dermaßen zu erschüttern vermocht, daß er Niemandem mehr ins Angesicht zu blicken wagte. Sein federnder Gang, die unternehmende Art, mit der er sich in der Taille seines

Gehrockes gewiegt, mit den Fäusten balanciert und die Augen gerollt hatte, die ungemeine Frische, mit der er von der Höhe seiner Unwissenheit und Unbildung herab seine Fragen und Erzählungen zum Besten gegeben hatte — Alles war dahin! Es war so sehr dahin, daß den Seinen vor so viel Gedrücktheit, Feigheit und dumpfer Würdelosigkeit graute.*5

Euphemisms like those of the other passage do not occur here, and there is only an occasional phrase that might indicate ironical detachment: 'von durabler Konstitution', 'es stand doch äußerst traurig um ihn', 'seinen Pfad gewandert', 'zu Ehr' und Vorteil unternommen'—only here do 'Fremdwörter' and a slight formality of expression suggest other than a serious note. They may induce the reader, however, to begin reading the passage as though the commercial practices of Weinschenk and his unaccused colleagues were being called into question. Hearing that 'his case was extremely sad', in those terms, one rather expects to have it implied that it wasn't; and the comment immediately following, that it was 'dreadful', consequently sounds also like an ironical invitation to believe the opposite. The reader accustomed to irony in Dickens or Swift or Defoe may expect to infer

---

* He had always had a hard-wearing constitution, and the prison life could hardly have impaired his physical health. But his condition was, none the less, pitiable in the extreme. This man had in all probability done no more than his business colleagues did every day and thought nothing of; if he had not been caught, he would have gone on his way with head erect and conscience clear. Yet it was dreadful to see how his ruin as a citizen, the judicial correction, and the three years' imprisonment, had operated to break down his morale. His testimony before the court had been given with the most sincere conviction; and people who understood the technicalities of the case supported his contention that he had merely executed a bold manœuvre for the credit of his firm and himself—a manœuvre known in the business world as usance. The lawyers who had convicted him knew, in his opinion, nothing whatever about such things and lived in quite a different world. But their conviction, endorsed by the governing power of the state, had shattered his self-esteem to such a degree that he could not look anybody in the face. Gone was his elastic tread, the enterprising way he had of wriggling at the waist of his frock-coat and balancing with his fists and rolling his eyes about. Gone was the ignorant self-assurance with which he had delivered his uninformed opinions and put his questions. The change was such that his family shuddered at it—and indeed it was frightful to see such cowardice, dejection, and lack of self-respect.

that a man who would have done very well for himself if he had not been caught is something of a rogue.

It soon becomes obvious, however, that if such a reading is implied at all it is not the only possible one. If one goes on with it, it must come to a halt towards the end at the description of Weinschenk's personal appearance. Up to this point, it is just possible to suppose that the views explicitly given are those of businessmen like Weinschenk, while the implicit attitude provides a contrapuntal note of disapproval. When the personal description is reached, this is no longer possible at all. Just as, in the 'Christian' passage, the final remark was inconceivable as coming from an assumed conventional mind, so here it is impossible to imagine the supposed spokesmen for conventionality as consciously wishing that Weinschenk had remained the dandified and ignorant bore he seems to have been. Weinschenk's relatives are horrified at his dispiritedness, as the last sentence shows, but this is surely an unreflective reaction, not a conscious regret that his former self has vanished.

Once again, a consistent reading of the passage must be based on other presuppositions. If we assume that the author is not critical of Weinschenk's business-morality, any more than he was, on one reading, of the morality of Christian's wife, the break in continuity of attitude does not occur. On that basis, the passage states quite straightforwardly that Weinschenk had offended against the lawyers' conception of right and wrong, not against that of most of his associates, and that it was horrifying to see his consequent loss of self-esteem. The implications now are that the moral issue was purely relative, and far less important than the preservation of a life-affirming confidence, of an acceptance of Weinschenk's own character without scruples or doubts. What ruined him was social condemnation and his own acquiescence in it: this, rather than the fact or the nature of his punishment, is the object of criticism.

If this reading is taken, there is no room at the same time or separately for an interpretation in terms of a Dickensian or similar morality. The 'Dickensian' interpretation indeed does not fit, whereas the other does—one cannot speak of an 'oscillation' between 'affirmation of the will' and 'moral denial' of it.[6] The 'moral denial' is a matter of inference only, which the passage as a whole does not bear out. Rather, Mann appears deliberately to portray a character who would normally incur disapproval, in order to present the opposite view of him as a man who fascinates by his vitality. At the same time, by informing us that Weinschenk's condition is the result of the accusation of fraud, Mann suggests that it is a moralizing society which is really at fault. There is in this no irony: Weinschenk is admired for what he was, although what he was is unattractive by normal standards.

However, in presenting this picture, Mann is guilty himself of some legerdemain, unless it is sheer forgetfulness that makes him say that 'Weinschenk had 'most probably' done no more than what most of his colleagues did every day with a clear conscience. It is true that we are not reminded at this point of the precise nature of the crime, so that the matter does indeed seem to be a mere difference of opinion between the prosecuting lawyers and Weinschenk himself. If, on the other hand, we do recall what was said in the novel over a hundred pages earlier, we shall look at the present passage rather more askance. The fact is that Weinschenk, as director of a fire-insurance company, had by means of an ingenious system obtained early warning about fires that had broken out on premises insured by him, and reinsured with other companies before the news had reached them, thus causing them to bear the losses. He had, then, practised deliberate frauds on his colleagues, frauds which can scarcely have been 'the accepted thing', as Mann describes them, and which were far more obviously against the general interest than Mann now implies. In persuading us of the lamentable loss of vitality in Weinschenk, Mann weights the balances against the moral evaluation we might otherwise make.

If we continue to speak of Mann's irony then, it must be in the special sense that he displays what he later called 'a destructive tolerance for everything', while at the same time recognizing what would normally be called faults or blemishes. Mann's recognition of these may mislead us into supposing that his tolerance is still critical, whereas in fact it is no more than aware. The 'faults' are recognized—we see that the hostility to Christian Buddenbrook is hypocritical and that Weinschenk is conceited— but they are stated merely as one element in the vitality that is admired. Weinschenk is not idealized, but he is accepted. The 'conventional' distaste for Christian is shown in its true colours but is not condemned: on the contrary. Mann adopts the attitude described by Schopenhauer, though not advocated by him, as 'affirmation of the Will'.

When we say that the Will affirms itself we mean that, although the Will becomes perfectly clearly aware of its own essence as being in the objective world of life, this awareness does not in the slightest degree inhibit its actions, but rather *the life it has thus grown aware of is desired by the Will just as it is*, although, whereas before it did so without being aware of its nature, as a blind impulse, it does so now with such awareness, consciously and deliberately.7

The essential point here is that life is recognized clearly, but consciously willed to be what it already is. We find Mann saying much the same thing when he writes in *Der Tod in Venedig* of Gustav von Aschenbach, the writer whose perceptiveness shows him the corruption of the world in sharp distinction, but who continues nevertheless to affirm. The melancholy conscientious- ness of a young man, Mann asserts there, is insignificant in comparison 'with the mature resolution of a master of his craft, who made a right-about-face, turned his back on the realm of knowledge, and passed it by with head erect, lest it lame his will or power of action, paralyse his feelings or his passions, deprive any of these of their conviction or dignity'.8 Allowing for certain differences of implication, this does declare that knowledge, by which is meant here knowledge of human corruption, must not be allowed to stand in the way of assertion of the will. Awareness of Weinschenk's fraudulence, by the same token, must not hinder admiration for the self-esteem which went with it. The 'irony' by which the immorality of Weinschenk is brought to our consciousness is thus only a preliminary to the affirmation which follows, and is in fact cancelled out by that affirmation.

That these passages should have occurred in a novel which quickly ran into editions of hundreds of thousands of copies in the first decade of this century is significant for the whole history of the period, as well as for this novel itself. The implicit amorality, sometimes upheld by what seems to be subterfuge, the artful surprises sprung on readers who must often have been unsuspecting, the uncertain tone of those passages which do seem to imply some moral frame of reference may seem trivial matters to find in fragments of no great consequence in themselves. They are, however, typical of a speculative atmosphere of much wider importance.

CHAPTER V

BUDDENBROOKS (2)

And you'll allow, as I expect,
That he was right to so object.
And I am right,
And you are right,
And everything is quite correct!

The features observed in the two individual passages from *Buddenbrooks* are also characteristic of the novel as a whole. It is, as the sub-title indicates, the story of the 'decline of a family', and its structure seems, accordingly, to outline an increasing debility. At the beginning there is the robust generation represented by the elder Johann Buddenbrook, untroubled by scruples, unreflecting, committed to what has been called 'blind living',[1] and standing no doubt for what Professor Heller calls, in the Schopenhauerian sense, 'the Will in its perfect integrity'.[2] With each successive generation, reflectiveness becomes greater: the younger Johann, his son Thomas and his grandson Hanno become increasingly self-conscious, increasingly hampered by doubts and conscientious objections to the harsh methods of the business-world. The blind, irresistible urge which, according to Schopenhauer, the Will is—self-seeking, power-grasping and brutal—is increasingly questioned and criticized, and with this comes an increasing inability to conduct the affairs of the family business with the calm efficiency of its earlier heads. Together with moral scruples goes a leaning towards art: Thomas marries the musically inclined Gerda, and at length the line dies out with the most artistically gifted of them all, the boy Hanno.

The structure of decline looks obvious enough. Yet, if we look more closely, we may hesitate to place the elder Johann at the upper end of a descending scale. We are told, quite early on, that his face is 'incapable of expressing malice', and there is indeed some idealization of his character. Yet, as the story unfolds, we perceive that the Buddenbrook ideal is nakedly egocentric: it is to 'exploit the situation without shame', to jib at nothing that will maintain the family's position in society. The development is very largely the story of the successive marriages of convenience through which, to the complete disregard of individual happiness, this is attempted. And thus, if there is a decline, it is a decline from a materialistic bonhomie, a conscienceless devotion to money-making, towards a moral awareness such as Thomas and Hanno have. From a different point of view it might be called an ascent, for the male line does end, even though disastrously, in the person of a boy who is perhaps a musical genius.

With all this in mind, it is tempting to regard the sub-title as itself a piece of irony. We are surely not meant, it may be argued, to regard the elder Johann as the summit from which the rest of the family declines. To make this assumption is, however, to make the same mistake as that implied in the 'first' reading of the passage about Christian: it is to assume a morality which the novel contradicts, and to ignore the signs that Mann invites such a reading only to 'transcend' it, that he registers awareness of immorality only as a preliminary to 'affirming' it.

That this is so—or, to be more accurate, that Mann wrote almost the whole of the novel in terms of such 'transcending'— may be partly seen from the very fact of the elder Johann's being idealized. We see him at the beginning of the story as a figure of Pickwickian geniality: 'His round, rosy, benevolent face, which could express no malice, no matter how hard he tried, was set in a frame of snow-white powdered hair, and the suggestion of a pigtail fell over the broad collar of his mouse-coloured coat.'3 The affectionately drawn picture is evidently meant to establish him in our minds as a benevolent old gentleman who will stand as a contrast, throughout the work, with the devious and increasingly self-torturing figures of his descendants. 'His mind', as Professor Heller says, 'is precisely what Schopenhauer says it [the will] is in its simple and harmonious adjustment to the needs of the Will...his will is wonderfully intact...he is, in so far as this state of innocence is attainable at all within the human species, that "perfect objectivation of the Will" and its "perfect enjoyment of itself" which Schopenhauer discerns in Nature.'4 In other words, he is the Will in its perfectly unreflective state, a man unconcerned with his own motives or with anything else but the here and now: 'he stood with both feet firmly planted in the present'.5 However, Professor Heller's phrase, 'in so far as this state of innocence is attainable at all within the human species', betrays some awareness of what I have referred to as an idealization. We are, in fact, asked to believe that such a state of unreflecting innocence is a possibility for a business man of seventy in the year 1835, that the elder Johann can conduct his business without the least trace of scruple and yet somehow still remain an honest citizen. And even if this possibility be granted, we find, when we look at the passages which treat of Johann, nothing at all about his business methods. We are left as much in ignorance of them as we are of the life of Christian Buddenbrook's wife—the assumption is made that all was well with them, but we never learn the details. (Indeed, what we do see of the elder Johann could contradict even the statement that his face is incapable of expressing malice, for the first expression we see on it is a snigger—'sein helles, verkniffenes Kichern'—at his granddaughter's recital of the catechism.) This absence of information, in view of the course taken by the rest of the novel, is a clear indication of Mann's intention. We are meant to accept the elder Johann as a paragon, and the slurring over of those difficulties which would present themselves if we looked more closely is a mark of Mann's sympathy with the ideal.

The consequences of the idealization are seen in the passage, much later on, when Johann's grandson Thomas is confronted with the problem of whether or not to buy the Pöppenrade harvest 'in the blade'. This is presented as a moral issue for Thomas: on first hearing of the deal he declares that only a cutthroat would take it up, and it is not until he realizes the perilous financial position of his own business that he begins to regard it as a serious possibility. Thereupon, the issue becomes for him a matter of proving himself a man unhampered by moral scruples, which he can only do, as it turns out, by buying the harvest at a bargain price, ruthlessly profiting from its owner's misfortune. 'Was he, Thomas Buddenbrook, a businessman, a man of untrammelled action, or was he a contemplative, riddled with scruples?...Did Thomas Buddenbrook, like his forefathers, stand firmly with his two feet in face of this hard practicality of life?'[6] The last phrase recalls that used of the elder Johann, 'with both feet firmly planted in the present', and suggests that the grandfather at least would not have been troubled as Thomas is: that he would have regarded the infliction of harsh conditions as a matter of course, 'not as harshness, but as something to be taken for granted'.[7] And as the inner argument develops, Thomas seems to come to that conclusion: 'Would his father, his grandfather, his greatgrandfather have bought the Pöppenrade harvest in the blade?...No matter!...No matter!...The thing was that they were practical men, more naturally, more vigorously, more impeccably practical than himself, that was the point!'[8]

Now it is true that Thomas was convinced, on first hearing of the deal, that nothing of the kind had ever been accepted by the Buddenbrooks for a hundred years. On the other hand, the firm has never been in the financial difficulties it faces now. What would in fact have been the decision in the present circumstances of the elder Johann? The answer given here—'No matter!'—evades this point, yet the issue remains. Would he have rejected the deal, and if he had done so, would he not have needed to reflect, to take a moral decision? Or would he have regarded the harshness as a matter of course, as somehow natural, in which case the genial picture of him presented in the opening pages was evidently misleading? We have nothing to go by. The earlier generations were, in some unexplained way, untroubled by such problems, and this is all we may know. The episode itself, however, is evidently constructed so as to suggest that it is precisely because Thomas has scruples that he finally accepts the deal. He accepts it in order to prove to himself that he is a ruthless businessman, and thus makes his action not only harsh but self-conscious and shabby.

If we bear in mind the way in which Weinschenk's deliberate fraud is defended, and his loss of self-esteem deplored, it must appear that the 'harvest' episode is included as an illustration of the evil of hesitant self-consciousness, an illustration somewhat weakened, it is true, by the evasiveness about the elder Johann. This interpretation, one affecting the whole structure and tendency of the novel, is borne out by reference to the climactic episode, that in which Thomas is momentarily caught up in a new vision of the world, as a result of his reading a philosophical work generally assumed to be the principal work of Schopenhauer (the book is never named). It is a matter of dispute whether this passage reflects Mann's own view or not. Although Mann did, by his own account,[9] read Schopenhauer while writing the novel, and was overwhelmed by him in much the same way as his namesake Thomas, it is contended by Professor Pascal, in company with Georg Lukács, that the account in the novel is presented ironically. (Henry Hatfield, on the other hand, takes it straightforwardly.) 'Schopenhauer', writes Pascal, 'does not appear here as the philosophy of the novel; it is only the outlook of this particular man in his particular situation.'[10] Now this is true enough, in that what Thomas derives from Schopenhauer is not at all like the thought of the philosopher. It is *not* true, in that Thomas's ideas fit very closely into the framework of the novel thus far hinted at: the framework within which un-reflecting self-assertion is preferred to self-doubting.[11]

First, it is not the case that Thomas 'gratefully accepts' the doctrine 'that life is suffering and that it is impossible to conquer life's difficulties except by withdrawing from the struggle into contemplation'.[12] His ideas have a much more Nietzschean ring; they are Schopenhauerian only in the sense of that 'affirmation of the Will' which Schopenhauer defined but rejected.[13]

Wo ich sein werde, wenn ich tot bin? Aber es ist so klar, so leuchtend klar, so überwältigend einfach! In allen Denen werde ich sein, die je und je Ich gesagt haben, sagen und sagen werden: *besonders aber in Denen, die es voller, kräftiger, fröhlicher sagen.* . . .

Irgendwo in der Welt wächst ein Knabe auf, gut ausgerüstet und wohlgelungen, begabt, seine Fähigkeiten zu entwickeln, gerade gewachsen und ungetrübt, rein, grausam und munter, einer von diesen Menschen, deren Anblick das Glück der Glücklichen erhöht und die Unglücklichen zur Verzweiflung treibt: — Das ist mein Sohn. *Das bin ich*, bald...bald...sobald der Tod mich von dem armseligen Wahne befreit, ich sei nicht sowohl er wie ich....*14

This is, taken straightforwardly, a reversion of Thomas's attitude to that of the ruthless businessmen he admires, although on a different plane. They stand, so to speak, at the beginning of the cycle, unreflective in their harshness, 'ungetrübt' as the boy is in this vision. But while they are unaware of the possibility of moral criticism, Thomas is aware of it and passes on to an affirmation of selfhood which includes it. Nor does he merely imagine this as the thought of a state 'after death', as Professor Pascal claims; he enjoys this state now:

Und während er es nun begreifen und erkennen durfte — nicht in Worten und aufeinander folgenden Gedanken, sondern in plötzlichen, beseligenden Erhellungen seines Inneren — *war er schon frei, war er ganz eigentlich schon erlöst* und aller natürlichen wie künstlichen Schranken und Bande entledigt.†15

His release into self-identification with those who affirm their egos, the healthy and cruel (the standard translation modifies 'grausam' into 'relentless'), the happy few who drive the unhappy to despair—is realized here and now, within his lifetime. (The definiteness of this is scarcely qualified at all by the slightly odd construction with 'während'.) At the same time, it is a self-

* Where shall I be when I am dead? Ah, it is so brilliantly clear, so overwhelmingly simple! I shall be in all those who have ever, do ever, or ever shall say 'I'—*especially, however, in all those who say it most fully, potently, and gladly!* Somewhere in the world a child is growing up, strong, well-grown, adequate, able to develop its powers, gifted, untroubled, pure, cruel and joyous, one of those beings whose glance heightens the joy of the joyous and drives the unhappy to despair. He is my son. *He is I, myself*, soon, soon; as soon as Death frees me from the wretched delusion that I am not he as well as myself.

† And in that he could now understand and recognize—not in words and consecutive thoughts, but in sudden rapturous illuminations of his inmost being— he was already free, actually released and free of all natural as well as artificial limitations.

identification with the ideal represented by his grandfather Johann, for while Johann stood 'with both feet in the present', Thomas now realizes that there exists 'nur eine unendliche Gegenwart', an endless present in which he himself is now able to participate. The wheel has come round full circle. What began, in Schopenhauerian terms, as the Will in its perfect integrity, has now become aware of itself in its own reflection, or 'Vorstellung': it has recognized its own creativity, vitality, cruelty and harshness, and has resolved not to take the self-annihilating course advocated by Schopenhauer but the self-affirming one advocated by Nietzsche. Thomas, could he remain at this level of vision, could become as resolute and as un-hampered by scruples as his grandfather was. The sole difference between them is that the grandson is aware, and reflects the Will perfectly in his 'Vorstellung', while the grandfather is unaware and simply *is* the Will, undivided and unconscious, having no 'Vorstellung' as yet. For a moment, the novel reaches a point where, if we could concede its assumptions, the decline might be halted.

Thomas, however, does not live up to his insight. Next day, he is already in doubt whether it was valid; his 'bürgerlich' (that is, here, his convention-regarding) instincts rebel, and he fears to appear ridiculous. Routine business takes his attention, and he never finishes the book to which the insight was owed. Should we, then, regard the episode as ironically narrated? Does Mann stand outside it, as Pascal suggests he does? 'When we read that [Thomas] relapses into his old bourgeois habits, after "his hands had reached out towards exalted and ultimate truths", we do not take these last words as an objective assessment of Schopenhauer, but ironically as the illusion of this worn-out man.'[16] Is that the case?

If it were, we should expect some indication from Mann that he means to be so read, but there is none. On the contrary, we learn that Thomas 'sinks back' from the 'exalted' truths into belief in those Christian concepts and images in which he had been brought up. These, for their part, are quite decidedly satirized:

Er ging umher und erinnerte sich des einigen und persönlichen Gottes, des Vaters der Menschenkinder, der einen persönlichen Teil seines Selbst auf die Erde entsandt hatte, damit er für uns leide und blute, der am jüngsten Tage Gericht halten würde, und zu dessen Füßen die Gerechten im Laufe der dann ihren Anfang nehmenden Ewigkeit für die Kümmernisse dieses Jammertales entschädigt werden würden.... Dieser ganzen, ein wenig unklaren und ein wenig absurden Geschichte, die aber kein Verständnis, sondern nur gehorsamen Glauben beanspruchte, und die in feststehenden und kindlichen Worten zur Hand sein würde, wenn die letzten Ängste kamen.... Wirklich?*[17]

The mocking note is unmistakable here and even overdone: the mere thought of Christianity releases it. But if we look for this mockery in the passage of Thomas's vision we shall find not a word or a construction hinting at irony. It is rather, perhaps, our own sense of the absurdity of these ideas in a man like Thomas Buddenbrook which makes us hesitate to believe that they can be seriously meant. If, in fact, Mann is ironically detached, from what viewpoint does he view that episode? It cannot be from a Christian one, so much is evident. It can scarcely be from a Nietzschean one, and there is no sign of irony here from a Schopenhauerian one. The biting attack implicit in our second passage is simply not conveyed by the first at all. Thus once again, the supposition that Mann somehow stands on both sides will not really help. The novel can only be interpreted in terms of traditional or Christian concepts of morality by refusing to take any sentence or episode in it as meaning what it appears to mean, and supposing that the opposite is intended. But, taking it as a whole or in its parts, the novel lends no support to such a reading.

There can be no doubt that Mann's own enthusiastic reception of Schopenhauer is reflected in his namesake Thomas's words, or

---

* He went about recalling that One, personal God, the Father of all human beings, who had sent a personal part of Himself upon earth to suffer and bleed for our sins, and who, on the final day, would come to judge the quick and the dead; at whose feet the justified, in the course of the eternity then beginning, would be recompensed for the sorrows they had borne in this vale of tears. Yes, he strove to subscribe to the whole somewhat confused absurd story, which required no intelligence, only obedient credulity; and which, when the last anguish came, would sustain one in a firm and childlike faith.... Really?

that it is presented as a solution by which the character in the novel fails to profit. Everything points to this: the personal experience, the italicizing of the important words (used similarly in *Der Zauberberg*), the unambiguous delight with which the revelation is narrated, whether in Thomas's own words or the narrator's. Indeed Thomas is, in Mann's own words, his 'Doppelgänger' and a 'man after my own heart'.[18] And yet there is still a forced solemnity, suggesting not irony but rather a certain self-consciousness, a desire to draw attention to the impressiveness of the revelation, rather than to let it impress by its own quality. The scene opens with Thomas reclining on his back and gazing into darkness, and at once the vision begins:

Und siehe da: plötzlich war es, wie wenn die Finsternis vor seinen Augen zerrisse, wie wenn die sammtne Wand der Nacht sich klaffend teilte und eine unermeßlich tiefe, eine ewige Fernsicht von Licht enthüllte.*[19]

The first words, 'And behold', strain after an effect; they lend a magisterial note which, far from being ironical, seeks to induce a reverent attentiveness and yet, by being an archaism, fails to do so. This quasi-biblical note is heard again in the course of this section:

Ende und Auflösung? Dreimal erbarmungswürdig Jeder, der diese nichtigen Begriffe als Schrecknisse empfand!†[20]

The high-flown expression, so strange in the mouth of Thomas Buddenbrook, reveals the spurious element of self-conscious pathos in him at this moment, which recurs from time to time:

In meinem Sohne habe ich fortzuleben gehofft? In einer noch ängstlicheren, schwächeren, schwankenderen Persönlichkeit? Kindische, irregeführte Torheit!‡[21]

Habe ich je das Leben gehaßt, dies reine, grausame und starke Leben? Torheit und Mißverständnis!§[22]

---

* And behold, suddenly it was as though the darkness were rent from before his eyes, as if the velvet wall of night parted wide and disclosed an immeasurable boundless prospect of light.

† End, dissolution? Thrice pitiable he who felt such vanities as terrors!

‡ Have I hoped to live on in my son? In a personality yet more feeble, flickering and timorous than my own? Childish, deluded folly!

§ Have I ever hated life? pure, cruel, stark life? Folly and misunderstanding!

These exalted linguistic gestures of refusal, thrusting away the offending thought as it were with a grand sweep of the hand and arm, have something theatrical about them: they belong to the melodrama of Schiller's stage, rather than to the world of either Thomas Buddenbrook or religious enlightenment. Yet our attention is not drawn to them, and when the narrator himself takes up the thread we have the impression that all this is approved.[23] That is, if we can define at all closely when the thoughts are meant to be Thomas's and when the narrator's: the passage moves frequently from the first person to indirect speech and then back to a present tense which can sometimes seem to be a general statement by either Thomas.

Perhaps, however, the theatrical gestures are themselves an indication of Mann's ironical standpoint? We may do him wrong to impute to him unawareness of what we perceive ourselves, and should rather suppose that he is at least as aware of such things as we claim to be? There is some weight to this argument, but not enough to counterbalance the impression formed by the passage as a whole. For the 'philosophical' outlook expressed in it (the 'Weltanschauung', rather) is highly paradoxical, not to say contradictory. On the one hand, Thomas Buddenbrook welcomes death, declares that every man is 'a mistake and a blunder', that death is 'the correction of a lamentable error'—namely the error of ever having been born at all. On the other hand, he rejoices at the thought 'I shall live', and affirms that he has never hated life, but rather hated himself for not being able to endure it. The transformation he envisages after death is not a transformation into a superhuman, angelic, or saintlike state, but into the form of all those who are glad to be themselves in this present life, and he quickly moves from this thought to the thought that he himself can welcome this present, mortal life, as it is, without change, in a mood akin to Nietzsche's in his teaching of the 'Eternal Recurrence'. Yet Thomas has no sooner realized his *present* freedom from 'all natural as well as artificial limitations', when he speaks of the liberation from such bonds which *death* promises to bring. All this may be the paradoxical kind of utterance which goes with most forms of religious belief: it would take us too far afield to examine the pros and cons of that. Yet it is at least as true to say of it that it is 'a little unclear' and 'a little absurd', and that it does not demand 'understanding', as it is to use these words of the version of Christian belief presented by Mann immediately after Thomas's vision. The point is, the words are not used, nor anything like them. The rational criteria advanced against Thomas's adherence to Christianity, and the condescending, even sneering, tone in which these are presented, are not used against Thomas's vision. We must surely conclude, then, that the vision is sincerely and straightforwardly intended to occupy the place in the structure of the novel we have assigned to it.

These are the terms with which the novel operates: an un-reflectiveness, which involves harshness and brutality as well as tolerance, but is unaware of itself; reflectiveness, which rejects all forms of harshness but thereby makes itself incapable of living; or a kind of second innocence, the 'miracle of innocence regained' as it is called in *Der Tod in Venedig*,[24] which passes through reflectiveness, through the moral world of 'Vorstellung', to a paradoxically conscious acceptance of the first attitude. No other moral terms are taken into account: there is no reference, for instance, to the parallel Christian concept of not letting the right hand know what the left hand is doing, which teaches a similar unawareness without forsaking the distinction between good and evil, or to the possibility of discrimination, rejecting certain actions in the name of morality without becoming thereby unfit to live. The concepts of the novel are extreme, and each development takes place within the confines of a rigid duality.

To say this, however, is not to exhaust the implications of the novel. Mann operates with these concepts; they have the consequences and the implications we have seen, and yet he does stand, in a special sense, outside them, and is in a certain way their seismograph. Nothing shows this so well as the episodes concerned with the youthful Hanno at the end of the novel. In Hanno, the male line of the Buddenbrooks dies out. His moral opposition to the harshness of business life is represented as part of his life-denying frame of mind, leaving him defenceless against the typhus which kills him. Before he dies, however, Hanno spends an afternoon at the piano, playing an improvisation which is in fact a rehearsal of all the themes of the novel, as though he were aware of the essential meaning of all that has gone on earlier, before his birth. To read the account of this improvisation is thus both to see the novel as it were in microcosmic form, and to realize the extent of Mann's self-distancing from it.

The playing begins with a fragment of a mere bar and a half, a motif which is soon repeated in the bass as though meant to be orchestrated for trombones, then again in the treble, mysteriously and yearningly, and then develops into a series of rapid passages 'torn by shrieks like a soul in unrest and tormented by some knowledge it possesses and cannot conceal';[25] this section ends with victory over the expressed disquiet in the form of a 'contrite, childishly imploring chorale'—'a sort of ecclesiastical cadence'.

It soon becomes clear that the disquiet is a reflection of Hanno's experience of the world, which he attempts to assuage with music in the style of Bach. (Later, he turns to Wagnerian music, reminding us of the discussion of the 'new morality' of Wagner earlier in the novel.) What, then, is the motif itself? It is first described as '*ein Nichts* [a trifle], das Bruchstück einer *nicht vorhandenen* Melodie [a fragment of a non-existent melody]'; when it is repeated in the bass, however, it is 'as the *source* and fount of all that was to come, as though it were to be announced in imperious unison by a burst of trombones'.[26] We are surely invited, then, to see it as a representation in music of the Will, in a Schopenhauerian sense, that Will which was for Schopenhauer precisely 'ein Nichts' and at the same time the origin of all things. It is also, in terms of the novel, the beginning, the symbol of the perfect integrity of the Will seen in the elder Johann. At the same time, it is the Will in its inevitable decline: in the treble it 'proved to consist essentially of a yearning and painful *sinking* from one key into another'—it has all the ambivalence of self-assertion and decline which we have seen running through the novel. The first section ends with an attempt at quelling the expressed emotions by traditional, Christian music: with a chorale.

After a pause, however, the first motif reasserts itself: 'a paltry invention, a figure either stupid or mysterious', as it is now described. Why 'dumm'; why 'stupid' as an alternative to 'mysterious'? Surely because the Will is ultimately to come full circle. It begins as unreflective living, as the vitality of, amongst others, a Weinschenk, and returns to affirm that vitality. Mann is as aware as Tonio Kröger will be in his later story, of 'life in all its seductive banality', 27 yet his solution never looks beyond this banality, always comes back to asserting its value. The motif, then, is stupid in so far as it stands for banal, unreflective, untransfigured life, and yet may be mysterious in so far as the secret key to living is to 'affirm' that life, still untransfigured. The banality remains banality and yet is accepted.

The difficulties inherent in such an attitude, if they are not already obvious enough, are brought out by the passage in which Hanno attempts a new theme, 'a bold improvisation, a sort of lively, stormy hunting-song'. With this he seeks to ignore the banality, to rejoice unfeignedly—'but there was no joy in it; its note was one of defiant despair. Signals sounded through it; yet they were not only signals but cries of fear...'—his moral consciousness will not let him proceed. Yet he is determined to triumph, and with this determination the Wagnerian music first makes its appearance: the notes begin to suggest the killing of dragons, the striding of Siegfried through the flames surrounding Brünnhilde. From here onwards, although the Christian music makes an ineffective attempt to reassert itself, there is a struggle to accept ambiguity. The first motif is heard again, its earlier dual aspect now pushed to extremes, if not developed out of all recognition: it appears now as 'a yelling laugh', or as 'an ineffably sweet promise', as though it were capable of being at one and the same time a source of hellish mockery and of heavenly bliss, like the music of Adrian Leverkühn in *Doktor Faustus*, or like the eyes of Goethe in *Lotte in Weimar*. The meaning here is surely that the motif, the Will, both mocks at human inadequacy and promises bliss as the reward for accepting it joyfully, and yet that the bliss is inseparable from the mockery, that the two must go together. We have heard something like the 'yelling laugh'— or at any rate a sneer—in the tone of Mann's description of Christian Buddenbrook and of the personal appearance of Weinschenk, and have seen that we must attribute this tone to the author rather than to the upholders of conventional morality. We have also seen how he welcomes people like Christian's wife, and Weinschenk as he was before prison crushed his spirit as well as his own self: in the acceptance of these lies the bliss—in fact for Tonio Kröger such acceptance of the 'Bürger' will be akin to Christian love at its highest. For Hanno, however, this dual mood is still hard to accept, as it still was for Thomas Buddenbrook before his vision.

Not until the end of the improvisation does the acceptance come, and when it does so, it is with all the marks of a solution and a resolution of Hanno's disquiet. 'The resolution, the redemption, the complete fulfilment—a chorus of jubilation burst forth'—yet hardly has it announced itself in harmonious tones than it slips into another harmony—'it was the motif, the first motif that sounded out!' Here, surely, is not only the discovery of Brünnhilde by Siegfried (we are told that it is as though walls of flame were sinking down), but also the moment of Thomas's vision, reflected in music. Just as Thomas returned momentarily to the spirit of his grandfather Johann, to the unreflective integrity of the Will at a stage where it has passed through self-knowledge, so in the music the moment of solution is the moment of return to the first motif. The motif has, it is true, been present throughout, with a kind of symbolical omnipresence, and yet the triumph consists in the return of the motif in an even more marked form.

In the final 'untrammelled orgy' of sound, however, the duality still continues: it is not transcended in some higher unity, if that were possible.

Es lag etwas Brutales und Stumpfsinniges, und zugleich etwas asketisch Religiöses, etwas wie Glaube und Selbstaufgabe in dem fanatischen Cultus dieses Nichts, dieses Stücks Melodie, dieser kurzen, kindischen, harmonischen Erfindung von anderthalb Takten...etwas Lasterhaftes in der Maßlosigkeit und Unersättlichkeit, mit der sie genossen und ausgebeutet wurde, und etwas cynisch Verzweifeltes, etwas wie Wille zu Wonne und Untergang in der Gier, mit der die letzte Süßigkeit aus ihr gesogen wurde, bis zur Erschöpfung, bis zum Ekel und Überdruß, bis endlich, endlich in Ermattung nach allen Ausschweifungen ein langes, leises Arpeggio in *moll* hinrieselte, um einen Ton emporstieg, sich in *dur* auflöste und mit einem wehmütigen Zögern erstarb.*[28]

The contrasted opposites, brutality and asceticism, faith and despair, stand side by side. If this is truly meant for a resolution, as it is said to be—and there is in all this as little evidence of irony as there is in the account of Thomas's vision—we are struck by the dichotomies rather than by their fusion. Yet the sexual overtones which this last passage certainly carries give us some reason to wonder just what Mann was really about. He can scarcely have been unaware of them. In fact, the scrap of dialogue between Hanno and his school-friend Kai shortly before the improvisation passage seems designed to prepare our minds for these overtones. Hanno has just confessed that he will probably 'play' this afternoon, and the word is given a special sense since he adds that he ought really to practise his *études* and sonatas and then stop—the playing of these is not what he means. Kai's reply can clearly still refer to the improvisation, and yet may be ambiguous:

'I know what you mean', said Kai after a bit, and then neither of the lads spoke again.

They were both at the same difficult age. Kai's face burned, and he cast down his eyes, though without lowering his head. Hanno looked pale and terribly serious; his eyes had clouded over and he kept giving sideways glances.[29]

* The fanatical worship of this worthless trifle, this scrap of melody, this brief, childish harmonic invention only a bar and a half in length, had about it something brutal and stupid, and at the same time something ascetic and religious—something much resembling faith and renunciation. There was a quality of the perverse in the insatiability with which it was produced and revelled in: there was a sort of cynical despair; there was something like a longing for joy, a yielding to desire, in the way the last drop of sweetness was, as it were, extracted from the melody, till exhaustion, disgust, and satiety supervened. Then, at last; at last, in the weariness after excess, a long, soft arpeggio in the minor trickled through, mounted a tone, resolved itself in the major, and died in mournful lingering away.

The shamefacedness is oddly inapposite if only the improvisation is meant, and seems to be linked with Hanno's secretiveness before he seats himself at the piano: he suddenly steps to the French windows and roughly draws the curtains, leaving the room in a yellow half-light. All this lends a suggestive note, so that the music becomes representative not only of a 'Weltanschauung' and of the course of the novel, but also of a perverse sexuality. The 'first motif' becomes phallic, and phrases such as 'source and fount of all that was to come', 'this short, childish, harmonious invention', 'this stupid or mysterious figure', 'under Hanno's labouring fingers', 'a swelling, a long, irresistible mounting', 'And it came; it could no longer be kept back', 'it came as though curtains were rent apart', 'complete fulfilment burst forth', 'with all the bursting, foaming, dripping magnificence', 'the last drop of sweetness', 'exhaustion, disgust and satiety', 'weariness after excess', 'died away with a melancholy hesitation' take on a sexual sense which need not, however, conflict with the interpretation of the motif as Will.

The improvisation remains a piece of piano-playing. Yet its total effect, whether or not the sexual overtones come into the reader's consciousness, is one of sly and secret self-gratification, and it is incredible that Mann, highly self-conscious writer that he was, can have been unaware of this; equally incredible, that he should not have been aware that he was writing a résumé of his own novel. (To complete the story, the lapse into decadence of Thomas Buddenbrook, and perhaps the death of Hanno, are mirrored in the final bars.) We must, then, ascribe to him as a writer the kind of destructive cynicism which he often puts forward in his characters for our awe. It is impossible, however, to ascribe to him also the praiseworthy features which he always links with the abominations, at least so far as these passages are concerned: impossible to see 'something ascetic and religious', 'something like faith and renunciation' ('etwas wie Glaube und Selbstaufgabe': the standard translation wrongly translates this as 'something that contained the essence of faith and renunciation'). We are told, in so many words, that there are these qualities, but we have no actions to go by. Rather, Mann presents us with a novel whose structure is already questionable—in the idealization of the elder Johann, for example, on whom so much of the 'argument' depends—only to recognize its nature and reject it. The rejection is not total, for Mann continues to operate with the same basic concepts throughout his life. It is, rather, ambiguously meant: both a rejection and an affirmation.[30] He holds by his novel, does not, apparently, regard it merely as an experiment within a given framework of thought, but at the same time sees more clearly into its nature than his readers are likely to do. This is the strangest aspect of his ambiguity.

For Mann does after all stand outside *Buddenbrooks*. The résumé in the final pages is not his own, it is Hanno's, the onanistic artist's, the improvisation of a boy who cannot face life and has not the strength to combat the typhus fever which kills him. Mann, for his part, is the artist who is able not merely to set down the suffering he sees, the attempt at triumph, and the failure to realize the triumph, but also to live on and narrate the whole story of these defeats. He sees what he himself has done, sees through it, and still goes on to record his failure and affirm it. But this can never, in the nature of things, be a wholehearted affirmation; it must always be a 'yes' and a 'no' in rapid alternation. Not only this, Mann can also withdraw more or less completely from the whole system of ideas within which he works—less in *Buddenbrooks*, more in *Der Zauberberg* and in *Doktor Faustus*, as will be seen. He put it on record himself that he felt his own personal life to be quite distinct from his role as a writer: that in the one he might feel tolerantly and benevolently disposed, while in the other he was impelled to deploy every cynicism at his command, and this 'personal' quality does frequently make its appearance within his fictional work (just as the 'writer's' quality appears in some of his political and social utterances—the distinction is never so complete as Mann would like to make it). The benevolence and tolerance are certainly the source of the humour which has helped to make him popular; we owe to it such figures as Permaneder and such scenes as his cursing of Tony Buddenbrook. It may also

be responsible for the epilogue in the Buddenbrook household
after the death of Hanno, a scene which seems, in mood, to be at
odds with the mood we have just been exploring.

The death of Hanno is described in an impersonal way: it is
an almost textbook-like account of the symptoms of typhus,
never referring to Hanno personally at all, so that the suffering is
brought home to the reader through the very dryness of the
narration, and is the more telling since he only gradually realizes
that this is the suffering of Hanno. The passage ends with the
comment that the invalid who cannot bring himself to return
with the feeling of 'a bond existing still between him and that
mocking, colourful, brutal business of living which he thought he
had left so far behind him' can only succumb: '...No, it is quite
clear, he will die'.³¹ The tone here is as ambiguous as ever. These
last words can be spoken either in sympathy or in supercilious
indifference. They are followed at once, however, after the interval
of a section heading, by the words 'it is not right, it is not right,
Gerda!' spoken by the aged Sesemi Weichbrodt, and since these
words are unexplained for several sentences to come, they seem
a comment on what has just gone before. In fact, as shortly
appears, they refer to the coming departure of Hanno's mother
Gerda, the widow of Thomas, but the delayed explanation allows
the impression to grow, that the injustice spoken of is the death
of the boy towards whom all feel such attachment. The remainder
of this, the concluding section of the novel, continues as it were
under the aegis of Fräulein Weichbrodt, with whose protest it
begins and with whose renewed protest it ends. The survivors are
assembled, all of them women: Sesemi herself, Gerda, Tony
Buddenbrook-Permaneder, her daughter Erika, her cousin
Klothilde, and the three daughters of Gotthold Buddenbrook.
In Tony alone does the real Buddenbrook tradition continue: she
carries her head high, and remembers her grandfather Johann
'who used to drive a four-in-hand'. Tony's presence is, in terms of
the structure of the novel, a reassertion, even though in humorous
style, of the ideas central to the whole. Yet the last word does not
remain with her, but with Sesemi Weichbrodt. The talk turns to

the recent deaths, to a lament for Hanno, Thomas, his father and his grandfather, at which one of the Gotthold daughters announces flatly and smugly that 'There will be a reunion'. Tony would like to believe it; she speaks of the times when she has lost all faith in divine justice and goodness, notions which have hitherto played no part in the novel. '...A reunion....If that were so—.' And at this, Sesemi rises in wrath, to speak the concluding words:

Da aber kam Sesemi Weichbrodt am Tische in die Höhe, so hoch sie nur irgend konnte. Sie stellte sich auf den Zehenspitzen, reckte den Hals, pochte auf die Platte, und die Haube zitterte auf ihrem Kopfe.

'Es ist so!' sagte sie mit ihrer ganzen Kraft und blickte Alle herausfordernd an.

Sie stand da, eine Siegerin in dem guten Streite, den sie während der Zeit ihres Lebens gegen die Anfechtungen vonseiten ihrer Lehrerinnenvernunft geführt hatte, bucklig, winzig und bebend vor Überzeugung, eine kleine, strafende, begeisterte Prophetin.*

Mann's brother Viktor believed that this ending displayed the 'true' Mann,[32] seeming to imply that the affirmation of Christian belief was more in his true nature than the ideas derived from Schopenhauer, Wagner and Nietzsche. This is more than can properly be said, at any rate from reading the novel. Sesemi's puny fury is portrayed with a sympathetic humour, but the ironical withdrawal from her is evident also. Yet these are the final words, and final words have an importance of their own in a novel. In this case, they hark back to the opening of the first chapter in which the elder Johann heard Tony's recital of the catechism, so that the whole is contained within these two affirmations of belief. At the beginning as at the end, the affirmations are mocked, though more gently than is Hanno's improvisa-

---

* But now Sesemi Weichbrodt stood up, as tall as ever she could. She stood on tip-toe, rapped on the table; the cap shook on her old head.

'It *is so*!' she said, with her whole strength; and looked at them all with a challenge in her eyes.

She stood there, a victor in the good fight which all her life she had waged against the assaults of her schoolmarm's Reason: hump-backed, tiny, quivering with the strength of her convictions, a little prophetess, admonishing and inspired.

tion through the undercurrent of suggestiveness. The fact that they are placed where they are, however, is at least a reminder, like the 'ecclesiastical cadence' which interrupts Hanno's playing, of a different scale of values. Probably one cannot say more than that. This is after all a novel, not a personal confession or a work of philosophy or theology, for all its philosophical themes. Perhaps, though, we might interpret more and say that in a detached way Mann does still keep one part of his mind, however ironically, in a vaguely Christian atmosphere. We shall see him doing so repeatedly in later works, in *Tonio Kröger*, *Der Zauberberg*, the Joseph novels, and *Doktor Faustus*, as also in *Der Erwählte*, and in most of these there is less justification than in *Buddenbrooks*, in so far as in them the vaguely Christian affirmations are made by the narrator, and apparently without irony. Unironical affirmation, where it occurs in these other works, makes a clean break with the ideas which are their main theme, and becomes a sudden, incoherent reversal. In *Buddenbrooks*, however, a better unity is preserved. That at least can be said.

The total impression is thus of a novel in which the author is sufficiently committed to Schopenhauerian and Nietzschean ideas to construct a slightly disingenuous plot in support of them, and to omit occasionally, again in a slightly disingenuous way, information which might tell against the points he is making; a novel which also is so destructively cynical at its own expense that we are compelled to see a perversity in its main intention, and yet also a novel in which the author detaches himself at least to some extent, as though rejecting the basis both of its assertions and its denials. Mann seems to feel that he can afford to make any self-exposure, allow his characters any form of self-gratifying fulfilment (which is what he means by feeling love for them) while at the same time, and as it were unwittingly, he sweepingly condemns himself and them out of hand. The one attitude is the complement and justification of the other, so to speak. Hanno's onanism is permissible, even to be gloried in, for it is after all an epitome of the whole novel, yet also to be punished ruthlessly with the 'inevitable' death which follows on Hanno's Narcissistic refusal to face Life. Knowing this also—not being purely and simply a reveller in boyish fantasies, Mann stands outside the moods of enjoyment and self-laceration, seeming at times to hold by neither. Whether he was aware of his disingenuities is doubtful: he does not either explicitly or implicitly draw our attention to them, but this is no proof. Nevertheless, the extent of his self-awareness is astonishing, so great in fact that one would hardly expect him to continue in the same vein—it is almost unbelievable that an author who had seen so clearly the Narcissistic basis of his work would go on building on the same foundations. Yet the fascination of the pattern of ideas set out in *Buddenbrooks* was evidently powerful enough to hold Mann as a novelist for the rest of his life. He had, perhaps, found the ideal key to permanent self-enjoyment.

CHAPTER VI

TONIO KRÖGER;
DEATH IN VENICE

In me there meet a combination of antithetical elements which
are at eternal war with one another. Driven hither by objective influences—thither by subjective emotions—wafted one
moment into blazing day by mocking hope—plunged the
next into the Cimmerian darkness of tangible despair,
I am but a living ganglion of irreconcilable antagonisms.

R. RACKSTRAW

Buddenbrooks appears to show the decline in self-assertiveness
which goes with moral consciousness and artistic leanings. *Tonio
Kröger* (1903) and *Der Tod in Venedig* (*Death in Venice*) (1911)
appear to show, respectively, how an artist may be reconciled
with 'the mocking, colourful and brutal business of living',[1] and
how an artist who is tempted away from such a reconciled mood
is doomed to destruction. The first, we might say, is in some
respects an explanation of how Mann was able to go on writing,
while the second shows the strength of the temptation to give
way to the desire for real perfection. Both stories, however,
achieve a verbal solution rather than one based on the exploration
of faithfully imagined realities.

TONIO KRÖGER

The structure of *Tonio Kröger* divides cleanly into three movements, the argument proceeding almost as though it were a
syllogism. First, Tonio's childhood isolation and yearning for
acceptance by the 'Bürger' is shown; then, as a young writer, he
is seen discussing in Munich with his friend Lisaveta Ivanovna
the relationships of the artist with society; lastly, he returns
north to his home and makes the journey to Elsinore, where his

137

reconciliation is realized. In the course of all this, a good deal
of entertainment is provided: the teenagers' dancing-class, the
orange-haired American boys who drink hot water, the Romantic
vision of Tonio's former loves, his embarrassment in the public
library are all vividly and sometimes amusingly drawn, in fact the
whole story has a relaxed atmosphere which is certain to please.
At the same time, however, it has the air of illustrating a point
which can be stated in abstract terms. It attempts to be more than
a series of vignettes and caricatures, and it is the total impression
gained from it that must concern us here.

The incidents are meant to add towards this whole. The scene
in which the Americans appear at Tonio's hotel table is more than
an observed moment, it is included for a purpose:

Dann waren nur noch drei große amerikanische Jünglinge mit ihrem
Gouverneur oder Hauslehrer zugegen, der schweigend an seiner Brille
rückte und tagüber mit ihnen Fußball spielte. Sie trugen ihr rotgelbes
Haar in der Mitte gescheitelt und hatten lange, unbewegte Gesichter.
'Please, give me the wurst-things there!' sagte der eine. 'That's not
wurst, that's schinken!' sagte ein anderer, und dies war alles, was
sowohl sie als der Hauslehrer zur Unterhaltung beitrugen, denn sonst
saßen sie still und tranken heißes Wasser.

Tonio Kröger hätte sich keine andere Art von Tischgesellschaft
gewünscht.*²

Tonio is content with this comically dull society not because he
finds it comic, but, more pretentiously, in connection with the
'Weltanschauung' he is beginning to formulate. At this point,
we have heard him discuss his situation with Lisaveta, and have
heard the strange defence he offers of a vaguely defined 'bürgerlich' life: briefly, it is this. For Tonio, humanity divides into
two classes, the unreflective, healthy-minded enjoyers of life,

---

* Besides him the company consisted only of three tall American youths with
their governor or tutor, who kept adjusting his glasses in unbroken silence. All
day long he played football with his charges, who had narrow, taciturn faces and
reddish-yellow hair parted in the middle. 'Please give me the *wurst*-things there',
said one. 'That's not *wurst*, it's *schinken*', said the other, and this was the extent
of their conversation and their tutor's, as the rest of the time they sat there dumb,
drinking hot water.
Tonio Kröger could have wished himself no other kind of table-companions.

among whom those with blue eyes and blond hair are supreme—
there is a touch of racialism about his preference—and the
critical, mistrusting destroyers whose perceptiveness fills them
with a disgust so deep that they become either satanical ironists or
helpless misfits. It is a fantastically exaggerated dichotomy: on
the one hand, the Army lieutenant, a 'lord of creation' in Tonio's
eyes, who demeans himself by reciting verses in public ('Ein Herr
der Welt! Er hätte es doch wahrhaftig nicht nötig');3 on the
other hand the artist, a criminal, a eunuch, a charlatan, a fake,
doomed to an onanistic excitation ('only the excitations and cold-
blooded ecstasies of the artist's corrupted nervous system are
artistic').4 The Russian woman, Tonio's partner in the conversation, does, it is true, put in amused objections from time to time,
but these are thrust aside with renewed outbursts of fanatical
assertion: Tonio is allowed to win the last trick, his initial
assumptions are allowed to remain unquestioned. 'Everyone
knows that artists are "sensitive" and easily wounded, just as
everybody knows that ordinary people with a good conscience
and a well-founded confidence in themselves are not.'5 The
'Bürger' possesses this good conscience and well-founded self-
assurance; that the artist does not is proof of his inferiority.
Tonio's argument is as unreasonable as that.

There is a point at which the discussion goes deeper than these
sweeping assertions, the point when Lisaveta advances a conception of literature as a 'guide to understanding, forgiveness and
love' and of the writer as 'perfect man, a saint'. Tonio's reply,
in which he sees such a conception as the basis of the Russian
novel, is, however, as irrational and evasive as the rest of his
comments. He sees the issue in a way which neither Dostoevsky
nor Tolstoy could have recognized as their own. For him, the
question is not whether human faults can be forgiven, or
humanity loved despite awareness of its imperfection, but rather
whether it is possible to feel a moral superiority in oneself: 'Not
to let the sadness of the world unman you; to read, mark, learn,
and take into account even the most torturing things and to be of
perpetual good cheer, in the sublime consciousness of moral

superiority over the horrible invention of existence—yes, thank you!'6 The concession in this 'yes, thank you!' (ja freilich!) indicates that this is how Tonio imagines the Russians to have felt: for him it is a matter of perceiving imperfection and yet continuing to pride himself on his distinctiveness, continuing to be in good spirits. The remainder of his reply then seeks to demonstrate that this, not love or forgiveness, is an impossibility. And, significantly enough, for such obliqueness and irrelevance in argument is typical of all Mann's work, Lisaveta fails to point out that her objection has been disregarded in a flood of words which, by the end of the paragraph, has become completely unintelligible.7

The best understanding we can reach of Tonio's attitude, in which he does nevertheless achieve a sense of superiority, comes from a passage a little further on. Having asserted that renewed insights into human nature constantly destroy such peace of mind as he can attain, Tonio comes to his solution. It is, in short, that life continues despite all criticism that may be made of it: 'You see, the literary man does not understand that life may go on living, unashamed, even after it has been expressed and thereby done with. No matter how much it has been redeemed by becoming literature, it keeps right on sinning—for all action is sinning, viewed with the eyes of the Spirit'.8 That is to say, that although the literary writer may 'express' life and thereby have 'done with' it; although he may point out its faults and thereby (in a sense understandable only in a way peculiar to Mann's thought) 'redeem' it, life will go on 'sinning', for any action is certain to be sinful if regarded from that 'spiritual' position which the artist occupies. With this, Tonio expresses himself in a confusion difficult to unravel. The term 'Literat', or 'literary man', is obviously pejorative: writers in general, we are to understand, fail to realize how pointless their criticisms of life really are. 'Geist', on the other hand, is a term of approval: from the viewpoint of the 'Spirit', which presumably some writers adopt, the criticisms are valid. The validity, however, is limited to the sphere of 'Geist', and has no real relevance to life. Thus the criticisms of the artist can be both praiseworthy and damnable (we recall the expression 'godlike-diabolical' used in relation to Goethe) and yet have no consequences for living. 'Life' goes on unashamedly just as did the elder Johann Buddenbrook, or Hugo Weinschenk before he went to prison. It 'sins boldly', to recall Luther's phrase, but not in his sense, that it does so through faith in its redemption, but rather because the sinning is of no importance. It is on these terms that Tonio now goes on to declare that he loves life, not as Nietzsche did,9 but for the sake of 'the normal, respectable and lovable', 'a little friendship, devotion, familiar human happiness'.10 The fact that 'the respectable', presumably, is also sinful from the standpoint of the Spirit, that he cannot use these terms at all from the position he has just adopted, does not occur to Tonio, nor does his exclusion of more passionate ways of living seem to him to require any justification. The 'disgust with knowledge', and the capacity of Life to go on sinning despite criticism have nothing to do with this conclusion, which merely reasserts a few values that were, earlier, implicitly supposed to be undermined by the artist's perceptiveness.

This discussion—or rather, assertion, for Tonio's partner does nothing of any consequence to hold him to the point—is the core of the story. The incidents before and after it are presented in such a way as to seem illustrations and confirmations of Tonio's conclusion. At times they please, and may invite us to side with him: a benevolent approval is easily given to the American boys, to Ingeborg Holm and Hans Hansen, even to the tipsy Hamburg businessman who contemplates the stars in sentimental mood after a lobster supper. If that were all the story amounted to, if it were simply a somewhat sentimental, slightly comic description of people in more or less happy circumstances, there would be nothing to complain about, or it would be overdoing things to complain. But the discussion and the conclusion make the story more ambitious. Tonio seems to claim that he has overcome his 'disgust with his perceptions', yet the fact is, we see nothing in the story that might cause him disgust, still less anything that might cause him a disgust so deep that he despairs of living. For all that we see of them, these people simply are 'ordinary, decent citizens', learning to dance, enjoying themselves at a week-end hop, going about their business in a 'normal' way. We know nothing of their motives, nothing even of their circumstances for the most part; we never see below the surface or have a glimpse of their minds.

The 'artist', on the other hand, is cavalierly dismissed. Tonio prefers the simple wonder of the Hamburg businessman to the writings of some unnamed philosopher who also contemplated the stars, but we are not told the reasons for this preference. He concedes, when the hotel authorities take him for a criminal, that they may be in the right to do so, although not on the grounds they allege, and here the justification seems to be simply that they are 'men of the social order', while he is not. Towards the end, seeing the young Danish woman who reminds him of his first love Ingeborg, he demeans himself to the point of declaring that, had he achieved the works of Beethoven, Schopenhauer and Michelangelo together, she would be entitled to laugh him out of court as she did in her childhood. This is mere self-abasement, the counterpart and justification of the self-assertion to come.

Yet it is on such a groundwork that Tonio reaches his final solution, communicated in his letter to Lisaveta:

Ich bewundere die Stolzen und Kalten, die auf den Pfaden der großen, der dämonischen Schönheit abenteuern und den 'Menschen' verachten — aber ich beneide sie nicht. Denn wenn irgend etwas imstande ist, aus einem Literaten einen Dichter zu machen, so ist es diese meine Liebe zum Menschlichen, Lebendigen und Gewöhnlichen. Alle Wärme, alle Güte, aller Humor kommt aus ihr, und fast will mir scheinen, als sei sie jene Liebe selbst, von der geschrieben steht, daß einer mit Menschen- und Engelszungen reden könne und ohne sie doch nur ein tönendes Erz und eine klingende Schelle sei.*II

* I admire those proud, cold beings who adventure upon the paths of great and daemonic beauty and despise 'mankind'; but I do not envy them. For if anything is capable of making a poet of a literary man, it is my *bourgeois* love of the human, the living and usual. It is the source of all warmth, goodness, and humour; I even almost think it is itself that love of which it stands written that one may speak with the tongues of men and of angels and yet having it not is as sounding brass and tinkling cymbals.

This contradicts what Tonio had said earlier: 'the artist is done for, the moment he becomes human and begins to feel at all', and it is not at all clear how Tonio passes from the one view to the other. So much is clear, that this is his reply to Lisaveta's objection on behalf of the Russian novelists, that he means this to be his own achievement of saintly love, embarrassing though it is to hear him claim it on his own behalf. Yet he cannot really mean the Pauline 'agapé' to which his words refer,[12] for that was never understood to be restricted to a particular class, or to 'the ordinary' and 'the decent'. He has in mind something more akin to a Nietzschean definition of love, whereby love consists in not reflecting deeply about others,[13] and the grounds for preferring this relationship with them are quite simply, as he himself confesses, that he has a 'fond weakness' for what is simple, loyal, pleasantly normal and decent. Indulging this weakness, if that is what it really amounts to (and what is weak about it, so far as it goes?), liking what is for the most part likable by definition, sounds a far cry from what Lisaveta described as 'the purifying and healing influence of letters'. So far as Tonio is concerned, the 'Bürger' remains stupid (one remembers how this word was used also of the first motif in Hanno's improvisation); he feels a certain contempt for him on this account, as well as a certain envy that the 'Bürger' should be 'in agreement with everybody'. But this contempt and envy are the twin effects of his desire to feel morally superior to the world he lives in. He swings from one to the other, as he swings from self-abasement to self-assertion, precisely because he misinterprets Lisaveta's words.

Tonio Kröger confusedly illustrates a confused argument. Being a story, it still remains interpretable as the intentional portrayal of such a confusion, and yet this view is unsatisfying. The reader is put to such pains, sorting out the evasions and the illogicalities, the story has so much the air of presenting a satisfactory solution (and has in fact been taken in that sense),[14] that he can hardly feel the author has given him enough help in penetrating his meaning, supposing the author to have maintained some deeply ironical reservations. We shall see this to be equally true of *Der Tod in Venedig*. What does emerge much more clearly from *Tonio Kröger* is Mann's concern to present the case for conformity with the Wilhelmine society of his day. The artist is suspect here because he is opposed to that society in which Army lieutenants generally were regarded as lords of creation, and in which liberal-minded citizens were expected to bow down to the 'men of the social order'—and if this could be justified in the name of established religion, so much the better. More than this, Mann gives a handle to anyone who needs his support in defence of the racial superiority of this society. Tonio, while avowing his affection for tragic and comic figures, confesses, 'But my deepest and secretest love belongs to the blond and blue-eyed, the fair and living, the happy, lovable and commonplace'.[15] This is essentially nothing else than Thomas Buddenbrook's preference for the healthy boy of his vision, whose unreflective happiness drove the unhappy to despair. The boy's cruelty has gone, or at least is not explicitly mentioned; the triumphant egoist has become more clearly identified with the 'Bürger'; in other respects the ideal remains the same. We can, then, readily understand the comment of a contemporary newspaper critic who found in Mann 'perhaps the finest German prose-writer of today'. 'His manner', said this contributor to the *Rheinisch-Westfälische Zeitung*, 'is absolutely Germanic, or alternatively Nordic. No sign of that Gallic quality, from which our literature suffers so much harm, is to be found in him.'[16] This was what Mann's readers expected, and this was what he gave them. 'What a victory there is here [in the story *Tristan*] for vital living', the same critic continued; 'how matter-of-course it is, how cruelly it persuades us. Robust concreteness is Life, all else but poetic imaginings, dreams. And men of finer mettle are here but to suffer.' It was not exactly Mann's meaning; it left out of account his perfunctory pretence at a confrontation with moral issues, and his reaffirmation beyond 'disgust with knowledge'. But it was what the normal and decent, simple-hearted and loyal 'Bürger', prospering without scruples in the Empire Bismarck had founded, most wanted to hear. To such people *Tonio Kröger*

offered no difficulties at all. To anyone who read it more subtly
it still said essentially the same thing, for as always in Mann the
end returns to the beginning. Even the conforming phrase with
which Tonio concludes in his maturity repeats exactly the phrase
used of him in his schooldays. He has done no more than reiterate
his condition with awareness.

DEATH IN VENICE

> Merely corroborative detail, intended to give artistic veri-
> similitude to an otherwise bald and unconvincing narrative.

Der Tod in Venedig presents the other side of the coin. Here, in
the person of Gustav von Aschenbach, whose works strongly
resemble those published or planned by Mann himself at the time,
is the finest German prose-writer of the day, seen from within.
We should hesitate, however, before identifying von Aschenbach
with Mann, seeing that he is frankly presented in so unfavourable
a light. Far from being a writer for whom artistic integrity
matters, Aschenbach is a man whose main concern is to secure
public recognition: 'his whole soul', we learn, 'was bent on
fame',[17] and he has already achieved world-wide fame by means
of a deliberate deception. He has realized, to be brief, that there
is no basis for morality, that to understand all is to forgive all,
and that consequently all forms of human conduct are acceptable.
To declare this openly would, he believes, deprive him of the
public's confidence; it would also cripple his activity as a writer
and have disastrous effects for his country. He has learned,
therefore, 'to administrate his fame',[18] to make kindly answers in
an imposing way to the hundreds of correspondents who approach
him, while at the same time catering for the discerning few who
welcome the deeper and amoral insights they find in his work. He
has determined to uphold morality, then, partly out of a desire
to protect the innocent from the full impact of his ideas, partly
to maintain his prestige.

   This might well be taken for an account of how Mann, having
written *Buddenbrooks*, went on to write *Tonio Kröger*; all the

more so, when he speaks of 'the yellow ugliness which, sensually at a disadvantage, could blow its choking heat of desire to a pure flame, and even rise to sovereignty in the kingdom of beauty',[19] for this could conceivably be an interpretation of Mann's intentions in the episode of Hanno's piano-playing, and thereby of his intentions in the whole novel. As a rule, we decline to associate an author with his fictional 'alter egos', preferring to see them as projections of his potentialities, explorations of possible selves—and indeed, as *Der Tod in Venedig* continues, it becomes clear that Aschenbach develops in a way that Mann himself never did. On the other hand, it may be essential to see that Mann is not so much out of sympathy with Aschenbach at this initial stage as might be supposed from the account of him just given.

Looking more closely at a single passage, we find clear indications in Mann's own style of this initial sympathy. He shares with Aschenbach the intention of pleasing the innocent and passing an amused nod of contempt for these to the discerning.

Gustav von Aschenbach [he writes] war der Dichter all derer, die am Rande der Erschöpfung arbeiten, der Überbürdeten, schon Aufgeriebenen, sich noch Aufrechthaltenden, all dieser Moralisten der Leistung, die, schmächtig von Wuchs und spröde von Mitteln, durch Willensverzückung und kluge Verwaltung sich wenigstens eine Zeitlang die Wirkungen der Größe abgewinnen. Ihrer sind viele, sie sind die Helden des Zeitalters. Und sie alle erkannten sich in seinem Werk, sie fanden sich bestätigt, besungen darin, sie wußten ihm Dank, sie verkündeten seinen Namen.*[20]

At a superficial reading, there appears to be pity and admiration here for the admirers of Aschenbach and their over-burdened lives. Closer attention reveals the irony. 'All dieser Moralisten

* Gustav von Aschenbach was the poet-spokesman of all those who labour at the edge of exhaustion; of the over-burdened, of those who are already worn out but still hold themselves upright; of all our successful moralists, with their modest stature and scanty resources, who yet contrive by skilful husbanding and prodigious spasms of will to produce, at least for a while, the effects of greatness. Their name is legion, they are the heroes of the age. And in Aschenbach's pages they saw themselves; he justified, he exalted them, he sang their praise—and they, they accorded him their thanks, they sounded forth his name.

der Leistung'—this is not straightforward admiration; there could be in it a Nietzschean scorn for those who think morality is a matter of achievements. 'Schmächtig von Wuchs' might as well imply praise for those who overcome physical weakness as contempt for the feeble body of the intellectual. 'Willensverzückung' suggests that a certain artificiality is being mocked, a straining for results rather than an effortless ease, and the fact that all this resoluteness achieves only 'die *Wirkungen* der Größe' seems to confirm the notion that the attainments of these people are merely illusory. Thus far, the passage is capable of a dual interpretation. As usual, the final sentences clinch the matter. The tone becomes absurdly lofty with 'Ihrer sind viele', with the effect that the heroes of the age are unambiguously belittled. The rhythms of the final sentence, the solemn breathlessness, the almost ecstatic repetitions, and the quasi-biblical grandeur of the last words—'they sounded forth his name'—these can never have been intended to be taken by all readers at face value. Mann himself is concerned here 'to win at once the adhesion of the general public and the admiration, both sympathetic and stimulating, of the connoisseur',[21]—although the connoisseur must in this case be rather slyly supercilious.

There can really be no doubt that Mann was, at this stage in the story, frankly putting his own case into the figure of Aschenbach. That he calls him a born deceiver, who concealed his own decay up to the last, should not deter us from maintaining this: we have seen plainly enough that deceit was no vice in his eyes. (Or, to be accurate, that it was, like all other actions in life, a sin in the eyes of the Spirit, but acceptable nevertheless.) For once, it is only by making such an identification between the writer and the fictional character that we can hope to understand the story.

Der Tod in Venedig, like *Tonio Kröger*, has the appearance of illustrating an argument, in the literary as well as the logical sense of the word. It seems to be about an artist of great distinction who abandons the disciplined life he has led, yielding to the elemental temptation of perfect beauty. Aschenbach, dissatisfied with the ambiguities of his situation as a writer, gives way to the impulse to seek a more untrammelled life, goes to Venice and there succumbs both to love of the boy Tadzio and to the plague which he is too infatuated to avoid. The whole seems to be summed up in Aschenbach's dream of Socrates, one or two pages from the end, in which he hears the philosopher affirm that all true poets and artists must inevitably come to disaster, by virtue of the very fact that it is beauty they pursue. 'Our magisterial style is all folly and pretence', Socrates is made to say, with evident application to Aschenbach, 'our honourable repute a farce, the crowd's belief in us is merely laughable. . .'.[22] If the artist abandons his pretence at dignity and his role as a leader of society, as Aschenbach has done—if he goes in search of beauty, he will come to disaster nevertheless. These thoughts are, it is true, introduced as 'the strange logic of dreams' and an examination of the argument would reveal the mass of illogicalities usually found in Mann's work, of which, here at least, he was evidently aware himself. Yet, standing where it does, the Socrates passage can easily give the impression of summing up the argument of the story as a whole.

Such an impression encounters difficulties as soon as the details are considered. The talk is always of 'the artist', and 'the poet', and evidently we must see Aschenbach as essentially representative if we are to make sense of the whole in this way. Here the difficulties arise. It is all too clear that Aschenbach is representative of no writer, unless of Mann himself. His fundamental desire for fame at the expense of truth is in itself enough to put him outside the conception of artistry as it had existed until his day. (It might be argued that both Aschenbach and Mann speak the truth as they see it, to those who have eyes to see, namely that there is no truth. But this paradox cannot be called a concern for truth; it is an abrupt denial of truth, overweeningly pre-judging the issue, and leads directly to the untruthfulness of this story.) Aschenbach's style, also, bears the mark of this desire for an acclaim not based on appreciation of his work but on conventional misreadings. It is not a genuine way of writing, not one which attempts to convey the author's perceptions, but rather one which is calculated to impress by its 'deliberate imprint of mastery and classicizing style'.[23] These words are carefully chosen; they express precisely the impression one has from reading *Death in Venice*: the 'imprint' of masterliness is there, and yet the writing has a curious pose, as though drawing attention to the quality; the whole thing is deliberate. The 'classicizing' is there too: neither 'classical' nor 'classic', but an imitation designed to deceive. Here is just such a passage as fits the description, a sunrise seen by Aschenbach from his bedroom window, though whether seen with his eyes or Mann's, whether in his style or the author's, is a question that might be interminably debated:

Das wundervolle Ereignis erfüllte seine vom Schlafe geweihte Seele mit Andacht. Noch lagen Himmel, Erde und Meer in geisterhaft glasiger Dämmerblässe; noch schwamm ein vergehender Stern im Wesenlosen. Aber ein Wehen kam, eine beschwingte Kunde von unnahbaren Wohnplätzen, daß Eos sich von der Seite des Gatten erhebe, und jenes erste, süße Erröten der fernsten Himmels- und Meeresstriche geschah, durch welches das Sinnlichwerden der Schöpfung sich anzeigt. Die Göttin nahte, die Jünglingsentführerin, die den Kleitos, den Kephalos raubte und dem Neide aller Olympischen trotzend die Liebe des schönen Orion genoß. Ein Rosenstreuen begann da am Rande der Welt, ein unsäglich holdes Scheinen und Blühen, kindliche Wolken, verklärt, durchleuchtet, schwebten gleich dienenden Amoretten im rosigen, bläulichen Duft, Purpur fiel auf das Meer, das ihn wallend vorwärts zu schwemmen schien, goldene Speere zuckten von unten zur Höhe des Himmels hinauf, der Glanz ward zum Brande, lautlos, mit göttlicher Übergewalt wälzten sich Glut und Brunst und lodernde Flammen herauf, und mit raffenden Hufen stiegen des Bruders heilige Renner über den Erdkreis empor. Angestrahlt von der Glorie des Gottes saß der Einsam-Wache, er schloß die Augen und ließ von der Glorie seine Lider küssen.*[24]

* Awe of the miracle filled his soul new-risen from its sleep. Heaven, earth, and its waters yet lay enfolded in the ghostly, glassy pallor of dawn; one paling star still swam in the shadowy vast. But there came a breath, a winged word from far and inaccessible abodes, that Eos was rising from the side of her spouse, and there was that first sweet reddening of the farthest strip of sea and sky that manifests creation to man's sense. She neared, the goddess, ravisher of youth, who stole away Cleitos and Cephalos and, defying all the envious Olympians,

The repeated dactylic rhythms constantly suggest verse, though never quite the hexameters that do occur elsewhere in the prose. The whole passage has an ecstatically mounting pulsation, and the classical references lend a touch of splendour. No sooner have they begun, however, than a certain falsity makes itself felt. 'Eine beschwingte Kunde' already strikes a slightly precious note, to be continued in the conceit whereby the reddening dawn is interpreted as the blush of a creation that realizes its sensual nature. ('Sinnlich' has the sense both of becoming evident to the senses and of enjoying sensual experience.) A little further on, this note becomes strident. 'Unsäglich hold' can only sound sentimental in conjunction with the strewing of roses, childlike clouds, and amoretti, and it now becomes clear that this is not the dawn as the Greeks might have seen it, but rather a rococo classicism deftly parodied to the point of introducing the clusters of golden spears which one sees decorating eighteenth-century churches. It is not a sunrise experienced with fresh eyes, but a pretty, literary mock-up designed for the connoisseur. 'It became fixed and exemplary', Mann writes of Aschenbach's style, 'conservative, formal, even made to formula':[25] it is easily seen on what formula this passage was based. 'Classicizing' was apt.

If it is true, then, that Aschenbach's claim to be thought an artist at all is so extremely doubtful, the reflections of Socrates lose some of their relevance. That part of the reflections which speaks of beauty is, however, just as irrelevant. We hear from the first moment, it is true, that Tadzio is beautiful, and even more than that: 'With astonishment, Aschenbach noticed that the boy had a perfect beauty.'[26] The boy's face and expression 'recalled the noblest moment of Greek sculpture. . . . Yet with all

tasted beautiful Orion's love. At the world's edge began a strewing of roses, a shining and a blooming ineffably pure; baby cloudlets hung illumined, like attendant amoretti, in the blue and blushful haze; purple effulgence fell upon the sea, that seemed to heave it forward on its welling waves; from horizon to zenith went quivering thrusts like golden lances, the gleam became a glare; without a sound, with godlike violence, glow and glare and rolling flames streamed upwards, and with flying hoof-beats the steeds of the sun-god mounted the sky. The lonely watcher sat, the splendour of the god shone on him, he closed his eyes and let the glory kiss his lids.

this chaste perfection of form it was of such unique personal charm that the observer thought he had never seen, either in nature or art, anything of quite such consummate achievement.'[27] Later, the description becomes even more emphatic, the implications more extensive:

What discipline, what precision of thought were expressed by the tense youthful perfection of this form! And yet the pure, strong will which had laboured in darkness and succeeded in bringing this god-like work of art to the light of day—was it not known and familiar to him, the artist? Was not the same force at work in himself, when he strove with a sober fury to liberate from the marble mass of language the slender forms of his art, which he saw with the eye of his mind, and would body forth to men as the mirror and image of spiritual beauty?[28]

The suggestion slips in here that Aschenbach's own prose may be as perfectly beautiful as the boy he loves, and although the statement is in the form of a question, the suggestion is likely to implant itself.[29] In addition, it is now intimated that the source of Tadzio's beauty as of Aschenbach's style is the Will: the Will, no doubt, in the sense of Schopenhauer and Nietzsche, an ambiguous Will, so that it ought not to surprise us to hear that Tadzio is also the 'instrument of a mocking deity'.[30] This is the same mocking Will which Hanno could not endure, a creator of seeming good as well as of seeming evil, yet capable of producing perfect, even divine beauty.

Here once again the interpretation of the story in terms of the Socrates passage will not fit. For very soon after Aschenbach has perceived Tadzio's beauty, it becomes apparent that the perfection is not to be understood in the terms proposed, certainly not in terms of 'the noblest moment of Greek sculpture'. Tadzio is himself, like Aschenbach, undermined with decay. His irregular, pale teeth, the suggestion of anaemia in his complexion, are the signs which induce Aschenbach almost gladly to predict his early death. His skin is clear, his nose classically modelled, his honey-coloured curls charming, but he is physically a weakling, easily defeated in the struggle with his boy-companion. Even at first sight, Aschenbach suspects and would rather like to believe that he is a cosseted pet, 'ein verzärteltes Vorzugskind'. His posture is negligent when we see him cupping his chin fondly in his hand as he rests his elbow on the table; his expression of hatred directed at the Russian family on the beach is fantastically melo-dramatic,31 suggesting some inner distortion; his only relation-ship with Aschenbach is the smile he gives him, 'the smile of a Narcissus', infatuated with the reflection of his own beauty, 'the lips just slightly pursed, distorted, perhaps half-realizing his own folly in trying to kiss the sweet lips of his shadow—with a mingling of coquetry and curiosity and a faint unease, enthralling and enthralled'.32

All this suggests an effete prettiness, a beauty—if the word may be used at all—rather akin to Aschenbach's classicizing prose than to the Charioteer of Delphi or the Doryphorus of Polyclitus. The story is reduced from one concerning the artist in his quest for perfect beauty to the account of a prolific writer whose artistry is never convincingly displayed, in his pursuit of a beauty which mirrors his own corruption, mockery and self-complaisance. As manifestations of the ambiguous Will, both the writer and the beauty are convincing, but neither lives up to the absolute terms used on his behalf.

What, then, can be the purpose of the story; was Mann aware of this seeming deception, or was he so identified with Aschen-bach for the time being that he could not stand outside him? The answer must be in terms of ambiguity, for the story does not, despite its ending, plainly conclude with Aschenbach's defeat and decay. From the outset, his position was ambiguously described: even in his initial situation he was described both as a born deceiver and as a martyred saint. His situation as a public man was, thanks to this dichotomy, unbearable, although it also seemed at times to be portrayed as an ideal one. Leaving Munich for Venice, Aschenbach looked for some escape, yet this situation too proved ambiguous. His love for Tadzio was felt, even by himself, to be iniquitous, and yet at the same time holy: 'he whispered the hackneyed phrase of longing—impossible in these circumstances, absurd, iniquitous, ridiculous enough, yet sacred

too, and not unworthy of honour even here: "I love you!"'.33
This dual image of a man who is both saint and devil persists into
the heart of the story, and continues through to the last page. In
his final moment, as Aschenbach sits in his deck-chair on the
beach, he sees, or thinks he sees Tadzio walking out into the sea
in the likeness of Hermes, the conductor of souls into the world
of the dead. It seems to him that the boy is beckoning him on, 'as
though, with the hand he lifted from his hip, he pointed outward
as he hovered on before into an immensity of richest expectation [ins Verheißungsvoll-Ungeheure]. And as he had done so
many times before, he made as if to follow him.'34 This is in fact
the moment of Aschenbach's final collapse, but the word 'Verheißung' ('promise', here rendered 'expectation') used in this
passage invites our attention. It is the word used by Mann at
those moments when his characters' visions seem on the point of
realization: it is used of Thomas Buddenbrook's vision and of
Hanno's music, and of course the word does have a more solemn,
religious import than the usual word for 'promise', 'Ver-
sprechen'. What, then, is this immensity or monstrousness
('Ungeheure' has both senses) which is full of promise? It must
surely be the sea, which had been for Aschenbach earlier the
object of his 'seductive allurement towards the unorganized, the
immoderate, the eternal—in short, towards nothingness'.35 The
sea was the symbol or living reality of that nothingness which is
the final goal of Schopenhauer's philosophy; Aschenbach had
longed to rest in it as in perfection, and, he or Mann had asked,
'is not nothingness a form of perfection?'36 If we can answer
yes to this question, then the story leads not only to Aschenbach's
ignominious collapse, his cheeks cosmetically tinted with the
appearance of youth, himself driven to the 'abyss' in his pursuit
of perfect beauty, but also to his assimilation at the very end into
a greater perfection, perhaps the Will itself which had produced
the perfection of his own style and of Tadzio's body. (The Will
was associated with 'the Naught' in this way in the interpretation
of Hanno's improvisation.) There is, in a way, no change. The
beauty and the perfection were themselves both ambiguous,

the Will is ambiguous in its promise and its monstrousness. Ultimately there is only the 'endless present' of Thomas's vision,37 the constant reiteration of the ambiguous Being which can only be either accepted or totally rejected, although even the rejection must lead to assimilation in the same Being.38

The apparent pattern of the story is thus of little consequence. We can, if we choose, read many patterns into it: Aschenbach can be seen as a Faust lured away from his study by diabolical promises of delight, as a symbol of Germany or of Europe succumbing to the 'disease' which spreads from the East, the 'yellow peril' perhaps, or neo-Buddhism; or again the disease may be the impending war of 1914. Hints here and there invite us to make such readings, but they are all a part of the world of appearances, a play of illusions. 'In this world of appearances', Schopenhauer wrote, 'there is as little possibility of genuine loss as of genuine gain. The Will alone exists, and it is this, the thing-in-itself, which is the source of all those appearances.'39 On these terms, the question whether Aschenbach loses by his decline or gains by his entry into the vastness full of promise is irrelevant. Mann draws the story together in such a way that contradictory readings are possible for some of his readers; for himself, he seems rather to stand like the camera seen on the beach shortly before Aschenbach's death: 'A camera on a tripod stood at the edge of the water, apparently with no-one to operate it [scheinbar herrenlos]; its black cloth snapped in the freshening wind.' The lens may be open, but there is, apparently at least, no one in charge. One image after another passes through on to the plate, but when the picture is sought there is, from over-exposure, nothing on the negative. We are left with nothing but the recording apparatus—a seismograph was the term used by Mann at another time—the black cloth, and the cold wind.

That *Der Tod in Venedig* records the fatalism which has pre-dominated in Germany for at least two centuries is undeniable. If Mann is right in his assumption that the artist's task is to be a 'medium of sensitivity', he has succeeded here supremely well, so far as certain tendencies in German thinking are concerned. His word does reveal, however, what seems to be an inevitable consequence of such an assumption, in its constant attempt at deluding the reader. The pretence is made, throughout the story, of dealing with issues familiar to the reader from long acquaintance: the nature of art, beauty, truth and so on. In fact, these are never properly dealt with: instead, some substitute is offered at every turn. The supreme qualities of Aschenbach's style are seen to be deceptive, the beauty of Tadzio is already corrupt. If the reader accepts these tokens of beauty at face value he is left with a pernicious sense of the corrupting influence of high ideals. If he does not accept them, he may be left with the impression, nevertheless, that there is something illusory about these ideals: he may be tempted to rank himself with the discerning few who see through to the heart of Mann's writing. But it is not a matter of illusion here, rather of delusion. Mann continually offers a suggested meaning which his incidents do not bear out, arguments whose evasiveness requires constant alertness, a style which is for the greater part of the story a mockery of the reader's ability to discern. It is not a matter of persuading the reader to perceive a genuine illusoriness in the world, but of tricking him into thinking he does. Or, to put it another way, Mann behaves here like a conjurer who, by means of hidden devices, tries to persuade his audience not merely that he is a first-rate conjurer, a first-rate deluder, but that reality is veritably as illusory as he makes it appear (whereas the real enjoyment of watching a conjurer lies in the wondering how he manages to trick us so well). Of course, if the trick fails to work, the grounds for mocking the reader disappear and no harm is done, or at least not so much harm. What is really pernicious, however, is the ease with which Mann implants his suggestions, the contempt which, with cause enough though little justification, he shows towards his audience. It is not because he shows a really corrupting power in truth and perfect beauty that he becomes so insidious a force for evil. Had he been able to show such a corrupting power, his regard for truth must still have counted for good: we should have been forced to a tragic recognition in which some uncorrupting truth would still have remained. But Mann does not do this: rather, he presents us with a highly suggestive story in the reading of which we need to keep all our wits about us, if we are not to be hypnotized into acceptance of its apparent purport. More, he offers an equally delusory (not illusory) refuge to those who look beyond his first level of meaning: the refuge of seismographic neutrality, from which one can observe the supposed imperfections of perfection with equanimity. The whole is deceivingly self-contained, and it is only by continual reminders of Aschenbach's and Tadzio's failure to correspond to the roles for which they are cast that its hermetic influence can be countered.

CHAPTER VII

THE MAGIC MOUNTAIN

KATISHA: And you won't hate me because I'm just a little
teeny weeny bit bloodthirsty, will you?
KOKO: Hate you? Oh, Katisha! is there not beauty even
in bloodthirstiness?
KATISHA: My idea exactly.

It will not be possible within the scope of this study to treat of
Mann's second major novel in a comprehensive way. A whole
book has been devoted to exploring its themes,[1] among them the
development of Hans Castorp to what has been called 'a philosophy of life, love of man and tolerance',[2] the drift of Germany
and Europe towards the First World War, the conflict of liberal
and totalitarian ideas, the relationship of Life and Art, Art and
Society, Love and Death, the meaning of music, and the contrast
between the contemplative and the active life. But since these are
treated in the same evasive way as the themes of Mann's other
works it would be wearying to demonstrate the same points over
again. As Henry Hatfield says, 'when one realizes that for spirit
one can substitute art, death, illness, or love; for "life" nature,
the normal, the material, or the naive, a certain looseness in
Mann's mode of thought becomes obvious enough'. And again,
'we sense perhaps that clever tricks have been used, but are
diverted from looking into matters too closely'.[3] A few score
pages of discussion between Settembrini and Naphta ought to be
sufficient illustration of the truth of that.

The more important point for my present purpose is that
Der Zauberberg represents Mann's contribution to the solution
of Germany's troubling problems in the period immediately
after the First World War. He had led himself into some difficulties in the Weimar Republic by his wartime advocacy of the
Imperialist cause both at home and abroad.[4] For some, he was

a symbol of an attitude which the new Republic would replace. The more liberal and humane beliefs, which *Der Zauberberg* was (and still is) thought to express, were thus seemingly in accordance with the change in the general mood.

Der Zauberberg is remarkable for the introduction of more explicit speculation than had hitherto appeared in Mann's fiction. There had been almost none in *Buddenbrooks*, in which the ideas expressed were on the whole incorporated into the incidents: into Thomas's vision, Hanno's music, the whole decline of the family. In *Tonio Kröger* the central passage is a fairly lengthy discussion about art and society; in *Der Tod in Venedig*, the first section contains a good deal of argument on the same topic, but again the story continues from there mainly in terms of incident and plot. In *Der Zauberberg*, by contrast with *Buddenbrooks*, one is struck by the very large amount of space taken up by reports of lectures and of the contents of books read, and by long arguments between the protagonists, all of which is relevant to the general themes of the novel and yet makes it less of a novelistic unity, more of a collection of essays and reflections loosely linked to the course of events. This tendency increases until in *Doktor Faustus* incident and plot play a very small part indeed, and some two hundred pages of reported lectures and discussions pass before the narration begins at all. (After *Doktor Faustus*, it is true, in *Der Erwählte*, *Felix Krull* and *Die Betrogene*, the story again becomes the real vehicle of expression.)

This tendency accords with that already observed, to adapt the incidents to the ideas, and yet to do so in such a way that there is often only an apparent correlation. It is clear, from the way in which Mann omits to give information from time to time, and the way in which he makes statements about his characters contrary to the impression we receive of them, that he was more concerned to set forth a pattern of ideas than to allow characters to develop more freely with their situations. His increasing use of abstract discussion is a further sign of his preference for communicating a group of extremely complex beliefs which he already holds, rather than for exploring an imagined situation to discover what its fullest implications may be. The comparatively few incidents in *Der Zauberberg* also show a disregard for the importance of events, which Mann seems increasingly to have treated as he treated human actions generally in his fiction, as irrelevant trifles from the standpoint of the Spirit. Thus it is noticeable, in a novel of which Mann said that its hero learned how 'knowledge of sin is a condition of salvation',5 and in which one principal form of sinning is taken to be sexual love, that very little of the action really concerns sexual love. Hans Castorp falls in love with Clawdia Chauchat, it is true; in his inward eye he sees her naked body projected on to the night sky, and engages in mystical speculations on its geometrical proportions. She becomes for him a symbol of the Body, which is associated with Life, and Death, and corruption and temptation and deliverance; she plays Venus to his Tannhäuser. But in the only scene of love between them, Mann literally puts a dunce's hat on Castorp's head, pushes him on to his knees, and has him pronounce an absurd declaration in French, partly a translation of a poem by Whitman, in which he worships her physical form in anatomical detail. 'Parler français', Hans is made to say, 'c'est parler sans parler': his passion seems to him too absurd for direct expression. More important, we never really get to know whether Hans sleeps with Clawdia or not. She leaves him after his declaration with a reminder to return her pencil, which sounds like an invitation to her bedroom—the pencil has played an obtrusively symbolical role for some time before this incident—but the chapter ends here, and the remainder of the novel gives only the barest ambiguous hints. Hans never thinks of that night again, nor does Clawdia refer to it, and we are left to suppose whatever we please. Yet, without expecting Mann to write as Lawrence did, we have good reason to experience a strange lacuna here. Hans and Clawdia do not strike us as people in love but rather as a man pretending devotion and a woman playing the part of a *femme fatale*. If any kind of salvation were to come from this play-acting it would need a careful definition which it does not receive from Mann.

The climax of *Der Zauberberg* is just as much a matter of

pretence and equivocation. As with the climax of Thomas Buddenbrook's vision, the point has been disputed whether it is really a climax or not,[6] and that there should be any dispute about the matter is in itself a sign of some uncertainty in the structure. Thomas Mann, in a lecture on his novel delivered at Princeton University, later printed as a foreword, was quite explicit: in the chapter entitled 'Snow', he told his audience, they would see Hans Castorp 'divine' (erahnen) the Grail: 'You will find out too what the Grail is—knowledge, initiation, that supreme summit in quest of which not only the "simple" hero but also the book itself is involved. You will find it particularly in the chapter entitled "Snow" where Hans Castorp, lost amid deathly mountain-peaks, dreams his dream of Man.'[7] In other words, while Hans Castorp does not himself truly find the Grail, only seeing it and failing to profit by the vision (or so we assume, for he forgets about his dream very shortly after it has happened), the Grail is made visible both to the reader and to him: it is 'the Idea of Man, the conception of a humanity of the future that shall have passed through the profoundest knowledge of disease and death'.[8] It is true, of course, that what the author said is not evidence, and Mann himself confessed that the idea that Hans's dream symbolized the Grail had come to him from reading a research thesis about his novel—'if I thought of it myself, it was both more and less than thinking'.[9] Nevertheless, his words do indicate the importance of this chapter in Mann's estimation; they underline a second time the italicized, didactic passage, which, like the passage on Thomas Buddenbrook's dream, it contains.[10]

In any case, the position of the 'Snow' chapter indicates its function as a fusion of the ideas which have gone before. So far, there has been a continual opposition between the ideas of Settembrini on the one hand and Naphta on the other, the Italian humanist advocating social reform, shunning all forms of ir-rationalism, which for him is symbolical of 'Death', and the Jewish, communistic Jesuit advocating a mystical and deathlike seclusion, together with a terroristic violence, in the interests of what he sees as true Life. Hans wearies at length of these diametrically opposed, yet often paradoxically similar standpoints. He perceives, as the reader has probably done long since, that there is 'no lack of inner contradictions' in the arguments of both sides, and that it is extraordinarily difficult 'not only to choose between the opposites, but even to keep them clear and distinct in one's mind'.[11] He objects to 'the general crossing over of lines, the great confusion',[12] and indeed the two opponents have taken so little trouble to sort out their positions that they do frequently appear to be holding identical views. The 'Snow' chapter, immediately following on these reflections of Hans's, thus represents the moment in which he seems to free himself from the confusion, at least temporarily. It is the end of that process which Mann described in his lecture as 'Steigerung', an 'intensification' and 'heightening' of the polar opposites towards a higher synthesis.

It is no longer by means of intellectual discussion that Hans foresees a solution. On the contrary, he abandons the society of his two mentors and the 'civilized' atmosphere of the hotel to confront the elemental powers of Nature. He sets out on an afternoon's skiing expedition in the mountains, in the course of which, temporarily halted by a snowstorm, he enjoys his dream. During the snowstorm, but before the dream, there occurs an episode which is evidently meant to have a suggestive significance. The sequence of events from the moment that he loses his way until he sinks exhausted by the Alpine hut is, like Hanno's improvisation, a résumé of the novel up to this point in symbolical terms, although without the same sexual undertones. Hans starts in a resolute mood, akin to that in which he first came to the Davos sanatorium, and quickly comes to enjoy the freedom of movement, unhindered by the need to keep to conventional paths, offered to him by the open snowfields—again, rather as he began to enjoy the contrast between the easy-going mode of life at Davos and the stricter code of his home in Hamburg. From here onwards, many of the words take on a double sense: 'he pressed on deeper into the wild silence, the monstrous and the menacing',[13] as he earlier pushed his way into troubled regions of thought; and as the snow begins to fall, obscuring his view, he reflects (or the author reflects for him), 'It was nothingness, white, whirling nothingness, into which he looked': one thinks here, perhaps (especially at the 'planted' words, 'kein Weg'), of Faust's descent to the spaceless, timeless world of the 'Mothers'. A little later, Hans begins to doubt whether he is making any progress: 'But whether in the right direction, whether there was any point in this progress, remained to be seen'—'he laboured deeper and deeper into this grim and callously indifferent sphere'. He begins to become indifferent whether he is making his way homewards or not, and trembles with excitement 'as often after a colloquy with Settembrini and Naphta, only to a far greater degree'. And at length, having continued to struggle onwards without hope of getting anywhere, he finds himself back at the Alpine hut which he passed an hour ago, having travelled round in a circle. 'That was the very devil' expresses Hans's first reaction to this, and although he certainly means to curse his bad luck, it seems quite probable that Mann would have us read this in a double sense also, for all his principal characters come back in one sense or another to the starting-place, and Mann would seem to count this as bad in one way, since they merely affirm an existence whose inadequacy they have already perceived, and good in another, since to make such an affirmation is wise. Thus Hans's further reflection, that for the last hour he has accomplished 'a sheer waste of time and effort', while it may sound severe if taken to refer to the recent happenings as a résumé of the novel, may yet be meant to read in this sense—it is, after all, no more severe than the sexual connotations of Hanno's music in its implications for the whole, and we have seen how low an estimate Castorp has formed of the arguments which take up so much of the preceding seven hundred pages.

As though to remove any doubt we may have about the symbolical nature of this passage, Hans himself now becomes aware of it. The succession of double meanings continues into explicit punning:

Wenn auch außen verklammt, habe ich doch innerlich Wärme gesammelt bei der Bewegung, die ich gemacht, und so war die Exkursion doch nicht ganz nutzlos, wenn ich auch umgekommen bin und von der Hütte zur Hütte geschweift...'Umkommen', was ist denn das für ein Ausdruck? Man braucht ihn gar nicht, er ist nicht üblich für das, was mir zugestoßen, ganz willkürlich setze ich ihn dafür ein, weil ich nicht so ganz klar im Kopfe bin; und doch ist es in seiner Art ein richtiges Wort, wie mir scheint.*14

The pun is naturally untranslatable, depending as it does on the fact that 'umkommen', normally meaning 'to die', can be divided into a verb and a prefix meaning 'to come' and 'round', although the whole word, as Hans remarks, is never used in any such sense. The dream-vision is about to come, and Hans must in some sense 'die' before it is vouchsafed to him; before he is reborn in the pure world of the Spirit, if only for a moment, he must deny the Will to live. But in fact he has only 'come round' in a circle, the significance is entirely in the pun. Hans has died neither in a physical nor in a metaphorical sense, neither in his life hitherto nor in the recent events which symbolize it. He had become confused by incoherent arguments to the point where he no longer knew what to think, but his mood after that has been a determined one: he meant to challenge the elements in his brief expedition, and having challenged them he has gone on struggling to keep alive at all costs. His pun is thus an empty formula, the proper move to make in a pattern which is known beforehand; there is no pain of relinquishment in it, no exercise of will. All that happens is, as he says, exactly what the books say should happen: 'But there it was, just as the books said'—he means the explorer's narrative in which he has read how lost travellers return to their starting-point, but he may equally well be understood to mean some religious or philosophical work. The strangest aspect of all this, however, is that Mann himself provides the words

* I'm rather stiff, naturally, but the effort I made has accumulated some inner warmth, so after all it was not quite in vain, that I have come round all this way, started at the hut and finished at the hut. 'Come round'—what am I saying? That's not the proper usage, not at all what people say for what has happened to me, I'm saying it quite off my own bat, because I'm not quite clear in the head, and yet in its way it's the proper word, I feel. [I translate literally, where the standard translation becomes free, in order to convey the sense of the pun.]

which reveal what looks like a rejection of his own accomplishment. Was he not aware of them, was some unconscious artistic impulse, at a level of integrity deeper than the conscious mind, responsible for such phrases as 'a waste of time and effort' ('nichtsnützigsten Unsinn', which also suggests wickedness)? He probably was aware; the motif in Hanno's music, it will be remembered, was both 'stupid' and 'mysterious', the 'Bürger' was in Tonio's eyes both 'stupid' and the supreme expression of unreflective life. These repetitions in various works seem to show that Mann consciously approved of what he thought unworthy of approval.

The dream-vision too shows bookish qualities, seeming to have been evolved from the last paragraph of Nietzsche's *Birth of Tragedy* rather than from experience in either the life of reality or an imagined world. Hans sees now a conventionally drawn Mediterranean landscape filled with happy people, the 'People of the Sun', Apolline in their serene composure and fraternal reverence for one another. At their backs is a Greek temple within which, he discovers when he enters, two grisly hags are silently crunching the bones and flesh of a small child, Dionysian in their savage and cruel indifference. The 'opposites' emerge in sharp contrast: Settembrini's clarity, and Naphta's devotion to dark mysteries, the dream of human happiness, and the evil which constantly frustrates it. Hans admires the one and shudders with horror at the other. What he remembers best, however, when the dream is over, is the expression on the face of one of the young men by the sea-shore, who turns round as though in recollection of the mysteries and gazes at the temple steps beyond which they are hidden. Or rather we should say not the expression, but the lack of any, for the young man's face, although 'grave' and showing a 'deathly reserve', is in the same sentence said to be 'expressionless' and 'unfathomable'.[15] It is clear at least from this paradox that the young man is in some way aware of the grisliness in the temple. It is also a disappointment that no more is said, for much depends on the attitude conveyed by this unfathomable gaze. As so often happens, Mann withdraws behind

164

a convenient vagueness. How necessary it was to penetrate a little further, if anything of value was to be had from the dream, is shown by the fact that the People of the Sun are shortly taken by Hans as inspiring models. These people, he concludes, were courteous and charming to one another not because they did not know of the 'blood-feast' in the temple, but because, knowing of it, they were able to regard it with equanimity and continue with their happy lives:

Mir träumte vom Stande des Menschen und seiner höflich-verständigen und ehrerbietigen Gemeinschaft, hinter der im Tempel das gräßliche Blutmahl sich abspielt. Waren sie so höflich und reizend zueinander, die Sonnenleute, im stillen Hinblick auf eben dies Gräßliche? Das wäre eine feine und recht galante Folgerung, die sie da zögen! Ich will es mit ihnen halten in meiner Seele und nicht mit Naphta — übrigens auch nicht mit Settembrini, sie sind beide Schwätzer.*[16]

It would have been interesting to know what this 'silent contemplation of the hideous' implied. So far as can be seen from the events of the dream, which is not to say very much, the happy people know to the full what is going on in the temple and quietly disregard it. (A more favourable, though ultimately no less objectionable phrase would be 'they accept it'.) Their attitude is not quite that of the happy people in Thomas Buddenbrook's dream, who drove the unhappy to despair: the deliberate cruelty has disappeared, and yet they are capable of indifference to cruelty. It is strange to find Mann describing all this as a dream of love. As in *Tonio Kröger*, his interpretation of the word seems to be based on the idea of preserving one's self-regard rather than on compassion or mutual forgiveness. At times, indeed, he seems to revert to the earlier notion, whereby all good and evil are parts of one whole which exists to be affirmed. 'The great soul of which we are a part', in Hans Castorp's words after

---

* I have dreamed of man's state, of his courteous and enlightened social state; behind which, in the temple, the horrible blood-sacrifice was consummated. Were they, those children of the sun, so sweetly courteous to each other, in silent recognition of that horror? It would be a fine and right conclusion they drew. I will hold to them, in my soul, I will hold with them and not with Naphta, neither with Settembrini. They are both talkers.

the dream, 'may dream through us, in our manner of dreaming, its own secret dreams, of its youth, its hope, its joy and peace— and its blood-feast.'[17] From this it might seem that the in- difference of the People of the Sun is the indifference of the 'great Soul' itself.[18] Theirs is a kind of godlike indifference.

It is not even clear, however, what Castorp himself makes of the dream. The scene described seems to make a sharp cleavage between the temple and the people on the beach, yet for Castorp it represents some form of synthesis. 'Man', he reflects, 'is lord of the counter-positions, they can be only through him, and thus he is more aristocratic than they.' Yet neither he nor the people of his dream are masters of the opposites, for they have no control over the happenings in the temple, nor can they except by some sophistry pretend that these do not happen. Certainly, Hans, whom we know to have been inside the temple and to have shuddered with horror at the gruesome rites, does not deny their existence; what he does deny and thrust out of his mind (or at any rate forget) is the recollection of the horror he felt. And when he comes to the thought italicized for our special attention, he generalizes so much that the origin of the thought is scarcely discernible. '*Der Mensch soll um der Güte und Liebe willen dem Tode keine Herrschaft einräumen über seine Gedanken.*' '*For the sake of goodness and love, man shall let death have no mastery over his thoughts.*' But it was not death which the scene in the temple brought to mind so much as savage cruelty, the 'blood-feast'. Settembrini, for that matter, would not allow death to have mastery over his thoughts, in fact his purpose was to promote all forms of healthiness. It is not clear why Castorp so emphatically rejected him, or why the paraphernalia of the dream was needed for so obscure or platitudinous a conclusion. The dream is now disregarded, or else, perhaps one should say, Mann's habit of making loose associations between ideas lets him down once again: 'death' means not only cessation of life but also every- thing that makes it more difficult to live in untroubled serenity. But whether we take the one view or the other, we are still in the dark as to the meaning of the dream as Hans interprets it: does he really side with the People of the Sun, as it were with Settembrini against Naphta, or does he associate himself with the 'great Soul', as it were combining Settembrini and Naphta in one? Is he another Tonio Kröger, rejecting the daemonic and all forms of intellectual inquiry or artistic scruple ('death' is occasionally associated with these in the novel), or is he still secretly hankering after the 'total acceptance' of Naphta?

Mann's own attitude to these events lends colour at times to the latter interpretation. The scene in the temple is a case in point, for it is not sheerly horrible, though it has the ingredients which make for horror. It is self-consciously portrayed, by one who looks with some detachment at the whole situation:

Da stand ihm die metallene Tür der Tempelkammer offen, und die Knie wollten dem Armen brechen vor dem, was er mit Starren erblickte. Zwei graue Weiber, halbnackt, zottelhaarig, mit hängenden Hexenbrüsten und fingerlangen Zitzen, hantierten dort drinnen zwischen flackernden Feuerpfannen aufs gräßlichste. Über einem Becken zerrissen sie ein kleines Kind, zerrissen es in wilder Stille mit den Händen — Hans Castorp sah zartes blondes Haar mit Blut verschmiert — und verschlangen die Stücke, daß die spröden Knöchlein ihnen im Maule knackten und das Blut von ihren wüsten Lippen troff. Grausende Eiseskälte hielt Hans Castorp im Bann. Er wollte die Hände vor die Augen schlagen und konnte nicht. Er wollte fliehen und konnte nicht. Da hatten sie ihn schon gesehen bei ihrem greulichen Geschäft, sie schüttelten die blutigen Fäuste nach ihm und schimpften stimmlos, aber mit letzter Gemeinheit, unflätig, und zwar im Dialekt von Hans Castorps Heimat. Es wurde ihm übel, so übel wie noch nie. Verzweifelt wollte er sich von der Stelle reißen — und so, wie er dabei an der Säule in seinem Rücken seitlich hingestürzt, so fand er sich, das scheußliche Flüsterkeifen noch im Ohr, von kaltem Grausen noch umklammert an seinem Schuppen im Schnee, auf einem Arme liegend, mit angelehntem Kopf, die Beine mit den Ski-Hölzern von sich gestreckt.*[19]

* The bronze door of the sanctuary stood open, and the poor soul's knees all but gave way beneath him at the sight within. Two grey old women, witchlike, with hanging breasts and dugs of finger-length, were busy there, between flaming braziers, most horribly. They were dismembering a child. In dreadful silence they tore it apart with their bare hands—Hans Castorp saw the bright hair

Phrases such as 'the poor soul', 'were busy...most horribly', 'their gory business' convey a certain detachment, 'placing' the scene for the reader as a classifiable phenomenon. The portrayal itself has a melodramatic note: the witches are in their appearance conventional figures calculated to impress rather than freshly perceived realities, and even the description of their actions, horrible as they are, strikes a note of unreality: 'und verschlangen die Stücke, daß die spröden Knöchlein ihnen im Munde knackten und das Blut von ihren wüsten Lippen troff'. There is an excessiveness about this onomatopoeic rendering which makes it capable, when read aloud, of sending even a large audience into a fit of laughter: it is too plainly a matter of deliberate 'artistry', with a 'deliberate imprint' akin to that of Aschenbach's style. The anticlimax of the witches' swearing at Castorp with 'the utmost vulgarity'—the contrast between this offensiveness to his social upbringing, reproved in such a phrase of lofty disdain, and the real offence to his deepest feelings—is a further indication of Mann's intentions. And this is capped by the words 'und zwar im Volksdialekt von Hans Castorps Heimat', in which 'und zwar' has an untranslatable note of pedantic exactitude. The progression downwards, from the savage cannibalism to the crowning insult of being obscenely sworn at in local dialect, from an offence against humane feeling to one against social convention, shows that despite the importance of this scene for the whole dream and thereby for the whole novel, Mann could either not resist the temptation to make it sound comic or else was not enough of an artist to avoid a clash of tones. His own attitude is not the indifference of the People of the Sun, but an amused contempla-

blood-smeared—and cracked the tender bones between their jaws, their dreadful lips dripped blood. An icy coldness held him. He would have covered his eyes and fled, but could not. They at their gory business had already seen him, they shook their reeking fists and uttered curses—soundlessly, most vilely, with the utmost vulgarity, and in the dialect of Hans Castorp's native Hamburg. It made him sick, sick as never before. He tried desperately to escape; knocked into a column with his shoulder—and found himself, with the sound of that dreadful whispered screech still in his ears, still wrapped in the cold horror of it, lying by his hut, in the snow, leaning against one arm, with his head upon it, his feet in their skis stretched out before him.

tion or an immature determination to compensate for melodramatic grotesquery by a snigger.

One notices, indeed, that the dream, and even Castorp's thoughts on awakening from it, the thoughts in which the famous italicized passage occurs, are not more esteemed by Mann than was the dream of Socrates in *Der Tod in Venedig*. Lying against the side of the hut, Hans is scarcely aware whether it is a hut or a temple, 'and after a fashion he continued to dream, no longer in pictures, but in thoughts hardly less fantastic and confused [kraus]'. The last word here should not be overlooked. Hans has sought to escape from the 'große Konfusion' brought about by Settembrini and Naphta in his mind, but both his dream and his reflections on it remain, as we have observed ourselves, in at least as much confusion. Mann is not seriously concerned to make anything else of them; from the heights of the Spirit it is all a sin or a bit of a joke, though any reader who cares to read deep meaning into this discovery of the Grail is welcome to do so. Small wonder that the dream has so little effect on Hans's later life, or that he forgets it so quickly.

The same indifference continues to the end of the novel. We need not refer, except in passing, to the intervening episodes, in which the same confusion of ideas spins on for another three hundred pages: to Hans's reflections on the 'nunc stans', which is the 'infinite present' of Thomas Buddenbrook's dream; to Mynheer Peeperkoorn, the symbol of Life who commits suicide by means of a poison derived from a life-giving substance; to the discussion of Hans's musical preferences, in which the same ambiguity of life and death is brought out. (One notices, however, that the epithet of 'the great Personality', attached to Peeperkoorn, is belied by the actual presence of this incoherent and amusing windbag—he is no more what he is said to be than is usually the case with Mann's characters). Let us move on, instead, to the final chapter, in which Hans takes what is often regarded as an important decision, to leave the Davos sanatorium and enlist in the German Army at the beginning of the First World War. Here, it is argued, is a resolution to act, a movement away from the irresolute speculations of the magic mountain: Hans ceases to sit on the fence or above it, and takes sides. And it is quite true, he does, though whether this has any decisive significance is still doubtful. He is last seen stumbling across a battlefield under shrapnel fire, singing the words of the 'Linden-baum' song, which have been analysed at length some pages earlier and shown to be the expression of a secret yearning for death. He does not know he is singing, this is made explicit more than once. And in this way, his decision to act and to take sides with Life is shown to be as ambiguous as any of his experiences on the mountain.

What, then, is to be made of the sentence with which the novel ends? 'Out of this universal feast of death', the author asks, 'out of this extremity of fever, kindling the rain-washed evening sky to a fiery glow, may it be that Love one day shall mount?'[20] Here at least—apart from the inflated expression, which may after all be Mann's own—there seems to be an unambiguous question, implying an unambiguous attachment. Yet it comes strangely from the pen of one who has just declared that he does not much mind whether Hans survives the battle or not ('We even confess that it is without great concern we leave the question open'), and who has just expressed an inclination, no more, to dab the corner of his eye at the thought of never seeing his hero again. The reasons for this indifference are also relevant but strange. Hans has, it now appears, experienced something of such great value that his mortal life is of no importance. 'Adventures of the flesh and in the Spirit, while enhancing thy simplicity, granted thee to know in the Spirit what in the flesh thou scarcely couldst have done. Moments there were, when out of death, and the rebellion of the flesh, there came to thee, as thou tookest stock of thyself, a dream of love.' In other words, the dream was supremely valuable despite the impression it made on us, Hans Castorp, and Mann himself; its confusions were not, or not only, grounds for rejecting it. In that case, however, what can be meant by the word 'love' in the final sentence? In terms of the dream it means for Hans the 'silent recognition of the horror'. It means continuing a life of happiness, as most people try to do anyway, while knowing that the blood-feast continues, perhaps knowing too that the blood-feast is merely one part of the dream of the 'great Soul'. There is nothing in it which would suggest any desire that the blood-feast should end, rather at best a grave resignation at its continuance. In terms of the ending of the novel, the battlefield is the blood-feast, and the attitude of the People of the Sun towards it would presumably remain what it was towards the knowledge of the temple's mysteries. Yet the final sentence clearly hopes for an end to the war; 'love' means here not acceptance of things as they are, and not an embracing of opposites in a single unity, but the triumph over, or the emergence out of death. The ending looks very much like a conventional bow to the proprieties, vaguely Christian like that in *Tonio Kröger* or the more ironically treated ending in *Buddenbrooks*. To take it at all seriously, we would have to disregard all the meaning accumulated by the word throughout the novel as far as the last sentence but one, and if we did that we should really have cause to ask why we had been led such a dance.

The answer to our difficulties must be that for Mann such contradictions are the very stuff of life as well as of art. Both life and art are in his eyes worthless and yet valuable, so that he constantly both denies and affirms the value of what he writes. But it is his own picture of things which he thus denies, not a picture to which we can attach a general validity. It is he who makes of the 'Snow' episode a confusion as great as that of the events and arguments preceding it. His account, nobody else's, makes the 'discovery of the Grail' a matter of contradictions, platitudes, and cruel mockeries, so that his ironical attitude towards it becomes tautologous. If we are not impressed in the first place, we are not likely to become more so when the author observes that he has written nothing that should impress us, and we can only be baffled when he then adds that it is highly impressive all the same.

To understand Mann better, however, we need to realize that, as he saw things, there was indeed a general validity attaching to the picture he drew, a validity which would be recognized by the greater number of his contemporaries in the German-speaking world, whether men of letters or politicians. In other words, Mann was and had a right to think of himself as being representative of his times, at least within the limitations described earlier.[21] In the tradition within which he wrote, such a form of argument as he used was commonly accepted, while the need to express it through concrete realities was scarcely felt. His language thus remains unfulfilled, a promissory note without valid backing. The consequences of such an attitude for the political events of his time are nowhere so apparent as in the short story in which Mann treated the most urgent peril of his day in the same traditional fashion.

CHAPTER VIII

MARIO AND THE MAGICIAN

Mann's opposition to the Nazis was made not only from the public platform but also in the cycle of four novels treating of the biblical Joseph, which occupied him for over a decade, and then in the novel *Doktor Faustus*, the epitome of all he had said and thought on German matters for nearly half a century. He had also, however, declared himself in a short story which, since it is so clearly an allegory of fascism, demands special attention here. It contains, as one might expect, both an implicit denunciation and a subtly expressed condonation, neither of which can be clearly disentangled from the other. And consequently, it is particularly useful in getting to understand the frame of mind in so many of Mann's contemporaries, who disapproved and yet approved the events of 1933 at one and the same time.

Mario und der Zauberer (1929) is an account, related in the first person, of a German's encounter with a travelling hypnotist in a performance at a small Italian seaside resort. The narrator is presented to us as a man of urbanity, tolerant and thoughtful, who witnesses with some misgivings the uncanny fascination exercised over his audience by the hypnotist, Cipolla, in whom the resemblance to Mussolini is unmistakable. It is fair to say, then, that while the story has many features of a general nature, it also presents Mann's forebodings at the movement already afoot on the Continent which might yet spread to his native land. The narrow-mindedness of the small town's population, its prudishness and its distrust of foreigners are first revealed in a series of incidents which might well have taken place a few years later in Germany itself. At the evening entertainment provided by Cipolla this rigidity and principled rectitude are seen to be the soil in which the hypnotist's powers can most readily take root. One after another of the inhabitants comes under his influence and is both literally and metaphorically made to dance to his tune, until at length a certain young man, Mario, driven beyond endurance, turns on his tormentor and shoots him dead.

Somehow or other [says the narrator] the atmosphere was lacking in innocence and unconstrainedness; this public 'thought well of itself'— one could not tell at first in what sense and in what spirit—it set out to be dignified, presented itself and the stranger with a show of seriousness and reserve, of an alert love of honour—but how? One soon realised that politics were in the air, that the idea of the nation was playing a part. In fact the beach was swarming with patriotic children—an unnatural and depressing sight.

In other words, there was a self-consciousness in these people, which, while it had something in common with the self-regard which Mann commonly admired in his other stories, was rather akin to that of Thomas Buddenbrook than that of his grandfather Johann—it was in this sense and in this spirit that the public's good opinion of itself was later to be revealed. In such an atmosphere Cipolla is best able to display his powers, for such subjects, neither integral in the innocent enjoyment of their will nor aware of the ambiguous nature of their desires, readily fall victims to him. The tricks he performs are a demonstration of the evil which underlies such attempts at virtue: all have in common the feature that a man or a woman who appears to will one thing is made to will its opposite.

Thus the young man Giovanotto, who makes a polite reminder to the magician that he has bored the audience by his tardy beginning, is swiftly brought under the hypnotic influence and compelled to stick out his tongue at the entire audience. Similarly, when the same young man returns to the attack a few minutes later with what looks like bold defiance, he is soon writhing on the ground with the physical manifestations of extreme fear, apparently doubled up with colic. Later still, the gentleman from Rome who is noted for his moral rigidity and his determination to expose Cipolla's trickery is defeated in much the same way. His rigidity is seen to be the obverse of his concealed desire for abandonment: he is, it is suggested, one of the 'Neinsager' whose affirmation is all in terms of 'Thou shalt not', and Cipolla's power over him derives from his fuller awareness of the double aspect of the human will. Cipolla is aware, as his subjects are not, of the relationship between the opposites known as politeness and contempt, defiance and fear, virtue and licentiousness, and he has the means to transform one into the other.

In this knowledge of human nature, however, Cipolla resembles Mann's 'artist' figures more closely than he does any dictator, and in fact he is frequently referred to in the story as an 'entertainment-artist', a 'magic-artist', and as 'the artist' pure and simple. Mann's use of this last term was always broad: men like Hans Castorp, who never engage in any strictly artistic work, are as likely to be called artists as those who are really poets, novelists, musicians or painters. In this generalized sense, Cipolla has much in common with, for example, Gustav von Aschenbach, or even Mann himself. His ability to read the thoughts of others is presented by the narrator as a result of secret sympathy with them, which is also the reason given for the success of Aschenbach. Where Mann spoke of himself as a seismograph, faithfully recording the trends of his times, Cipolla 'lives himself into' the situation of his audience, and in guessing the nature of a hidden object is led to success by just this sympathy: 'He groped about like a visionary, guided and borne along by the public, secret will.' He is successful just as Aschenbach is successful, because he fulfils the requirements made on him by 'mass-confidence': he can make Giovanotto seem to experience the pains of colic because he is, in imagination, experiencing them himself. There is even something of the martyr about him in his own estimation, which recalls the description of Aschenbach as the Saint Sebastian of his times. When the audience calls out in pity for one of his subjects Cipolla claims that pity for himself: 'Poveretto!', he mocks bitterly, 'That is addressed to the wrong man, gentlemen! Sono io, il poveretto! I am the one who is bearing all that.' Just as remarkable is his profession of love for Mario, whom he calls his Ganymede as Aschenbach does Tadzio, and the way in which he is brought to his death through this homosexual attachment.

The title of 'cavaliere' which he claims recalls the patent of nobility which Aschenbach acquired, on doubtful merits. His display of patriotism, which looks assumed, has affinity with Aschenbach's seemingly hypocritical love for Germany, and with Mann's own incredible moment of jingoism during the First World War. More important, his style of speech, if not of writing, is one of the things which most endear him to the audience at the outset. He is in his own way a master of language, so far as rhetorical influence is concerned, as much as Aschenbach was. In all these ways Mann suggests that he expected the appellation 'artist' to be taken with some seriousness, for all that he is much more obviously detached from his fictional creation than he had been in *Der Tod in Venedig*. He is still drawing an aspect of himself, a possible development of his own personality, although another self, the narrator, is now more decisively set over against the first.[1]

All this is little more than one would expect from any writer obliged to draw a good deal on his knowledge of himself in order to create characters of fiction. It is only the implicit suggestion that Cipolla is in some way typical of 'the artist' that is likely, so far, to cause us any hesitation. Looking more closely, however, it grows clear that Mann is not so much divided between the hypnotist and the narrator, seeing the one aspect of himself through the other, as he is actually sharing himself out between them, so that features of the one appear in the other. In the light of the first few pages of the story the reader is inclined to sympathize with and to put a considerable trust in the narrator, who is after all his only means of knowing what went on. The civilized tolerance of this man is highly attractive, and may even dispose us to accept all he says as true. Yet there are times when he seems concerned not merely to provide an account of the evening's happenings, but also to confuse the reader in such a way that he too is lulled into acknowledging a mysterious omnipotence in Cipolla.

There is the incident in which the gentleman from Rome goes up to the platform resolved not to yield to the hypnotic influence, and yet succumbs after a brief resistance. This the narrator explains as being due to the gentleman's lack of any positive will of his own: 'If I understood the event correctly', he observes, 'it was the negative character of the young man's fighting position that was his undoing.' The Roman, by simply 'not-willing', was doing the very thing that Cipolla required of him, providing the blank sheet on which the hypnotist could write: we are reminded of Cipolla's claim that he could enforce subdual 'even if you do not will'—words which, the narrator says, have rung in his ears ever since. Yet only in the preceding paragraph the narrator has offered a precisely opposite explanation. 'This fine fellow', he said of the same gentleman from Rome, 'wanted to rescue the honour of the human race'; there was, then, after all an effort of will and the man was not simply 'not-willing'. Yet the narrator offers his contradictory explanations as though both were equally valid, creating thus the impression that there is no possibility of evasion, and that whether the subject does or does not exert his will-power, he is lost.

Taken alone, this incident has little significance. We might well write it off as a momentary slip on the narrator's part, were it not that such contradictoriness is a feature of all Mann's writing and that it occurs again within this same story. A similar instance occurs in the episode of the colonel who, under the hypnotic influence, was unable to raise his arm. Rather earlier than this, Cipolla had put forward a subtle philosophical theory justifying or explaining the basis of his power. 'Freedom exists', he had said, 'and the will also exists; but freedom of the will does not exist, for a will that is directed towards its own freedom thrusts into emptiness.' The point had not seemed particularly clear to the reader at the time: it certainly did not seem to disprove the existence of free will, and even the hesitations of the most scrupulous would have been dispelled by the narrator's immediate disclaimer. 'One had to admit', he observed on this occasion, 'that [Cipolla] could not have chosen his words better, in order to obscure the issue and institute intellectual confusion'. At this, we naturally pass on, assuming that the argument is not to be understood except as part of the hypnotist's usual duplicity. Yet when the story reaches the episode of the Italian colonel, the narrator himself reverts to the idea in surprising fashion:

I can still see the face of that stately, moustachioed colonel, smiling and clenching his teeth as he struggled to regain his lost freedom of action. What confusion! He seemed to be exerting his will, and in vain; the trouble, however, was probably simply that he could not will, and that freedom-crippling entanglement of the will in itself, which our conqueror had scornfully prophesied earlier on to the gentleman from Rome, was in full operation.

This can only refer to Cipolla's theory, or to its summary re-statement in the phrase 'Even if you do not will'. The earlier dismissal of that theory has now been forgotten; the narrator accepts and uses it himself, despite his avowal that it creates intellectual confusion. And this is done so nonchalantly that in the course of a normally attentive reading one inclines to let it pass unnoticed. In short, the narrator is apparently concerned to persuade his reader that freedom to resist Cipolla is non-existent, and is either confused in his own mind or prepared himself to use duplicity for the purpose.

It is hard to say which of these two possibilities is the more likely. In view of the actual preference for ambiguity and contra-dictoriness in so much of Mann's work, it seems probable that the narrator's oscillation between two points of view is the product of his philosophy rather than of deliberate dishonesty. On the other hand, it does bear a resemblance to the dishonesty of the hypnotist which is explicitly criticized in the story. At all events, there can be no question of confusion in the narrator's mind in one other episode, that of Cipolla's mind-reading act, in which he guesses with seemingly miraculous intuition that a member of the audience was formerly very much attached to the famous actress Eleonora Duse. The point about this particular instance of Cipolla's powers is that the person in question, Signora Angiolieri, runs a boarding-house in the town, known as the Casa Eleonora. It is thus perfectly possible that Cipolla has made discreet inquiries before his performance, and that his amazing knowledge is just extremely astute guesswork. This the narrator acknowledges, in fact he draws our attention to the idea. 'There was only the question', he remarks, 'how much he knew of all this himself, how much he might have heard in his first professional eaves-dropping after his arrival in Torre.' Having raised this doubt, however, he breaks off, inserts three dots, and continues with remarkable disingenuousness: 'But I have no reason whatsoever to render rationally suspect faculties which brought about his downfall before our very eyes.' At first sight, this seems highly cryptic. Why should not faculties which brought about Cipolla's downfall be rationally suspect as well? Why is the narrator reluctant to press the point he has just made? The answer to these questions is probably to be found in the opening paragraph of the whole story. Cipolla is not merely a hypnotist, nor yet a dictator, or an artist, or a reflection of one aspect of the author: his story is meant to convey also a metaphysical significance. Thinking over the events before unfolding them, the narrator observes in parenthesis that their terrifying ending was one which 'resided in the essence of things'. This remark is never expounded, nor is it ever referred to again, but in view of the frequent talk of 'the Will' throughout the story we may guess that Cipolla is meant to stand in an unusually close relationship to the Will as we hear it spoken of in such works as *Buddenbrooks* and *Der Tod in Venedig*: the brutal, ruthless, relentless Will whose ultimate goal is both self-affirmation and self-destruction. It is to this close relation-ship, if not identification with the Will that Cipolla owes his uncanny mastery over the crowd, for in a sense he is the Will of which they remain always unconscious, and his assertions thus correspond to their own Will, whether they acknowledge it or not. To cast rational doubts on his powers, to suggest that he is, even in a single instance, an ordinary trickster, would thus be to detract from the suggestion that his downfall is the outcome of an essential process in the very heart of things. The narrator must, therefore, suppress such doubts, although at the same time he is frank enough to admit their possibility. He must induce the reader to believe that Cipolla is invincible, that neither willing nor 'not-willing' is of any avail, that his powers are super-rational and, as we shall see, liable to destruction only at his own, the hypnotist's volition. Hence the disingenuousness, the cryptic allusiveness, the plain statement of Cipolla's weakness in argument and the subsequent adoption of the same argument. The reader himself must be lulled into acceptance by the apparent recognition of his possible objections.

This aim once achieved, the implications of the story become more convincing. They are, briefly, that Cipolla and the Will which he represents or embodies are both evil and irresistible, and yet doomed to destruction by their essential negativity. In the final long episode, which culminates in the shooting of Cipolla by the youthful Mario, it becomes apparent that, while the hypnotist still holds the whip-hand, it is a hand which he uses almost deliberately for encompassing his own downfall. We see him first taunting the young man with the realization that his sweetheart Silvestra is deceiving him with another man, then with his memories of her as an 'angel of paradise'. Having awakened in Mario, who remains in a hypnotic trance, this ambiguous feeling towards Silvestra, a feeling normally suppressed, Cipolla offers him his gruesome cheek for a kiss, suggesting at the same time that the cheek is Silvestra's. Mario accepts the substitution, being perhaps in that frame of mind where distinctions are no longer possible: seeing that the angel can be a deceiver, it is surely possible that the deceiver Cipolla may represent an angel. Yet the physical expression of love for his tormentor suddenly takes a surprising turn. Awakening from the trance, Mario turns on Cipolla and shoots him dead.

In the context of the other incidents in the evening's entertainment it seems probable that we should also see this awakening in terms of the ambivalence of emotions. Just as earlier politeness was transformed by Cipolla into rudeness, courage into fear, resistance into compliance, so here love is turned into hatred. Yet to make this interpretation is difficult, since it might imply that Cipolla had for once made a fatal error, and one he was not likely to make. This difficulty can, however, be met, at least in reasonable measure. For from the very first moment of Cipolla's encounter with Mario, when he silently beckons him to come out of the audience and mount the steps of the platform, the hypnotist seems to have foreknowledge of his end. His words to Mario, though not out of keeping with the situation, have overtones of almost symbolical import.

Well, ragazzo mio? [he said]. How comes it we make acquaintance so late in the day? But believe me, I made yours long ago. . . . Yes, yes, I've looked you in the eyes a long while now, and assured myself of your excellent qualities. How could I forget you again? . . .

There is a strange impressiveness about these words, something that is not quite called for by an ordinary conversational remark preluding a display of hypnotism. If Cipolla has met Mario before, and has actually looked into his eyes for a long while, it is strange that Mario should have no recollection of it. Indeed, Cipolla's initial failure to remember, his suggestion that they are meeting for the first time now, indicates that he only afterwards realizes in what sense he has made Mario's acquaintance. The 'excellent qualities' in the young man are not qualities of character but, surely, those of the death which he symbolizes in Cipolla's eyes, and which the hypnotist now sets out to encompass in the manner we have seen. He encourages Mario to love him in the knowledge that the feeling experienced in the state of trance will, as in the other cases, be the opposite of that experienced in full consciousness. Or so we may reasonably conclude from the structure and symbolism of the story.

Mario, for his part, is not so much the agent as the tool of the Will: it is not because of any determination on his part that Cipolla dies, but rather by an instinctive revulsion, on the certainty of which Cipolla has calculated. It is not even Mario who is thought of as the destroyer, but rather 'the small, squat, metal, scarcely pistol-shaped piece of machinery dangling from his hand, whose almost non-existent barrel had steered Destiny in so unexpected and strange a direction'. And the pistol itself is evidently described in such periphrastic fashion in order to suggest a further level of meaning, a symbolical agent. That the barrel should be not merely short, but 'almost non-existent' is a reminder that the Will is often equated in Mann's writing with 'the Naught'— Mann goes as near as he may within the limits of realism to suggesting that Cipolla's death was due to an agent as null as his own Will, while the genital overtones in the description recall the fleeting associations of phallus and Will in the final climax of *Buddenbrooks*. The pistol is deliberately made to look as little like a pistol as possible, in order to bring out the idea that conscious human agency and even material objects had only an ancillary part to play in the defeat of the Will by itself.

Mario und der Zauberer is a work of great subtlety whose ramifications of meaning could lead to reams of exposition. All that is possible here is to indicate certain essential features. In the context of Mann's development, it is clear that he no longer emphasizes the value of self-assertiveness as he had done, however ironically, in pre-war days, but is alarmed at the consequences of such an attitude as they now loom on the horizon of real life. Yet he still holds to the essential framework of his earlier thought: there is for him the same ambiguity at the heart of things, with the difference that stress is now laid on the self-destructiveness inherent in it. In many ways, the change of attitude is hard to perceive. As in the earlier stories and novels, Mann remains curiously aloof from all that happens, despite his tendency to identify himself also with both sides. He is, in fact, still represented in much the same way as ever by the narrator in this story who is present at the entertainment, who expresses horror, disgust, and admiration at what he sees, yet remains throughout unattached, calmly setting down the catastrophe as one might record an earth tremor. There is little sign here of the 'wholly unequivocal "No"' which Mann was impelled to utter as a human being against the dictatorship in his own country; the writer who saw some justification on all sides is much more in evidence. But the result of this continuing attachment to Mann's earlier modes of thought and feeling is not that just appraisal and balance which we could properly expect from a story of this kind.

Without demanding that Mann should have composed a moral tract on the subject of hypnotists or dictators, we have a right to insist as readers that the sympathy of a writer with his own creations should not turn into a spurious defence of them. The disturbing element of the story is the way in which the narrator, wittingly or unwittingly, tends to delude the reader into acknowledging the invincibility of Cipolla, and the way in which this delusiveness serves the underlying 'Weltanschauung'. It may well be, after all, that the metaphysical implications of the story are true: that the evil which Cipolla represents is inherently bound to destroy itself. A story which made the reader feel the truth of that might well be gratifying. But a story which arouses such a feeling by hoodwinking the reader to some extent, loses impact. The narrator has to persuade us that Cipolla is possessed of supernatural powers, or powers that are often thought of as supernatural, and he has to persuade us that nothing can resist these powers, in order to make the ending the more impressive. To the extent that he fails in this attempt he fails to round off the narrative satisfyingly.

So, at least, we should judge according to traditional standards. In reading a story by Mann, however, we must be constantly aware that for him these standards do not apply. He does not regard truth as a matter of fidelity to facts or logic, but rather as a life-giving myth, a fiction in which it is better to believe than to disbelieve—better, that is, because it enables men to live more intensely and with greater enjoyment both of their suffering and their happiness, and better because it is more in keeping with the irrational and even delusory ways of the Will, or Providence, or God. There has been plenty of evidence so far of Mann's disregard of logic, the tricks which he seems to play on the reader, the inconsistency of his attitudes to various moral and religious issues. The question that remains before us now is the one that ought to be in any critic's mind all the time: the question whether he may not after all be wrong. For what Mann set out to do throughout the whole period of Nazi rule in Germany was to construct a myth which would stand over against their myth, a series of memorable stories in which a view opposed to theirs, yet taking full cognizance of it, should be embodied. The 'Joseph' novels and *Doktor Faustus* are the two principal works in which this myth-making took shape, and, like *Mario und der Zauberer*, they contain a good deal that must be described as delusion of the reader. At the same time they contain a defence of such a proceeding which we shall now need to look at. If a myth is required at all in these days—and the chaotic results of much of our scrupulous truth-seeking, whereby we often arrive at less and less certainty on every issue, might incline us to think the idea worth trying—must we not be prepared to allow a certain amount of bluff or deliberate evasiveness? Are we not being prudish and prim in our demand for solemn dedication to the truth and nothing but the truth? This is the point at issue in the next few chapters.

CHAPTER IX

THE 'JOSEPH' NOVELS

The trend of the most powerful tradition in German thought and literature had been towards an all-embracingness which the Nazis were easily able to invoke for their own purposes. Scorn of reason as the weapon of trivial minds, praise of self-assertion and amoral self-realization, and the advocacy of a united German nation in which critical opposition was treachery to the common myth—all this was potentially a preparation for the dictatorship. Yet the fact remains that the majority of German men of letters, Nietzscheans or not, were in exile from 1933 onwards, and Thomas Mann himself was the foremost in conducting opposition. He was never, of course, the spokesman for Communism, or for liberals outside the Nietzschean tradition. His own task, as he saw it, was to create out of that tradition a myth which would show its potentialities not for criminal aggressiveness but for more human ends.

In choosing to embody his myth in the story of the biblical Joseph, however, Mann might seem to have picked on intractable material. The biblical tradition is of all traditions the one most opposed to the ambiguous ideas typical of all Mann's earlier work: its insistence on the uniqueness, transcendence, and righteousness of Jehovah, and on the insignificance of man in the world of his creation, certainly sounds as though it could never be reconciled with the ambivalent, immanent, antinomian trend of thought, and the deliberate cultivation of the ego in a quasi-divine self-assertiveness, which we have encountered so far. At first sight at least it must seem that there is a choice or a preference to be made, and that the two traditions are incompatible.

This Mann recognized. For the first time in his work, we find in the Joseph novels cognizance of a form of belief in which good and evil are differentiated, in which a divine pattern of events is perceived, and individual men are aware of their lowly position in the whole scheme of things. Mann takes the short narrative in Genesis, with its essential theme of Joseph's service to God's purposes, and develops it into a tetralogy which is not only crammed with historical detail but also has immediate topical relevance. We see not only the divine pattern in which the events occur, but also the lives of Joseph's ancestors, Abraham, Isaac and Jacob; we see Abraham's discovery of the One God, Jacob's continuance in that discovery, Joseph's dreams of being set above his brothers, their jealousy, their casting of Joseph into the well, his rescue and journey to Egypt, his life in the house of Potiphar, his interpretation of Pharaoh's dreams, his rise to eminence, and the careful husbandry by which he is at length enabled to save not only Egypt but his own brethren and father from famine. Through all this, we are continually reminded of the hand of God, leading Joseph on through imprisonment and mortal peril to the day when he both saves and is reconciled with the men who had cast him out. At the same time, the topical hints from time to time suggest that Mann has something of himself in mind here: that this story, although begun before 1933, is close to his own, especially after that year, and Joseph's years in exile are in many ways a parallel with his. In short, we can if we choose see the Joseph novels as a myth not only about Palestine and Egypt, but also about Germany in recent times.

All the same, the biblical framework should not lead anyone to suppose that it is essentially a Judaic pattern that Mann traces here. There is certainly cognizance of the tradition without which the Joseph story would be unintelligible, but it is cognizance rather than affirmation. What has really happened is that the supreme and almost unapproachable Lord of Genesis has been transformed into a being rather more like the Will of Schopenhauer and still more like the Will to Power of Nietzsche: a being who develops, who is as yet not fully himself and will not become so till the end of days. This is a being for whom 'supreme' and 'unapproachable' are fit terms, so far as they go, but yet scarcely at all in the sense understood by the prophets and historians of Israel. The God who appears in the early pages of *Die Geschichten Jaakobs*, the first novel in the tetralogy, is a God for whom the praises of the angelic hosts are not enough to give that glow of self-approval which he needs. It takes the ingenuity of Satan to see that this dissatisfaction is due to the fact that angels are creatures having no moral choice: that praise from their lips is automatic and thus worthless, whereas, by creating a being able to withhold his praise, God might have the full delight of knowing that praise from him is praise indeed. To this 'diabolical' temptation (the inverted commas are needed, since the word is not meant in its usual sense) God succumbs, or rather, he accepts it with considerable relish. The world begins, Man is made, and time moves on towards the climax with which it is to end.

What that climax is likely to be, we learn from a chapter in the second novel, *Der junge Joseph*, entitled 'How Abraham discovered God'. Once again, the emphasis lies on an astute self-regard. Abraham, in this account, seeks to know what god he may most fitly worship, and having considered many alternatives decides that only the highest is good enough for him, or for any man worth the name. Only the supreme controller of all will suffice, and while this choice contains some danger for the chooser, since if he is abandoned he can turn to no other god, it also contains great promise, for if Abraham is not abandoned, he can count on untold blessings. It is in this spirit of a wager, then, that Abraham makes his choice. He risks a great deal, but, like a man paying court to an earthly king, he stands to gain even more. Nor is there any question of moral greatness in the choice he makes. The God of Abraham here is not righteous, or not only righteous, but evil also, embodying the contradiction that he is 'not good, or merely good along with other things, but evil as well, including evil as well in his abundant vitality, and yet holy too, holiness itself, demanding holiness'.[1] He is not even necessarily superior to men in his goodness, for Mann conceives of him as standing in a dialectical relationship to mankind: God and man are partners, standing on opposite poles of the rolling sphere of time, so that now one, now the other is uppermost, now man must teach God to forgo his ancient barbarism, now God must perform the same service for man. But at the end of time—of this Abraham is confident—God will achieve his aim at last, and men will worship him not from angelic and automatic acquiescence but freely and by their own choice. What a day that will be is revealed through Abraham's imagination: a day of great splendour and yet inescapably comic:

In the blare of ten thousand trumpets directed slantwise at the skies, in the singing and thundering of the flames, in a hailstorm of lightnings, He, clothed in majesty and terrors, would pace away to His throne across a world praying with forehead in the dust to take possession in sight of all and forever a reality which was His truth.[2]

That is the cosmological basis of the novel, the groundwork of the myth Mann presents. At the origin of all there is a kind of roguish good-nature (not wholly remote from the character of the elder Johann Buddenbrook) bent on asserting itself unscrupulously but not maliciously, and looking forward tongue in cheek to the day when men will actually do reverence to such audacious and impudent vitality. By virtue of one of his loose associations, however, Mann also suggests that all this is tantamount to a combination of good and evil, creativeness and destructiveness, God and Satan, within the divine nature, and thus gives a serious purport to his comedy which it will scarcely sustain.

This may be seen from the life-story of Joseph himself, with which the bulk of the novels is concerned. For one further paradox must now be added to the cosmological picture, the paradox that God and man are not merely partners on the rolling sphere but that it is often impossible to distinguish one from the other. Mann introduces many myths of men and gods from the ancient world of the Middle East, to lend weight to this suggestion, and in particular to invest Joseph with both a human and a god-like quality. Indeed a great part of the novel is taken up with speculations on the nature of time and progress, separate individuality and ancestral identity, all tending to create the impression that there is not so much a history unfolding itself as a single, eternal 'now', whose total manifestations in the course of time have a pattern exactly similar to that of the essential patterns of any period: what happens in the godlike whole also happens in the human part.

Thus we hear early on of God's intention to provide a blessing which shall give the 'blessings of heaven above' and at the same time 'blessings of the deep that lieth under', and the words, which are from Genesis (xlix. 25), suggest in their context in the novel a kind of dual blessing from God and Satan together, if such a thing were possible. By the end of the tetralogy, however, when we learn that Joseph is blessed with this blessing, the meaning has subtly and unavowedly changed. It is no longer a matter of divine and diabolical sources but rather of divine and human ones—Joseph is not only approved by the Almighty, but acclaimed by men also. He is the benevolent ruler of Egypt who has not only remained faithful in spirit to the one God of Israel, but also provided materially for the physical needs of his brethren. (It is true that Joseph is also excluded, as a merely material saviour, from the line that leads to Christ, and this has been thought to rank his achievement as more lowly—though it is not clear why Mann should be thought to esteem Christ more highly. However, the ambiguities on that score must be reserved till later in this chapter.)

Some such shift of meaning is typical of all Mann's work. By virtue of his habitual division of all things into two polar groups of opposites, he was constantly misled, and prone to mislead his readers, into supposing that something profound was being asserted. He liked the idea of the God–Devil, and possibly also the idea of himself acting in such a role. But in order to maintain it he was often driven to untenable associations, so that what was 'below' could be the devil at one moment and human beings at another, and 'blessing' could equally well be a promise of prosperity as an expression of general approval. So it was with Joseph, for Mann's intention with regard to him seems quite plainly to have been the demonstration of a kind of self-regard which was not blameworthy—a reasonable aim which is only obscured by the attempt at maintaining the paradox of a good–evil (not, of course, good *and* evil) nature.

Joseph, Mann tells us, was not one of those who from sheer humility cannot believe themselves chosen by God, who even feel a slight to their unbelief if ever they find themselves exalted. He was rather one of those 'conscious darlings of the Gods', to whom nothing comes as a surprise, who accept their good fortune with what looks to others like presumptuousness and yet is really trust.3 The story of his descent into slavery and ascent to the highest eminence under Pharaoh is thus told in a way that shows his assurance as not at all presumptuous but charmingly naïve and for the most part quite disarming. In relating his dream of the sheaves which bowed down to his sheaf, Joseph is not made to look vain—he is merely telling his brothers something he feels to be true and which turns out to be so, however little they may be pleased. Mann uses this incident, in fact, to point the difference between the jealously moral, egalitarian attitude of the brothers and the insouciance of Joseph, in whom there is perhaps that very childlike innocent self-assertion of which Nietzsche wrote.4 Joseph accepts men for what they are, and himself for what he is; as it happens, he is gifted far more than the common run. The brothers, however, unable to accept this natural fact, conspire against him, and at length throw him into a well, abandon him, and return home to their father with the bloodstained 'coat of many colours'. He, for his part, bears them no resentment for this treatment: he recognizes that he has brought it upon himself by claiming to be set above his fellows, and that he was half aware of willing his own downfall when he told his dream. He was no more wrong in telling it than they were in opposing him—each is fulfilling his part in the play of conflicts which is the nature of the all-embracing whole.

In this awareness of the whole, however, Joseph is made to appear quite godlike. It is not only that he is frequently described as though he were a precursor of Christ, riding to meet his brothers on a white donkey, waiting within the well until the heavy stone covering it is rolled away as though from the mouth of a tomb. It is also that he himself sees his fate with an equanimity which comes from his perfect assurance and knowledge of the ways of the gods. Cast into the well, Joseph utters no cry of forsakenness, he knows that God will not allow his chosen one to suffer corruption, just as he knows that the gods always are resurrected after their several deaths. He endures some bodily suffering, but his mind laughs at the whole situation as though it were a joke: his attitude, in contrast to that of his father, is said to have a 'witzig berechnenderes Gepräge'5—it is intelligently and wittily calculating, and a 'rational gaiety' gleams through 'the horror of his soul', so that he is always in reality beyond what happens to him. Knowing that the life of men and the life of gods intertwine so much as to be indistinguishable, he is certain of the outcome.

Thus, while Joseph is presented as a self-assured and self-seeking young man, these qualities in him are often endearing. He succeeds in Egypt, moreover, not by any importunacy, but by his ready sympathy, thanks to which he can read the characters of the butler and the baker so well that the meaning of their dreams is immediately apparent to him. He flatters Potiphar, it is true, but so charmingly that Potiphar can only feel flattered. On the other hand, he preserves his chastity from the attack on it by Potiphar's wife, even at the risk of being thrown to the crocodiles: he is not merely a chameleon, adapting himself to whatever circumstances chance to arise.

The nature of Mann's counter to the Nazi 'myth of the twentieth century' thus begins to emerge. It is to be a myth which draws on the same tradition of thought, dealing in terms of polarity and synthesis, emphasizing equally all aspects of human nature, accepting good and evil on equal terms, even incorporating the cult of egoism of which so much was heard in Germany from the time of Max Stirner onwards. But all this is to be modified. Like Tonio Kröger, Mann will have nothing to do with philosophies of ecstasy and intoxication, nor will he, through Joseph at least, deliberately cultivate barbarism. So far as Joseph is concerned, he puts forward an ideal (which is, ambiguously, also not an ideal) of harmonious sympathy coupled with unpretentious self-awareness, a man who is a god and yet not a god, a chameleon who is also a leader. Joseph saves Egypt by peaceful, not warlike means, and yet seems to remain within the ambience of Mann's dualistic thought.

It is, however, a matter of seeming. For some while during the early pages of the tetralogy, Mann continues to speak of a God who could well succumb to the temptation of Satan, and of human beings in a way that accords with such a conception of divinity. The God of Abraham, as he is presented here, is the victor over other gods of evil propensities: Bel, Dagon, Moloch; and he incorporates in himself their wickedness. Thus far, the un-differentiated whole containing good and evil in one continues to be represented. It is still represented when Mann comes to relate the story, again taken from Genesis, of the treacherous slaughter of the Shechemites by the sons of Jacob. In presenting to his readers the view that Israel could not have become great but for this willingness to act treacherously, Mann seems to adopt the view still current in Germany before 1914 that the vitality of a nation overrides all need for strict fidelity. Similarly, in the long digression on Tamar,[6] he makes much of the point that this woman's self-assertive determination to conceive a child by Judah, who was not her husband, resulted in the flourishing House which later went by his name and ultimately gave birth to Jesus Christ: her flouting of morality and her egoism were, he implies, a part of the divine purpose. Again, while it is true that Mann relates Joseph's rejection of Potiphar's wife to his devotion to the One God of Israel, so recognizing, apparently, an absolute obligation, he adds later in the story that the reader should have been indignant at Joseph's lack of charity, seeing that the wife, being married to a eunuch, needed sexual fulfilment so strongly. A relativistic morality, based on human needs, thus alternates with an absolute and more demanding one, and comments are made now in the spirit of one, now of the other.

On the whole, however, the amoral, dualistic mood is perhaps meant to be seen as an early stage of development. The episodes of Tamar and of the Shechemites both occur before Joseph is born, and it is only rarely that even remote appeals to amorality are heard in the later pages of the tetralogy. To trace such appeals in detail would in any case be beyond the scope of this study. In order to define a little more closely, therefore, what new developments Mann now had in mind, it will be convenient to consider one complete episode which occurs towards the end of the whole cycle, an episode which, like the passages from *Buddenbrooks* and *Der Zauberberg* already discussed, is in itself a recapitulation of the whole. This is the long section describing the journey of Joseph's brothers, long after his supposed death, into Egypt in search of food; his cold reception of them, his insistence that they return home and bring back their brother Benjamin, their second visit, and the trick by which Joseph accuses them of stealing a silver goblet. It ends with the brothers' confession of guilt in having made an attempt on Joseph's life, whereupon he reveals to them that he himself is their lost brother. In Genesis, a number of these events are obscure: they are of course not psychologically motivated and stand merely as facts. In Mann's version, all are woven into the situation and add to the total meaning of the novel. Particularly in the chapter 'Das heilige Spiel', the Sacred Game, the relationship of the brothers to Joseph is made to resemble that of the Israelites to Jehovah. The journey into Egypt, the land of plenty, of which Joseph has foreknowledge, is like the later journey into the Promised Land. A special 'providence' watches over them: they are allowed, by Joseph's intervention, an easy passage through the Egyptian customs, and a seemingly miraculous swift passage to Pharaoh's capital. Their brother watches over them as though they were a chosen people. Yet when they arrive and imagine themselves specially favoured, they meet with nothing but rebuffs. They are accused of being spies, and sent home again—with corn, it is true, but with their own money returned inside the sacks, a bounty which fills them with horror, for they have no hold over a man who accepts no recompense. They suspect that some dreadful fate is in store for them when they go back to Egypt a second time. Indeed, they see in the return of the money both a sign of goodness and a sign of evil, and attribute this ambiguity to God himself. 'There was something pleasant about it and yet again something spiteful—how could one tell, and who could say why God had done this to them?'7 They have the views on God's nature formerly ascribed to Abraham, although this is a fairly late moment in the story we are reading.

These views remain with them even on their return to Egypt with Benjamin, even when Joseph treats them with munificent hospitality. For all the while they are reminded of their guilt, which they have concealed from the man whom they take to be a powerful Egyptian only, and the thought of it hinders all enjoyment. Moreover, when they leave a second time, and are caught by Joseph's men not far from their starting-place, with Joseph's goblet in Benjamin's sack of corn, it seems quite evident that they are the victims of a cat-and-mouse game. Judah, who speaks in the name of all of them, sees that no purpose is served by opposing so omnipotent a ruler. Although all are convinced that they had no part in this theft, they are obliged to adopt the policy of affirming their own insignificance and avoiding any attempt at self-justification. Judah speaks as though he were addressing the Almighty himself:

Was sollen wir meinem Herrn sagen, und welchen Sinn hätte wohl der Versuch, uns vor ihm zu rechtfertigen? Wir sind schuldig vor dir, mein Herr — schuldig in dem Sinne, daß dein Becher bei uns gefunden worden, bei Einem von uns, das ist: bei uns....Ein Gewaltiger bist du, und bist gut und böse, erhebst und stürzest. Wir gehören dir, keine Rechtfertigung lohnt sich vor dir, und töricht der Sünder, der auf gegenwärtige Unschuld pocht, wenn der Rächer Zahlung fordert für alte Missetat....*8

* What shall we say unto my lord, and what sense would there be in trying to clear ourselves before him? We are guilty before you, O lord, guilty in the sense that your cup was found among us, with one of us and that means with all. How the cup came into the sack of the youngest and most innocent of us all, who was always safe at home, I do not know. We do not know. We are powerless to speculate about it before your seat. You are a mighty one, you are good and evil, you raise up and cast down. We are your servants. No defence of ours has any worth before you, and foolish is the sinner who presumes upon present innocence when the avenger demands pay for old misdeeds.

There is in this already an inkling of what Joseph intends to hear—the recognition and public affirmation of the brothers' guilt. But the basis of the speech is dualistic. In the brothers' eyes, the evil of which they are accused was not their own, but that of their lord. In terms of the mythological framework God himself has willed the evil in the world: Joseph's placing of the goblet in Benjamin's sack is a human repetition of the divine act. Guilt is implanted in the men from outside.

Judah accepts this belief since no other course is open to him, in view of Joseph's power. But this does not prevent him from making his human and humane protest at Joseph's demand that Benjamin, the apparent thief, should remain behind when the brothers return home. This is a piece of eccentricity which he cannot tolerate, seeing what the loss of a second son would mean to their father Jacob. Judah senses, indeed, that some secret is being withheld from him by Joseph, and that the eccentric demand has some relation to the secret. He resolves to make the secret reveal itself by revealing a secret of his own. He 'atones' ('sühnt') for all the brothers by revealing the crime of which all are guilty and offering himself as a hostage in Benjamin's place.

Only at this point does Joseph reveal who he is and welcome the brothers. The secret is out, released by the revelation of the brothers' secret. There is no evil intention in Joseph towards them, only love. The ambiguous nature they had thought to see, and which had made the world seem crooked to them, is not there. They want to send a swift messenger to their father, to tell him 'that the crookedness has vanished from the world', as though the fact that their brother has forgiven and loved them had a significance beyond itself. And so it has, for Joseph has played this 'Sacred Game' with them in much the same spirit as that of the 'Godly jest' which has been played in his own life. Just as God has apparently allowed him to die, at least so far as his father Jacob is aware, so Joseph has apparently shown a stern face to his brothers. Just as God has seemed even to Joseph himself a deity of unfathomable ambiguity, so has Joseph seemed to Judah. But in reality, Jacob has no cause for grief: his son Joseph is alive;

and in reality God has not acted harshly, even though, it is conceded, he has been over-rough in his playfulness, being unaware of the pain he has caused. And similarly the brothers have no cause for fear: the suspense in which they have been placed was Joseph's way of ensuring that they repented their cruelty to him. In Joseph as in God there is ultimately good will: there is no 'crookedness' in the world of either, no fundamental ambiguity or ambivalence.

It seems, then, that the novel ends on this note of realization. The ambivalent world gives way at length to a world in which love and good-will reign, or are at least prevalent. And whereas in *Der Zauberberg* there is no more than a breath of such single-ness—the merest mention of it in a final sentence—here in the Joseph novels there is a much longer development and an embodying of the idea in the action of the story.

But is that really so? Is it true that the unequivocal 'No' which Mann felt impelled to utter in real life is paralleled by an ultimate unequivocalness in his novel? If it is, we should expect to find in these pages something that we could properly call human: genuine grief or genuine rejoicing, real fear or love, rather than the seemingly superhuman detachment from emotions which we find in Joseph in, for instance, his moments of peril. It is human to feel intensely because it is human not to know the answers, to suspect or hope or believe at most, but not to have that godlike certainty which comes from identifying oneself with 'the Whole'. If, however, we look at the final paragraphs of the chapter in which the recognition-scene occurs, we shall find something difficult to define, but not quite so moving as we might have expected. For one thing, we have been constantly reminded that for Joseph all this is a game, a means of bringing the greatest possible pleasure to his brothers and himself, so that his prepa-rations for their reception take on the appearance of rehearsals for a stage-part. We are explicitly told that his behaviour is like that of actors, their make-up complete, running about before the curtain goes up, and that he has stage-fright. Thus the scene is set in a somewhat formal and thereby, in the context, a somewhat comic atmosphere. While the brothers imagine that the solemnity of the occasion could scarcely be surpassed, Joseph has his tongue in his cheek all the while, and so has the narrator, as we observe from the carefully placed archaism or the minutely observed rhetorical gesture. Thus, when we come to the end of Judah's speech, in which he offers himself as a sacrifice on behalf of the remaining brothers, there is a curious sense of seriousness and humour at one and the same time. We are aware that for Judah this is a moment of great self-conquest, that Joseph would not reveal himself, as he shortly does, if the confession were not made, and yet that Joseph means no harm whatsoever:

So und nicht anders endete Juda seine berühmte Rede. Wogenden Leibes stand er, und bleich standen die Brüder, wenn auch tief erleichtert, weil es heraus war. Dies kommt sehr wohl vor: die bleiche Erleichterung. Aber zwei Rufe ertönten: sie kamen vom Größten und Kleinsten. Ruben rief: 'Was hör ich!' und Benjamin macht' es genau wie vordem, als sie der Haushalter eingeholt: die Arme warf er empor und schrie unbeschreiblich auf. — Und Joseph? — Er war aufgestanden von seinem Stuhl und glitzernd liefen die Tränen ihm die Wangen hinab. Denn es war so, daß die Garbe Lichtes, die vorhin von der Seite her auf die Brudergruppe gefallen war, nach stiller Wanderschaft nun durch eine Luke am Ende des Saales gegen ihm über gerade auf ihn fiel: davon glitzerten die rinnenden Tränen auf seinen Backen als wie Geschmeide.*9

There is a note of humour running all through this passage, from the teasing of the reader in the first sentence onwards. 'Thus and not otherwise'—this insertion is made because the end of Judah's speech, his confession of guilt, is pure invention on Mann's part,

* Thus did Judah end his famous speech, thus and not otherwise. He stood there weaving to and fro. The brothers had gone pale; yet they were deeply relieved that the secret was out at last. For it is not impossible to go pale and yet feel relieved at the same time. But two of them cried out, and they were the oldest and the youngest. Reuben shouted: 'What do I hear?' And Benjamin did just as he had done before when the steward overtook them: he flung up his arms and gave an indescribable cry. And Joseph? He had got up from his seat and glittering tears ran down his cheeks. For it happened that the shaft of light which had been falling aslant upon the group of brothers had now moved round and was coming through an opening at the end of the hall. It fell directly on Joseph's face and in it his tears glittered like jewels.

not at all like the 'famous speech' in Genesis xliv, as those will find who look it up. (Mann keeps up a running fire against those of his readers who are tempted to check with the 'original'.) Similarly the Latinism, 'wogenden Leibes' makes Judah's appearance slightly ludicrous, the more so by contrast with the colloquial end of the sentence, 'weil es heraus war', thanks to which the brothers look a little like naughty schoolboys. The faint note of persiflage then continues in the way in which our attention is drawn to the fact that the two cries came from the biggest and the smallest of the brothers, and that Benjamin's reaction is exactly like his reaction on an earlier occasion. (Thanks to this, Benjamin looks something of a marionette, an actor who in given circumstances will always perform the same gesture.) We know this is a solemn occasion, but we are being invited to see it as a scene in a play on the great world's stage, an incident in the divine–human present which is always with us. And this extends even to Joseph's joy, which even now is given a deliberately artificial description. That the shaft of light happens now to fall on his cheeks and to make his tears glisten like jewels is an aesthetically pleasing touch which, for that very reason, a careful artist would have wanted to avoid. Mann surely knows this: we see from phrases like 'Denn es war so', with its deliberately archaic flavour, and the even more archaic 'glitzerten...als wie Geschmeide' how conscious he is of the artificiality of his art. But then, of course, it is his point that life is a work of art, in the sense that it is something artificial, to be contrived so as to give pleasing results to the aesthete. He does not see either art or life as capable of witnessing or producing unadulterated, unmockable humanity, or indeed unmockable anything. And so, just as the 'perfect beauty' of Der Tod in Venedig proved to be corrupt from the outset, so here the simple scene of reconciliation between the brothers is deliberately made to have a certain air of artificiality: in neither case are we given anything purely human or humanly pure.

In the reconciliation scene itself, which follows immediately, there is very little irony, although it is introduced by a scene comical enough, that in which all Joseph's servants stand in the room outside and lean towards the door, each with one hand behind his ear. (It is the repetitiveness of the action that makes for comedy, as it does earlier in the case of Benjamin.) Let us try to establish the mood as accurately as possible:

Dort aber breitete Joseph, ohne des Geschmeides auf seinen Backen zu achten, die Arme aus und gab sich zu erkennen. Er hatte sich oft zu erkennen gegeben und die Leute stutzen gemacht, indem er zu verstehen gab, daß ein Höheres sich in ihm darstellte, als was er war, so daß dies Höhere träumerisch-verführerisch ineinanderlief mit seiner Person. Jetzt sagte er einfach und trotz der gebreiteten Arme sogar mit einem kleinen bescheidenen Lachen:

'Kinder, ich bin's ja. Ich bin ja euer Bruder Joseph.'

'Aber er ist's ja natürlich doch!' schrie Benjamin, fast erstickt von Jubel und stürzte vorwärts, die Stufen hinan zur Erhöhung, fiel auf seine Knie und umfing mit Ungestüm die Knie des Wiedergefundenen.

'Jaschup, Joseph-el, Jehosiph!' schluchzte er zu ihm hinauf, den Kopf im Nacken. 'Du bist's, du bist's, aber selbstverständlich bist du's natürlich ja doch! Du bist nicht tot, umgestürzt hast du die große Wohnung des Todesschattens, aufgefahren bist du zum siebenten Söller und bist eingesetzt als Metatron und Innerer Fürst, ich hab's gewußt, ich hab's gewußt, hoch erhoben bist du, und der Herr hat dir einen Stuhl gemacht, ähnlich dem Seinen! Mich aber kennst du noch, deiner Mutter Sohn, und hast im Winde gewedelt mit meiner Hand!'

'Kleiner', sprach Joseph. 'Kleiner', sagte er, hob Benjamin auf und tat ihre Köpfe zusammen. 'Rede nicht, es ist nicht so groß und nicht so weit her, und kein solcher Ruhm ist es mit mir, und die Hauptsache ist, daß wir wieder zwölfe sind.'*10

---

* And Joseph, heedless of the jewels on his face, stretched out his arms and made himself known. Often before now he had done the same and made people stare, giving them to think that some higher power moved in him other than what he was himself and mingled in his single person with a dreamy and seductive charm. But now quite simply—and despite the outstretched arms with a deprecating little laugh—he said:

'Children, here I am, I am your brother Joseph!'

'Of course he is, of course he is!' shouted Benjamin, almost choking with joy. He stumbled forwards and up the steps, fell on his knees, and stormily embraced the new-found brother's knees.

'Jashup, Joseph-el, Jehosiph!' he sobbed, with his head tipped back to look

Only once or twice does the ironical tone appear, and then it is not strongly marked. (It is present at 'und gab sich zu erkennen. Er hatte sich oft zu erkennen gegeben...', where once more the element of repetition creates a smile, and, for the same reason, in Benjamin's 'aber selbstverständlich bist du's natürlich ja doch!', although what we really smile at here it is probably impossible to say.) Essentially, this scene seems to be about Joseph's abandonment of pretence: he is descending from his often-adopted godlike role to reveal himself as the man he is.[11] *Although* his arms are outstretched in the godlike posture he is able to give a modest laugh. Yet it is just this insistence on Joseph's modesty that helps to make the scene less moving—our attention is being drawn to Joseph's condescension rather than to any brotherly feeling he may have for Benjamin, and that modest laugh, revealing as it does how much Joseph has his own motives in mind, rather than concern for Benjamin, undermines the real joy we might have felt with him. (Let the reader try saying, with a modest laugh, 'Kinder, ich bin's ja. Ich bin ja euer Bruder Joseph.') And strangely enough it seems to undermine Benjamin's joy also, for it is strange that Benjamin should so quickly go on from his stumbling words of welcome, themselves a trifle comic, to a speech in which he is mainly concerned with the metaphysical implications of Joseph's high office within the Cabbalistic system. We are being offered in this scene less of a meeting between brothers than a demonstration of how natural and human Joseph can be despite his claims to divinity.

The attempt at making this demonstration continues into the next chapter, which takes up the story exactly where we just

up in his brother's face. 'It's you, you are, you are, of course you are! You are not dead, you have overturned the great abode of the shadow of death, you have risen up to the seventh threshold, you are set as metatron and inner prince— I knew it, I knew it, you are lifted up on high, the Lord has made you a seat like to his own! But me you know still, your mother's son, and you fanned the air with my hand!'

'Little one!' said Joseph. 'Little one!' He raised Benjamin up and put their heads together. 'Do not talk, it is none of it so great nor so remote and I have no such glory and the great thing of all is that we are twelve once more.'

left it. In this, the attitudes ascribed to the brothers deserve
special attention, and not only for their comic aspect:

Und er schlang den Arm um seine Schulter und trat hinab mit ihm zu
den Brüdern — ja, wie stand es mit denen und wie standen die da!
Einige standen, die Beine gespreizt, mit hängenden Armen, die viel
länger schienen als sonst, knielang beinahe und suchten offenen
Mundes mit den Augen im Leeren herum. Andere preßten die Brust
mit beiden Fäusten — die wuchteten auf und ab von ihrem gehenden
Atem. Alle waren sie bleich gewesen vor Juda's Bekenntnis, nun
waren sie dunkelrot im Gesicht, rot wie Kiefernstämme, rot wie einst,
als sie auf ihren Fersen gesessen hatten und Joseph daher gekommen
war im bunten Kleid.*12

That the brothers should stand around like gorillas or caricatures
in a Disney cartoon is funny, after a fashion, but it prevents the
story from having any human significance at this fairly significant
moment. The gap between Joseph and his brethren is now made
so large that communication between them seems scarcely
feasible—it is as though Thomas Mann, having allowed Joseph
to become so condescending, felt obliged to push the brothers
still further down the scale, lest some real contact might be made.
Yet the brothers are no fools: Reuben has always felt uneasy in
Joseph's presence, and Judah has just made a daringly self-
sacrificial proposal. The description of them at this moment in
these terms looks almost vindictive. Joseph himself, however,
does not come out of the encounter well:

'Tretet doch her zu mir', sagte Joseph, während er selber zu ihnen trat.
'Ja, ja, ich bin's. Ich bin Joseph, euer Bruder, den ihr nach Ägypten
verkauft habt, — macht euch nichts draus, es war schon recht. Sagt,
lebt mein Vater noch? Redet mir doch ein bißchen und bekümmert
euch nicht! Juda, das war eine gewaltige Rede! Die hast du für

* He put his arm around Benoni's shoulders and went down with him to the
brothers—ah yes, the brothers: how was it with them as they stood there? Some
stood with their legs apart and arms dangling awkwardly down almost to their
knees. They stared open-mouthed into space. Some held their clenched fists
upon breasts that heaved up and down with the fury of their panting. All of
them had gone pale at Judah's confession; now they were crimson, a deep dark
red like the colour of pine-trunks, red as that time when squatting on their hands
they had seen Joseph coming towards them in the coat of many colours.

immer und ewig gehalten. Innig umarm' ich dich zur Beglückwün-
schung, wie auch zum Willkomm und küße dein Löwenhaupt. Siehe,
es ist der Kuß, den du mir gabst vor den Minäern, — heute geb' ich
ihn dir wieder, mein Bruder, und nun ist ausgelöscht. . . .'*13

Perhaps inevitably, since the brothers are so apish, Joseph speaks
in the manner of a careful expounder of the situation. His
question about his father is almost curt, and the plea that they
should talk with him a little (as though telling him about his
father would be fit matter for a chat) sounds oddly embarrassed.
When Joseph turns to Judah with praise for his speech, however—as though Judah was concerned at that moment, or would
have been at any moment, about his fame as an orator—the fact
that this scene is for Joseph a thing for aesthetic enjoyment
rather than plain feeling recurs to mind. It is in congratulation
for the speech that Joseph first embraces Judah—the welcome to
a brother implied in the embrace is an afterthought. But the final
tactlessness occurs when Joseph, in kissing Judah, reminds him
of the kiss at the time when Joseph was betrayed. (If it is not
tactlessness, it is a deliberate flick on a raw spot, despite Joseph's
disclaimer, 'es war schon recht'.)

Contrast with this the biblical narrative:

Then Joseph could not refrain himself before all them that stood by
him; and he cried, Cause every man to go out from me. And there
stood no man with him, while Joseph made himself known unto his
brethren. And he wept aloud: and the Egyptians and the house of
Pharaoh heard. And Joseph said unto his brethren, I am Joseph; doth
my father yet live? And his brethren could not answer him; for they
were troubled at his presence. And Joseph said unto his brethren,
Come near to me, I pray you. And they came near. And he said, I am
Joseph your brother, whom ye sold into Egypt. Now therefore be not
grieved, nor angry with yourselves, that ye sold me hither: for God

* 'Come here to me', said Joseph as he approached. 'Yes, yes, I am your
brother Joseph whom you sold down in Egypt; but never mind about that, for
you did me no harm. Tell me, my father is truly alive?—Speak to me, don't be
afraid. Judah, that was a great speech you made. You made it for ever and ever.
I dearly embrace and congratulate you, I greet you and kiss your lion's head. See,
it is the kiss you gave me in front of the Minaeans; today I give it back, my
brother, and it is all blotted out.'

did send me before you to preserve life. . . . And behold, your eyes see, and the eyes of my brother Benjamin, that it is my mouth that speaketh unto you. And ye shall tell my father of all my glory in Egypt, and of all that ye have seen; and ye shall haste and bring down my father hither. And he fell upon his brother Benjamin's neck, and wept; and Benjamin wept upon his neck. Moreover he kissed all his brethren, and wept upon them: and after that his brethren talked with him.[14]

Mann has made this event amusing by making it into a caricature. But in so far as he also has a serious purpose, he only renders it impossible to achieve by this treatment. He is really more concerned to keep up the teasing game with the reader, inviting him to see divinity in Joseph while at the same time denying the implication, than he is concerned to move or please. And so, a little later, when Joseph asks his brothers, laughingly, 'Bin ich ein Gott?' we do not have the sense we have in Genesis, when the same moment arises, of a sincere disclaimer. Rather, the question seems to invite an answer that oscillates continually between negative and affirmative.

Similarly also, in the chapter entitled 'Of Withholding Love' ('Von absprechender Liebe'), there is an apparent turning away from ambiguities and a firm declaration in the name of the One God of Israel. Here, in a scene between Joseph and his father Jacob, it is made clear that Joseph has merely served one of God's purposes: he has provided earthly bread in a time of famine, but this is merely a means towards God's spiritual end for man. The true line of descent in Israel will not pass through Joseph. He is rejected, though still loved. And with this moment once again the novel seems to move away from the ideas of the 'rolling sphere' with which it began, the alternation of man and God, so that either could be superior to the other. These are, it is suggested, attractive ideas. As Jacob says 'I know very well that the two-in-one has no part in the Spirit whose representatives we are, that it is merely the folly of the nations. And yet I succumbed to its powerful fascination.'[15] But they are not, as he observes, consistent with the true tradition of Israel in which he has always felt himself to stand, and thus even Joseph, despite his own devotion to the same tradition, is not truly within it. The One God, in whom goodness is unmixed with evil, who is wholly distinct from his creation and never to be confused with it as he seems to be in the person of Joseph, does not admit of ambiguousness and duplicity. Or so we would suppose, were it not for the note of irony which accompanies these pages also. The morally exacting 'Spirit', we see from this, is still no more than one facet of the whole which is God. Jacob, its representative throughout the tetralogy, is not without his own ambiguities: he knows how to play his part in the comedy as well as any other. And thus, just as on hearing the news of Joseph's death he went through the motions of grief with all the required formalities, so here he seems conscious that he is merely acting one of the many roles that have to be performed. From the moment when he asks the name of 'the man of medium physical stature', and is told that it is Joseph who is approaching, Jacob is self-aware. Rising to meet his son, he deliberately exaggerates the limp, the 'limp of honour' which he has had since he wrestled with the angel: he is determined to keep at least on terms of equality with his distinguished son. Again, when Joseph asks (a little deliberately) whether he may call him 'Väterchen', Jacob replies with a formal assumption of dignity that he would prefer to be called 'Vater'. 'Let our hearts compose themselves in earnestness, and not jest.' There is a polite, tacit understanding between the two, to observe all the proprieties consonant with their positions, and this extends even to propriety of expression about the God of Israel. Thus Joseph, having explained the view which, otherwise, Jacob would no doubt have put, that God has acted in much the same way as he himself has acted towards his brothers, asks whether he has expressed himself 'more or less decently' (annähernd schicklich), to which Jacob replies: 'more or less'. And so, when the father explains further how Joseph is called, yet not called to the highest rank of God's servants, we remember how very godlike Joseph seemed (and yet did not seem) in his own eyes, and we observe his reception of the message with curiosity. Jacob, almost exhausted, can speak only in a whisper. Joseph, to hear him, must place his ear close to his father's mouth, and to reply must take it away again and place his own mouth to Jacob's ear. The gesture or movement is repeated over and over again at almost every interval in the dialogue, giving an impression of filial piety that is assiduous in its desire to respect propriety, and at the same time a little comic in its excessiveness. For Joseph knows, and knows that Jacob knows, that the position is more subtle than either of them will admit. To quote Erich Heller's words on this scene, 'the blessing will go to Judah, the great sinner and the unhappy son. He needs it. . . .'[16] Joseph, for his part, has the blessing from heaven above and from the earth beneath, the blessing which, as an earlier part of the novels foretold, was God's ultimate purpose for man. Should he ask for more? And is the blessing that will pass to posterity through Judah not a less desirable one than his? Yes and no: the novel oscillates once again at this point, and so remains within the tradition of ambivalence, the tradition which, given its biblical subject-matter, it seemed about to reject.

There remains a 'knowingness' about these characters, then, which keeps them from straightforward emotions even in their most humanly moving situations. They have their emotions, but, knowing the pattern as they do, they have them with a certain artfulness, realizing the part allotted to them. Joseph in the well must 'die' so that he can rise again, and in fact he dies as little, and as punningly, as Hans Castorp in the snow. Jacob, mourning for his son, goes through the motions until the formalities of tearing his robes and falling flat on his back become occasions for laughter. Joseph's joy at the return of his brethren to Egypt is not so much joy as an excited arranging of the most aesthetically pleasing reunion, an artistically tasteful composition of events.

A pretence at reality, a real pretence: this is how Mann envisages the outside world and his own art. The Joseph novels are fiction, yet the reader goes through the motions of living through the events as though they were real. To persuade him that they are truly real, Mann assumes that pedantic air of scholarship which makes long sections of the books tedious;

he sets forth his astonishingly detailed historical knowledge as though it confirmed the version of the Joseph story he has amusingly invented. The effect is twofold. On the one hand, the reader is impressed by this technique to the point of looking up the Bible and finding out whether Joseph 'really' said or did this or that (and Mann as often as not taunts the reader into doing this). On the other hand, by the same technique Mann reminds us that this *is* a fiction which we are being deluded into taking for a reality. Further, he suggests that reality outside the novels is also like this: a fiction, a 'Vorstellung', a great work of art to be enjoyed as one enjoys a tragedy or a poem. His system of thought is apparently quite self-sufficient; within it art and reality coalesce in every possible sense. Only by comparison with some view of reality not already conditioned by the system does the whole appear not real at all, but artificial where it most needs reality. Only by such a comparison is it seen that the jewel-tears on Joseph's cheek are 'right' only in the convention of a cheapened art, just as the words used to suggest horror in Hans Castorp's dream are appropriate as onomatopoeia, but not really horrifying, or as Aschenbach's prose is classicizing but not classic. In each case there is an element of 'going through the motions', of behaving 'just as the books said', to quote *Der Zauberberg*.[17] A son is supposed to show due deference to his father: Joseph does. A man is supposed to die before being reborn into wisdom: Hans Castorp dies. Horrific passages are supposed to have certain ingredients: they are provided. Yet with all this there is a complete absence of real grief, real longing or hope, real love, real horror, and instead of these a knowing complicity in the supposed indifference of the creator which separates the novels from the conditions of real living. For Mann, fiction is not a portrayal of reality, inadequate perhaps, but still attempting a faithful likeness. It is itself, by the very fact that it is a fiction, a proper likeness, for the world of reality is a fiction, an illusion in which the polar opposites must always hold sway. Thus his irony, continually bringing reminders of the fictitious nature of his narrative, is not a criticism, but an integral part of his view of the real. The pretence is real, the reality pretended, and there is no more, within the system, to be said, for there is no place within it for the view that what is conventionally appropriate can be really and absolutely misplaced. There is room only for the view that a mock grief, an aesthetic love, a corrupt beauty, or whatever other diminutions of reality can be adduced, are in accordance with reality in the very ground of its being.

CHAPTER X

DR FAUSTUS

While the 'Joseph' novels provided a kind of positive counter-myth to Nazism, or were meant to do so, *Doktor Faustus* took a more negative form. The Joseph tetralogy was a defence of self-regard within the philosophical tradition to which Nazism itself was in strange ways indebted; it was mainly concerned with the life of a man who trusted completely in God's loving purpose for himself, and who seemed to know that purpose as if it had been his own. *Doktor Faustus*, on the other hand, provided a reverse to this obverse, dealing with a man whose whole being rested on the supposition that he must be damned, and who rejected the universe of God's creation in every morsel and atom. The two novels thus form a duality in themselves, an extreme positive and an extreme negative, the man who knows to the utmost that he is saved and secure, and the man who knows equally well that he is abandoned. We shall not be surprised, therefore, to find that there is a certain sense in which both novels are alike. For just as Joseph is the man blessed from above and below, and his God is both good and evil at once, so Leverkühn, the Faust of the later novel, is supposed to be a wicked man who is yet a saint. The emphasis is different in each case, but the paradox of the 'holy sinner' remains, if paradox is the right word for it.

The whole of *Doktor Faustus*, directly related in time to the period which gave rise to the Nazis, and indirectly related to it through a symbolism which makes the central character look like the epitome of his age, gives clear evidence of Mann's continued adherence to ambiguity. In the person of Adrian Leverkühn ('Livebold'), the musical composer who plays here also the part of a Faust, disposing of his soul to the devil in return for a new access of creative power, Mann represents the German nation in its self-abandonment to Nazi rule. At the same time, a wide array of further suggestiveness is included. Not only is Leverkühn's childhood upbringing portrayed, but also his university career, and the intellectual circles in which he moved, in short the whole background of German thought which he later came to represent; in addition, hints are woven in, resemblances between his life and that of Nietzsche, and others recalling that of Thomas Mann himself. Indeed, so far as Mann is concerned, Leverkühn is all that part of him which sympathized with Nietzsche and adopted his way of thought.

Leverkühn is not, however, the whole of Mann, any more than he is the whole of Germany. Interposed between him and the reader is the narrator, Serenus Zeitblom ('Time's flower'), the solid pedant and worthy citizen, 'bieder' and 'tüchtig' (to use untranslatable words), in whom other German qualities which Mann admired and shared come to the fore. It is perhaps significant that a narrator appears here for the first time in Mann's novels as a technical device: by this means the author himself remains in the background entirely uninvolved, while at the same time he alternately lives out the implications in the two existences of his protagonists.[1] For Zeitblom is as much a part of Mann as Leverkühn is, and the contradictory natures interlink in a remarkable and sometimes oppressive manner. At the same time, Mann remains, like Tadzio in *Der Tod in Venedig*, 'unverbindlich', attached neither to the one nor the other. Zeitblom may show a reverent and horrified admiration for his daemonic friend, as Mann did for Nietzsche. He may also speak of the path of German history which had led to the concentration camps and the Gestapo as 'wickedly godless ["heillos"] in every respect, at every twist and turn',[2] again as Mann was able to do. Yet admiration and condemnation play into one another's hands, at times seeming even to coalesce.

The choice of Zeitblom as narrator means that the novel cannot be read with aesthetic enjoyment. Zeitblom has no talent for writing a novel, and says so repeatedly; indeed the second sentence of the first chapter becomes so involved that he breaks it off with an apology and begins again—a frank and so far amusing indication that felicitous prose is not the main object. Other sentences, later in the book, become so turgid that they need to be followed with some doggedness if they are read at all—and these too are sometimes offered with an apology. Periphrasis, abstraction, a pedantic show of scrupulousness, redundancy, digression, the complex adjectival phrase, and the lengthy relative clause which withholds its verb till several lines of print have passed— these are some of Zeitblom's favourite devices. All characters speak, with rare exceptions, in the same professorial prose: even the beautiful Marie Godeau refuses a suitor in language more likely to come from a government official, and the greater part of the dialogue is given in reported speech, with its distancing, disillusioning subjunctive. Little of what is said is in the form of conversation: people hold forth for pages at a time, and the first two hundred pages give, in reported speech, the substance of lectures and discussions heard by Leverkühn in his early years. From time to time Zeitblom intervenes, in a way reminiscent of *Tristram Shandy*, to observe what the reader already knows, that he is not writing well, that this is not a novel, that the point of these digressions will be realized later, or that he is afraid the reader may have skipped the last few pages. There is no formal pattern to speak of, almost no plot, and the main character is realized largely by a description of his intellectual background and musical compositions. All this does serve a purpose. By the very fact that Zeitblom is so dull, the dynamism he attributes to Leverkühn looks the more attractive. At the same time, the novel whose deficiencies he so frequently deplores does ironically seem to set forth an interpretation of Leverkühn which would, it might have been thought, be beyond Zeitblom's power to convey.

The bulk of the novel is presented as a foil to the two principal events—Leverkühn's conversation with the devil, and his collapse into madness twenty-four years later.[3] Everything contributes in some way to the understanding of these two moments. German culture is surveyed in almost every aspect: social life, politics, painting, architecture, literature, philosophy, and above all, two of its most notable contributions to civilization,

German theology and German music. (There is curiously little about Marxism.) From all this, two features emerge which have the closest relevance to Leverkühn's situation: the tradition of ambiguity and paradox, and an idea best given in its German form, 'Durchbruch', or 'breakthrough'. The first of these is familiar enough. Leverkühn lives in a world where opposites coincide, where theologians are preoccupied with diabolism, musicians speak of the 'sensuality' of their 'most unsensual work', and life and death constantly intermingle. The second is concerned with the sense of isolation which appears to result from this way of seeing things. Where there is unity-in-duality there is also aloneness, from which escape is sought by a breakthrough into a wider world. Politically, German history is seen as the attempt to make this breakthrough, to make contact with other nations even at the price of dominating them. Spiritually, it is seen as the attempt to escape from a fundamentally ambiguous relationship with the world into a true unity.

The dilemma of Leverkühn's situation in his youth, which resembles that of Mann, is that his works are all in some sense parodies. Being parodies, they are twofold: Leverkühn is self-conscious in everything he does. There is the mood he sets out to express, and the ironical contemplation of it which finally makes the work as it emerges parodistic. To escape from parody, to break through into single-hearted feeling, is one of the motives which lead to his meeting with the devil, for with the devil's help he imagines the possibility of at least a temporal success. Ecstasies and terrifying despairs are the offers made, the heights and depths of emotion, and with them the possibility of unheard-of creativity. Damnation is to be the final outcome, intense heat and intense cold, the heights and depths of consciousness, in fact a life after death which will closely resemble, if it is not identical with, the one Leverkühn will lead from now on, so that he observes already that what is being offered is 'hell in advance'. There is nothing enticing about the devil's proposals, nor is Leverkühn deceived by them; he sees them with complete clarity. Nevertheless, like Goethe's Faust, he inserts a proviso into any possible pact that may be made. The devil, for his part, imagines that he will win the bargain, since Leverkühn's pride will never allow him to make the act of contrition which might save him in spite of everything. Leverkühn retorts that the devil's theology is defective. There is such a thing as proud contrition: 'Contrition without hope at all, complete unbelief in the possibility of grace and forgiveness, the unshakable conviction of the sinner that he has been too wicked, and even infinite goodness is insufficient to forgive his sins—only that is true contrition, and I would point out to you that it stands closest of all to redemption, being the most irresistible claim on goodness.'4 With this in mind, Leverkühn puts forward his proviso: 'A sinfulness so graceless that it makes a man utterly despair of grace, that is the truly theological path to grace.'5 The devil, it is true, is quick to point out the absurdity of this over-cunning speculation on divine forgiveness. Hell, he says, is full of ingenious contrivers like Leverkühn, who have insured in this way against the fruits of their wickedness. Nevertheless, the narration continues as though Leverkühn's proviso had gone uncountered.

The narration continues, but no pact is made. For the remainder of the novel this can easily be forgotten: everything takes place as though there were a pact, but in reality Leverkühn has done no more than consider the implications of a pact with a devil who is perhaps no more than a projection of his own unconscious desires. The absurdity and fruitlessness of the pact has been observed, even the absurdity of Leverkühn's proviso has been noticed, and he has not committed himself to it.6 The contrast with the pact of Goethe's play, with its 'Topp!' 'Und Schlag auf Schlag!', is striking. In Mann's work nothing so definite occurs: the devil is a shadow, perhaps not supernatural at all; what he offers is neither accepted nor rejected, what Leverkühn objects is neither affirmed nor denied. The motions of making a pact are gone through, much as Hans Castorp goes through the motions of dying in order to be reborn, but the decisive act is never made in reality. What appears to be a climax is not one. The 'consequences' provide no change in Leverkühn's manner of composition, and his last works are parodistic like his first. Sameness rules throughout, the sameness of ambiguity. This is the more damaging to the novel as a whole, in so far as it reflects an outside world of German history where concrete evil was in no way indecisive. Where the outside world was really committed, Leverkühn remains in an atmosphere of shadowy unreality.

A distinction should be made here between Leverkühn's proviso and the concept of 'abandonment' to the divine will, often mentioned in studies of mystical authors, and especially by de Caussade. Leverkühn's argument is in effect that by the fact of being an extreme sinner he ensures his salvation. He is, as he puts it with seeming arrogance, 'closest of all to redemption'. Contrast with this the conviction of the Cambridge Platonist, Henry More, meditating on the Calvinist doctrine of pre-destination: 'I did thus seriously and deliberately conclude within my self, viz. If I am one of those that are predestinated unto Hell, where all Things are full of nothing but Cursing and Blasphemy, yet will I behave my self there patiently and sub-missively towards God....Being certainly perswaded, that if I thus demeaned my self, he would hardly keep me long in that place.'[7] More's carefully worked out phrases (not, for instance, claiming salvation for certain, though not doubting it either) are echoed in modern times by Simone Weil, considering her own dilemma that, while baptism would mean salvation for her, she is also irresistibly impelled to feel that it is not God's will for her to be baptized. 'If it were conceivable', she says, 'that in obeying God one should bring about one's own damnation, whilst in disobeying him one could be saved, I should still choose the way of obedience.'[8] The whole difficult concept is treated at length by Ronald Knox, especially in relation to St Francis of Sales, who as a young man made a resolution to go on loving God, even though he knew himself damned. For St Francis, conditions could be imagined in which a soul ought to throw up its salvation and run eagerly to perdition if, 'par imagination d'une chose impossible', it believed that to be God's intention for it. His most faithful disciple taught that a man should acquiesce in his own damnation, 'la grâce de Dieu toujours sauve, au cas où Dieu le voudrait', and this was incontestable for some of the greatest saints, including Catherine of Siena and Ignatius Loyola. 'Truly humble souls', Knox adds, 'might consent to God's will, even if, on a wholly imaginary supposition, it were his good pleasure to keep them in eternal torment, without the loss of his grace and love.'9 Leverkühn's contention, in contrast, is avowedly proud and calculating, being more concerned with salvation than with love. It should not be confused with the delicate notions of people who really believe themselves damned and would rather not be.

Like all Mann's work, *Doktor Faustus* rests on nothing: there is no pact and nothing is at stake. To see the whole nature of the novel, however, it will be necessary to ignore this temporarily and pursue the progress of events with which it seems to be concerned. The stage is set as though in illustration of Leverkühn's proviso, that a completely despairing sinfulness, proudly persuaded of its own damnation, is the truly theological path to salvation. The outward events of his life, few as they are, are presented so as to suggest the extent of his sin, and so have the air of bearing out his argument. Like the events in Tonio Kröger's life, however, which equally seemed related to an argument concerning the position of the artist in society, they are delusive. First, before ever the pact with the devil is propounded, comes the incident based on accounts of the life of Nietzsche, where Leverkühn contracts syphilis from a prostitute. This is, perhaps, the beginning of the pact itself, for it is presented as a deliberate act, made by Leverkühn for the same purpose as the one mentioned in his discussion with the devil. In contracting the disease, he looks for that heightening of his creativity in artistic invention which it is supposed to bring: he physically brings about the intense ecstasies and despairs promised to him by his imagined devil. Or so at least Zeitblom is inclined to surmise at times. At other times he puts a different interpretation on his friend's actions. He suggests by remote allusions that it was not such a 'daring temptation of God', not a perverted form of self-aggrandizement, but an act of compassion. Leverkühn was not willing to live a healthy life while others were diseased, and took on himself this evil in order to experience it in his own person to the full. In Blake's lines from 'Silent, silent night', which Zeitblom quotes,

> ...an honest joy
> Does itself destroy
> For a harlot coy.

With this motive, Leverkühn appears in a different light. But whether or not it was his motive is left obscure. The episode of his journey to meet the prostitute in a remote part of Austria is briefly related, and no more of it is said than that it happened. The rest is Zeitblom's speculation; Leverkühn's thoughts and emotions remain unknown except for the fact that motifs using the letters of the woman's name as musical notes recur throughout his work. Thus the apparently sinful act remains capable of being interpreted in two ways. It is no more possible to say that Leverkühn evilly contracts a disease for the furtherance of his own projects than it is to say that he contracts to serve and be served by the devil. The whole episode, on the face of it so vital for Leverkühn's proviso about extreme sinfulness, is allowed to remain in darkness.

The same is true of the other events of Leverkühn's outward life, after the pact has been propounded. It is, outwardly, a sheltered life, the life of a recluse. Shortly before his final collapse, however—that is, while he still remains sane—Leverkühn accuses himself before his friends of several monstrous sins. He has committed murder and incest, has brought about the death of his young nephew, and has indeed, as he foresaw in his speech with the devil, been so great a sinner that divine forgiveness must remain a perpetual impossibility. In these last words of his sane life, Leverkühn recalls the proviso, and thereby suggests the possibility, though he cannot for himself claim it, that he has in fact found the true theological path to salvation. The paradox seems to have been driven to its utmost, and the man despairing of grace may yet come to grace despite the absurdity of his speculations. But again, it is only a matter of seeming. The murder of

Rudi Schwerdtfeger of which Leverkühn accuses himself is not in fact committed by him, but by a woman, Ines Roddes. It is true that Leverkühn was at one time involved in an intricate love affair, in which Schwerdtfeger and Ines Roddes also played a part, and that he might have helped to bring about a situation in which her jealousy of Schwerdtfeger would not have led to this disastrous end. But his part in the murder is so extremely remote, if indeed it can be said to exist at all, that his self-accusation appears as the exaggeration of an over-scrupulous conscience.[10] One is inclined to feel, because he accuses himself so violently, that he is really innocent. Of the second charge which he brings against himself, incest with his sister, nothing else is said in the novel; certainly it does not form an episode in the narration. What Leverkühn appears to have in mind is the mermaid in Hans Andersen's story, who has always had a strange fascination for him, and whom he confuses with his sister at this point in his confession. Thus once again the accusation looks like a scruple expanded to monstrous proportions by the onset of insanity. And the third charge is equally unrelated to the reality of the novel. Leverkühn's nephew has died at an early age from a horrifying attack of meningitis. This, Leverkühn believes, was a direct outcome of his pact with the devil, who had put venom in his eyes, so that when he gazed lovingly on the boy he unwittingly became the agent of the disease which destroyed him. At this point, no one is likely to feel that this is properly a confession of extreme sinfulness. On the contrary, one is moved rather by the horrifying self-torture of a diseased mind. Leverkühn, one feels, needs to believe himself guilty, whether he is so or not, in order that the very proviso he has made may be fulfilled. For only by fulfilling this proviso can he reach the 'truly theological path to salvation'. More and more strongly comes the feeling that this is a man who may believe himself extremely sinful, but who has in fact led a comparatively blameless life.

With this, of course, the paradox of Leverkühn's proviso is reduced to meaninglessness. If what was meant by sinfulness was not sinful deeds but a subjective conviction of having sinned, whether or not this bore any relation to facts, then no more was affirmed than that a man of blameless life who thought he had done wrong would be saved nevertheless. The paradox becomes a tautology. It did not, however, seem to be presented as one. It looked as though Leverkühn by his pact were being portrayed as a parallel to the evil-doing of the Nazis, as though in some way he were an explanation of what they had done. Later in the novel, the German people are in fact said to have entered on a pact with the devil, and it will be seen that yet further parallels are to be drawn between Leverkühn and them. In portraying Leverkühn, however, Mann has had recourse to his customarily ambiguous technique. A situation is outlined which might be described, though remotely, as evil. At the same time so little definition is provided that an entirely different interpretation is equally possible. This, in a story professedly dealing with diabolical matters, cannot be expected to sustain interest. Mann withdraws here as always from the definite statement, and as he veers away from perfect beauty in *Der Tod in Venedig*, so he veers away here from absolute evil.

Leverkühn's inward life, seen almost entirely through accounts of his music, is lived in terms of a similar ambiguity. It is, however, an ambiguity which does seem to lead, in his final work, to a single, unitive absolute, and to explore the way in which this comes about must be the preoccupation of the next few pages. Unfortunately, whatever may be said in words, these are after all verbal accounts of music, not the realization of music itself, as indeed they could not be unless the novel were issued with an accompanying album of gramophone records. It is taken for granted that the 'meaning' of music can be alternatively expressed in words, so that what is in fact received by the reader is Zeitblom's philosophical interpretation, not the mysterious communications of musical sound. As a result, there is once again not reality—not the reality of witnessing a composition through the ear—but the interpolation of the narrator's speculative point of view. The reader can no more hear for himself what Leverkühn's music was like than he can see the events of his life: both are screened first by Zeitblom. Granted, however, this mode of narration, what emerges from the music is what might be expected. In the oratorio 'Apocalipsis', for example, there seems to be confirmation of Leverkühn's own paradox. Believing (yet not believing) that the extreme, proud, unrepentant, yet contrite sinner is on the right path to salvation, he writes a work which contains both a diabolical chorus and a serene choir of angelic children. They are as different as could well be imagined: the first a 'sardonic gaudy of Gehenna', fifty bars of swelling laughter, screeching, howling and neighing, 'a salvo of the mocking and triumphant laughter of Hell'; the second a piece from the music of the spheres, 'icy, clear, glassily transparent, astringently dissonant, it is true, but full of what I might call a distant, strange, unearthly loveliness of sound, filling the heart with hopeless longing'.[11] Yet Zeitblom notices with a fascinated horror that 'in musical substance' the two sections of the work are identical. The angelic chorus is in an entirely different rhythm, played by entirely different instruments, yet the notes of which it is composed are the same, and follow one another in the same order, as in the laughter of Hell ('zwar völlig uminstrumentiert und umrhythmisiert; aber in dem...Engelsgetön ist *keine Note*, die nicht, streng korrespondierend, auch in dem Höllengelächter vorkäme').[12] It may seem strange to describe the mere sequence of notes as musical substance, without regard to rhythm, phrasing, instrumentation, dynamics. It is rather like speaking of two sentences as identical in substance because the words in them have exactly the same sounds.[13] One is more inclined to say that they are substantially different and only superficially alike. Moreover, the implication within the context of the novel, that here a unity in duality exists, suggests a certain contrivedness. However, Zeitblom affirms that for those who had ears to hear, this identity could not only be seen in the score but heard in the performance. Within the novel you can only take his word for it.[14]

This 'substantial identity of the most blissful with the most hideous', this 'inward oneness of the choir of angelic children with the laughter of hell',[15] is preliminary to the realization of Leverkühn's final work, the cantata, 'Lament of Dr Faustus', in which the combination of opposites 'becomes universal'.[16] Here, in the cantata, Leverkühn takes over from the original 'Volksbuch' certain words of the dying Faust, and gives to them a melody, composed of all twelve notes of the chromatic scale and thus itself all-inclusive, which forms the basis of the whole composition. The words are 'For I die as a wicked and a good Christian', and thus themselves express a paradoxical combination. The melody, meanwhile, with its pervasiveness 'creates the identity of extreme multiplicity—that identity which operates between the crystalline angel-choir and the howls of hell in the "Apocalypse"'.[17] In this work, however, there is no such contrived identity as there is in the earlier one, if indeed an identity can be spoken of at all in either. On the contrary, it is from first to last a work of lament, a deliberate counterpart to Beethoven's Ode to Joy, and a determined refusal to accept the 'lie', that the world is a blessed creation of God.[18] There is not, however, as might be expected, any hellish laughter on the part of Faust, any laughter which is mysteriously united in substance with the song of angels. On the contrary, there is only Faust's despair and lament over a world which does not fulfil the perfection due to its divine origin—and this is far from being a matter of diabolical concern. The terms of reference have, as in the 'Joseph' novels, subtly shifted. Hellish delight at imperfection, and triumphant mockery over it, have become confused with Faust's desperate lament that the world is not perfect as it ought to be. Zeitblom, suggesting that the ambiguity of the 'Apocalipsis' carries over into the cantata, makes it impossible to appreciate the later work adequately even through his ears, for his own abstract account contradicts the details as he narrates them. His own purpose, clearly enough, is to indicate the unity of opposites and persuade the reader of its existence in both works. Yet the cantata as he describes it is evidently of a different nature. Here the Leverkühn who perhaps took on the disease of the prostitute out of compassion, not the man who evilly contracted syphilis for its creative gifts, is in the foreground: the figure of Faust in the musical work represents this aspect of the composer. For Zeitblom, there is no clear distinction: it is all, vaguely, a pact with the devil, and thus equally vaguely identical with blessedness. In short, Zeitblom himself is inclined to accept the paradox of Leverkühn's proviso in the pact, and to persuade the reader of its value.

While the 'Lament of Dr Faustus' thus contains no identity of opposites, it does end on a note which almost permits of hope. There is, Zeitblom says, to the very end no comfort, no reconciliation, no possibility of transfiguration. Nevertheless, in its very hopelessness, there is perhaps a budding hope, if only as the barest suggestion:

Hört nur den Schluß, hört ihn mit mir: Eine Instrumentengruppe nach der anderen tritt zurück, und was übrig bleibt, womit das Werk verklingt, ist das hohe g eines Cello, das letzte Wort, der letzte verschwebende Laut, im pianissimo-Fermate langsam vergehend. Dann ist nichts mehr, — Schweigen und Nacht. Aber der nachschwingend im Schweigen hängende Ton, der nicht mehr ist, dem nur die Seele noch nachlauscht, und der Ausklang der Trauer war, ist es nicht mehr, wandelt den Sinn, steht als ein Licht in der Nacht.*19

Here there is not identity but change, not reconciliation but something like the mystery of tragedy. From hopelessness comes hope: there is no similarity between the two, though the one could not be known without the other. The idea of a substantial identity is clearly impossible, yet Zeitblom's account continues to speak as though Leverkühn's life and music were still under the sign of the paradox. Zeitblom cannot approve Leverkühn: his feeling towards him is ambivalently one of love and hatred, and

* Listen to the end, listen to it with me: one section of instruments after another withdraws, and all that remains, the last note of the work, is the top G of a 'cello, the final word, the last hovering sound, slowly dying away in a sustained pianissimo. Then there is no more—silence and night. But the note that hangs vibrating in the silence, the note that no longer exists, which only the soul goes on hearing, that echo of mourning mourns no more, changes its meaning, stands like a light in the darkness!

he would have preferred, he says, not to hear the dreadful identity of hideousness and bliss. Yet he cannot deny the admiration he feels for a man greater than himself in his probing of heights and depths, nor can he rid himself, despite his own account of Leverkühn's 'Lament', of the feeling of a unity of the opposites. In his description of Leverkühn's physical appearance in his final years of sanity, he finds something Christlike ('etwas Vergeistigt-Leidendes, ja Christushaftes').[20] Yet at the same time, he speaks of a habit of rolling the eyeballs in a frightening way, so that a suggestion of diabolical intensity lies not far off. In the light of the 'Apocalypse' music, it is easy to suppose that here too some kind of identity is implied. And indeed the whole scene of Leverkühn's final speech, with its suggestion of a 'Pietà' at the end, seems bent on bringing the reader to feel that here is an extreme sinner who is at one and the same moment a saint. The paradox of von Aschenbach, 'iniquitous yet holy', is repeated once more. Leverkühn accuses himself of murder and incest, charges in which Zeitblom apparently believes; he affirms that it was the desire for fame (not compassion with human suffering, which for his part he does not mention) that drove him to make his pact; he makes no repentance, but claims that the spirit of his times compelled him to lead the life he has led, and dies with just such a cry of lament as that which ends the Faust-cantata. Yet by the terms of his proviso, this very pride in the magnitude of his sin—he despises and envies moderate sinners, ordinary men—is the prerequisite of salvation. By his obduracy in proud contrition, if his proviso means anything at all, he does nevertheless ensure his place among the saints. And Zeitblom does what he can to suggest that the paradox does emerge triumphant.

There remain, within the novel, the last links to be forged with the history of Germany in Leverkühn's era. This has already been prepared in the documentation of his earlier life, and in the chronological sequence of dates. Born in 1885, Leverkühn enters on his pact towards the end of the Wilhelmine Empire, eight years before the outbreak of the First World War. He becomes insane in 1930, the year in which the strength of the Nazi party first showed itself in the elections. He dies in 1940, on 25 August, when the Nazi conquest of western Europe was complete. Throughout the novel, Zeitblom has interspersed reports of what has happened in Germany since that time, of the mounting pressure that is bringing her to her knees, and at length, writing in 1944 after the landings in Normandy, he looks back in a final paragraph to the situation at the time of Leverkühn's death:

Deutschland, die Wangen hektisch gerötet, taumelte dazumal auf der Höhe wüster Triumphe, im Begriffe, die Welt zu gewinnen kraft des einen Vertrages, den es zu halten gesonnen war, und den es mit seinem Blute gezeichnet hatte. Heute stürzt es, von Dämonen umschlungen, über einem Auge die Hand und mit dem andern ins Grauen starrend, hinab von Verzweiflung zu Verzweiflung. Wann wird es des Schlundes Grund erreichen? Wann wird aus letzter Hoffnungslosigkeit, ein Wunder, das über den Glauben geht, das Licht der Hoffnung tagen? Ein einsamer Mann faltet seine Hände und spricht: Gott sei euerer armen Seele gnädig, mein Freund, mein Vaterland.*[21]

The phrasing here is identical in places with that used by Zeitblom in writing of the conclusion of Leverkühn's 'Lament'. He had spoken there of a hope beyond hopelessness, a miracle transcending faith, expressed through or beyond the last note of the 'cello, and he now allows his own story, the novel *Doktor Faustus*, to end in the same way. The parallelism is maintained to the end, as if to imply that the pact made by Leverkühn were aligned with that made by Germany—and at the same time to imply that both pacts might end in a miraculous new uprising, that both were the truly theological path to salvation.

The implications of this are absurd or horrible. If they are not taken as meant, the parallelism in the novel can only be regarded

---

* Germany, its cheeks in a hectic flush, was swashbuckling at that time at the height of its savage triumphs, on the point of conquering the world by virtue of the one pact that it was minded to keep, and which it had signed with its blood. Today it plunges down, surrounded by demons and with a hand over one eye as it stares with the other into shuddering horror, down from despair to despair. When will it reach the bottom of the abyss? When will there dawn, from this utter hopelessness, a miracle transcending faith, the light of hope? A lonely man joins his hands together and says: God be merciful to your poor soul, my friend, my Fatherland.

as fortuitous: the two 'pacts' are then not to be seen as related at all, and there was no particular point in referring to them both by the same name. Yet if they are taken seriously, with Germany cast in the role of Faust, as everything in the novel seems to imply, a vast national perversion tends to be seen as an ambiguous saintliness. And the roots of these implications can be traced at least as far back as *Der Tod in Venedig*.

The confusion of *Doktor Faustus* derives from the fact that Zeitblom operates always with a dual conception of Leverkühn. There is the man who makes no pact, who consorts with the prostitute out of compassion, and who falsely accuses himself of monstrous crimes; and there is the man who somehow does make a pact, who contracts syphilis in order to achieve fame, and commits murder and incest. Neither of these comes to life in described action, both remain possibilities on which Zeitblom can speculate. Equally, he operates with a dual conception of morality. He condemns evil in the strongest terms, especially the evil committed by Nazi Germany; at other times he suggests, as Mann himself was always prone to do, that evil and good are indistinguishable, or that the one is the proper path to pursue in order to attain the other. To use his own words: 'Belief in absolute values, illusory though it be, seems to me a condition of life.'[22] He feels it necessary to condemn evil as though holding by an absolute distinction between it and good, but he feels at the same time that such a distinction is mere illusion from the standpoint of a Whole which is committed to neither good nor evil. In this way it comes about that a book which seems to be written in condemnation of a whole tradition—the tradition in which Mann stood, and which is here interpreted as leading to disaster—can also be read as providing a seeming justification for the same tradition. A more oppressive conclusion, for Germans and non-Germans alike, to a work by so prominent and as some have thought so representative a figure, can scarcely be imagined.

PART III

RILKE

CHAPTER XI

RILKE'S POETRY

Mehr nicht sollst du wissen als die Stele
und im reinen Stein das milde Bild
beinah heiter, nur so leicht, als fehle
ihr die Mühe, die auf Erden gilt.

Mehr nicht sollst du fühlen als die reine
Richtung im unendlichen Entzug —
ach, vielleicht das Kaltsein jener Steine,
die sie manchmal abends trug.

Aber sonst sei dir die Tröstung teuer,
die du im Gewöhntesten erkennst.
Wind ist Trost, und Tröstung ist das Feuer.

Hier- und Dortsein, dich ergreife beides
seltsam ohne Unterschied. Du trennst
sonst das Weißsein von dem Weiß des Kleides.*

After the war, Rilke retired to almost complete isolation in the château of Muzot, waiting for the time when he would be able to write again. It was not until February 1922 that the moment came, in a sudden burst of inspiration that brought with it not only a large part[1] of the *Duino Elegies* but also the whole of the *Sonnets to Orpheus*, all within a few weeks. This sonnet was written at that time, but was not included among the Orpheus sonnets, though it is in harmony with them in thought and mood.

* No more is yours to know than this one stela, and in its pure stone the kindly form, almost serenely gay, and yet so slender as though ignoring the toil that counts on earth for all.

No more is yours to feel than the pure direction in the infinite withdrawal—alas, and perhaps the coldness of those stones that at evening sometimes went with it.

But also let the comforting be dear to you, that you find in most accustomed things. Wind is comfort, comforting's in fire.

Existence here or beyond, let both enfold you strangely and without distinc tion. Else you will separate the whiteness from the white of the garment.

It may be, then, that the one here was not wholly satisfactory to Rilke, and a closer reading may indicate more than a likelihood of this; it may be also that, by comparison, the nature of his greater achievements will stand out more clearly.

This is not a poem that yields its sense quickly, but then that is true of many of the Orpheus sonnets. The words have acquired overtones of meaning, sometimes specialized uses, from the remainder of Rilke's poetry, and to come upon them for the first time, apart from this wider context, is almost baffling. The stela itself, in the first quatrain, has a special, intimate significance in Rilke's experience, recalled by the lines from one of the Elegies:

> Erstaunte euch nicht auf attischen Stelen die Vorsicht
> menschlicher Geste? war nicht Liebe und Abschied
> so leicht auf die Schultern gelegt, als wär es aus anderm
> Stoffe gemacht als bei uns? Gedenkt euch der Hände,
> wie sie drucklos beruhen, obwohl in den Torsen die Kraft steht.
> Diese Beherrschten wußten damit: so weit sind wirs,
> *dieses* ist unser, uns *so* zu berühren; stärker
> stemmen die Götter uns an. Doch dies ist Sache der Götter.*
>
> (2nd *Duino Elegy*)

The delicate restraint of this carving is 'das milde Bild' in the poem, and the gesture portrayed by it is in accord with the sense of the sonnet as a whole. This combination of love and leave-taking, strength and gentleness, the control which permits a touch but withholds an embrace, is one theme of the poem, briefly brought to mind by the first image.[2] It is reinforced by the word 'rein', a favourite one, which Rilke often uses in a sense closely connected with this. To be 'rein', 'pure', is to exist in a replete sufficiency, unneeding, self-contained, effortless; it is to be so much in unity with oneself that any unity that might be

---

* On Attic stelae, did not the circumspection
  of human gesture amaze you? Were not love and farewell
  so lightly laid upon shoulders, they seemed to be made
  of other stuff than with us? Oh, think of the hands,
  how they rest without pressure, though power is there in the torsos.
  The wisdom of those self-masters was this: hitherto it's us;
  ours is to touch one another like this; the gods
  may press more strongly upon us. But that is the gods' affair.

gained from association with others can be dispensed with.3 The 'pure' stone here is as replete as are the gestures of the human beings carved on it. To know this image and this stone is thus all that there is to 'know' (in a very wide sense), it is the 'thing in itself'. Yet—the form of the first line suggests this—there is something not wholly satisfying in this knowledge. 'No more is yours to know...': a limit is both affirmed and a little regretted.

The regret becomes stronger in the second quatrain. There is no more to be felt than the 'pure direction'—again the word recurs—of an 'infinite withdrawal'. Here again favourite words are used. The sense of 'direction' here can be better understood by comparison with a phrase Rilke had used much earlier: 'God is only a direction of love, not love's object.' The primary sense is again one of unity rather than duality. The love of God is meant here solely as a subjective, not as an objective emotion; it is immanent, not transcendent, and recalls Spinoza's saying that God is a circle whose centre is everywhere and whose circumference is nowhere. There is no object of love here, no circumference, only radiating directions of love, all of which God is. Thus 'pure direction', in the sonnet, is the self-contained emotion which goes out from the subject yet always remains the subject, and never is aimed at any external being. It is not direction towards anything, but simply movement. Movement, moreover, 'im unendlichen Entzug', where 'Entzug' means withdrawal, regression. Whatever might seem to be the goal of the direction is constantly being withdrawn, in an infinite recession that never allows attainment: the direction is everlasting, as is the pursuit on the frieze of Keats's Grecian Urn, but not static as it is there—the movement itself continues infinitely. The thought becomes more complex still, however, when you note that the direction is 'in' the withdrawal. Here Rilke is already thinking in terms of the words he uses at the end of the sonnet, letting 'here' and 'there' seize hold of him without distinction. The direction is 'here', it is the subjective movement of the poet, without object, and pure. The withdrawal, however, is 'there', it is the movement away which makes his own movement infinite.

With the word 'in', Rilke brings both these movements together, or attempts to do so, for to envisage a direction which is in any sense within that which recedes from it baffles imagination. In fact the comfort which might be had from that 'in', the feeling that some relationship could exist between the living and the dead, lover and beloved, beholder and beheld, is scarcely noticed in the sweep of the lines. Regret predominates in them, as is seen in the thought that follows. At most there is the coldness of the stones, this may be felt; these stones may be borne along at times with the pure direction, and there may at least be some sense of contact, if not with them, yet with one of their qualities.

The first eight lines are concerned, then, with the thought expressed by the first Elegy in the words 'Ach, wen vermögen / wir denn zu brauchen?' Whom or what can we use, with whom can we make contact? Neither angels nor men, is the reply in the Elegy: we are isolated individuals seeking to interpret the world, and by that very act of interpretation increasing our isolation from it. Only the brute creation, another Elegy goes on to say, sees the world without interpreting and thereby maintains unity with it. For us there is only some tree or some habit to which we have grown accustomed, and these, it seems, are not enough. In the opening of the sonnet, there is both regret at the isolation and a certain welcoming of it. In the remaining tercets, however, another side is given. There is comfort in all things, even in those we are most accustomed to see and meet; there is comfort also in wind, which, as the first Elegy says, sweeps past our features consuming them and destroying our identity, and there is comforting in fire. This is all to be valued, for, as the last tercet declares, it is only by accepting, being willing to be seized by both 'existence here' and 'existence there', that things come truly alive. Just as Rilke's Angels are often unaware whether they are among the living or among the dead, and as his Orpheus has knowledge of both the underworld and the living earth, so in this poem he speaks of experiencing both what is close at hand, the things of ordinary everyday life, and what is distant and remote, the 'pure direction', the almost mystical detachment. Not to do this, the last line adds, is to separate the quality from the thing. Like a medieval scholastic, Rilke contrasts now the quality of being white, 'Weißsein', something like the idea of whiteness, with the white of a particular garment, but only in order to bring them together again. Existing 'there', in the region of ideas, and 'here', in the region of matter, at one and the same time, he restores the synthesis which idealist philosophers were prone to lose: the white garment becomes vividly white again, not a mere reflection of a supernal whiteness.

The quatrains and the first tercet thus stand in contrast with one another, setting the pure isolation against the familiar intimacy of daily intercourse; the last tercet asserts that both must be allowed to work together without distinction. Yet on closer examination the contrast and the synthesis are seen to exist within the separate parts: knowledge of the stela *is* given—the intimacy is there already; and the pure direction is 'in' the regression from it. As in the Taoist symbol of the universe, a unity-in-duality exists throughout the whole. It is possible to know the thing-in-itself and yet remain distant from it and in isolation, for as Schopenhauer said, 'we *are* the thing-in-itself'.

The sonnet is characteristic of Rilke's philosophical outlook not only in his maturity, but from his earliest years. It is, however, almost a private note, comprehensible to the writer as a reminder, and to others in so far as they are acquainted with him, but not primarily a communication. What is gained from reading it, moreover, is not dependent on its poetic form. A philosophical statement, helped out by metaphor, would serve almost equally well. There are, it is true, many features that stamp this as a poem by Rilke. The frequent alliterations and assonances, the curious enjambements that let the thought hover at the end of a line and lend at first glance a mysterious significance to the first word in the line that follows, are among these. But here they do not, as they do in other poems, contribute to the statement more than a certain solemnity. Sometimes indeed the poetic form seems to add an obscurity: the 'white of the garment' comes rather surprisingly in the last line, and is perhaps a result of the need to rhyme. The philosophical content also stands out crudely against the imagery. A poem that includes in its first line a beautiful word like 'Stele' passes with difficulty to such conceptual expressions as 'Kaltsein', 'Hier- und Dortsein', 'Weißsein'— and 'Entzug'. Nor are the abstractions given any form of imagery that brings them to life. The 'pure direction' is said to 'bear' stones at evening-time, but becomes thereby so much the more difficult to comprehend. Image and thought are linked in only a strained and contorted fashion.

It is not so with one of the poems written in the same month which Rilke did include among the *Sonnets to Orpheus*:

> O Brunnen-Mund, du gebender, du Mund,
> der unerschöpflich Eines, Reines spricht, —
> du, vor des Wassers fließendem Gesicht,
> marmorne Maske. Und im Hintergrund
>
> der Aquädukte Herkunft. Weither an
> Gräbern vorbei, vom Hang des Appenins
> tragen sie dir dein Sagen zu, das dann
> am schwarzen Altern deines Kinns
>
> vorüberfällt in das Gefäß davor.
> Dies ist das schlafend hingelegte Ohr,
> das Marmorohr, in das du immer sprichst.
>
> Ein Ohr der Erde. Nur mit sich allein
> redet sie also. Schiebt ein Krug sich ein,
> so scheint es ihr, daß du sie unterbrichst.*

> *   O fountain mouth, you mouth that can respond
> so inexhaustibly to all who ask
> with one, pure, single saying. Marble mask
> before the water's flowing face. Beyond,
>
> the aqueducts' long derivation. Past
> the tombs, from where the Apennines begin,
> they bring your saying to you, which at last,
> over the grizzled age of your dark chin,
>
> falls to the waiting basin, crystal-clear;
> falls to the slumbering recumbent ear,
> the marble ear, with which you still confer.
>
> One of earth's ears. With her own lonely mood
> she thus converses. Let a jug intrude,
> she'll only think you've interrupted her.

232

The sense of this is not wholly different from that of the other poem, despite the gap between them. Here once again is that idea, which Rilke never tired of evolving in new forms, of the repleteness of things. The fountain-mouth speaks continually one thing, one pure thing—the word 'rein' has the same sense of unity and self-sufficiency as it had before. The water which is this speech flows continually from the mouth to the sleeping ear of the fountain-basin, passing thence back into the cycle and sustaining the eternal converse of the earth with itself. To this idea, shared with the cruder poem, are added features that link it more firmly with the Orpheus legend as Rilke interprets it within the whole collection. The mouth suggests a face, a marble mask, perhaps even a carved representation. The mosses or dark streaks below it dimly suggest a venerable figure, they become 'the black ageing of thy chin'. When many of the sonnets treat of the speech of poets, and of Orpheus himself as the supreme poet, the ideal who becomes metamorphosed now in this man, now in that, it is not hard to see here an image of some poet of antiquity and indeed of all poets. The 'Sagen' of the fountain-mouth becomes linked with the true poetry of which Rilke has spoken earlier:

> In Wahrheit singen, ist ein andrer Hauch.
> Ein Hauch um nichts. Ein Wehn im Gott. Ein Wind.*
>
> (I, iii)

It is incommunicable, existent for itself alone, or within the God alone (which is not to say something essentially different). It has come also, as the song of Orpheus has come, past and from knowledge of the realm of the dead. 'Weither an / Gräbern vorbei...'—the image is drawn in perhaps a little arbitrarily, though it still seems apt: this speech comes past the graves, as the water does down the slope of the Apennines sometimes through ancient sarcophagi which are used as conduits. And again in the image of the sleeping ear, Rilke harks back to a familiar idea of

* Far other is the breath of real singing.
An aimless breath. A stirring in the god. A breeze.

233

both *Sonnets* and *Elegies*: that of the spirit receptive to the message
that comes from complete attentiveness to silence:

> Stimmen, Stimmen. Höre, mein Herz, wie sonst nur
> Heilige hörten: daß sie der riesige Ruf
> aufhob vom Boden; sie aber knieten,
> Unmögliche, weiter und achtetens nicht:
> *So* waren sie hörend. Nicht, daß du *Gottes* ertrügest
> die Stimme, bei weitem. Aber das Wehende höre,
> die ununterbrochene Nachricht, die aus Stille sich bildet.*
>
> (1st Elegy)

This unbroken discourse is heard by the ear that lies passively
sleeping beneath the one, 'pure' speech coming from above it.
The whole poem, or almost the whole, is a realization in visual
terms of the outlook conveyed philosophically in 'No more is
yours to know...'.

It is, however, a realization, not an abstract statement. The
detailed aspects of the fountain, though they need the context of
all the Sonnets to reveal their fuller implications, are used naturally
and without distortion. Similarly, the diction plays its part, and is
not decorative only. The internal rhyme here of 'Eines, Reines' is
not vapid as the assonance tends to be in 'im reinen Stein das
milde Bild'. It bodies forth the uninterrupted, only minutely
varying sound of the water. It also serves to associate the two
words meaningfully, linking unity with purity, one-ness with
repleteness. The carrying over of the sense between the first and
second quatrains, hovering on 'im Hintergrund', brings in the
massiveness of the aqueducts with power. That between the fifth
and sixth lines soars out with the words' literal meaning to
the distant sources whence the water flows. From the fourth line
('Und im Hintergrund...') the sense has been carried strongly

---

* Voices, voices. Hearken, my heart, as only
saints have done: till it seemed the gigantic call
must lift them aloft; yet they went impossibly
on with their kneeling, in undistracted attention:
so inherently hearers. Not that you could endure
the voice of God—far from it. But hark to the suspiration,
the uninterrupted news that grows out of silence.

along, as in a steady channelled course, and now, with 'Voruberfällt in das Gefäß davor' it tumbles into the first tercet with the sound and movement of the water's own fall. 'Vorüberfällt' comes at the beginning of a tercet which forms as it were a new receptacle for this falling. The poem begins with passionate admiration and sinks to a quiet repose all of which is guided and formed by its rhythmic structure. It uses the body of the language, its physical feel, to convey meaning, as well as the bare definition of words in isolation.

The thought expressed is not, however, quite the same as in the more abstract poem. There is an image of self-enclosing unity which corresponds well, but the final lines introduce a new thought.

> Schiebt ein Krug sich ein,
> so scheint es ihr, daß du sie unterbrichst.

The converse of earth with itself is incommunicable to others, it remains mystery, and although the outline of the mystery can be drawn, it can never be entered into. Interposing a jug interrupts the flow, alters the speech. The poem thus lacks that intricate involvement of abstractions, where 'here' and 'there' inter-mingle, the 'direction' is in the 'withdrawal', and opposites are distinguished only to be reconciled in the same breath. There before you are the fountain and its basin with their continual cycle, distinct and separate, and the jug that brings the cycle momen-tarily to a halt. The physical realities do not permit the ambiguities which were achievable by words alone. Only at one point in these final lines do the ambiguities begin to emerge, in the words, 'so scheint es ihr'; and this is puzzling. To say that it merely 'seems' to the earth that her discourse is interrupted looks a little dis-ingenuous, as though Rilke intended to suggest that a possibility of deception remains. The interruption seems to take place, but the flow continues undisturbed nevertheless—some such thought as that is vaguely suggested. It would accord well with Rilke's philosophical outlook to make such an interpretation. And yet to do so is to go against one's knowledge of the way things behave, to suppose a purely metaphysically continued flow such as Rilke would have rejected at other times, as being out of accordance with the nature of 'things'. The word 'scheint' is imposed on the poem. Jugs do catch water, with all that the word implies in terms of the living spirit.

The reasons for the inclusion of the one, and the exclusion of the other of these two poems can then be readily understood on grounds of technique only. The two also show, however, the deepest preoccupations of Rilke's thought and the difficulty of conveying them in poetry. Rilke stands quite clearly in the tradition of Schopenhauer and Nietzsche, so far as philosophy is concerned. Though he seldom admires cruelty and barbarity as Nietzsche did, his whole temperament being gentle even to the point of languour at times, he works within the same framework of thought where opposites coalesce and divide again within a unity that subsumes them all. As a poet, meanwhile, he was also concerned to find the concrete image of reality which should express his thought without imposing a merely subjective vision. Writing in 1907 of his earlier work, he accused himself of just this form of solipsism: 'It was not Nature I saw, but the visions she suggested to me.'4 From Rodin, whose secretary he was for a time, he learnt to pay closer attention to things, 'Dinge', a word which he was to use more and more frequently. He learned, or attempted to learn, to restrict himself to the sayable, writing of Rodin's sculpture: 'His art was not built up on a great Idea, but on a small, conscientious realization [Verwirklichung], on what could be achieved, on a technical ability. There was no arrogance in him.'5 And this was also one of the conclusions he reached in the *Duino Elegies*, when he contrasted the activity of the human poet, representative of all mankind, with the super-human awareness of the Angel, at home in both realms:

> Preise dem Engel die Welt, nicht die unsägliche, *ihm*
> kannst du nicht großtun mit herrlich Erfühltem;...
> sag ihm die Dinge. Er wird staunender stehen.*
>
> (9th *Duino Elegy*)

> *   Praise this world to the Angel, not the untellable: you
>   can't impress him with the splendour you've felt;...
>   tell him *things*. He'll stand more astonished.

But this human, distinguishing, interpreting mode of writing was always in conflict with Rilke's sense of a transcending unity in which all differentiation disappeared. The kind of poetry which holds back from 'the unsayable' is at variance with the kind described in the Sonnets as 'An aimless breath. A stirring in the god. A breeze'. Rilke's own mystical experience of identity with living and dead Nature outside himself urged him to attempt direct expression of the mystery, unsayable as it was, and at the risk of mere arrogance in the display of 'herrlich Erfühltes'. As he wrote in the poem, 'Ausgesetzt auf den Bergen des Herzens', this meant passing beyond words: it was the climbing of a mountain, leaving far below 'the last village of words...the last farmstead of feelings'. Yet in poetry words still had to be used, and the attempt to make them serve his purpose in saying even the unsayable was the main occupation of Rilke's later years.

So long as the words remained abstractions, this remained a possibility. Rilke could convey the ambiguities inherent in his way of thinking with comparative ease. His poem 'An Hölderlin', interpreting the work of a poet who had greatly influenced Rilke's own writing, and seeing in it just that wholeness in incompletion which Rilke himself admired, begins with a line that sets the tone for the remainder:

> Verweilung, auch am Vertrautesten nicht,
> ist uns gegeben.*

'Verweilung', with its overtones of Faust's 'Verweile doch, du bist so schön', is the possibility of remaining at home in the world, content with things, finding a relationship with them. 'Das Vertrauteste', the most intimate, recalls 'das Gewöhnteste', the most accustomed, in the first poem discussed above: Rilke is thinking once again of the comfort to be had from the things of daily life. Whereas before, however, he had called this comfort dear, and naturally granted to men, here he denies it. There is no staying to be had, even with the things we know best. Yet the

---

*   Tarrying, not even with what is most close to us,
is granted to us.

grammatical structure reveals the fuller sense. The 'not' is contained in the parenthesis, 'auch am Vertrautesten nicht'; the main clause enveloping it reads 'Verweilung...ist uns gegeben'. Much as Joyce wrote sentences containing several layers of sometimes contradictory meaning, Rilke here both affirms and denies that 'sojourning with things' is granted to us.

Similarly, in the poem just quoted, 'Ausgesetzt auf den Bergen des Herzens', he makes a play on words which seems to bring two opposites into unity. The whole of this poem is concerned with the exposure of utter isolation: in the ascent of the mountain there is conveyed a sense of the mystic's dereliction, his confrontation of a summit in his experience that meets him with sheer denial. He is exposed, here on the 'mountains of the heart'. Yet, it has been suggested, the last line conveys also an idea of protection.[6]

> Und der große geborgene Vogel
> kreist um der Gipfel reine Verweigerung. — Aber
> ungeborgen, hier auf den Bergen des Herzens.*

The bird circling round the peak is protected, 'geborgen': it has that unity with Nature which Rilke found in all the brute creation. The man endowed with reflective consciousness, however, has not this unity, he is exposed, unprotected, 'ungeborgen', and the poem concludes with the refrain that comes four times in all in just over a dozen lines: 'here on the mountains of the heart'. Yet it occurs this time with a slight difference: where before it had read 'exposed on the mountains...', it now reads 'unprotected here on the mountains...'. The new verb is perhaps intentionally linked by sound and derivation with the word that follows. 'Bergen', the verb, is the infinitive from which 'geborgen' derives and the whole line may perhaps now have an ambiguous ring: 'ungeborgen, hier auf den Bergen des Herzens'— there is protection, 'bergen', even in these mountains of complete exposure. Is the pun intended? It has an unpleasing triviality or distortedness about it. Yet it does suggest, by a verbal conceit,

---

* And the great bird, secure, circles about the summits' pure refusal.—But insecure, here on the heart's mountains.

238

something that Rilke had expressed much earlier in lengthier form in the poem 'Herbst':

> Wir alle fallen. Diese Hand da fällt.
> Und sieh dir andre an. Es ist in allen.
>
> Und doch ist Einer, welcher dieses Fallen
> unendlich sanft in seinen Händen hält.*

The dreaded experience of falling, comparable to the exposure which forms the subject-matter of the later poem, is accepted with the sense of a comforting presence: it is a fall, yet God gently sustains it in its downward rush, there is protection in it. It is true that the sustaining hands must be falling too, so that ultimately there is nothing but fall, and the sustaining does not really sustain. The thought is, however, very typical of Rilke, forming the conclusion of the last *Duino Elegy*, and it may well have given rise also to the pun on 'bergen'. Or, to take a further instance of this use of words, there is the word 'brauchen' in the First Elegy. 'Ach, wen vermögen / wir denn zu brauchen?' is the question with which Rilke introduces the dilemma that the Elegies set out to solve. Whom can we use, with whom can we stand in a mutual relationship, are we condemned to the isolation of selfhood, or is contact possible? This would seem to be the sense implied, as Rilke's best English translator also takes it: 'Alas, who is there / we can make use of?' Yet 'brauchen' does not primarily have this meaning; it is 'gebrauchen' that means 'to use', while 'brauchen' more often means 'to need', and there is no regular metre here which might have required the dropping of a syllable. The word Rilke chooses thus has a double sense: needing, passive receptivity, subjective lack on the one hand; using, active intervention, objective acquisition on the other. His mind continually furnishes instances of such twofold usage, whether in single words, in rhymes, rhythms, or other technical devices of poetry. In the lines immediately preceding these, he achieves much the same effect through assonance alone. Since

---

* We are all falling. See, my hand here falls. And look at others. It's in every one. And yet there's One who holds this falling infinitely gently in his hands.

contact with angels is impossible, he writes here, the yearning for them must be restrained:

> Und so verhalt ich mich denn und verschlucke den Lockruf
> dunkelen Schluchzens.

The cry uttered to the Angel is held back, the sobbing is stifled. Yet the English translation cannot give the full sense of the German:

> And so I repress myself, and swallow the call-note
> of depth-dark sobbings.

The relationship of 'swallow' and 'sobbings' does not have the intimate closeness of sound in 'verschlucke' and 'Schluchzens'. In the original, the sorrow continues despite the attempted stifling, the sound of the one is still heard in the other. Or again, in a passage where Rilke speaks of the protection afforded by a mother to her child, he writes:

> Wo, ach, hin sind die Jahre, da du ihm einfach
> mit der schlanken Gestalt wallendes Chaos vertratst?

—which is correctly translated 'where are the years when you barred the way for him...to the surging abyss?' The mother shields the child from knowledge of the chaotic world that lurks beneath adult consciousness. Yet the word chosen to convey this meaning, 'vertratst', means not only to bar the way, but to 'represent': to 'stand for' as well as to 'stand in the way of', and indeed 'to represent' is the more usual sense. The mother both protects and becomes for the child the very image of his fears. By countless devices like these, some trivial, some within the sphere of genuine poetic technique, Rilke conveys the sense of a duality in unity.

It is in the applications of the concrete imagery that the sense most often breaks down. So long as abstract statements alone are made, it is possible to have the impression of understanding. 'Verweilung...ist uns gegeben' sounds like a paradox, to be understood much in the same way as the saying of Heraclitus, 'we step and do not step into the same river'. The pun on 'bergen', far-fetched if meant at all, can similarly be grasped intellectually. But the intellect cannot understand fully, standing alone. As Rilke was well aware, the physical, sensual impressions play a part in understanding, particularly in poetry: 'Denn auch der Leib ist leibhaft erst im Geiste'[7] ('For the body itself is bodily only in the spirit'). Comprehension must come not only through speculation but through things; Rilke sought, as he described Ibsen as seeking, 'equivalents for his inward vision', and these equivalents had to correspond with the external world of Nature, they could not be merely the subjective visions Nature suggested to him. When he turns to things, however, to express the ambiguities of his philosophy, they will not serve his whole purpose. They will express a part of it, as the 'Brunnen-Mund' sonnet does, but not the whole complexity that he strives after. Thus in the First Elegy he looks for a simile to convey the sense of love as he wished it to be understood, love from which 'everything transitive has been removed',[8] having no object and existing 'purely' in self-sufficiency. An intransitive love, which is not of someone or something, but directed rather at nothing, 'auf Nichts zu', is indeed impossibly hard to imagine; a concrete image might well provide a clue. It is given in these lines:

> Sollen nicht endlich uns diese ältesten Schmerzen
> fruchtbarer werden? Ist es nicht Zeit, daß wir liebend
> uns vom Geliebten befrein und es bebend bestehn:
> wie der Pfeil die Sehne besteht, um gesammelt im Absprung
> *mehr* zu sein als er selbst. Denn Bleiben ist nirgends.*

The thought, paradoxical in itself, is linked with the image only in a paradoxical way that does not illuminate either. The ideal expressed is that of a love which remains loving while yet being

---

* Ought not these oldest sufferings of ours to be yielding
 more fruit by now? Is it not time that, in loving,
 we freed ourselves from the loved one, and, quivering, endured:
 as the arrow endures the string, to become, in the gathering out-leap,
 something more than itself? For staying is nowhere.

entirely detached from the beloved. It is an emotion that needs no reciprocity, as Gaspara Stampa or Marianna Alcoforado, women whom Rilke deeply admired, had no need for their own love to be returned to them. And this separation from the lover is to be endured, 'quiveringly', as being a means of spiritual enhancement. To be alone and detached like this is to be like the arrow flying magnificently through the air, 'more than itself'. Or so the sense seems to run. Looking again, however, you see that the comparison is not between the isolation of the lover and the flying arrow; the simile is of the arrow while it still remains on the bowstring:

> ...und es bebend bestehn,
> wie der Pfeil die Sehne besteht....

The quivering tension felt by the lover in separation from his beloved is compared with the trembling of the arrow against the taut bowstring, with which it is in the closest possible contact. Only after the arrow is released, and this trembling has ceased, does it present an image related to the thought of isolation that Rilke has in mind. The simile offers in illumination of the thought the exact opposite of what the thought seemed to express. One may ask whether to speak of a transferred epithet here would not be to go counter to Rilke's paradoxical intention.

Words unattached to things can be used in such a way as to suggest a dual sense in one sound. Words referring to things are limited by our experience of physical behaviour: we cannot imagine an arrow which is simultaneously on the bowstring and flying through the air, and such an imagining is perhaps only possible for the Angel as Rilke conceived him. The image used here is not, however, a fortuitous choice. Similar images recur quite frequently in the later verse. In the Second Elegy, where the definition of the Angel is given more fully, a passage reads:

> ... — Pollen der blühenden Gottheit,
> Gelenke des Lichtes, Gänge, Treppen, Throne,
> Räume aus Wesen, Schilde aus Wonne, Tumulte

stürmisch entzückten Gefühls und plötzlich, einzeln,
Spiegel, die die entströmte eigene Schönheit
wiederschöpfen zurück in das eigene Antlitz.*

The movement of these lines in itself suggests a certain dual aspect of the Angels: they are both ecstatic, tumultuous manifestations of the Godhead, and silent, contemplative beings whose whole glory lies in themselves. The image of the last two lines, moreover, repeats an idea expressed much earlier in the *Stundenbuch*, that of a beauty which passes out from the creator only to return to him. The song of the poet, Rilke had written there, was not truly his, but God's, who seeks to come to fuller knowledge of himself from them:

> Er schweigt hinterm bebenden Barte,
> er möchte sich wiedergewinnen
> aus seinen Melodien.
> Da komm ich zu seinen Knien:
>
> und seine Lieder rinnen
> rauschend zurück in ihn.†

In Schopenhauerian terms, the Will comes to self-knowledge by becoming an object to itself, and this is true both of the individual and of the cosmic Will as a whole. God hears from the poet his own melodies; 'his' songs, not the poet's—or only the poet's in so far as he is aware of his own godlikeness—are the flow which returns to its source. As in the sonnet on the fountain, this cycle is closed to all external interposing; true song is 'A stirring in the god. A breeze'. So in the Elegy also, the beauty of the Angels streams out from them to return again to their own countenances,

---

*   . . . —pollen of blossoming godhead,
hinges of light, corridors, stairways, thrones,
spaces of being, shields of felicity, tumults
of stormily-rapturous feeling, and suddenly, separate,
mirrors, drawing up their own
outstreamed beauty into their faces again.
† He is silent behind his quivering beard; he would like to regain himself out of his melodies. Then I come to his knees, and his melodies run swirling back into him.

and their repleteness is so great that Rilke asks, a little later, whether any part of our human nature can ever be joined with it:

Fangen die Engel
wirklich nur Ihriges auf, ihnen Entströmtes,
oder ist manchmal, wie aus Versehen, ein wenig
unseres Wesens dabei?*

The image with which Rilke supplies this thought must seem, however, inapposite. '*Spiegel*, die die entströmte eigene Schönheit...': mirrors do not give out and receive back, just the opposite. Only by reversing the nature of mirrors as we are acquainted with them does the image coincide with the thought.9 Once again, Rilke seems obliged to do violence to the external world of things, to compel them to serve the purposes of his 'great Idea'. In speaking of Rodin, he had admired the art which began not with the Idea but with the tiny detail of observed reality. Here, he is so purposeful in his expounding that reality is ignored. Striving for an understanding of Rilke, one may imagine him to have meant that all angels are like identical mirrors reflecting one another: each reflects the beauty that is in fact its own since all are one. The lines do not clearly have this meaning, but perhaps the best comment on it, if it were intended, would be that of Yeats, in his partly ironical contemplation of Oriental religions:

Empty eyeballs knew
That knowledge increases unreality, that
Mirror on mirror mirrored is all the show.

('The Statues')

The image lacks that central source of light or being which would make the reflections more than a continual void.

One last instance from the Elegies, again from the opening lines of the First, to indicate the cleavage between idea and visual representation. To the questions, whom can we make use of,

* Do the angels really
only catch up what is theirs, what has streamed from them, or at times,
as though through an oversight, is a little of our
existence in it as well?

244

with whom can we have contact, comes the answer, 'at most a tree, or a street, or some habitual action'—and the night, the dreaded time when our sense of personal, separate identity may be annihilated. We may attach ourselves to this experience and savour all its 'gently disappointing' terror. Is it then easier, the thought continues, for lovers to bear the knowledge of this destruction? It is not; lovers merely hide from one another their fate, each offering to the other a momentary masking of the void that awaits them both. 'Ach, sie verdecken sich nur miteinander ihr Los.' ('Alas, with each other they merely conceal their lot.') Then, as though in impatience with himself at his own blindness, Rilke breaks out into lines that conclude the opening section with an apparent solution:

> Weißt du's *noch* nicht? Wirf aus den Armen die Leere
> zu den Räumen hinzu, die wir atmen; vielleicht daß die Vögel
> die erweiterte Luft fühlen mit innigerm Flug.*

It is not enough merely to love intransitively, without object, embracing emptiness. The emptiness itself must be cast away, the last sacrifice made, so that it is no longer possible to speak even of an embrace. The space once occupied by the loved one joins with all other space, becomes part of the air which we breathe in-differently, no longer conscious of any personal claims on any part of it. Yet at the same time this casting away of emptiness is said perhaps to expand the air, so that birds may feel its pressure more intimately beneath their wings: our loss may be their gain. Once more the physical implications of the image become impossible to follow. One might understand how the air became expanded by the addition of some new entity to it, increasing its density and making its presence more felt; one cannot understand how this might come about through the addition of emptiness. The loss is easily appreciated, as so often in Rilke's verse: the suggestion of a gain, however, passes into confusion and dark-

---

* Don't you know *yet?*—Fling the emptiness out of your arms
into the spaces we breathe—maybe that the birds
will feel the extended air in more fervent flight.

ness. It is not so much that the imagery breaks down here: rather, Rilke uses words without relevance to the physical connotations they normally have.

The difficulties, and sometimes even the limitations of Rilke's verse result from the attempt at saying the unsayable. By this I do not mean that what he attempts to say is of course true, but not conveyable in words. Nor do I mean that his poetry is comparable to that of the 'symbolistes' in their quest of the absolute. I mean instead something closer to what Wittgenstein expressed in the words, 'There is indeed the inexpressible. This *shows* itself; it is the mystical'.[10] The poetry of Mallarmé sought to *show* the inexpressible and so also does Rilke's on occasions. But on other occasions, Rilke's also attempts to say, by means of paradoxes, puns, assonances and so forth, what the inexpressible is. And when he finds images for it, these prove to be in contradiction with reality, forcing it to assume an unwonted shape for the sake of the philosophy to be expressed. One has the impression then that the philosophy, like the Angels themselves, is self-contained, and can make no use of objects in the external world, or only in so far as they can be radically altered into conformity with it.

This arises from the ultimately unitary, 'eindeutig' nature of much of Rilke's thought, which attempts to fuse opposites into a single whole. For while these fusions can be followed intellectually, as one follows the logical pattern of a pun, without supposing it to have any profound sense, they cannot be followed in relationship to physical objects. There the attempted fusion divides again, and Rilke is seen to be at home not in 'both realms' ('beide Bereiche', to quote the First Elegy) but in one only, that of the mind. 'The body 'does not become truly 'bodily', 'leibhaftig', there, but is remoulded into a nature foreign to its own. On the other hand, when Rilke is content to let the mystery exist, as he is in the fountain-sonnet, these contradictions do not arise. His verse gains 'body', it is no longer 'ein Wehn im Gott', or not in such a way that it can be seen to be so. Rather, it stands outside the mystery, recognizing it but not identical with it.

CHAPTER XII

RILKE AND MYSTICISM

'Ay' and 'no' too was no good divinity.

King Lear

Rilke's thought stands not only in the tradition of Schopenhauer and Nietzsche, but also in that of the mystics. From almost his earliest writing onwards, the mystical element is clear. When he writes in the *Stundenbuch*:

> Was wirst du tun, Gott, wenn ich sterbe?
> Ich bin dein Krug (wenn ich zerscherbe?)
> Ich bin dein Trank (wenn ich verderbe?)
> Bin dein Gewand und dein Gewerbe,
> mit mir verlierst du deinen Sinn,*

he echoes one of the most famous lines of the seventeenth-century mystic, Angelus Silesius, in *Der cherubinische Wandersmann*:

> Ich weiß, daß ohne mich Gott nicht ein Nu kann leben,
> Werd ich zu nicht, er muß von Not den Geist aufgeben.†[1]

This bringing together of God and man, making each dependent on the other, is in tune with much mystical speculation for centuries past. In some of its forms, it makes of the Incarnation not a unique event in history, but one which recurs in every age with every individual. In these forms, the immanence of God in man is stressed, at the expense of all notion of God's transcendence. The contrast between human and divine, which men imagine they perceive, is an illusion, removable only by the

---

*   What will you do, God, if I die?
        I am your jug (if I should break?)
        I am your drink (if I should spoil?)
        I am your garment, and your trade,
        With me you lose your meaning.

†   I know that God cannot live an instant
        If I become naught, he needs must give up the ghost.

complete annihilation of any sense of personal identity and differentiation.

Not all mystics, however, speak alike. Despite the impression given by Mr Aldous Huxley of a 'perennial philosophy' whose content is identical in almost all parts of the world, and has been expressed by mystics of every race and time, there are essential differences. There are those mystics whose experience can be called theistic, and there are those for whom it is more apt to speak of a 'natural mystical experience', or a 'pan-en-henic' one. For the latter, Nature and God are in effect identical terms. The All is one, and one is the All; there is no perception of a reality transcending the 'hen kai pan', nor is any sought after. The experience of oneness with the whole of Nature, had by so many, is held to be equivalent to the greatest experience that can possibly be had. Moreover, this experience commonly leads to the kind of philosophizing of which so much can be found in the German literature of the last two centuries. As Professor Zaehner, to whom I am indebted for these distinctions, writes,

The nature mystic identifies himself with the whole of Nature, and in his exalted moments sees himself as being one with Nature and as having passed beyond good and evil. This feeling of being beyond good and evil, which has always shocked Christians, is characteristic of the nature mystic; and were he not concerned with something quite other than the theistic mystic, his experience would indeed point to a non-moral God who would thus be, like Nature itself, neither good nor evil, but beyond and indifferent to both.[2]

The Nietzschean trend is clearly recognizable in these words, and indeed it goes back far beyond Nietzsche to the German Romantics, and in a certain degree to Goethe himself. The pan-en-henic experience has various effects: it may lend a certain strength and solidity, or it may have a quite opposite result. To quote Professor Zaehner again:

though we may be prepared to concede for the time being that this experience, this blissful realization of all things in oneself, may be what the Zen Buddhists understand by 'enlightenment', and though it may lead to an integration of the personality as it appears to have done in the case of Proust, it may equally result in a complete breakdown of all accepted values, in a total indifference to good and evil, in madness and schizophrenia.3

It is not too much to see this potential evil consequence in the history of Germany in recent times, leading as it did to the madness of Nazism.

The 'theistic' mystic apparently finds this repose in the natural world, this emptying oneself of all desire, even of love, either abhorrent or at best a possible step on the way to a greater knowledge. The difference between him and the 'nature' mystic can be illustrated from the terms which each uses. For the theistic mystic, the highest stage in his progress is not the sense of a god-like unity with the All, but the Beatific Vision. It is, then, not a permanent identity, but a state in which there is direct apperception of God: it is not merely nature transfigured, but awareness of the divine outside nature. The essential feature of this theistic mysticism is that it does not only transform the natural world, seeing it in a new way, but that it adds to this transformation a sense of the immeasurable infinitude of love beyond the world. It is, then, not only concerned with the world as we see it ordinarily, and as we may see it in a state of enlightenment, but also with an entirely new dimension of which we have no possible knowledge in any other state, enlightened or unenlightened. In T. S. Eliot's words from 'Burnt Norton':

> ...both a new world
> and the old made explicit, understood...

'Nature' mysticism may well give the sense of the old world, the world we know ordinarily, being understood. It never claims, however, to add to this knowledge that of the divine creator who is not merely in the world but exists to eternity, before and after his creation. This claim is made by theistic mysticism alone. And through this claim, a driving force enters into the theist's doctrine which is absent from that of pan-en-henism. For the latter, the end of the quest is always in sight, always thought of as achievable, if only in an ironical sense. In repose and emptiness the world may be allowed to roll on along its ambiguous path. Nothing new can be added to it save the awareness that it is as it is, and to have wisdom is to come to this awareness. For the former, there is no such terminus: 'how', as a Muslim mystic asked, 'could one ever come to the end of the Godhead?' Theistic mysticism pays a due respect to such words as infinity and eternity; it does not suppose that infinity can ever become finite, or realizable by finite minds, but preserves both the sense of distance and the ever-renewed endeavour that ensues from it. The possibility of growing in love always remains open, and the hubristic temptation to imagine the development as complete is countered. Whatever the vision, it is still not an unchanging identification: Mr Eliot's lines, which I quoted only fragmentarily, make this quite evident:

> . . . *Erhebung* without motion, concentration
> *Without elimination*, both a new world
> And the old made explicit, understood
> In the completion of its *partial* ecstasy,
> The resolution of its *partial* horror.
> Yet the enchainment of past and future
> Woven in the weakness of the changing body,
> *Protects mankind from heaven and damnation*
> Which flesh cannot endure.[4]

Neither extreme, heaven or damnation, is capable of being endured by human beings, and it is this sense of proportion that the theists preserve. Yet the theists are not all in one camp, do not all profess one religion. To quote Professor Zaehner once more, 'This is not a question of Christianity and Islam *versus* Hinduism and Buddhism: it is an unbridgeable gulf between all those who see God as incomparably greater than oneself, though He is, at the same time, the root and ground of one's being, and those who maintain that soul and God are one and the same and that all else is pure illusion'.[5] Both forms of mysticism are found in all the great religions.

Rilke's mystical experience finds its most complete expression in the *Sonnets* and *Elegies*, the outcome of that extraordinary flood of inspiration at Muzot in February 1922. Some of the implications and limitations of these have already been explored, and there will be a time to return to them again. Here, however, it is appropriate to speak not of the poetic embodyings of his experience, but of the experience itself which came to him in the garden of Schloß Duino, in 1912, and at another time in Capri. The accounts of these, which can be given only in excerpts here, are remarkable not only for their content, but also for a certain contrast between them. At Duino, the experience was above all one of detachment. It began, it is true, with a sense of intimate relationship. Reclining against the fork of a shrub-like tree, the feeling grew of being 'completely received into nature, in an almost unconscious contemplation':

Little by little his attention woke to a feeling he had never known: it was as though almost imperceptible vibrations were passing into him from the interior of the tree....It seemed to him that he had never before been filled with more gentle motions, his body was being somehow treated like a soul, and enabled to receive a degree of influence which, given the normal apparentness of one's physical conditions, really could not have been felt at all....Nevertheless, concerned as he always was to account to himself for precisely the most delicate impressions, he insistently asked himself what was happening to him then, and almost at once found an expression that satisfied him, saying to himself, that he had got to the other side of Nature....Everywhere and more and more regularly filled with this impulse that kept on recurring in strangely interior intervals, his body became indescribably touching to him and of no further use than to be cautiously present in, just as a ghost, already dwelling elsewhere, sadly enters what has once been tenderly laid aside, in order to belong once more, even though inattentively, to this once so indispensable world. Looking slowly round him, without otherwise changing his position, he recognized it all, recalled it, smiled at it with a kind of distant affection, let it be, like something much earlier that once, in circumstances long gone by, had had a share in his life...he was looking, over his shoulder, as it were, backwards at things, and that existence of theirs that was closed to him took on a bold, sweet after-taste, as though everything had been spiced with a trace of the blossom of parting.—Saying to himself from time to time that it could not last, he nevertheless had no fear about the cessation of this extraordinary condition, as though, just as from music, all that was to be expected from it was an infinitely legitimate close.[6]

The paradox of this mood, or perhaps only of Rilke's account, is that it gives at once a sense of being 'received into nature', and at the same time of being completely remote. Neither his own body, nor the bodies of things around him, are present in the usual sense: the one is belonged to inattentively, as a ghost might return to its past scenes, the others have an existence that is closed to him. He is outside, 'on the other side of Nature', not at one with it, but rather in that deathly state that Rilke describes in his verse:

> Freilich ist es seltsam, die Erde nicht mehr zu bewohnen,
> kaum erlernte Gebräuche nicht mehr zu üben,
> Rosen, und andern eigens versprechenden Dingen
> nicht die Bedeutung menschlicher Zukunft zu geben;
> das, was man war in unendlich ängstlichen Händen,
> nicht mehr zu sein, und selbst den eigenen Namen
> wegzulassen wie ein zerbrochenes Spielzeug.
> Seltsam, die Wünsche nicht weiter zu wünschen. Seltsam,
> alles, was sich bezog, so lose im Raume
> flattern zu sehen.*   (1st Elegy)

This experience has its parallel in the fountain-sonnet, in the respect that there, also, was an enclosed cycle impenetrable from outside. In the garden at Duino, Rilke had that sensation deeply, of being beyond and separate from the created world. Writing of his experience in Capri, however, he seems to take a different view, make a different interpretation. The extract from

---

*   True, it is strange to inhabit the earth no longer,
to use no longer customs scarcely acquired,
not to interpret roses, and other things
that promise so much, in terms of a human future;
to be no longer all that one used to be
in endlessly anxious hands, and to lay aside
even one's proper name like a broken toy.
Strange, not to go on wishing one's wishes. Strange,
to see all that was once relation so loosely fluttering
hither and thither in space.

his notebook which follows below, and may be regarded, Mr Leishman says, as an addition to the fragment7 that has just been quoted, having probably been written at the same time, reads thus:

Later, he thought he could recall certain moments in which the power of this one was already contained, as in a seed. He remembered that hour in that other southern garden (Capri), when, both outside and within him, the cry of a bird was correspondingly present, did not, so to speak, break upon the barriers of his body, but gathered inner and outer together into one uninterrupted space, in which, mysteriously protected, only one single spot of purest, deepest consciousness remained. That time he had shut his eyes, so as not to be disconcerted in so generous an experience by the contour of his body, and the infinite passed into him so intimately from every side, that he could believe he felt the light reposing of the already appearing stars within his breast.

It is notoriously difficult, as all mystics declare, to give any real notion of their experiences to those who have no knowledge of them, and it will not do to press too hard on these accounts. What may be observed, however, is that while Rilke apparently linked the two in his recollection, finding the seed of one in the other, the interpretations he makes are quite contrary to one another. At Duino there was separation, leave-taking, inattentive sojourning in a body to which he no longer belonged; other existences were closed to him. At Capri there was unity, birdsong and starlight were at once within and without, his body was no longer felt as an obstruction to the intermingling of all with all. For Rilke the two experiences were essentially related, the 'power of the one' was already in the other, and it is indeed easy to see how the almost complete loss of a sense of separate consciousness may bring about in the remaining glimmer of awareness a feeling of unity with all existences. Equally well, however, the same loss, with the same remaining glimmer, may give rise to a feeling of deathlike separation from all the manifold life of the created world. This is in fact the dilemma of nature mysticism and its fundamental ambiguity. When the envelopment of the natural world is conceived as nothing, as the Naught, the escape from selfhood leads not to the rapturous contemplation of the one eternal, as it does with theistic mystics, but either to a state best compared with a consciousness of death, or to a sense of identity with the universe, in which all distinctions vanish. The latter brings with it the sense of integration that may be greatly valuable to the soul; the former, however, can be terrifying, dreadful in its promise of total annihilation, and there is no means of choosing between the two. They interchange without the possibility of control by a directing mind, and either may emerge in the fore-front at any instant. For Rilke in the Duino garden the terror was not present: he speaks of a 'bold, sweet after-taste', not of a bitter one. Yet it was always capable of making its presence felt.

It may be that mystical experience is largely conditioned by the interpretation placed on it at the time. Certainly there is a remarkable general similarity among all accounts, and it is also remarkable how interpretations accord with the traditions in which the mystic has been reared. We should be astonished, for instance, to read of Christ appearing in a vision to a Muslim or Hindu mystic who had no knowledge of or concern with Christian beliefs. This need not mean, however, that interpretation is solely a subjective and relative matter. The question of interpretation may rather be resolved as other similar questions are, by testing the fruits, by rational inquiry, and by sympathetic imagining, courses which are as much open to the mystic himself as to others. The one vital quality must be complete fidelity to the experience, recognizing at what points, if any, interpretation does not cor-respond, and seeking to modify it so that it does. Where dark-nesses remain, they must be left as darknesses which an incomplete comprehension on the part of the interpreter makes necessary.

With Rilke, there are here two experiences which correspond closely with the general outline of his habits of thought as we know them to have existed at the time. His poetry had already for several years been occupied with very similar ideas of com-plete detachment from, and unity with the world as a whole, and it continued to be so up till the time of his death. We cannot know more of his mystical experience than his accounts, already interpreted by him, will allow: there is only, beside this, the outcome in his creative work, and this we must receive as we would any other work of literature, without dogmatic presuppositions or any other yardstick determining in advance what it ought to be. On the other hand, we need not remain with the bare statement that it is what it is; we can also compare it with other possible forms, as we have compared natural with theistic mysticism. This is, after all, the fundamental business of literary criticism, not to be only expository, but to consider what else has been achieved in a similar field, and to serve as a reminder of alternative qualities that may be preferred.

The difficulties of a non-dogmatic consideration are great, however. They involve a temporary neutrality, a suspension of disbelief, which is sometimes next to impossible to achieve. This is especially the case, in Rilke's verse, in those poems where he interprets the life of Christ in such terms as to run counter to the whole trend of interpretation for centuries past, various though it has been. One may decide, as T. S. Eliot did in comparing Dante and Goethe, to contrast the traditional element in the one with the more personal statement of the other. 'Goethe', T. S. Eliot once observed, 'always arouses in me a strong sentiment of disbelief in what he believes: Dante does not.' For Dante, writing within 'a coherent traditional system of dogma and morals like the Catholic, is not merely an individual propounding his own ideas'.[8] This argument will no longer serve in the case of Rilke's work. It stands not only in a coherent and traditional German system of thought, but in one much older than Catholicism, for it is closely linked with the religious beliefs of Buddhism. We can no longer today balance the traditions of Europe against those of the rest of the world and merely assert their superiority. We are compelled to consider all these possible modes of living with the fullest awareness that we can bring to bear.

Rilke's poems on the person of Christ, of which there are quite a number,[9] reinterpret the traditional accounts in such a way as to fashion them into illustrations of his own way of thought. The raising of Lazarus thus becomes not one of Christ's

255

mighty works, by which he made physically evident the new life
he had brought to men. It is undertaken reluctantly, in order to
show that the power is there, but with the feeling that it is an
outrage on Nature:

> Und da ging er hin, das Unerlaubte
> an der ruhigen Natur zu tun.*

For Nature is the whole, in which being dead or being alive is
a matter of indifference. The clamour of the crowd for a sign,
a miracle restoring Lazarus to life, fills the Christ of this poem
with repugnance and 'hostility in every limb'. The differentiation
which they make between death and life is for him pointless; like
Rilke's Angels, these are for him not different spheres but equally
part of the same whole:

> . . . — Aber Lebendige machen
> alle den Fehler, daß sie zu stark unterscheiden.
> Engel (sagt man) wüßten oft nicht, ob sie unter
> Lebenden gehn oder Toten.†   (1st Elegy)

Christ, Angels and Nature know nothing of these differences, and
it is only with extreme reluctance that he summons up his powers,
slowly raising his hand to summon Lazarus from the grave, as a
concession to human ignorance. At length, fearing that not the
one man, but all the dead will come pouring out, he allows his
outstretched hand to curl down like a claw, threatening all that
remain in the recesses of the tombs. Hostility, and determination
that the dead shall remain dead, are the chief motives of Christ as
Rilke portrays him at this point. Lazarus is risen, it is true, but
this is without further significance:

> und man sah: das ungenaue vage
> Leben nahm es wieder mit in Kauf.‡

---

* And then he went to perform on passive nature the impermissible.

†   Yes, but all of the living
make the mistake of drawing too sharp distinctions.
Angels (they say) are often unable to tell
whether they move among living or dead.

‡   And they saw: imprecise, vague life
swept it up along with itself again.

Christians may incline to call this a travesty. It is hard to see, however, how an undoctrinal literary criticism can be opposed to it. The poem is dramatic, vivid, the language runs with the thought, conveying an almost physical sense of the intensity of movement with which Christ acts. One might indeed ask whether there is any motive given at all for this display of miraculous power, whether the poem makes sense in that respect. And so far as can be seen, the answer is that Christ means to demonstrate his astonishing faculties to those who will not take him at his word: he manifests his superiority for the sake of manifesting it, in a way that the Christ of the Gospels was always careful to avoid. The point of the miracle is this self-glorification; its teaching is the reverse of what this Christ would presumably want people to believe on questions of life and death. But if that is what Rilke means to say, there is nothing purely literary to be urged against it.

The poem treating of Christ in the garden of Gethsemane presents him in a more traditional guise. Its purpose, however, is once again to pour scorn on those who seek to heal suffering or gain victory over death. Here Christ is one of those for whom Rilke's unity of life and death means nothing. He has sought for a god beyond creation and found none; now there is nothing to be found of God either in Nature, in other men, or in himself:

> Ich bin allein mit aller Menschen Gram,
> den ich durch Dich zu lindern unternahm,
> der Du nicht bist. O namenlose Scham....*

There is no answer, then, to Christ's agony. The tradition that an angel from heaven appeared, to strengthen him,[10] is dismissed as a fancy: all that came was the night, with the threat of annihilation that it commonly has in Rilke's verse. Nor was it a particularly remarkable night—'ach eine traurige, ach irgendeine'— for Christ had done nothing to magnify it. His attempt at assuaging human grief was a betrayal of human nature and

---

*   I am alone with all men's grief, which, through you,
        I proposed to assuage, you, who do not exist.
        O nameless shame....

nature in general: only the full perception of an unredeemable suffering could have made this night distinguished:

> Denn Engel kommen nicht zu solchen Betern,
> und Nächte werden nicht um solche groß.
> Die sich-Verlierenden läßt alles los,
> und sie sind preisgegeben von den Vätern
> und ausgeschloßen aus der Mütter Schoß.*

Angels for whom both life and death are of equal stature have no contact with the man who seeks the victory of one over the other. The night which might have become great through wholehearted acceptance of its eroding darkness, as one facet of the ambiguous whole, remains ordinary and untransfigured.

The remaining poems all deal, however, with a Rilkean Christ by whom this acceptance is made. The descent into hell is not, as it was formerly presented, a proclamation of victory to the 'spirits that are in prison'. The spirit of the crucified Christ is presented as released from the body, and seeking inactivity now that its suffering is complete:

> Sein entlassener Geist gedachte vielleicht in der Landschaft
> anzustehen, unhandelnd. Denn seiner Leidung Ereignis
> war noch genug.†

He reaches beyond himself to the sad fullness of things around him, and for a moment he seems content to remain so. But the call of Hell reaches him, demanding knowledge of his achievement:

> Er, Kenner der Martern, hörte die Hölle
> herheulend, begehrend Bewußtsein
> seiner vollendeten Not: daß über dem Ende der seinen
> (unendlichen) ihre, währende Pein erschrecke, ahne.‡

---

* For angels do not come to such as pray thus, nor do the nights achieve greatness through them. Those who yield all are yielded up by all, delivered up by their fathers and excluded from their mothers' wombs.

† His released spirit thought perhaps it might wait in the landscape, inactive. For the event of his suffering was full.

‡   He who knew torments already heard Hell howling,
    demanding awareness of his perfected, completed
    distress, that seeing the end of his own (unending)
    pain their own, still lasting, might feel terror, and guess.

Christ's suffering is complete—not 'swallowed up in victory', but at its furthermost limits, infinite though it is—and thus Hell too can glimpse the completion of its own suffering. The glimpse is not of eventual release or redemption, it is true: the sight of this final state is frightening even in Hell. Yet it is to show this completion that Christ sinks, with the whole weight of his exhaustion, into the depths. No greeting awaits him. He hurries past indifferent or astonished shades, glances hastily upward at Adam, and descends into yet wilder levels of tumult. From there, however, as though some yet further limit had been reached, from which there could be only a return and a reversal, he ascends again:

> ...Plötzlich (höher, höher) über der Mitte
> aufschäumender Schreie, auf dem langen
> Turm seines Duldens trat er hervor: ohne Atem,
> stand, ohne Geländer, Eigentümer der Schmerzen. Schwieg.*

Traditional conceptions of Christ may lead to a misreading here. This is not the ascent of a redeemer but rather of one who finds his fullest realization only in the deepest regions of hell.[11] Here he becomes for the first time the complete possessor of all suffering, and rises to dominate the scene by virtue of his endurance. There is no compassion here—this is what makes the poem Rilkean and eventually Nietzschean—nor is there any contact between Christ and these shades; there is only the showing forth of suffering at its furthermost limit, isolated and mute. And thus the way is prepared for the resurrection poem (written earlier), in which the risen Christ seeks to impart to Mary Magdalene some hint of his own replete self-enclosing.

It is the attributing of these motives and actions to Christ, however, which makes them appear untrue, not any inherent contradictoriness in them. Related of some other, they could bring home forcibly the experience of isolation and extreme

---

* Suddenly (higher, higher) over the middle of foaming shrieks,
on the long tower of his patience he emerged, breathless,
stood, with no railing, he the possessor of sufferings.
And was silent.

suffering. (I am thinking here mainly of 'Christi Höllenfahrt'.) Related of Christ they are inapposite both on account of their lack of compassion (the suffering of Rilke's Christ must be of some wholly different nature) and of their lack of faith. But then it is usual for poets to refashion history, or beliefs about historical facts, in such a way as to reveal some new mode of experience. Their concern, on such occasions, is not the historian's search for 'what really happened', but the forming of a new statement, utilizing those elements of history which prove amenable. So we have tended to regard the work of poets since Coleridge defined its function as pleasure-giving rather than truth-proclaiming. While this possibility remains, of regarding the name of Christ here as a superficial adjunct, not to be understood in the traditional way, the difficulties of Rilke's Christ-poems for Christians may disappear: no truth is intended to be conveyed, rather a new myth, with no necessary foundation in reality. So long as we are content to think that Rilke's purpose is fully expressed in this formulation, the poems may be received as we might receive the delineation of a character in a play. It soon becomes clear, however, that Rilke intends more than that. The poems express too closely his own philosophical-religious outlook to allow doubt on that score. They are not poetry only, in Coleridge's rather limiting and probably artificial sense, but poetry *and* a proclamation of prophetic import. As much as Blake, Rilke calls for assent as well as appreciation. And here one of the dilemmas of modern criticism shows itself plainly. We attempt on the one hand to give a purely literary appraisal, excluding all doctrinal considerations. On the other hand, a great deal of the literature we are concerned with—most of the literature of the past hundred years—actively propagates or implicitly derives from ethical and religious doctrines almost diametrically opposed to those of earlier European tradition. We do not feel ourselves allowed, by the rules we acknowledge, to make any purely doctrinal observations here, and are thus likely to be confined to fragmentary accounts of experiences, deprived of the opportunity to understand these as parts of one whole.

We may, however, inquire what purely literary pattern emerges from a work, and this is a method which may be applied, if not to these Christ-poems at this particular moment, to a rather larger and more far-reaching work, *Malte*, composed at about the same time. The thought and the mood conveyed by the Christ-poems is essentially one of a complete wholeness in self-containing isolation. Suffering is embraced, as it was by Nietzsche, as an inevitable part of the whole that is to be endured, and it becomes endurable through the replete nature of the self, desiring no reciprocity or contact. In other words, Rilke remains here within the natural world, in the sphere of nature mysticism, where the world remains unredeemed and can only be experienced at its full intensity of good and evil, suffering and joy. The 'old world' becomes explicit, understood, but there is no 'new world' standing beyond it. Here, however, a curious fact draws attention to itself. Nowhere does Rilke say that the Angels of the Duino Elegies, those most complete realizers of the unity of life and death, are divine or in any way truly comparable to God. They are 'pollen of blossoming Godhead', it is true, and so apparently share in some divine quality. Yet they are part of a hierarchy of spirits, it seems, of whom the highest may well be the 'Archangel', dangerous to behold, spoken of in the Second Elegy. And at one point, Rilke seems to distinguish the smooth, uninterrupted converse of angelic spirits with themselves from the voice of God who has created them:

> Nicht daß du Gottes ertrügest
> die Stimme, bei weitem. Aber das Wehende höre,
> die ununterbrochene Nachricht, die aus Stille sich bildet.*[12]

(1st Elegy)

It is as though Rilke were momentarily aware of a distinction between the purely life-and-death embracing ideal represented by the Angels, and a reality transcending them. Within the Christ-

---

*   Not that you could endure
the voice of God—far from it. But hark to the suspiration,
the uninterrupted news that grows out of silence.

poems this distinction is not even remotely present. It will be seen, however, in the wider framework of Rilke's prose work, *Malte Laurids Brigge*, that it recurs, and that Rilke's own view of the purport of his writing at this time was strangely hesitant and contradictory. It may well be that some sense of dissatisfaction that he had with the fruits of his seeking, finding no proper solution within the godless beliefs he tried to hold, showed itself in these momentary glimpses and hesitations. For his beliefs were godless in the sense that they were derived from the 'pan-en-henic' experience, an experience in which Hell and suffering are as much a part of the whole as anything else is, and in which there is no escape from the eternal recurrence.

CHAPTER XIII

MALTE LAURIDS BRIGGE;
THE DUINO ELEGIES

Die Aufzeichnungen des Malte Laurids Brigge, written between 1904 and 1910, is almost the equivalent of Rilke's diary during those years. The first quarter of the book is mainly a direct transcript of his diary-entries and letters; the young Danish poet Malte, whose reflections are recorded here, is a very thinly disguised portrayal of Rilke's own self. The form, which owes something to Goethe's *Werther*, owes more to Gide's *Cahiers d'André Walter* and the Norwegian Obstfelder's *Diary of a Priest*: it is the classic means of unfolding the innermost thoughts of the heart.

From the beginning, Malte is determined to reject no experience that comes to him, and in particular no experience of that overwhelming power, both within and outside himself, threatening his own and every other existence, which he calls 'das Große'. In fact he deliberately sets out to experience this power, believing, like Rilke himself, that he is one of those who are sent out, not in order to proclaim heaven to men, but 'to be among human kind, to see everything, to reject nothing, not one of the thousand transformations in which the uttermost extreme disguises and blackens and makes itself unrecognisable'.[1] And again like Rilke, he is one of those who 'go about with a desire to comprehend all things, and who (still not yet understanding) make the excessively great [das Übergroße] into an activity of the heart, that it may not destroy us'.[2] The greatness, or excessive greatness, of which Rilke speaks here is above all the fact of death and annihilation. Malte seeks it in the memories of his childhood, when his own shadow, cast by his bedside light, would loom up behind him, threatening him with extinction. He recalls it in the death of his grandfather, Kammerherr Brigge, 'the great death' whose immense dimensions were fully apparent to the old man, and which bore no relationship to those 'little deaths' experienced by men who regard their end with as little emotion as they do their life. He recalls also people he has seen on the streets, a man seized with a fit, as though 'the greatness' were bursting out of him and destroying him. There are also scenes from Malte's present life: his entry into a hospital, where the same childhood experience sweeps over him again; the day when he sees a wall horrifying in its ugliness, and feels the wall present with its horror as an aspect of himself. All this Malte describes with a vividness and sensitivity which, it seems, can only lead to madness. In fact, while Rilke was still writing the book, he observed to a friend that if it was ever completed it would be the account of a man for whom the trial of facing the greatness of suffering was too immense. For unlike Kafka, with whom some similarities will be noticed here, there is no question for Malte of this suffering ever being seen as good. He attempts rather to take the facts of death and suffering into himself without hope of release or victory or transformation: to make them into an 'activity of the heart' as they are an 'activity' of the external world, and thereby establish an identity between his own life and that of the whole.

In so far as there is progression in the *Notebooks*, it is towards a containing of these terrors, a living in equanimity with the certainty of extinction. Significantly, however, this comes about in association with a decreasing concern with Malte's day-to-day experiences and encounters, and his own personal memories. Towards the end of the first half of the book, and increasingly in the second half, the diary-entries refer to people and events of which Malte has no direct knowledge, and which evidently represent Rilke's own reflections on his reading at the time. The reality of the environment yields place to literary sources, and sections are now devoted to thoughts evoked by Michelet's *History of France*, by accounts of Cézanne, Beethoven, Ibsen, Sappho and others. The main impressions to be had from these are twofold. There are further reflections on men who are represented as having lived the same kind of life in the past as Malte is living now. There are also reflections on women whose lives present a kind of solution for his fears. These predominate more and more, and all point towards that ideal of repleteness which Rilke was later to stress as one aspect of the *Elegies* and *Sonnets*. The lives of women such as Gaspara Stampa, Marianna Alcoforado, Louïze Labé are all drawn upon for examples of a love which endures in spite of the complete absence and indifference of the lover. They are women who so little needed any return of their love that at length their isolation became their fulfilment: 'who did not desist until their torment was reversed into an austere, icy glory that could no longer be restrained'. It is this reversal of suffering into glory that Malte himself, near the end, seems to attain or foreshadow. The attainment of these women is the projected image of his own desired condition. Like Bettina von Arnim, the unrequited lover of Goethe, each of them 'spread out into the whole from the very beginning, as though she were past her death'; each of them 'lay down outstretched in Being, belonging to it, and whatever took place in her was eternal in all Nature'. They thus needed no requital, for like Rilke's Angels they were at one with the whole of Being, they had that 'stärkeres Dasein' that the Angels possessed, and lived on as though already in death.

With the last two sections of the book, Malte seems very close to the realization of a similar condition in himself. If the book has a pattern, it is one that leads towards this new development, whereby the suffering endured in the earlier part is taken up, 'reversed' into the austere glory of self-fulfilment. Once again, the reflections on which this discerning of a pattern might be based are concerned not with Malte's personal experiences, but rather with his reinterpretation of an old and long familiar story, the parable of the Prodigal Son. They are, then, not so much a realization of the new condition by Malte himself as an imaginative account of how the condition would reveal itself in another. These considerations put aside, however, there remains the essentially literary question, in what sense these final sections may be regarded as a climax, in what way they affect the structure of the work as a whole. That Rilke was disposed, on at least one occasion, to see a climax in the last pages, may reasonably be concluded from his letter to his publisher, written when the book was just completed: 'Poor Malte begins so deep in misery and reaches, if you want to be particular about it, as far as eternal bliss; he is a heart that spans a whole octave; after him very nearly every song is possible.'3 On this reading, the *Notebooks* reveal the progression through which Malte comes, like the Christ of Rilke's poems, to a complete possession of suffering, and thereby, on these terms, to perfect fulfilment.

The parable of the Prodigal, however, as Malte retells it, no longer has the import it has in the Gospels. It has an interpretation evidently influenced by André Gide's *Retour de l'Enfant Prodigue*, in which the prodigal comes home not to be received with love and feast-making, but to encourage his younger brother to do as he himself has done. Life in the wilderness, hazardous as it is, is preferred to the humdrum pleasures of conventional society. Malte's prodigal is conceived in similar terms, in so far as he also can find no share in the society to which he returns. His story is, Malte is persuaded, 'the legend of one . . . who did not wish to be loved'. He has learned during his absence to maintain the 'inner indifference of his heart', so that he acts now freely, in his own right, and is no longer beholden to the love which his relatives attempt to bestow on him. He has also learned 'never to love, so as never to bring another into the horrible situation of being loved'. For in the Nietzschean terms in which Rilke is surely writing here, to love is to express the will to power over another; it is a means of subduing the other to one's own desires, a form of that subtle 'Christian' undermining of the other which Nietzsche abhorred. The return of the prodigal is therefore described in these terms:

Those who have told the story usually try at this point to remind us of the house, as it used to be: for there only a little time has passed, a little recorded time, anyone in the house could tell you just how much. The dogs have grown old, but are still alive. Report has it that one of them set up a howl. The whole daily round is interrupted. Faces appear at the windows, faces grown old and matured, with a touching resemblance. And in one quite old face recognition suddenly pales through. Recognition? No more than that?—Forgiveness. Forgiveness of what?—Love. My God. Love.

He for his part had ceased to think of it, busy as he had been: to think that it could still exist. Understandably, of all that then ensued this alone was handed down by tradition: the gesture, the astonishing gesture, never before beheld, the gesture of entreaty with which he flung himself at their feet, imploring them not to love. Taken aback and hesitant they lifted him up into their arms. They interpreted his impetuous act in their own fashion, forgiving him. It must have been an indescribable liberation for him that all misunderstood him so, despite the desperate unambiguousness of his bearing. He probably felt able to stay. For he perceived more and more each day that the love of which they were so vain, and in which they gave each other such secret encouragement, had no concern with him. He was almost obliged to smile as they exerted themselves and made it the more clear, how little they meant it for him.

What did they know of him? He was terribly hard to love now, and he felt that One alone could still do so. But He did not wish to as yet.

In these sentences, concluding the *Notebooks*, Malte portrays through the reinterpretation something of himself. The prodigal has reached that state of total indifference in love, which is one of the ideals set out in the earlier part of the book. He does not need the offer of human contact made by his father's people; he has come to terms with his loneliness in a way unimaginable by them, he is complete within himself. In terms of the Nietzschean 'reversal of values', he has reached a summit of his experience, a state which Rilke describes as reaching as far as eternal bliss. On the other hand, in traditional terms Malte could hardly be worse placed than in this lack of contact with other men. A somewhat supercilious tone towards the 'bien pensant' well-wishers, a perverse pleasure at their misunderstanding, and a touch of smug self-praise are the qualities most likely to be seen from this older viewpoint. And apart from such contrasting interpretations, there must remain a sense of unease at this as a portrayal of bliss. It does not have the feeling of blissfulness about it, rather of a cold indifference stemming from a psychic defect, and on this account the *Notebooks* seem to end on an uncertain note.

This is, or can be, a purely literary question. The pattern of the *Notebooks* as a whole depends on the interpretation of this final passage: if it is a climax, the book will be seen progressing upwards towards it; if it is a final defeat the book trends 'downward' in that direction. Either way, Malte seems to have come to terms with suffering not so much by enduring it as by cutting himself off from contact with all others. But does Rilke present this as an ideal or as a deplored end? His own comments at different times, both while the book was being written and afterwards, are inconclusive, and in part this was due to his own uncertainty as to the extent to which Malte's life could be identified with his own. It has been seen how the earliest passages of the book are direct transcripts of some of Rilke's personal diary-entries and letters. By the time the book was finished, however, Rilke could speak of having diverged from his 'alter ego', much as Goethe had from Werther: Malte had 'developed into a figure, completely distinct from myself, which acquired a particular existence of its own and which interested me the more strongly, the more it differed from me'.4 By this account, Malte was a sheerly literary character through whom Rilke explored the possibilities of a situation, without committing himself to the ideas expressed. He did in fact intend, in the middle of writing the book, that Malte should die at the end,5 and had he done so, the work would have remained quite certainly a work of literature in which the consequences of a given course of life were followed through to their inevitable outcome. The question of an author's self-identification with his characters is, however, a delicate one. Rilke was decidedly more involved in Malte's explorations than his avowal of a distinction would lead one to suppose, even to the point of foreseeing his own early death: 'Sometimes it seems to me', he wrote of the book while still at work on it, 'that I could die, once it is finished.'6 And when it was in fact finished, he was to make clear, only a few months after his disclaimer, how much Malte's attitude had been his own all along: 'I am somewhat

horrified when I think of the high-handedness [die Gewaltsam-
keit] I have shown in Malte Laurids, how I had gone on with him
in a deliberately consistent despair [konsequente Verzweiflung]
till I was beyond everything, beyond even death in a sense, so
that nothing more was possible, not even dying.'7 This would
make of the *Notebooks* much more of a personal statement by
Rilke, a continued publication of what might still have gone into
his own private diaries, a non-fictional statement of views which
he held himself. At the same time, the passage reveals another
part of Rilke's self that stands opposed to what he has accomplished. He is a little horrified; he speaks of his own high-
handedness: he may well mean to imply that he was aware of
some falsity in the attitude represented by Malte, that he had in
some way done violence to the truth of life as he knew it to be.
Within a week of making this self-accusation, indeed, he uses
much stronger terms. 'As for myself, I breathe again whenever
I think that this book is in existence; it had to be, I was so
indescribably under obligation to write it, no question of choice.
But now I feel a little like Raskolnikov after the deed, I don't
know at all what is to come now, and I am even a little horrified
when I reflect that I have written this book; with what strength,
I ask myself, with what right, I might almost ask.'8 The suggestive
overtones of these final questions, the feeling of having been not
only high-handed but almost murderous, reveal Rilke's sense of an
evil deed accomplished. Far from having brought Malte to span
a whole octave between deepest misery and eternal bliss, he seems
to perceive here how Malte's final isolation and repleteness cuts
him off from all living contacts and is, like the isolation in suffering
of 'Christi Höllenfahrt', more akin to a state of damnation. His
attitude towards his own work in the year that it was completed
was thus ambiguous and vacillating, and it is not surprising if these
qualities are read out of the book itself. In later years, at Muzot in
fact when a new attitude began to make itself more intensely felt,
there were occasions when he was obliged to forbid young people
to read *Malte*. Its purport was too difficult to grasp, and only an
extremely careful reading would distil the true sense: 'For this

book, which seems to have its issue in the proof that life is impossible, must be read so to speak against the current. If it does contain bitter reproaches, they are not at all aimed at life. On the contrary, they are a statement that, for want of strength, through distractions and inherited misconceptions, we lose almost entirely the countless earthly riches that were intended for us.'9 In other words, the book must be read resistingly, not in sympathy with the views Malte expresses, but with a constant determination in the reader to maintain from his own resources an awareness of the 'earthly riches' that the book does little or nothing to foster. This too is of course a possible mode of reading, though the reader may be tempted to reply as Goethe did to an interlocutor, 'Don't tell me about your doubts, tell me about your beliefs. I have enough doubts of my own.' At the same time, to read in this fashion is to resist one of the ideals which Rilke was still proclaiming at Muzot, at the time when he wrote his corrective. The state of pure Being, hinted at in Malte's portrayal of Bettina von Arnim 'as though she were past her death', like Rilke's own experience of inhabiting his own body like a ghost, is that of Malte himself in the final pages, so far as one can judge, and it is also the state of the angelic beings as they are depicted in the First Duino Elegy.

The final lines of the *Notebooks* contain one further ambiguity. Hitherto, Malte has spoken of God as 'a direction of love, not love's object'; in tune with his own desire not to be loved, he has said 'no return of love need be feared from Him'. The love of God, as he conceives it, and as many Christian mystics have conceived it, is inspired with the purpose of schooling human beings to the point of exerting a godlike love themselves: 'quietly postponing the pleasure so that we, slowly learning, may give vent to our whole heart'. For in thus giving full vent to human aspirations, the 'direction of love' will be realized at its fullest intensity. The outcome of this belief, however, as it is seen in the final passage, looks more contemptuous than loving; if Malte does love these people it is quite intransitively. And the last two sentences of the book appear to recognize this inadequacy: 'He was terribly hard to love now, and he felt that One alone could still do so. But He did not wish to as yet.' In one sense, the words may be taken as indicating the final postponement of reciprocal love, as though Malte had expressed his aspirations so intensely that no return was needed, and it was no doubt this sense that Rilke had in mind when he spoke of Malte reaching to eternal bliss. On the other hand, the words also imply a love in the more usual, transitive sense of the word: one which can surmount even the greatest obstacles. As so often happens in the novels of Thomas Mann, there is reintroduced here at the end a meaning of the word 'love' which is quite unconnected with the meaning it has acquired during the course of the work. In so far as this second sense is taken, Malte appears as the deliberate self-excluder from love, the man who realizes in himself the state which some theologians have regarded as the self-imposed punishment of the unbeliever. The last words of all, 'But He did not wish to as yet', thus give a curiously vacillating quality to the ending. Malte must both welcome this seeming denial, since to do so must on his terms enhance his spiritual status, and at the same time fear it and long for it to come to an end. The 'as yet' betrays this yearning in its paradoxical intensity: like the sustained 'cello-note in Mann's *Doktor Faustus* it echoes on with a hope beyond hopelessness.

There does not seem to be any way out from this dilemma except in the abandonment of self-enclosing isolation as an ideal. The self-enclosing may have wide bounds; it may, as Rilke believed, establish a sense of enclosing far more than is normally meant by 'the self'; yet it leads inexorably back to acceptance of an un-redeemed world, not to the vision of a new earth. Since the world so accepted remains with its dualities, the acceptance itself remains ambiguous, and it is never really apparent whether it is acceptance or not:

> Wissen wirs, Freunde, wissen wirs nicht?
> Beides bildet die zögernde Stunde
> in dem menschlichen Angesicht.*
>
> (*Sonnets to Orpheus*, I, x)

* Knowing it or not, friends—which is our case?—
Both alike has the lingering hour
graved in the human face.

Within the compass of the 'zögernde Stunde', the lingering hour, it is true that this hesitancy must continue. Rilke's own vacillation between his two interpretations of *Malte Laurids Brigge* is integral to his outlook at this time. Nor does he abandon it later, although the *Sonnets to Orpheus* do introduce also an entirely new note. The consistent desperation of Malte did not bring with it the liberation Rilke hoped for. It did not prove immediately true that, as Rilke had said, 'after him very nearly every song is possible'.[10] Instead, two years later, the earliest parts of the *Duino Elegies* continued to express an ambiguous attitude that both looked for release and spurned it.

The opening lines of the Tenth Elegy, coming as they do almost at the end of the cycle, seem with their powerful rhythms to announce the resolution of the suffering that has formed the main theme of the whole. They were not, however, written at Muzot together with the *Sonnets* and a great part of the *Elegies*, but at Duino itself in 1912.[11] They thus continue very closely from the mood in which the final passage of the *Notebooks* was written in 1910. Yet the spirit of triumphant hope with which they begin does suggest the first signs of that 'reversal', *Umschlag*, into an austere glory that Malte had looked for earlier in the course of his meditations:

Daß ich dereinst, an dem Ausgang der grimmigen Einsicht,
Jubel und Ruhm aufsinge zustimmenden Engeln.
Daß von den klargeschlagenen Hämmern des Herzens
Keiner versage an weichen, zweifelnden oder
reißenden Saiten. Daß mich mein strömendes Antlitz
glänzender mache: daß das unscheinbare Weinen
blühe. O wie werdet ihr dann, Nächte, mir lieb sein,
gehärmte. Daß ich euch knieender nicht, untröstliche Schwestern,
hinnahm, nicht in euer gelöstes
Haar mich gelöster ergab. Wir, Vergeuder der Schmerzen.
Wie wir sie absehn voraus, in die traurige Dauer,
ob sie nicht enden vielleicht. Sie aber sind ja
unser winterwähriges Laub, unser dunkles Sinngrün,
eine der Zeiten des heimlichen Jahres —, nicht nur
Zeit —, sind Stelle, Siedelung, Lager, Boden, Wohnort.*

*   Translation on opposite page.

The triumphant note is not sustained; by the end, a quiet resignation has taken its place, concluding on a note of renewed and repeated sorrow. The contrast between the vigorous and excited sweep of the opening rhythms and the heavy tread of the final line marks the similar contrast in the sequence of thought. For, despite the hope of a final emergence so forcefully expressed in the first line, the expectation is slowly eroded as its proper implications come to be perceived. With the word 'Ausgang' Rilke suggests something like the image of the man in Plato's myth, standing at the entrance to the cave in which he has before seen nothing but the shadows of reality. The grim and terrible insight into the nature of things seems about to end here, to give place to a new mode of vision, and the triumphant note accords well with that. In the lines which follow, this impression continues: the truth of the vision is to be guaranteed by the clarity of the heart, by the absence of doubt, when every part is in tune, and the whole thus capable of sustaining the song of praise that is hammered out on it. This, too, remains vigorously emphatic; the enjambement from 'oder' to 'reißenden' swoops down on the offending thought of a possible hesitation in praise, and the continuing distant suggestion of a hexameter lends the memory of a tradition of strength in German verse. At once, however, a modification of the opening impression enters. 'Daß mich mein strömendes Antlitz / glänzender mache.' The figure

---

*   Some day, emerging at last from this terrifying vision,
may I burst into jubilant praise to assenting Angels!
May not one of the clear-struck keys of the heart
fail to respond through alighting on slack or doubtful
or rending strings! May a new-found splendour appear
in my streaming face! May inconspicuous Weeping
flower! How dear you will be to me then, you Nights
of Affliction! Oh, why did I not, inconsolable sisters,
more bendingly kneel to receive you, more loosely surrender
myself to your loosened hair? We wasters of sorrows!
How we stare away into sad endurance beyond them,
trying to foresee their end! Whereas they are nothing else
than our winter foliage, our sombre evergreen, *one*
of the seasons of our interior year,—not only
season—they're also place, settlement, camp, soil, dwelling.

of speech is introduced, whereby tears themselves make the countenance more radiant, as though their glistening in itself were the source of glory. Already the thought is moving away from 'emergence' towards quietistic acceptance of the terrifying insight, and away from jubilant praise towards a radiance that comes entirely from tears. At the same time, the rhythms become less vigorous and more fervent. The enjambements thrust forward the initial words of the lines in a movement of longing rather than one of decision:

> Daß mich mein strömendes Antlitz
> glänzender mache: daß das unscheinbare Weinen
> blühe. O wie werdet ihr dann, Nächte, mir lieb sein,
> gehärmte. Daß ich euch knieender nicht, untröstliche Schwestern,
> hinnahm....

The sense meanwhile is moving continually further from the idea of emergence. The 'nights', in the sense they have come to acquire from earlier passages in the *Elegies*, are the calm destroyers of men, consumers of their identity:

> O und die Nacht, die Nacht, wenn der Wind voller Weltraum
> uns am Angesicht zehrt —, wem bliebe sie nicht, die ersehnte,
> sanft enttäuschende,...*

(1st Elegy)

Still unable to bear with the complete loss that they impose, Rilke looks forward to a time when he will receive them more reverently, unconsoling as they are.[12] Here, for the first time fully, the thought shows its affinities with Nietzsche's. Comfort, consolation, 'Trost', is the name of the invidious reward, the external aid, which the self-enclosing can never permit. There can be no consolation, in fact no emergence from the grim vision, since the

---

* Oh, and there's Night, there's Night, when wind full of cosmic space
  feeds on our faces: for whom would she not remain,
  longed for, mild disenchantress, painfully there
  for the lonely heart to achieve?

vision endures continually. This the ensuing lines indicate, as they completely reverse the expectation of emergence:

> Wir, Vergeuder der Schmerzen.
> Wie wir sie absehn voraus, in die traurige Dauer,
> ob sie nicht enden vielleicht.

To look forward, as the first line seemed to do, to a time when the vision will come to an end, is now renounced, and the remainder continues on a quite different basis. The rhythm too has begun to drag, slowing towards the almost halting utterance of the last line.[13] We are at fault in seeking an end of sorrows, as Rilke was at fault in refusing the soft erosion of night. Sorrows are wasted thus. As the First Elegy had asked:

> Sollen nicht endlich uns diese ältesten Schmerzen
> fruchtbarer werden?*

There is further to go, before sorrow bears fruit, and the journey is not shortened by looking towards its end. At this point, however, the thought begins to waver uncertainly between the two poles so far made visible. Sorrows, the lines continue, are 'unser winterwähriges Laub, unser dunkeles Sinngrün'. With 'winterwährig'—winter-lasting—comes the thought that sorrows do end: there is spring after winter, and a season of blossoming. Equally, however, the word recalls that 'winter-foliage' is foliage that remains the year through, and this is reinforced by 'Sinngrün' (literally, the periwinkle flower), with its suggestion of 'Immergrün'. Sorrows are the evergreen leaves that never vanish so long as we remain in the world of the senses. The lines become filled with shifting meanings that constantly replace one another, hinting now at emergence, now at everlasting continuance, and this continues into the last two lines. Sorrows are '*one* of the seasons of our interior year': the first suggestion in 'winterwährig' is confirmed, and the reminder of spring is made. But then again, '—not only season'. The suggestion is withdrawn once more, and there follow only images of a permanence that lasts the year through. By this time, however, the initial trium-

---

* Ought not these oldest sufferings of ours to be yielding more fruit by now?

phant impulse is spent. Jubilation and praise, which went with the idea of emergence, have no place in this solemn confirmation of the enduring nature of sorrows, and the rhythms convey now an entirely contrasted mood.

These opening lines of the Elegy thus set the tone for the remainder, written at Muzot in 1922. Here the world is seen allegorically as the City of Pain, duly provided with its 'market of consolation', its closed and disappointed Church, its advertisements for the deceptively named, bitter beer known as 'Deathless'. All the comforts of the conventional world are rejected by the youth who passes, in the allegorical narrative, beyond these preserves of hypocrisy into the Land of Lament. In his own deathlessness (for he is already dead) there is no consolation but only the increasing intensity of pain, the awareness of a whole land once ruled by the Lords of Lament, forgotten now in the human striving for the wrong kind of happiness. With his guide, he comes at length to the foot of the hills, where the spring of Joy rises. But this is no turning-point. Joy may rise out of deep sorrow; it cannot be tasted by the youth, who must press on further still. The guide shows him the spring and names it with reverence, perhaps in awareness that its source is valid:

> In Ehrfurcht
> nennt sie sie, sagt: 'Bei den Menschen
> ist sie ein tragender Strom.'*

But while men may be borne along by it, ignorant of its origin, the youth can only mount higher still into the Mountains of Primal Pain. So the concluding lines of the Elegy and of the whole cycle return to an ambiguous happiness, to be found not in joy but in sorrow, and not springing from sorrow, but identical with it:

> Aber erweckten sie uns, die unendlich Toten, ein Gleichnis,
> siehe, sie zeigten vielleicht auf die Kätzchen der leeren
> Hasel, die hängenden, oder
> meinten den Regen, der fällt auf dunkles Erdreich im Frühjahr. —

> *   With awe
> she names it, says 'Among men
> it's a carrying stream.'

Und wir, die an *steigendes* Glück
denken, empfänden die Rührung,
die uns beinah bestürzt,
wenn ein Glückliches *fällt.**

The essential mood of 1922, as revealed by the *Elegies*, remains finally what it was in 1910, when *Malte* was completed. The bliss in isolation of the one is akin to the paradoxical happiness in sorrow of the other. The triumph fades away into an infinite death that still remains conscious of its own sorrow, and calls this sorrow by the name of its opposite. The contrast between this and the theistic mystic's vision of ultimate bliss shows Rilke's attachment to a stage in mystical progress less advanced than the extreme: it is as though he had determined to stop at some penultimate point in the dark night.

* And yet, were they waking a symbol within us, the endlessly dead,
  look, they'd be pointing, perhaps, to the catkins, hanging
  from empty hazels, or else they'd be meaning the rain
  that falls on the dark earth in the early Spring.

  And we, who have always thought
  of happiness climbing, would feel
  the emotion that almost startles
  when happiness falls.

CHAPTER XIV

THE SONNETS TO ORPHEUS

Rilke had looked forward, on completing *Malte*, to the new access of lyrical power that should come with this complete yielding of himself to thoughts of death. It did not come then, nor for many years to follow, and the *Elegies* continue the involvement with death still further. Yet the *Sonnets to Orpheus*, written at the same time as at least half of the *Elegies*, do reveal in part that lyrical rejoicing for which he had otherwise looked in vain. This was, perhaps, the reversal he had longed for, the emergence that had seemed at other times impossible. Yet, attractive as the thought may be, it is hard to reconcile with the fact that the allegory of the Land of Lament was written at the same time as some of the most lyrically resplendent poems among the *Sonnets*. If the reversal could come, could it not also lead Rilke through the Tenth Elegy in a way that would have sustained the note of triumph?

The *Sonnets* are in fact remarkably close to the *Elegies* in the framework of ideas that upholds them. The similarities between Orpheus and the Angels have often drawn attention, and they are so close that a cursory reading might overlook the differences that also exist. Like the Angels, Orpheus is equally at home in the realm of the living and of the dead. As the would-be liberator of Eurydice he has descended into the land of the shades, and Rilke takes over from ancient mythology the intuitive knowledge that he is 'own cousin to the dead'.[1] As the singer of human longings, he is also of this earth:

> Ist er ein Hiesiger? Nein, aus beiden
> Reichen erwuchs seine weite Natur.*　　　　　(I, vi)

*　　　　Does he belong here? No, his spreading nature
　　　　from either domain has sprung.

278

And in these lines can be heard an echo of those in the *Elegies*, where the nature of Angels is hinted at:

> Engel (sagt man) wüßten oft nicht, ob sie unter
> Lebenden gehn oder Toten. Die ewige Strömung
> reißt durch beide Bereiche alle Alter
> immer mit sich und übertönt sie in beiden.*

Yet in turning to the figure of Orpheus at all, Rilke at once brings in the influence of an established myth, with all the powerful aura of suggestiveness that myths have. Orpheus is not to be identified solely with the Angels of the *Elegies*; his nature will not permit of it. Almost insensibly, the trend of Rilke's thought and imagery changes. Orpheus is not, like the Angels, one of the 'early successes, favourites of fond Creation', nor does he share their aloofness from the human condition. He is a man, who has taken part in human destinies, and thus at once bridges across the gap that existed between men and the Angels. The self-enclosing cycle of their outgoing and return to themselves, in which human beings could have no part, is no longer apparent in him. Yet while Orpheus was a man—a hero or at most a semi-god in classical antiquity—he is, in Rilke's poems, also a god. Rilke both uses the elements in the legend that refer to his mortal existence, and speaks of him throughout as either 'ein Gott', or 'ein Göttlicher'. Whether Rilke conceived Orpheus to have been always a god, epiphanized for a span of mortal existence which his divine life had always preceded, is not apparent from the poems: it was not a point which concerned him. It is apparent, however, that Orpheus is still alive and present in men wherever there is song:

> Errichtet keinen Denkstein. Laßt die Rose
> nur jedes Jahr zu seinen Gunsten blühn.
> Denn Orpheus ists. Seine Metamorphose
> in dem und dem. Wir sollen uns nicht mühn

---

*   Angels (they say) are often unable to tell
whether they move among living or dead. The eternal
torrent whirls all the ages through either realm
for ever, and sounds above their voices in both.

um andre Namen. Ein für alle Male
ists Orpheus, wenn es singt. . . .*   (I, v)

The divine Orphic nature is still capable of being not merely
transmitted to men, but of being metamorphosed into human shape.
Where the Angel could only stand in amazement at the greatness of
human achievement, sung by the poet, Orpheus is himself the
poet's song. And with the song comes order and peace, again one
of the chief gifts to men of the god in the myth of antiquity.
Ancient Orphism, it has been said, came to establish a new religion
and transform the older religion of Dionysus. Where the Bacchic
rites had inspired ecstasies, orgies of delight, and the fervent sense
of identity with the godhead, Orphism informed them with 'the
spirit of music, order and peace'.[2] Thus it is that in Rilke's sonnets
Orpheus appears as 'der Ordnende': pursued by the fanatical
Maenads, followers of Dionysus, he has 'outsounded their cries
with order'. In this again, moreover, Orpheus stands contrasted
with the Angels. It would certainly be going too far to associate
these with the revellers of Dionysus, for they have none of the
Dionysian fury and savagery. They are, however, ecstatic beings
in whom something of the Dionysian is still apparent:

> Räume aus Wesen, Schilde aus Wonne, Tumulte
> stürmisch entzückten Gefühls.†   (2nd Elegy)

There is nothing tempestuous or tumultuous in the Orpheus
either of the *Sonnets* or of ancient myth. The mood of the *Sonnets*
is often joyful, but never violent, and it is as though Rilke,
moving himself from one ideal towards another, repeated the
historical movement which sought to take up the best in a former
religion and purify it in a more spiritual form.

* Raise no commemorating stone. The roses
shall blossom every summer for his sake.
For this is Orpheus. His metamorphosis
in this one and in that. We should not take
thought about other names. Once and for all,
it's Orpheus when there's song.

† spaces of being, shields of felicity, tumults
of stormily-rapturous feeling.

Taking Orpheus for his guide, then, Rilke begins to turn away from the Nietzschean, Schopenhauerian framework of belief that had inspired much of his earlier work. This is not to say that he abandoned it. It remains in many subtle forms, much as Dionysianism permeated Orphism, and as the religion of the Old Testament permeated that of the New. (I mean no more than the broad comparison of permeations here.) But a new element is introduced, the world is no longer conceived of as an array of self-enclosing Angels; instead, the god is said to have become a man, and to become man again wherever there is song: the bridge is established through an incarnation. In addition, this bridging is said to come about not through the striving of the individual self, but through the god's sacrifice. Orpheus was killed and torn in pieces by the Maenads who, as Rilke interprets, were maddened by his scorn of their rites. Yet the head and the lyre of the god could not be destroyed: as tradition has it they continued to sing and play from the shores of Lesbos, and it is this enduring of indestructible song that Rilke takes at one point for this theme:

> O du verlorener Gott! Du unendliche Spur!
> Nur weil dich reißend zuletzt die Feindschaft verteilte,
> sind wir die Hörenden jetzt und ein Mund der Natur.*
>
> (I, xxvi)

The idea of an enabling sacrifice contained in these lines is wholly removed from anything that might have been said of the Angels. But for the death of Orpheus at the hands of his enemies, a death which could have meant nothing in the angelic sphere, there could have been neither ears to hear his song, nor mouths to utter it. Indeed, while the treatment of the legend remains aesthetic and never ethical, it is not hard to see many parallels with the religious ideals of Christianity. Nor is it at all incomprehensible that the figure of Orpheus himself, the preacher of monotheism, immortality, purity of life, and the possibility of attaining divine

---

* O you god that has vanished! You infinite track!
Only because dismembering hatred dispersed you
are we hearers today and a mouth which else Nature would lack.

life on earth, the bringer of peace, order, gentleness, was regarded
by the early Church as a prototype of Christ. The gift of Orphic
religion to the Greek world, and the mark which distinguishes it
from the Dionysian religion that preceded it, have been described
by Jane Harrison in these terms: 'Dionysus is drunken, Orpheus
is utterly sober. But this new spirit of gentle decorum is but the
manifestation, the outward shining of a lambent flame within,
the expression of a new spiritual faith which brought to man, at
the moment he most needed it, the longing for peace and purity
in this life, the hope of final fruition in the next.'3 Something of
this spirit passes almost unconsciously into Rilke's poetry as the
myth expands its transforming influence. Rilke does not acknowledge any such resemblance with Christ and no doubt was unaware of any, and yet, yielding momentarily, he begins to speak
in unaccustomed terms.

This is felt from the beginning of the cycle: in the first of the
Sonnets there is already that contact with the god which the
Elegies denied between men and the Angels. At once also,
through the power of song, the distance between ourselves and
the outward creation is established. Where before there had been
the sense of pain and loss, of distinctness from our 'interpreted'
world, there is now the felt presence of the visible world in the
invisible world within. Orpheus creates the 'tree' that had
formerly been a companion at most, so that it is no longer
separate but immediately felt:

> Da stieg ein Baum. O reine Übersteigung!
> O Orpheus singt! O hoher Baum im Ohr!
> Und alles schwieg. Doch selbst in der Verschweigung
> ging neuer Anfang, Wink und Wandlung vor.

> Tiere aus Stille drangen aus dem klaren
> gelösten Wald von Lager und Genist;
> und da ergab sich, daß sie nicht aus List
> und nicht aus Angst in sich so leise waren,

> sondern aus Hören. Brüllen, Schrei, Geröhr
> schien klein in ihren Herzen. Und wo eben
> kaum eine Hütte war, dies zu empfangen,

ein Unterschlupf aus dunkelstem Verlangen,
mit einem Zugang, dessen Pfosten beben, —
da schufst du ihnen Tempel im Gehör.*

From the outset, there takes place that transformation of the world into the invisible, which, Rilke wrote to his Polish translator, was announced also in the *Elegies*. It is accompanied now, however, by a quite different background of beliefs. Orpheus appears already as the creator not only of things but of order: the maze of lairs in the wood which the beasts inhabit becomes 'clear' and 'unravelled', as though the one tree that has now risen had established its influence over all the trees that before existed. Again, there is no fear of the singing god, as there had been of the Angels. The beasts assemble without subtly cunning hindthoughts of the consolation to be acquired, nor out of fear, but with attentive ears for the silence. There is, it seems, no audible song, rather perhaps something akin to the 'uninterrupted message that forms itself out of stillness', of which Rilke had written in one of the *Elegies*. Most notable of all, however, are the last lines, where it is made clear that the ability to hear at all is itself given by the god. In a way, a closed circle is suggested here also. The song is made, but remains unheard or inadequately received, so long as there is only the desire for it. Till Orpheus comes, there is only a 'refuge' in the hearing of the beasts, a place

* A tree ascending there. O pure transcension!
O Orpheus sings! O tall tree in the ear!
All noise suspended, yet in that suspension
what new beginning, beckoning, change, appear!

Creatures of silence pressing through the clear
disintricated wood from lair and nest;
and neither cunning, it grew manifest,
had made them breathe so quietly, nor fear,

but only hearing. Roar, cry, bell they found
within their hearts too small. And where before
less than a hut had harboured what came thronging,

a refuge tunnelled out of dimmest longing
with lowly entrance through a quivering door
you built them temples in their sense of sound.

to which they can withdraw from real or imagined dangers. With the coming of Orpheus, this is changed: he himself creates temples in which his song may be heard at its fullest. And so both the hearing and the song are his creation: the cycle is closed, as it is in the fountain-sonnet, where the speech pours forth from the mouth into the sleeping ear. Whereas in the fountain, however, there had been no means of penetrating this endless converse without interruption, there is now participation. Just as Orpheus can become metamorphosed now in this man and now in that, so here he allows the beasts to participate in the silence of his song, while yet providing himself all the means whereby they do so. The closed cycle continues, transcending human powers to comprehend it, as it does also in the converse of the Holy Trinity, yet at the same time it is capable of entering into life and of fashioning it, as life is fashioned by the Holy Spirit. The question asked of the Angels, whether they 'only catch up what is theirs, what has streamed from them', is answered here, of Orpheus, negatively: he does enter, if not the spirit of men, then at least that of the brute creation.

Later in the sequence, it becomes apparent that there is, however, no such limitation. Orpheus is not only the master of beasts but the uniter of men, and in some sense their justification. The sonnet which begins 'Heil dem Geist, der uns verbinden mag', is surely meant to refer to Orpheus, and the sense of unity brought by his spirit. It is notable also for the lines:

> Ohne unsern wahren Platz zu kennen,
> handeln wir aus wirklichem Bezug.*

Rilke affirms here, what he had often seemed to deny before, that while mystery still remains, there can be nevertheless a reality in our relationships with it, which is not nugatory for being inexplicable or unutterable. Much of his earlier writing seems not content with this: he looks for the realization, the paradoxical statement of the mystery, and despite his own misgivings

* Literally: 'without knowing our true place we act from real relationship'.

attempts to say the unsayable. The world of 'things' then suffers violence at his hands, or he affirms a unity-in-duality by purely verbal means, punning, grammatical subtleties and the like. Now he falls back on complete trust and dependence, not seeking to add a cubit to his stature. Human effort, in this sonnet, is seen as action that depends for its fruition on powers outside its control:

> Selbst wenn sich der Bauer sorgt und handelt,
> wo die Saat im Sommer sich verwandelt,
> reicht er niemals hin. Die Erde *schenkt.** (I, xii)

Where Orpheus creates temples through which alone his song can be heard, the earth gives the full life that the sower of the seed cannot produce of himself. All this is a part of the new realization that comes in the *Sonnets*, attributing power not to the individual self, but to the gift of the god who momentarily transforms it. With it arises a sense of the comparative ineffectuality of human effort, and a recognition from outside the mystery that the effort is hallowed nevertheless. The language in which this belief is expressed becomes extremely simple, no longer paradoxical in the former sense of holding together two opposites that are straining apart. One of the simplest of all the sonnets runs in this vein:

> Wandelt sich rasch auch die Welt
> wie Wolkengestalten,
> alles Vollendete fällt
> heim zum Uralten.
>
> Über dem Wandel und Gang,
> weiter und freier,
> währt noch dein Vor-gesang,
> Gott mit der Leier.
>
> Nicht sind die Leiden erkannt,
> nicht ist die Liebe gelernt,
> und was im Tod uns entfernt

* Does the farmer, anxiously arranging,
ever reach to where the seed is changing
into summer? Does not Earth bestow?

285

ist nicht entschleiert.
Einzig das Lied überm Land
heiligt und feiert.*

The simplicity of this derives from its lack of paradox. Rilke denies here what he had suggested in the Tenth Elegy and in 'Christi Höllenfahrt', that suffering is capable of being realized at its fullest extent by men. The belief which had guided him before, that only a tasting of the cup down to the bitterest dregs could rightfully lead to a 'reversal', had led only to further unending spirals of wretchedness: the youth in the Tenth Elegy is finally seen still climbing into the mountains of the Land of Lament. Now, while suffering still remains, it is not 'erkannt', not fully known with intimacy. Similarly love is not learnt, and the mystery of death is not unveiled. Rilke, who had claimed to have been 'beyond death, in a certain sense', gives up this claim in these lines, and returns to a world of infinite possibilities. He seems to say that there is no limit either to love or suffering, but that the celebration of human living does not depend on the ability of each man to love or suffer infinitely. The celebration, the 'hallowing', stems from the song that spreads over the land when Orpheus sings, and wherever there is song, it is his singing.

With this awareness that the sanctification of life is a gift, not an attainment, Rilke must abandon the ideal of self-enclosure. Self-enclosure, however wide its scope, had always meant the

*   Change though the world may as fast
as cloud-collections,
home to the changeless at last
fall all perfections.

Over the thrust and the throng,
freer and higher,
echoes your preluding song,
god with the lyre.

Sorrow we misunderstand,
love we have still to begin,
death and what's hidden therein

await unveiling.
Song alone circles the land,
hallowing and hailing.

imposition of an inward pattern on the outward world, and the ultimate hope that in the widest range of the embracing circle a limit would be reached where sorrow and happiness were one. Now, as a later sonnet has it, 'the circle is nowhere closed' ('Nirgends schließt sich der Kreis', II, xx). There is no finality, and no ultimate point of 'reversal' or of synthesis. Rather, the song of Orpheus, mysterious itself, sustains a pure, unambiguous note of praise which continues unaffected by human efforts to attain to it. There may be more suffering to undergo, and more of love to be learned, but neither of these can describe the full circle; the glorifying of earth exists independently of them.

Thus there is no longer striving or assertion but belief, no longer an all-embracing desire but attentiveness, and no longer the final vision but glimpses here and there. Orpheus is not the imposer of an ultimate reality but the fleeting appearance that enlivens for a moment with a new awareness, and vanishes again:

> Ein für alle Male
> ists Orpheus, wenn es singt. Er kommt und geht.
> Ists nicht schon viel, wenn er die Rosenschale
> um ein paar Tage übersteht?*　　　　　　　(I, v)

In this coming and going there is surely a much truer representation of our experiences of poetry, music, and perhaps also of something like mystical insights. They are not compelling revelations that persuade us of the truth of a system, not final or all-embracing, but almost instantaneous glimpses that do bring nevertheless a conviction of hearing or acting 'from real relationship'.

The self-evident joyful quality of many of the sonnets may thus owe a great deal to the new element introduced into Rilke's thought by the figure of Orpheus. It seems as though, under the influence of the proto-Christian myth, he unwittingly departs from the characteristic thought of most of his poetry even if only

---

*　　　　　　　Once and for all,
it's Orpheus when there's song. He comes and goes.
Is it not much if sometimes, by some small
number of days, he shall outlive the rose?

for a short while. Untrammelled joy comes from the momentary return to a Christian framework. On the other hand, the prominence given here to the distinctness of Orpheus from the angels may easily give a false impression. For Rilke, both *Elegies* and *Sonnets* were part of one whole, and of the two, the *Elegies* were by far the greater, more comprehensive work. 'Elegies and Sonnets', he wrote, 'support each other continually—and I see an infinite grace in the fact that I was permitted to fill these two sails with the same breath: the little rust-coloured sail of the *Sonnets* and the gigantic white canvas of the *Elegies*.'4 The *Sonnets* were originally not even a part of his plan; he had set out in February 1922 to complete the *Elegies* after eight years' interruption, and the *Sonnets* thrust themselves between in a 'tempestuous self-imposition'.5 This complete unexpectedness of the *Sonnets* may or may not be significant: since Rilke was so unprepared for them it might well be thought that they stem from a deeper level of inspiration, less guided by his conscious presuppositions. At all events, however, it has to be recognized that for him the distinctions so far outlined were not perceptible. In particular, the thought of any similarity between Orpheus and some aspects of Christian belief would have been unacceptable: Rilke, believing that Christianity was concerned with the preaching of otherworldliness alone, withdrew from it in his last years more and more passionately. In what sense, then, could he have held that the *Elegies* and the *Sonnets* continually support one another?

First, there can be no doubt that the Seventh and Ninth Elegies, two of the *Elegies* wholly composed at Muzot,6 do have the belief in the validity of human creations and earthly sights that characterizes the *Sonnets*. The Seventh in particular, in the lines near the beginning that evoke the lark mounting into the sky, have a joyful quality that is seldom to be found in the rest of the *Elegies*. And this quality is certainly related to the new relationship to the Angels that enters at this point in the composition: the desire to present human achievement as worthy even of their contemplation:

...Engel,
dir noch zeig ich es, da! in deinem Anschaun
steh es gerettet zuletzt, nun endlich aufrecht.*

Already here, there is a sharing with the Angel, for all that he remains distinct. The cathedrals, the monuments of ancient Egypt which Rilke has in mind can be shown by him to the Angel, but it is only when they stand 'within his gaze' that they are 'saved', and thus valid. Again, a few lines later, the means of glorifying these creations is relinquished by the poet himself and handed to these greater beings, who, like Orpheus, are more truly able to praise:

War es nicht Wunder? O staune, Engel, denn *wir* sinds,
wir, o du Großer, erzähls, daß wir solches vermochten, mein Atem
reicht für die Rühmung nicht aus.†

Angels and Orpheus begin here to coalesce. Both are the wholly replete beings from whom alone true song is possible and through whom the reality of finite endeavours is assured. As always, however, the Angels remain ultimately aloof. Whereas Orpheus is metamorphosed in the song of the human poet, at one with it in its transitory glimpses, the Angel must take over where the poet can no longer summon up the strength to continue. Or in another passage, from the Ninth Elegy, it is the poet who speaks of human achievements, while the Angel, unaware of them despite his familiarity with the realms both of the living and the dead, hears with amazement:

Preise dem Engel die Welt, nicht die unsägliche, *ihm*
kannst du nicht großtun mit herrlich Erfühltem; im Weltall,
wo er fühlender fühlt, bist du ein Neuling...
Sag ihm die Dinge. Er wird staunender stehn....‡

*   Angel,
    I'll show it to you as well—there! In your gaze
    it shall stand redeemed at last, in a final uprightness.

†   Was it not miracle? Angel, gaze, for it's *we*—
    O mightiness, tell them that *we* were capable of it—my breath's
    too short for this celebration.

‡   Praise this world to the Angel, not the untellable: you
    can't impress him with the splendour you've felt; in the cosmos
    where he more feelingly feels you're only a novice....
    Tell him *things*. He'll stand more astonished.

Perhaps equally significantly, Rilke speaks in these passages not of singing, as he does in the *Sonnets*, but of saying, telling, showing—'sagen', 'erzählen', 'zeigen'. The lyrical element is acknowledged not in relationship to the Angels, but to Orpheus, in whom the poet no longer remains distinct.

Similarly, the contrast may be illustrated from the Fourth Elegy, written in 1914. In this earlier work, the distinctness of the Angels from humanity becomes apparent in the imagery of the marionette. Rilke sees himself here as a child, waiting in front of the puppet-stage for some reality to take place. The stage, in which an allegory of life may be seen, remains lifeless and dull, till the concentrated gaze of the child, determined that at last something shall happen, draws down an Angel:

> Wenn mir zumut ist,
> zu warten vor der Puppenbühne, nein,
> so völlig hinzuschaun, daß, um mein Schauen
> am Ende aufzuwiegen, dort als Spieler
> ein Engel hinmuß, der die Bälge hochreißt.
> Engel und Puppe: dann ist endlich Schauspiel.
> Dann kommt zusammen, was wir immerfort
> entzwein, indem wir da sind. Dann entsteht
> aus unsern Jahreszeiten erst der Umkreis
> des ganzen Wandelns. Über uns hinüber
> spielt dann der Engel.*

This is another statement, only slightly modified, of Rilke's earlier expectations of a 'reversal'. Where he had spoken before of 'rejecting nothing' that came to him in the way of experience, here he envisages a complete concentration on the lifelessness

---

*   When I feel like it,
to wait before the puppet stage—no, rather
gaze so intensely on it that at last
a counterpoising angel has to come
and play a part there, snatching up the rags.
Angel and doll! Then there's at last a play.
Then there unites what we continually
part by our mere existence. Then at last
can spring from our own turning years the cycle
of the whole going-on. Over and above us,
then, there's the angel playing.

and emptiness of the scene before him. And where before he had waited for the transformation into an 'austere glory', he waits now for the Angel to take up the strings controlling the puppet, and to begin the play. Only then will the union of opposites be accomplished, and the final unity be established. Yet it is doubtful whether the image Rilke uses here carries any conviction to the reader. The train of thought can be followed: that a lifeless thing begins to act as though it were alive. But the image itself, once again, seems inadequate. It is surprising, and at first glance perhaps incomprehensible, that the sight of an Angel manipulating the strings of a puppet should represent so deep an impression of cosmic unity. It is a help, of course, to remember the well-known essay of von Kleist, 'On the Marionette-Theatre', which may very well have been in Rilke's mind at this moment. In this, the unthinking, unreflective behaviour of puppets, entirely responsive to the controlling hands of the operator, is put forward as one mode of acting with the grace of a god, and so Rilke may have meant the image in the Elegy. On the other hand, the very notion of puppetry as a model of human behaviour has a certain repellence. It denies all sense of freedom of action, and suggests a stiff manneredness that can never be as graceful as the movement of a truly human body. And this manneredness surely comes from the artificial way in which the movements are brought about: the operator, or here the Angel, is distinct from the puppet, dictating its movements from outside, not informing its limbs with his own spirit. Rilke uses this image because the angels are for him still eternally remote, and capable of influencing human life only by forcing it into conformity with their own self-enclosure.

In the imagery of the *Sonnets*, this distinctness and manipulative control disappears, to be replaced by that of the dancer. As 'saying' gives place to 'singing', puppet-movements give place to the fullest measure of human gracefulness, and this becomes possible with the belief that Orpheus can be, not distinct, but metamorphosed in human nature. It also becomes possible on account of the second source of inspiration that gave rise to the *Sonnets*: the memory of the young woman, Wera Ouckama

Knoop, whose dancing forms the theme of several of them. Nothing could be further removed from the heavy, broken rhythms of the puppet-passage in the Elegy than the light sweeping motion of the sonnet, 'O komm und geh'. In the Elegy you have

> Dann kommt zusammen, was wir immerfort
> entzwein, indem wir da sind. Dann entsteht
> aus unsern Jahreszeiten erst der Umkreis
> des ganzen Wandelns. Über uns hinüber
> spielt dann der Engel.

Rhythmically, the consciousness is still with the divided state, the fragmentary experience. In the sonnet, however, you have

> O komm und geh. Du, fast noch Kind, ergänze
> für einen Augenblick, die Tanzfigur
> zum reinen Sternbild eines jener Tänze
> darin wir die stumpf ordnende Natur
>
> vergänglich übertreffen. Denn sie regte
> sich völlig hörend nur, da Orpheus sang.
> Du warst noch die von damals her Bewegte
> und leicht befremdet, wenn ein Baum sich lang
>
> besann, mit dir nach dem Gehör zu gehn.
> Du wußtest noch die Stelle, wo die Leier
> sich tönend hob —; die unerhörte Mitte.
>
> Für sie versuchtest du die schönen Schritte
> und hofftest, einmal zu der heilen Feier
> des Freundes Gang und Antlitz hinzudrehn.*

> * Oh, come and go, you almost child, enhancing
> for one brief hour the figure of the dance
> to part of that pure constellated dancing
> where, subject as we are to change and chance,
>
> we beat dull nature. For she only started
> hearing with all her ears at Orpheus' song.
> And you still moved with motion then imparted,
> and shrank a little if a tree seemed long
>
> in treading with you the remembered pace.
> You knew it still, that passage where the lyre
> soundingly rose, the unimagined centre,
>
> and practised all your steps in hope to enter
> that theme again, whirling to one entire
> communion with your friend both feet and face.

Thematically, there is the difference here between movement controlled from above, as it is in the Elegy, and movement freely evolved in time to music. A dancer is restricted by the kind of music played, but her steps are freely invented, and need never be quite the same from dance to dance. So much is worth noting in general terms, apart from the poem, to indicate the combination of freedom and harmony that may be achieved. Within the poem, a great deal more is suggested. In the first words, 'O komm und geh', there is already a reminiscence of the words used of Orpheus earlier, 'er kommt und geht', and thereby a hint of his presence in the person of the dancing girl is given. It is not a statement, however; it is no more than a dim recollection of words that have gone before: suggestion rather than affirmation. Again, there is none of the finality that there is in the words of the Elegy: 'dann ist endlich Schauspiel', nor is there any note of reservation, as there must be in thinking of the unreality of a 'spectacle'. The dancing achieves its perfection only 'for a moment', although in this moment the order of dull nature is surpassed—the dance becomes a 'pure constellation', having the ordered brilliance of the changeless groupings of the stars. A 'new world' is being realized beyond the natural one, and in this the ambiguities of ordinary living no longer exist. All depends on the enlivening influence of Orpheus' song; it was only in hearing this song that Nature stirred into true life. But the dancer still has ears to hear the silence of the song, and still dances with that harmonious movement which is always seeking to sweep Nature with it into transfiguration. The relationship of Orpheus, as this poem expresses it, is never a rigid control but a constant invitation, and never a submission but a harmony in momentary identity.

Although, then, there are signs in the *Elegies* that the figure of Orpheus subtly alters the conception of the Angels Rilke already had in mind, bringing them into a certain relationship with men, there remain essential differences, so essential as to influence his whole mode of writing. Equally, however, the earlier conception of the Angels continues to influence that of Orpheus. The *Sonnets* themselves do not remain wholly by the new conception, and features of self-enclosing isolation continue to appear. At times, these seem even contradictory. These lines from a sonnet in the First Part show Orpheus (in contrast, one might say, to the Christ of 'Christi Höllenfahrt') actively going forward to greet the dead, offering them the means of praising:

> Er ist einer der bleibenden Boten,
> der noch weit in die Türen der Toten
> Schalen mit rühmlichen Früchten hält.*   (i, vii)

These, however, from the Second Part, show a god who remains remote and almost indifferent, in an ambiguous way:

> Selbst die reine, die geweihte Spende
> nimmt er anders nicht in seine Welt,
> als indem er sich dem freien Ende
> unbewegt entgegenstellt.

> Nur der Tote trinkt
> aus der hier von uns *gehörten* Quelle,
> wenn der Gott ihm schweigend winkt, dem Toten.†

Once again, the rhythm changes with the changed conception from dactylic gaiety in the first passage to a slow rise and fall in the second, with unequal lines that mark the heaviness of heart. Orpheus is no longer the spirit that unites, but the motionless contemplator who will not so much as touch the gift men bring to him, and indicates that it is taken 'into his world' by a dumb action that is almost an opposition.

So it is whenever the self-enclosing ideal, which is certainly still present in Rilke's conception of Orpheus, gains pre-

---

*   He is a messenger always attendant,
reaching far through their gates resplendent
dishes of fruit for the dead to praise.

†   Even gifts of purest consecration
only find acceptance in so much
as he turns in moveless contemplation
to the end we do not touch.

Only those who dwell
out of sight can taste the spring we hear,
when the god has silently assented.

dominance. The possibility of metamorphosis is forgotten, and Orpheus becomes associated with only the transcendent qualities of the Angels. Narcissus becomes an ideal figure, isolation and separation are conditions that are once again not to be overcome but accepted as in themselves fruition. And whereas one of the sonnets declares that 'Only within the sphere of praise may there be lamentation', this seems now to be reversed. It is not a question of lament being permitted only within the sphere of praise, but of praise being permitted within the sphere of lament. Indeed Rilke's words on the relationship of the *Elegies* and *Sonnets* indicate this: the 'gigantic white canvas' of the *Elegies*, devoted almost wholly to lament and ending with affirmation of it, overshadows the 'little rust-coloured sail' of the *Sonnets*, as though the praise of the latter were justified only by the questionings of the former. The glorifying of the world becomes once more, if Rilke's interpretation be adopted, an accomplishment of the individual self, not an independently existing praise in which the individual may participate. It depends once again on the individual's paradoxical attainment of the furthermost limits of an infinite degree of suffering, rather than on the enabling sacrifice of the incarnate god.

The new note that enters with the *Sonnets* is thus not sustained, and was probably not recognized by Rilke, for whom Christian thought clothed in Christian rather than Orphic garb would have been unthinkable. The framework of beliefs with which Rilke had begun, a Nietzschean and Schopenhauerian framework, broadly speaking, reasserts its structural influence, and absorbs the Orphic revelations into itself:

> Wir stehn und stemmen uns an unsre Grenze
> und reißen ein Unkenntliches herein.*

Rilke had indeed strained himself against the limits of his experience, but the new element that entered remained 'unrecognizable', and seemed to be no more than a confirmation of

---

* We stand and strain against our limits, and drag an unrecognizable something within the pale.

what he had already expected. The first of the *Sonnets* at once establishes the means of communication with the self-enclosing cycle from which he had felt excluded; the old myth, with its proto-Christian features, begins to afford the possibility of praise, union with other men, justification, while at the same time not suggesting that suffering is unreal or to be avoided. With the last of the *Sonnets*, however, affirmation has undergone a subtle change:

Stiller Freund der vielen Fernen, fühle
wie dein Atem noch den Raum vermehrt.
Im Gebälk der finstern Glockenstühle
laß dich läuten. Das, was an dir zehrt,

wird ein Starkes über dieser Nahrung.
Geh in der Verwandlung aus und ein.
Was ist deine leidendste Erfahrung?
Ist dir Trinken bitter, werde Wein.

Sei in dieser Nacht aus Übermaß
Zauberkraft am Kreuzweg deiner Sinne,
ihrer seltsamen Begegnung Sinn.

Und wenn dich das Irdische vergaß,
zu der stillen Erde sag: Ich rinne.
Zu dem raschen Wasser sprich: Ich bin.*

It *is* affirmation, not lament. But it is affirmation against a background of nothingness, darkness and death, not of the all-

*   Silent friend of those far from us, feeling
how your breath is still enlarging space,
fill the sombre belfry with your pealing.
What consumes you now is growing apace

stronger than the feeding strength it borrows.
Be, as Change will have you, shade or shine.
Which has grieved you most of all your sorrows?
Turn, if drinking's bitter, into wine.

Be, in this immeasurable night,
at your senses' cross-ways magic cunning,
be the sense of their mysterious tryst.

And, should earthliness forget you quite,
murmur to the quiet earth: I'm running.
Tell the running water: I exist.

THE SONNETS TO ORPHEUS

enlivening yet otherworldly presence of Orpheus. It affirms existence in awareness of the limitation imposed by non-being, 'des Nicht-Seins Bedingung', poised over a void, not validated as it is elsewhere in the *Sonnets* by the 'permanent powers'. Rilke addresses here a friend of Wera, perhaps her mother with whom he had been in correspondence, and the soft alliteration of the first line suggests already an assuagement of loss. He counsels her to yield herself to the power that controls her, as a bell is yielded to the bell-rope: to let her praise or lament ring out unchecked. Yet the surroundings whence these peals come are dark, threatening. In preparation for the thought that is to follow, Rilke sets the sound against the background of sombre belfry-beams. For the outcome of this ringing is seen not as a communication to men, but as a strengthening of the mysterious being that devours the friend. There is an ominous note both in the impersonality of this being—'Das, was an dir zehrt', and in the word that portrays its activity. 'Zehren' is always associated in Rilke's verse with that consuming of personality spoken of in the First Elegy—'when the wind full of cosmic space feeds on our faces'. Here, it seems inevitable to associate it with the concluding lines of a sonnet that comes a short space before this one:

> Und nur der schweigsame Tod, der weiß, was wir sind
> und was er immer gewinnt, wenn er uns leiht.*   (II, xxiv)

All human praising serves to strengthen the power that destroys men. To be reconciled with this human condition there is need to accept both existence and annihilation, to be both the actor and the sufferer, the drinker and the wine. In the words of the Sanskrit formula, there is need for the realization, 'That art thou': only complete identity with all forms of existence can suffice. And with this, self-enclosing returns once more as an ideal: the friend is counselled to be the 'sense' of the meeting of his 'senses'. Through punning allusion Rilke seeks again to present the individual self as his own validation, giving no more

---

*   And only taciturn Death knows what we are worth,
        and how much it always pays him to lend us.

meaning to himself than he already possesses potentially, but affirming this meaning with a greater intensity that seems to derive from the double accent on 'sense'. It is true that this self-enclosing widens again in the final tercet. Here, the feeling of identity between the one and the all is underlined by the crossing of images: towards the fixed earth, there is the self-association with running water; towards the running water, the self-association with the enduring earth. Yet it remains an identity in separation; it is not affirmed except when 'earthliness' forgets the existence of earthly creatures. As a whole, the last sonnet embraces once more the ideal of natural mysticism, self-identification with the changing earth, while the void of death stretches below. And thus Rilke's mysticism continually vacillates between theistic and natural mysticism, emerging only momentarily into an acceptance of unambiguous realities, unambiguous fulfilments. The unambiguous can after all only be affirmed quite unambiguously, and for this Rilke's poetry was not equipped. For the purpose of the tradition we are seeking, Rilke provides only tenuous footholds which quickly crumble away.

PART IV

RESHAPING THE TRADITION

CHAPTER XV

HOFMANNSTHAL AND
'DER SCHWIERIGE'

Perhaps none of Hofmannsthal's plays is so difficult to stage as his social comedy, *Der Schwierige* (published 1921). It is true that it has none of the resplendent scenic effects of *Die ägyptische Helena* (1928) or of the intensely dramatic moments of *Elektra* (1904). It is not laden with allegorical significance as is *Der Turm* (1925). But the enchanted atmosphere of many of his works, from *Der Tod des Tizian* (1892) onwards, was a comparatively simple matter for the Viennese stage of his day, with its long tradition of 'Märchendramen' extending back to Mozart's *Magic Flute*, and beyond. The fairy-tale world of magic transformations, richly luxuriant settings and mystic revelations was an Austrian inheritance deriving ultimately from the Jesuit drama of the seventeenth century, and in the hands of a producer of genius like Max Reinhardt it could be realized to perfection. *Der Schwierige*, on the other hand, does not belong to this fairy-tale world. It has the elegance, the refinement, the tact and the wisdom of Hofmannsthal's libretto written for Richard Strauss, *Der Rosenkavalier* (1911), and with that there goes a certain enchantment which is not alien to the 'Märchendrama'. But *Der Schwierige* is not set in the heyday of Austria's rococo glory; the moment of which Hofmannsthal chose to write was a day late in the year 1918, when the Austro-Hungarian Empire had just been defeated and was about to disintegrate into the separate nations which continue to exist today. 'Do you remember what Novalis said?' Hofmannsthal asked a friend at that time, as revolution flared up in Munich and Budapest. '"After losing wars you must write comedies." Comedy, the most difficult of all literary art-forms, which can express everything in a complete balance, which can say the most difficult, the most alarming things in that balanced state of highly concentrated energy which always gives the impression of playful ease.'[1] *Der Schwierige* is clearly the outcome of that remark, and it is the very ease of its mood, of its concern with love-affairs, bridge-parties and marriage in the lower ranks of an apparently effete aristocracy, which makes it so difficult to produce. On the surface, this is, though unusually refined, a play of the kind that makes a West End success. It has the brilliance of Oscar Wilde, whose work Hofmannsthal knew well, but little of his wit and none of his cynicism. It has the warmth and humanity of Lessing's earlier masterpiece in the same vein, *Minna von Barnhelm*, whose theme it echoes. With these qualities, however, it combines a concern with other issues such as is found in T. S. Eliot's *The Cocktail Party* and *The Confidential Clerk*. Not that these are made to look prominent: one does not have the uncomfortable feeling at the suggestions dropped by Eliot, that some of the characters on stage are really guardian angels, or that a Harley Street psychiatrist is almost a supernatural being. The deeper concern is revealed with such tact that it may escape attention as easily as ordinary life does off-stage: the play is as real as that. Nor does Hofmannsthal indulge in the profundities which have often marred German literature. As Richard Alewyn has said,

he was spared the fatal tensions of the German: the nihilistic idealism, the fanatical pursuit of the absolute, the Titanic defiance, the strivings of Faust and the enthusiasms of Werther, the desire for the All and the aspiration for the Naught, the preponderance of Will over Being, the overstraining and the tautness, as well as the unfortunate heartiness and brutish lack of humour—all this was always very strange to him, indeed embarrassing.[2]

It may prove true to say of Hofmannsthal, as he said of Lessing, that 'he was of a different stock: he showed a potential German quality which had no descendants; he mastered his material, instead of allowing it to master him. His importance for the nation lies in his contradiction to it. In a people whose greatest danger is the artificial character, he was a genuine character.'[3]

For Hofmannsthal's material was certainly of the kind which has always engaged the attention of German authors. His entire work, plays, poems, literary and political essays, is intimately connected with the mystical experience—there seems to be no other name for it—which came to him at an early age. The maturity and poetic mastery which brought him fame while he was still a schoolboy would not have existed without the knowledge, reflected in almost every poem, of an identity between himself and the whole of the surrounding world. In his later notes serving for an interpretation of his work, the *Ad me ipsum*, he refers to this always by the term 'Praeexistenz',4 although the word has not quite the same meaning for him as it had for Plato. It is not the condition of the soul before birth, dwelling in the realm of Ideas, but rather a condition experienced during life, a state of mind and body in which something comparable to the Platonic pre-existence is felt in the here and now: 'das Ich als Universum' is Hofmannsthal's briefest summary of it, and in his earliest lyric plays, in *Gestern* (1891), *Das kleine Welttheater* (1897) and *Das Bergwerk zu Falun* (1899), it is a recurrent theme. Moreover, this preoccupation did bring with it some of the 'fatal tensions' whose presence Professor Alewyn denies (for all that, broadly speaking, his characterization of Hofmannsthal is just). For this 'pre-existence' was felt by Hofmannsthal as a 'glorious but dangerous condition'.5 The sense of identity, paradoxically, also brought a strong sense of isolation: he was 'allem nah, allem fern',6 and the experience, while it seemed to spread over all things, was also a withdrawal from the world of sensual reality. It was, like Nirvana, a condition comparable to death, and could be preserved only by a 'Supposition des quasi-Gestorbenseins',7 yet this death must also be somehow seen as life. As Claudio put it in *Der Tod und der Tod* (1893):

Da tot mein Leben war, sei du mein Leben, Tod!8

And meanwhile, life was constantly asserting its brutalities and uglinesses, reminding the mystic of the fragility of his dreams. The blissful communion of self with itself, apparently a communion with all things, was continually confronted with the realization, 'Die Welt besitzt sich selber' ('The world owns itself')9—standing over against it was something wholly other, something senselessly destructive, vindictive and capricious. So in the story, *Märchen der 672. Nacht* (1895), the young man who attempts to live in luxurious isolation is suddenly enticed out of his home and guided—almost by Fate, it seems—to an ignominious death. And in *Die Frau im Fenster* (1897) the woman who lives in mysterious concord with every living thing about her is suddenly strangled by her jealous husband. The soul still enjoying its primal bliss is abruptly brought to a realization of its present condition:

> Nun spür ich schaudernd etwas mich umgeben,
> Es türmt sich auf bis an die hohen Sterne,
> Und seinen Namen weiß ich nun: das Leben.*10

The earliest plays escape the fanaticism which might easily arise from the extremity of these contrasts. They are lyrical rather than dramatic, resigned or fatalistic in mood, slow-moving like a long dream, with rich and exotic colouring, luxurious imagery and rhythms, languorous, limpid. Only after the turn of the century did a note of frenzy enter the plays, in the ecstatic savagery of Hofmannsthal's *Elektra* and the brutal sadism of his adaptation from Otway, *Das gerettete Venedig* (1905), though something of the kind had been heard in the short story of a cavalry episode, *Reitergeschichte* (1898). Hofmannsthal was experimenting here, perhaps, with a mode of being far from his own proper nature, the wilful amorality of the Nietzschean Superman which he was later to feel as 'Reich-German' rather than Austrian. This too was, after all, one manifestation of an all-embracing attitude such as his own had been, and had he followed it up it might have made of him a writer of whom Alewyn's characterization would be quite untrue. In fact, he wrote only one further play in this vein, *Ödipus und die Sphinx* (1906), in

---

* Now with a shudder I feel something surround me,
  towering above to the high stars, and now I know its name,
  it is Life.

which the 'pre-existent' hero lives a life of charmed innocence. The guilt of Oedipus, as this work shows it, is an illusion, for in the pre-existent world there is no differentiation, neither night nor day, death nor life, self nor not-self, guilt nor innocence. Oedipus accepts the murder of his father and prepares to marry his mother in the knowledge that what the gods have ordained must come to pass: there is the thrill of experience, but no remorse, no conflict. Yet already the note of frenzy has disappeared: the language of *Ödipus* is restrained by comparison with *Elektra*, and the 'affirmation' in it, to use a Nietzschean word, is unforced. There followed a curious gap of some four years—a time of reflection, perhaps, for the earlier plays had been written at much smaller intervals—before *Cristinas Heimreise* (1910) appeared, and this, for the first time, proved to be a light-hearted comedy. It is true that it took up a theme which had appeared earlier, that of the amorous adventurer who had emerged in *Der Abenteurer und die Sängerin* (1899) and was to reappear in *Der Schwierige* itself.[11] It is also true that the Casanova-figure of these plays, with his indifferent love for all women, was a reflection of the mystic's universal embrace. But *Cristinas Heimreise* is also notable for its gaiety, its departure from the world of myth and fairy-tale, and for its new emphasis on the serenity, even the sanctity, of married life. Out of the mystic's indifferentism and his awareness of a hostile reality comes a crystallized realization: the adventurer goes on his way untrammelled, but the heroine 'returns home' to the enduring love of one man. The new moral attitude gained in this play did not bear immediate fruit, however. Hofmannsthal's next play, an adaptation from an English medieval morality, *Jedermann* (1912), although it has proved a great popular success, is over-naïve. After Nietzsche, it was no longer possible to put forward Christian ideals, as this play does, with so little regard for the complexities of self-seeking they bring with them. Hofmannsthal had resort here to an over-simplification which is still apparent in his post-war attempt at a similar resuscitation from the past, the adaptation from Calderón, *Das Salzburger Große Welttheater* (1922).

During the course of the First World War, Hofmannsthal wrote no plays, although his thought was still directed along the channels prepared by his earlier work. In place of the mystic's fulfilment, however, or rather branching from the same aspiration, he looked outwards now, politically, to the state whose last days he was witnessing. The Austro-Hungarian Empire with its variety of nations straddling across the centre of Europe and defending it against attack from the East was, in his eyes, the direct descendant of the Holy Roman Empire, with its nominally all-embracing dominion. The Empire of his own day, decadent as it was and split by nationalisms, might yet be restored to a truly united central block in which Austrians, Czechs, Slovaks, Hungarians, Italians and others would form a single whole. With this in mind, he wrote his war-time essays on such representative figures as the dramatist Grillparzer, Prince Eugène, and the Empress Maria Theresa, attempting to recreate a sense of traditional values, generosity, audacity, humanity, and an aristocratic outlook combined with a genuine respect for all classes. His play *Jedermann* was also a contribution to this end, for it aimed at both the intellectual and the 'Volk' and was meant to bridge the gap between them by recourse to a combination of folk-art with Baroque tradition. The political aim was doomed to failure, and within a few years Hofmannsthal saw Austria shrivel to one of the smallest states in Europe. Nevertheless, some awareness of his ideals in their political aspect is necessary for a full appreciation of his post-war plays.

The war over, Hofmannsthal continued to write in the fairy-tale vein of enchantment to be found in *Die Frau ohne Schatten* (1919) and *Die ägyptische Helena* (1928); this too was a part of the Austrian, or at least the Viennese tradition, which he could not abandon. At the same time, these libretti reveal even more than his earlier works his preoccupation with mysticism and the occult. Delightful as they are, they are not sheer entertainment, and flashes of mysterious symbolism hint at a continuing search for real selfhood. Similarly the uncompleted novel *Andreas*, published posthumously in 1930, shows many signs of an interest in Rosicrucianism, alchemy, Freemasonry and the symbols derived from them. Hofmannsthal still moved in a world of 'Doppelgänger', hermaphrodites, magical sympathies and strange forebodings. Only in his most ambitious work of all, *Der Turm* (1925, and in a revised version for the stage, 1927) did he attempt to bring together the romantic world of his imagination and his practical political aims. *Der Turm* is a vast network of symbols seeking to portray not only the inner development of its hero but also the essence of European history in the last three hundred years. Based on Calderón's play, *Life's a Dream*, it hints at connections with Oedipus, Hamlet, Schiller's Don Carlos, at the story of Adam's fall and the Second Coming, at the threat of Bolshevism (or of Fascism) and the possibility of realizing Hofmannsthal's ideals for Austria; features of Christ and of Nietzsche flit across the face of its hero, and a prophetic vision of a man in whom we can now recognize a Hitler arises to dominate the scene at the end. The play is an imposing attempt to gather into one fable the purely personal aspirations of Hofmannsthal and his insights into the state of Europe and the aspirations of mankind as a whole. Yet as a whole it fails to communicate: the associations of ideas are too complex and arbitrary, the symbols interfere with the characterization, the realities mingle incomprehensibly with abstractions. Here, at least, and perhaps for the only time, Hofmannsthal was not the master of his material, which he had allowed to become so immense as to be beyond any man's grasp.

So much the more remarkable is *Der Schwierige*, in that here Hofmannsthal completely abandons symbol and allegory, and presents for once an immediately contemporary scene, in terms of sheer realism. Inevitably, his other and possibly deeper preoccupations influence the play. Yet nobody in it 'stands for' any particular quality or abstraction, and if there is symbolism at all it is at that level of reality where it cannot be discerned or pointed out without a sense of impropriety. To pursue 'deeper meanings' in this elusive work is at once a temptation and a folly, and not even the bare outline can be stated with confidence. There is perhaps no better introduction to it than to quote the words near the beginning of Emil Staiger's perceptive essay.[12]

It is not possible even to 'give the contents' in the usual way to anyone who does not know the play, and to begin by saying: Hans Karl, a gentleman of upper Viennese society, has had a liaison with Antoinette Hechingen, but broken it off out of regard for her husband.... We would at once come to a halt and feel obliged to ask ourselves whether we were not going astray. And whatever form we gave to our account, the doubt or rather the certainty would remain, that we were doing violence to the author's viewpoint. For the question whether the mind of man is ever able to appreciate correctly any human event, to see every detail in its true context, to ascertain the why and the wherefore, is an essential ingredient of the play and needs to be treated with tact.

The appreciative critic is indeed in the position where he can scarcely avoid the blunderings of those characters within the play who are all too ready to explain and interpret, and thereby repeatedly demonstrate their incomprehension. On the other hand, there is also a sense in which even the blunderers have their contribution to make towards the total meaning, and this may serve as some kind of pretext for the interpretation attempted here.

The play begins with a time-honoured device, presenting the master Hans Karl through the eyes of his servants, the faithful retainer Lukas and the inquisitive newcomer Vinzenz; the picture soon emerges of a fastidious man-about-town who cannot endure the sight of a picture hanging awry or the unannounced entrance even of close relations. Through the suspicious observations of Vinzenz, moreover, certain questions are aroused in the spectator's mind. Why has Hans Karl, as his fortieth birthday draws near, decided to share his house with his sister Crescence and her son, Count Stani? The war in which he has served is now over; what are his intentions? Does he mean, in middle age, to renounce the society of pretty women, and is it for that reason that he has invited his relations to live with him? Or does he intend to marry, in which case there will be no place for Vinzenz in the house? Vinzenz's suspicions, trivial and gossipy as they are, at once introduce an essential theme, for the question of intentions, whether it is better to have them or to live without them, what they are, and whether they exist at a level different from that of consciousness, recurs frequently later on. There will be occasion to think again of Vinzenz in this opening scene when the full picture is unfolded.

Meanwhile, with the entry of Hans Karl himself, the sceptical view of him as an elegant but irresolute ladies' man seems to be confirmed. His conversation with Crescence is apparently aimless, like so much of the play, although it also reveals the bases on which the plot is, almost casually, to be built up. The vital question of the moment is whether or not Hans Karl intends to go to a soirée at the residence of his relations, the Altenwyls, and on the whole it seems that the answer is no. 'If it were all the same to you', he tells Crescence, 'I should quite possibly have decided later on, and quite possibly have phoned from the club to cry off. You know I can't bear to tie myself down.'[13] Already what Crescence calls Hans Karl's 'Wiegel-Wagel' begins to show itself, his inability to come to any firm decision, for we learn a little later that he has telephoned a few hours ago to refuse the invitation. As so often it is yes and no with him at the same time, and this indeterminate mood, swaying between both opposites, continues as the scene progresses. It soon appears that, at least in Crescence's view—but then she is always jumping to wrong conclusions—Hans Karl's unwillingness to attend the soirée is due to his reluctance to meet the youthful daughter of the house, Helene Altenwyl, who—again according to Crescence—has been head over heels in love with him for years past. Moreover, Crescence urges, if Hans Karl insists on staying away, Helene will in all probability marry the upstart Baron Neuhoff. At this, he begins to waver again, although his motives are not quite clear, indeed they never are. Whether he inclines to go to the soirée from jealousy, or whether it is because, as he says, he will lend credibility to the rumour of his attachment to Helene if he stays away, remains undetermined. In any case, a further complication arises, for Crescence is much concerned that her son Stani is mildly flirting with the beautiful Antoinette Hechingen, a married woman who is, in her turn, devoted to Hans Karl: a word from him would be enough to remind Antoinette of her duty to her husband and rescue Stani from possible future scandal. With this, a new 'motive' enters. For the time being, Hans Karl remains irresolute. Only when Antoinette's maid has called, to collect the large sealed bundle of letters from her mistress which Hans Karl has preserved for more than two years, does he make up his mind to attend the soirée after all. And by now it is most uncertain whether he does so in the awareness of the complete break with Antoinette implied by the return of her letters—for he will now have the opportunity of seeing her again at the Altenwyls'—or whether he really does intend to talk her into marital fidelity, or whether he has discovered here a better pretext for seeing Helene. This last, however, seems the least probable of all, for Crescence, taking Hans Karl's denial of love for Helene 'au pied de la lettre', now hits on a further use for his diplomacy. Rather than that Helene should marry Neuhoff, let Hans Karl propose to her on behalf of Crescence's son Stani, who, having been carefully fended away from Antoinette, will be free to make a splendid match. To this Hans Karl agrees, leaving Vinzenz to draw the obvious conclusion as the curtain falls on the first act: 'He's sent back his love-letters, he's marrying off his nephew, and himself he's decided to live as an elderly bachelor along with me. Exactly as I thought!'[14]

The dilemma of almost all the characters in the play is, however, that things are always turning out exactly as they thought, while at the same time contradicting all their expectations. They confidently read their own motives into the actions of others, but since their own motives are so inconstant they are not greatly surprised when the outcome of those actions shows their interpretation to have been inaccurate: but the feeling of having been right remains with them almost all the time. Stani, in his own eyes, is a young replica of his uncle, whom he studies with care and whose manner he reproduces almost to perfection. He is also, however, in contrast to Hans Karl, a man of decisive action, a perceptive observer for whom the world divides itself into neat categories and who is never at a loss for words or deeds. Yet by the end of the play he has done nothing and gained nothing. Crescence too is a skilful intriguer, constantly making tactful adjustments to situations, reliant on her instinct and good sense, while in successive scenes she shows a total misunderstanding of every situation that arises. Hans Karl alone is indecisive, never knows what he wants or intends to do, and is continually horrified at the unforeseen results of his actions. Like the spider in Hofmannsthal's epigram, he spins out a thread from his own body, and this same thread is his own path through the air:[15] the direction seems arbitrary or random. If the rest live in a world of self-reflecting illusion, he scarcely knows of a self to reflect; living as it were in a pre-existent world he does not know how to differentiate as they do, and yet this indeterminacy yields no advantage. When he comes to deal with reality he too makes blunder after blunder, and his very indifferentism is the cause of misunderstanding.

The first act shows Hans Karl as it were in the isolation and safety of his home (somewhat as Sigismund in *Der Turm* is secure temporarily in his tower). The second act brings him out into the world and confronts him with the reality of the soirée, where confusion and misinterpretation almost immediately begin. Before they do so, however, Hans Karl has the opportunity of a brief conversation with Helene, in which something more of his character is revealed. On his way to the soirée he has called at the circus to see his favourite clown, Furlani, and in recounting his admiration he unwittingly recounts his own ideals. As so often happens, Hans Karl's reflection of the outside world is a reflection of himself, although he cannot observe that. And so when Helene inquires whether Furlani is perhaps a knockabout, a 'Wurstel', he is a little hurt:

No, that would be piling it on too thick. He never piles it on, and he never caricatures. He plays his part: he's the one who wants to understand everybody, who wants to help everybody yet brings everything into confusion. He makes a complete buffoon of himself, the gallery doubles up with laughter, and for all that he keeps up an elegance and a tactfulness—you can see that he respects himself and everything else in the world. He turns everything topsy-turvy; wherever he goes it's sheer Bedlam, and yet you want to call out all the time, 'He's right, you know!'[16]

At this point, attention turns to a conversation between the blue-stocking Edine, of whom there will be more to say shortly, and the master of the house, Poldo Altenwyl. When it returns (it has not been concentrated on this fairly vital speech of Hans Karl's, but allowed to wander in the way talk will at a party) it is to find Hans Karl distinguishing Furlani from the acrobats and jugglers, who need a fabulous concentration for their tricks:

HANS KARL: What Furlani does is at a completely different level from what all the others do. All the rest let themselves be led by some purpose, and they won't look left or right, in fact they scarcely breathe till they've achieved their purpose: that *is* their trick. But he seems to do nothing on purpose—he always joins in with the purposes of other people. He wants to do whatever it is the others are doing, he has so much good will, he's so fascinated by every single turn that any of them does: when he balances a flowerpot on his nose he balances it as it were from sheer politeness.
HELENE: But he drops it?
HANS KARL: But how he drops it, that's the point! He drops it out of sheer enthusiasm and delight that he's balanced it so well up to now. He thinks if you could do it really nicely it would stay up on its own.
HELENE (*to herself*): And as a rule the flowerpot won't stand for that, and down it comes.[17]

Hofmannsthal does seem to hit off here one of the preoccupations of his times. The man who joins in with the purposes of everybody else and has no proper self to speak of is of course also Felix Krull, whose story Thomas Mann had begun but not published, at the time Hofmannsthal wrote this play. He is also, as Franz Mennemeier has observed, reflected again in 'The Man without Qualities', in Robert Musil's Austrian novel of that name,[18] which sums up the tendencies of its epoch. And it is remarkable how both Rilke and Kafka, not to mention Nietzsche, employ the figure of the acrobat to convey the incredible feats of mental agility required by the spiritual adventures of the age. The new age, with its 'all-embracing' philosophies, did in fact require either a knife-edge balance between opposites or a chameleon-like adaptability to them all, and most German writers swung one way or the other, or in both. Yet Helene's final observation is just as relevant for understanding the play as a whole. Does she relate Hans Karl's imagery to her own condition when she remarks that the flowerpot usually will not stand such treatment, but falls down? The stage direction reads 'to herself': she does not intend Hans Karl to hear what sounds like an implied criticism. But she may sense in his admiration for Furlani's combined sympathy and detachment a certain ultimate isolation (such as is inherent in all the post-Nietzscheans) which still lacks or does not even want real and fruitful contact with other human beings. At all events, Helene's later actions tend to bring Hans Karl out of his isolation towards such a contact. The aesthete's ideal of 'doing it really nicely' does not appeal to her entirely.

But the indelicacy of emphasizing such thoughts is quickly exposed in the person of Edine, the keen student of philosophical books and fine literature, who asks nothing better than to be introduced to the famous professor who has graced the party with his presence. She is unfortunate, of course, in that she first praises to his face the profound thought and beautiful style of his published work, only to find that she has mistaken the name, and that the work she has read, on 'The Origin of All Religions', is by the professor's detested rival. Yet it is not so much this contretemps that stays in the mind, as the moment when Edine, greatly daring, puts to him a question that has long weighed on her mind:

EDINE: But I'm so hideously sorry you aren't the author. Now I can't ask you my question. And I would have laid any amount of money that you are the only one who could answer it satisfactorily.

NEUHOFF: Won't you ask the Herr Professor your question all the same?

EDINE: I'm sure you are much more profound and learned than the other gentleman. (*To Neuhoff*) Shall I really? I do so terribly want to know. I do so want satisfaction. I can't tell you how much.

THE FAMOUS MAN: Won't your ladyship sit down?
EDINE: (*anxiously looking round to see whether anyone is coming, then quickly*) What do you think Nirvana is like?[19]

This is the kind of conversation that old Altenwyl deplored when he spoke of his guests asking their neighbours, as soon as soup was served, whether they believed in metempsychosis. In his day, one conversed to bring out one's partner, to make him at ease and thereby to make him pleased with oneself. In these days, as Helene remarks, there are only 'words that flatten all reality'.[20] Yet the function of this passage, satirical of such conversation as it is, is not exhausted in satire. Nothing here is quite fortuitous, and Edine's question stays in one's mind like those absurdities posed by Zen masters to their pupils. It can be dismissed, but it will recur.

The remainder of the second act consists essentially of two more conversations—although in saying this one becomes aware that nothing is inessential, and that every omission detracts from the sense of the whole. Hans Karl has first to meet Antoinette, in accordance with Crescence's suggestion, and dissuade her from encouraging Stani. His purpose seems clear enough, and he does begin by urging on Antoinette the propriety of remaining faithful to her husband Ado von Hechingen, for whose naïvety Hans Karl, unlike others, has a great regard. But Stani is soon forgotten in the general reflections on marriage which take hold of Hans Karl, and he never arrives at the point which for Crescence is so important. He reverts to his habitual indeterminacy as he seeks first to persuade Antoinette of the complete relativity of all feelings of love between men and women. For his own part, he declares, he has no conscience, which seems to confirm Antoinette's accusation that he thinks all things permissible. 'Nothing is evil', he adds; he has been very attached to Antoinette, in the past—just how much we never discover—and in that there was nothing wrong. It would be wrong only to attempt to hold on to such moments. All that happens is mere chance, and so far as chance is concerned any man could live with any woman. It is not surprising that, after this, Antoinette feels both insulted, at his attaching so little importance to her, and subtly tempted to suppose that he is not withdrawing his affection completely after all. Nor is this impression of hers altered when Hans Karl continues his reflections. To live as chance dictates, he says, is to live in horror: human beings have found the chaos of sheer relativity impossible to bear, and have therefore invented 'the institution which turns chance and unchastity into necessity, permanence and value: marriage'.[21] But although Hans Karl goes on now to emphasize not chance, but 'a necessity which chooses us from moment to moment',[22] Antoinette at once suspects, perhaps from the solemn emotion with which he speaks of the sanctity of marriage, that it is not her marriage with Ado so much as his own with Helene that he has in mind. This Hans Karl hotly denies: he intends this evening to say goodbye for ever to Helene, and at length Antoinette accepts this assurance. She will not be talked into going back to Ado, but she will believe that Hans Karl seriously wants her to, and that he is not, as she a moment ago suspected, merely sending her back to her husband in order the better to pursue an *affaire* with her clandestinely. But what is she to think when, as she is about to leave, he tells her she has never been so close to him, and in answer to her plea that he should come and see her often, kisses her 'almost without knowing it', on the forehead? Hans Karl may really be the innocent, generous, disinterested lover, incapable of concealing the affection he feels for so many people, men and women alike, that he often appears to be. Yet there are also not unreasonable grounds for calling him, as Antoinette and Neuhoff openly do (and his secretary Neugebauer implies), a cynic, an egoist, an inconsiderate trifler who seeks the best for himself in every situation.

This interview reveals something of the 'dangerous condition' which Hofmannsthal also discovered in 'pre-existence'. Hans Karl may speak confidently of the non-existence of evil or of his own conscience, he may distinguish between loving Antoinette and being in love with her, but he can scarcely expect either this knife-edge distinction or his balanced antinomianism to meet with ready comprehension, and it may just be that his rejection of Antoinette is after all, perhaps against his will, a subtle wooing of her. Certainly, from her point of view, it seems like that, and she rushes away to give Crescence a distracted embrace which Crescence all too readily interprets as the emotion of renewed dedication to marital fidelity. A point in the play has been reached, in fact, where Hans Karl's indecisiveness begins to look a little alarming. He himself has spoken of the horror that comes with complete uncertainty, the complete lack of any sense of values (the 'anhedonia' spoken of in *Andreas*),[23] and the complete confusion of all concepts—it is the horror to be felt frequently in Nietzsche, in Rilke and in Kafka—and a little of it comes into consciousness even through the laughter of the comedy. It begins to be a matter of some degree of urgency, for others' sake as well as his own, that Hans Karl should gain greater insight into his own motives, concealed and denied though they may be.

As Helene tells Hans Karl, when she meets him again a half hour later, 'you use the poor women in your own way, but you really aren't very fond of them. It needs a good deal of self-respect, or else a touch of ordinariness, to go on being your friend.'[24] And as he has just told her, words are all very well, but everything really depends on the inexpressible. So long as he continues to believe only that—Helene agrees with him about it, so far as it goes—he has no hope of contact, for communication depends on expression, and within 'the inexpressible' there seems to be only unity and isolation, 'allem nah, allem fern'. Language, words, expressions, are essential despite their inadequacy, and Helene's desire is to help Hans Karl to use them despite his misgivings, just as the play itself uses words for what really cannot be said. Her task, however, is an extraordinarily difficult one, for Hans Karl is if anything more tactless with her than he was with Antoinette, and this despite his great reputation for tact. Almost at once, he advises her to marry whom she likes, Neuhoff for instance, or rather not Neuhoff, but 'the first nice young man that comes along, a man like my nephew Stani, yes really, Helene, marry Stani, it would please him so much, and nothing could possibly harm you'.[25] This is no doubt meant as genuinely disinterested friendly advice, but it has the same ring of unconcern for Helene as a person as had the similar remark to Antoinette. Indeed it is just this disinterestedness of Hans Karl's, his almost mystical detachment, Goethean 'indifference', that precludes him from real humanity. While his attention is really fixed on the inexpressible, the All (or as Stani says, on 'the absolute, the perfect'),[26] he has no perception of people as individuals. Once again it is not surprising that Helene should gently deprecate Hans Karl's indelicacy. But although he withdraws the suggestion about Stani, it is only to substitute 'someone quite different, someone good and noble, someone who is a man: that's to say, everything that I'm not'.[27] And the reason for his blindness, to what everyone else including Helene can see plainly enough, becomes apparent when he begins to recount the vision of her he saw when he was momentarily buried by a shell-burst in his dugout during the war. In that moment of apparent annihilation he lived through a whole lifetime, and in that lifetime it seemed to him quite clearly that Helene was his wife—not his future wife, but quite simply his wife, as a *fait accompli*. Yet in his self-effacing way, he still could not envisage this as an account of his own marriage; he felt himself rather as an onlooker at some wedding ceremony in which Helene was involved with someone other than himself. And thus, although he has approached as close as he is ever likely to do to a proposal, Hans Karl is in the end covered with confusion at his tactlessness, bids adieu to Helene, and leaves her to an overwhelming desperation which Crescence once again interprets in her own favour, as a sign of Hans Karl's second success of the evening.

Hans Karl's account of his vision has one feature in common with the attitude of most people towards their dreams: they cannot bring themselves to see that they themselves are the principals in these unconscious narrations, any more than they can see themselves in their conscious interpretations of waking reality. The vision shows him with all possible clarity as the husband of Helene, but he still makes a distinction between the self who appears in the vision and the self who dreams it. In the same way, he distinguishes between chance and necessity, illusion and reality, relative standards and the absolute, and it is of course immensely difficult to see how he could very well do otherwise. And yet by this time almost every member of the audience must be urgently expecting him to realize his identity with the self of his vision, and not only amused but even slightly vexed at the self-enclosing illusion that prevents him from seeing it. It is the task of the third act to show how he escapes at least momentarily from this curious dualism of a divided selfhood in which we all exist for most of our time.

Before we come to the third act, however, it will be enlightening to cast a backward glance over some of the other features of the play up to this point. A very clear impression is given, in the course of the first two acts, that no character really ever understands another character: confusions and misunderstandings follow quickly on one another's heels and are the main source of comedy. On the other hand, a great many of the interpretations of motive are surprisingly shrewd or close to the point. Agathe, Antoinette's maid, is convinced, despite Hans Karl's denials, that he wrote in his letters to her mistress that love was a matter of pure chance, and in his scene with Antoinette herself we hear him saying as much. Neugebauer, the secretary, manages by his unbending formality to imply a severe moral judgment on the adventurer whom he sees in his master, and Hans Karl is not at all certain whether he has not a right to do so. But it is the unspeakable Neuhoff, of all people, who comes nearest to giving a verbal definition of Hans Karl's quality which can scarcely be denied. It is he who perceives in him the childlikeness whose presence Helene later, in a different context, confirms. It is Neuhoff again who describes the quality of Austrian culture— 'value without pretentiousness, nobility tempered with infinite grace'[28]— which receives its stamp from such men as Hans Karl, and Neuhoff who defines the truth and naturalness of Hans Karl's character. That he does so to his face is of course the first mark of his insincerity, and that he says precisely the opposite behind his back is the second. Yet it should not be overlooked, when Stani fumes at these indiscretions, that Hans Karl remarks 'It was probably all very much as he said it was'.[29] This refers, it is true, to Neuhoff's account of his conversation with Helene, and Hans Karl adds at once, 'But there are people in whose mouths every nuance is altered, willy-nilly'. However, it is not false to say that every remark of Neuhoff's in this scene has a certain ring of truth. The circumstances in which he makes them render them difficult to accept, and yet he is not plainly wrong for all that. In a not dissimilar way, the cynical Vinzenz has right on his side when he affirms that Crescence and Stani do as they please with Hans Karl, bending him to their own desires. And towards the end of the play, there is a curious scene in which misunderstanding leads to apparently complete accuracy of interpretation. Antoinette, abandoned by Hans Karl to her husband, is wooed now by Neuhoff with unheard-of effrontery. As she determinedly rejects him, Ado von Hechingen appears momentarily on the balcony above; he is seen by Neuhoff, whose expression at once changes, but not by Antoinette. At once, however, she 'misinterprets' this changed expression in a manner which surely hits him off exactly. It was Helene, and not Ado, she believes, who just passed by, and the sight of her has aroused in Neuhoff spite and impotence, anger and shame that he has failed to win her, together with the determination to conquer Antoinette for want of a better prey. 'Edine tells me off for not being able to read complicated books. But that was very complicated, and I read it in a flash.'[30] She has read quite wrongly, of course, and yet it cannot be doubted that such feelings were at the heart, whether Neuhoff let them come to the surface at that moment or not. In short, no interpretation need be put on one side as irrelevant. Subjective, obtuse, insincere misunderstandings can hit the mark as well as others, and in this particular scene at least illusion comes very close to reflecting reality. Similarly, reality can easily be mistaken for illusion, as is clear in the ensuing scene between Antoinette and her husband. Ado's pathetic attempts at protesting his fidelity and love, clothed entirely in words evidently borrowed from his memories of conversations with Hans Karl about his wife, have all the hallmarks of a second-hand fervour, and succeed only in increasing Antoinette's distress. Yet one would swear that no husband was ever more genuinely devoted than Ado, and it is one of the subtlest ironies in the play that the words which might have sounded so well, coming from Hans Karl, here have the ring of insincerity.

By the last act, the dividing line between illusion and reality, which the earlier scenes seemed to emphasize, has begun to be erased. Not only that: the dividing line between chance and necessity, desire and will, conscious self and unconscious self, becomes increasingly difficult to perceive. For now that Antoinette has misunderstood Neuhoff, and understood her husband much too well, Hans Karl himself returns to the house which he left only a short while ago in the full determination never to impose himself on Helene again. His conscious motive, as he explains it to himself, is the desire to restore to Helene her freedom; he realizes that the mere mention of marriage with her, even in allusion to a past vision, was a kind of proposal which he now wants formally to withdraw. He realizes at once, of course, that by the mere word 'freedom' he implies some earlier claim to Helene's love, and substitutes 'disinterestedness' instead: he wants, then, to restore her disinterestedness. By now, however, it is clear that no substitution will do; every evasion brings him to a further level of self-contradiction. He has come back to Helene in order to tell her that he is not coming back, that in seeming to propose to her he had no intention of proposing, but that the mere seeming in itself implied a reality which he will not acknowledge, and which his presence now does nothing to confirm. His return is a final token of his departure. To this, Helene can only reply that she will tell him why he has come back:

HANS KARL: Oh my God, you think there's no understanding me. Say so straight away.

HELENE: I understand very well. I understand what it was that drove you away, *and* what it was that brought you back again.

HANS KARL: You understand? I don't even understand myself.

HELENE: We might talk a little more softly, if you wouldn't mind. What drove you away from here was your distrust, your fear of your real self—are you annoyed?

HANS KARL: Of my self?

HELENE: Your real will, a long way down inside you. Yes, it isn't very agreeable, it doesn't lead you the easiest way. It's just brought you back here, for instance.

HANS KARL: I don't understand you, Helen'!³¹

But he quickly does understand, when Helene shows by repeated insights her understanding of him, and when he confesses her to be in the right time after time. It is true that, when she commits the 'enormity' of actually proposing to him, he still hesitates, convinced as he is that he has nothing but misunderstandings on his conscience. Yet although they are both tenderly and deeply distressed by now, Helene displays to perfection that quality of 'indifference' or disinterestedness which Hans Karl had hitherto displayed in vain. She would not have lifted a finger, she says, to attract him away from another woman, and as she says so, we are reminded of Neuhoff's clumsy observation, made to her face, that her simplicity is the result of a tremendous tension: 'Motionless as a statue, you vibrate within yourself, and no one can suspect it, but anyone who does suspect it vibrates with you.'³² And 'Everything about you is wonderful. And at the same time, like all lofty things, almost terrifyingly matter-of-fact.'³³ Hans Karl, though he will not and may not say it, perceives the quality of indifferent love in Helene which exists also in himself and which, when expressed to Antoinette, led only to misunderstanding: he begins to share in the movement of her being. He also appreciates the matter-of-factness in Helene, which is not deceived in him, does not idealize him, but wants to know and love him as he is. At the same time, there is something mysterious about matter-of-factness of this kind, belonging almost to genius. To quote a countrywoman of Hofmannsthal's, the nineteenth-century novelist Marie von Ebner-Eschenbach: 'Say something that goes without saying for the first time, and you will be immortal.' It is this kind of realistic insight that Helene has into Hans Karl, and he acknowledges it by a remark which has little enough to do with the obvious: 'What is this magic in you? Not at all like other women. You make a man so quiet in himself.'³⁴ Matter-of-factness to this degree looks like magic. It has also the quality of bringing Hans Karl to live for the first time in contentment with himself. Being accepted by Helene as he is, he is able to accept himself as he is. And although Hofmannsthal is careful not to intrude into this conversation piece more than a little suggestion of the matters which concerned his mind outside it, it is not inapt to quote here the words which were perhaps intended to conclude his unfinished novel, *Andreas*. 'He was what he was able to be, and yet never, or scarcely ever, had been. He saw the sky, the small clouds over a wood, he saw beauty and was moved—but without the feeling of selfhood on which the world needs to rest as on an emerald—with Romana, he said to himself, it could be his heaven.'35 The lost Romana of the novel is found here in the play.

But Helene has also spoken of the 'will' in Hans Karl, a word easily used and in fact frequently used, by Neuhoff, throughout the play. No concept has so permeated German literature and thought as this has, or been so often substituted 'wo Begriffe fehlen'. It is the simplest thing in the world to let it stand in difficult places for a whole vague metaphysical system, and trust in its imposing weight of accrued suggestiveness to explain the ineffable. This Hofmannsthal does not do. Helene's remark (more natural in a cultured Austrian woman than in an English counterpart) is not a mere token of meaning. If we look back over the play, the sense to be attached to it, on a little examination, becomes clear. From the beginning, Hans Karl has been moving 'against his will', as we might say on some occasions, or 'by his own will', as we might say on others, towards this point. He has seen events taking place against his will in the same sense that he has seen only a strange self reflected in his vision. Possibly Vinzenz was right, in his cynical way, to suppose at the outset that Hans Karl had invited Crescence and Stani to live with him in order to make a life of amorous adventures more difficult for himself. This may have been, unconsciously, a necessary first step, although Hans Karl could never have properly recognized it at the time. And then again, his motives for going to the soirée were subtly complex. He decided to go, not because he would see Helene: though he seemed to yield on that point to Crescence, he made it clear later on that he did so out of mere politeness, and had in fact decided to the contrary. The immediate occasion of his decision to go was the visit of Antoinette's maid Agathe, and the occasion it offered of seeing Antoinette again. So far as conscious motives were concerned, it was the desire to see another woman than Helene which prompted Hans Karl. For all he knew, it was the genuine desire to restore Antoinette to her husband and woo Helene for Stani that sent him to the Altenwyls. It was also the genuine desire to restore to Helene her freedom or her dis-interestedness that both sent him away from the house and brought him back to it. All this we can interpret, from outside his situation, as the working of one aspect of himself which in fact does not lead him the easiest of paths. What we do not so quickly realize, however, is that this path may have been the only possible one by which he could win Helene. A deliberate wooing of her might have had quite different results. Helene, like Hans Karl, will make no pursuit, and yet it is this very indifference that leads Antoinette to accuse her of secretly running after him. As Neuhoff says, and he seems once again to be proved right by the course of events: 'She is like you: one of the sort that can't be wooed, that have to give themselves to you.'[36] Helene cannot be wooed and will not woo, yet in her last scene with Hans Karl she does give herself to him. And it may be that Hans Karl knew this, in some sense, as she knew it too, and that both were guided by an instinctive sympathy towards one another. Or as each of them has said at different times, the whole experience has been present from the beginning for them both, and has merely come to light as, in Hans Karl's image, the lower part of the statue did in the drained fountain. The purposelessness of Hans Karl's conduct that evening can also be seen as purposeful, in what is still a proper sense of the word, or it can all be seen as an enduring condition.

Hans Karl is not, however, immediately cured of his in-decisiveness or his almost mystical leanings. That would be rather much to expect from a single evening's conversations. He remains on stage after Helene has left, to deplore the fact that he has shortly to stand up in the House of Lords, of which he has been a hereditary member for years without uttering a word, and make a speech on international reconciliation:

—I, a man who is convinced of one thing at all events, that it's impossible to open your mouth without causing the most disastrous confusion.... But everything we say is indecent. The simple fact of saying anything at all is indecent. And to be particular, my dear Ado— but nobody ever is particular about anything—there's even something shameless in daring to experience some things at all. To experience some things and not feel indecent takes such a monstrous self-infatuation and a degree of self-delusion as a grown man can perhaps hide in the innermost corner of his heart, but never can admit to himself.[37]

The defence of the unsayable remains, though one remembers that Hofmannsthal himself did dare to speak on international and other political issues of his day, and that Helene has just revealed to Hans Karl the possibility of decency. But that is the way it is with this play. Nothing is ever quite fixed and definite: it never reveals authoritatively what motives have been, what Nirvana is like, what is success and what failure, what is reality and what illusion, or where the true self lies. Like *Der Turm*, *Der Schwierige* affords a sympathetic critique of European culture, especially in its German aspects, and advances a statement of Austrian qualities, civilized values, which provide the possibility of a crystallizing point in a chaotic world. It is a strange irony that the month which saw the end of an empire that had existed in one form or another for at least four hundred years also saw the conception of a play which embodied the social character of that empire at its best. *Der Schwierige* does more than that, however. It takes up the recurrent themes of German literature, the nihilistic idealism, the pursuit of the absolute, the desire for the All, the preponderance of Will over Being, but without fanaticism, defiance, overstraining or lack of humour, and it places them in a context where they have genuine validity. No one can point with assurance to any part of it and claim the right to perceive that the pursuit has been ultimately successful or the desire fulfilled. It remains completely elusive. As Ernst Robert Curtius has said, however,

> Since Plato's day there has been an eternal struggle between the poet and the thinker. But the poet has the upper hand, for with him problems are solved not in concepts but in shapes. The labour of thinking is never finished, but the creation of the poet is perfected form. He says the unsayable in the language of symbols. We receive from him an ordered structure of the world, purified of all the tangle of philosophic concepts. 'We can love only individual forms, and when we say we love ideas, we love them always as forms. Form settles the problem, it answers the unanswerable.'

The particular achievement of this play, in comparison with the more ambitious *Der Turm*, is its formal excellence. It is more limited, and yet its scope is almost as great, and its total sense much more definite. As with every other artistic construction, however, indeed with every reality, the sense is definite only in terms of the whole, and all commentary can only serve to refer back to the original.

There is little point, then, in trying to decide whether, as Crescence says, people are simple if you take them simply, or whether in some way all the characters, false and genuine alike, receive a kind of justification of their existence. One wants to say on questions like these, as Hans Karl often says of himself, that every statement in the play needs to be taken 'au pied de la lettre': that it needs to be received as a sheer existent. Yet seeing the confusions which arise for Hans Karl from offering precisely this advice, one wants to turn again to the deeper strata of meaning and make them pre-eminent. Neither course is completely satisfying, and thus the play continues to flash from its many facets in unapproachable isolation. At times a Schopenhauerian or neo-Buddhist interpretation seems to offer itself more readily, at others a fundamentally Christian one. When Neuhoff tells Helene, in the vein of one for whom all the world is illusion, that she herself endows Hans Karl with all his qualities, 'even the power with which he holds you', one thinks of an Oriental subjectivism which may after all be justified. When Helene replies, 'The power with which a man holds you—that must be given him by God',[38] one remembers that Hofmannsthal was buried at his own request in the habit of a Franciscan tertiary. There is perhaps a kind of subtle fusion even in this snatch of talk.

The last word, or almost the last, is thus best left with Hofmannsthal, in the charming scene with which he ends the play. Here Crescence is left with Stani, not at all abashed that her plans have gone completely awry, but rather delighted that her brother and Helene are betrothed. Yet she feels too overjoyed to accept with equanimity the fact that the pair have separated without an embrace, and seeks to remedy their unconventional leave-taking by advancing to embrace her son. Stani retreats in dismay at this threat of overt emotion, and points out that there are two categories of demonstration, the one private, the other public, for which recognized forms of expression have existed for thousands of years. At this moment old Altenwyl descends the staircase with a number of departing guests, as Stani continues to Crescence:

What we have seen here today was, *tant bien que mal*, and to call a spade a spade, an engagement. An engagement is supposed to culminate in an embrace by the couple engaged. In our case the couple engaged is too bizarre to observe this formality. Mama, you are Uncle Kari's next-of-kin, and there's Poldo Altenwyl, the father of the bride. Go up to him *sans mot dire* and embrace him, and the whole thing will look correct and official.[39]

Altenwyl, as the stage direction requires, has come down the steps with some of the guests. Crescence rushes up to him and embraces him. 'The guests stand back in astonishment' and the curtain falls. Society has done its level best to accept and justify the conduct of its two most genuine representatives. It has supplied their lack as they supply its own. And while astonishment is the inevitable outcome of the bringing together of such disparate elements, the laughter it also arouses is of the deeply satisfying kind.

CHAPTER XVI

ENGLISH RESISTANCE TO GERMAN LITERATURE FROM COLERIDGE TO D. H. LAWRENCE

'This has been the confusion and the error of the northern countries, but particularly of Germany, this desire to have the spirit mate with the flesh, the flesh with the spirit. Spirit can mate with spirit, and flesh with flesh, and the two matings can take place separately, flesh with flesh, or spirit with spirit. But to try to mate flesh with spirit makes confusion.'[1] In these words Lawrence expresses in his own special terms a view which had been current in those English writers and critics concerned with German literature for a century and a half. What follows is an account of the opinions expressed by these Englishmen (and Scots and Irishmen), and an attempt at showing how they culminate in a work of Lawrence's, *Women in Love*, which at the same time assimilates much of the German tradition[2] in a distinctive and impressive way. It may even be that something essential to the health of that tradition is to be found in that novel.

Can we appeal to tradition in the way we have been prone to do, in forming impressions of literary works? A purely English tradition is insufficient basis; the 'European mind' will not serve either. One thing that must strike any reader of German literature and thought is the complete difference between the standards of its main tradition and the English ones. German thought is rarely empirical or pragmatic: in Goethe, Hegel, Fichte, Schelling, Schopenhauer, Marx, Wagner, Nietzsche, Mann, Rilke it is 'synthetic', it deals in terms of a universe where all individual phenomena are ambivalent and where a solution is to be found only in escape from the phenomenal world into the Naught, or into the all-embracing yet transcendent Absolute, or into the joyful affirmation of ambivalence, or into some similarly ambiguous haven. German literature, so far as this tradition is concerned, sets out to illustrate the relevant 'Weltanschauung' rather than to explore a given situation or mood to ascertain what it will bring. It is true that these modes of thought and writing have had great influence in France and Russia, not to mention the Scandinavian countries and others. But they have had no comparable influence in England, indeed many English writers were unaware of the far-reaching 'Weltanschauungen' underlying the German works. Goethe had his heyday in mid and late Victorian times, when George Lewes's *Life* appeared (in 1855), and when Irving could pack the Lyceum night after night with a melodramatized *Faust*. Hegel was still a name for Yeats to conjure with in his youth. The close similarity of preoccupations in Nietzsche and D. H. Lawrence is self-evident. And Coleridge was deeply indebted for his critical ideas to contemporary Germans, who thus continue to influence us today. Yet by and large the response to German literature of English poets and critics, novelists and dramatists has been wary, to say the least. The writers most profoundly influenced have been, with few exceptions—Blake and Coleridge are the chief—those who have aroused the least interest in recent generations. Shelley's warm, devoted enthusiasm3 for Goethe's *Faust* has never been echoed here. Scott, who translated *Götz* and took over Goethean themes in novel after novel, seems to be more read in Russia today than in England. Bulwer-Lytton, comparable in respect of German influence, is known far less. Carlyle, to whom the widespread respect for Goethe's genius was largely due, has had little more subsequent success than Walter Pater or George Meredith. Shaw, who tumbled German thought into his plays along with everything else, shows in his ironical ambivalence more affinity to, say, Thomas Mann, than to any of his British contemporaries. Perhaps significantly, it is in Germany that Shaw has retained the greatest share of his reputation. The parodistic reversals of Oscar Wilde, fundamentally akin to Shaw's, may explain something of his almost equal popularity in the German-speaking world.

Of other influences it is hard to speak with much assurance. Joyce, in *Finnegans Wake*, develops a theme with great affinities to German schemes of thought, but much else besides went into the making of that unreadable experiment. The plays of Auden and Spender owed something, sometimes a great deal, to Ernst Toller and the German Expressionists. Brecht has helped to shape plays by Robert Bolt and John Whiting as well as John Osborne's *Luther* and the recent productions of the Royal Shakespeare Company; Kafka must have led Rex Warner to write *The Aerodrome* and *The Wild Goose Chase*. But these are hardly to be reckoned influences in the main stream. Nor has any German writer found a following here comparable to Schiller's influence on Dostoevsky, Hoffmann's on Gogol, Nietzsche's on Gide, Sartre and Camus, Kafka's on Ionesco and Beckett, or the more general German influence in Ibsen. It is often by a more devious route, *via* such authors as these, that German literature has really made itself felt.

Even within the stream of those British writers most receptive to German ideas, there has often been a hesitancy. Coleridge, though he translated Schiller's *Wallenstein*, and had read all the German literature thought worth the reading in his time, was frankly and accurately critical of the one generally acclaimed masterpiece it contained. 'There is neither causation nor progression in *Faust*; he is a ready-made conjurer from the beginning; the *incredulus odi* is felt from the very first line. The sensuality and the thirst after knowledge are unconnected with each other. Mephistopheles and Margaret are excellent; but Faust himself is dull and meaningless.'[4] True, this is table-talk, and Coleridge found a few things to praise in *Faust*; like Ezra Pound and many others he singled out Goethe's lyrics and ballads as truly excellent. Even so, despite the presence in *Faust* of such elements, Coleridge could go on to say 'there is no whole in the poem; the scenes are mere magic-lantern pictures, and a large part of the work is to me very flat'.[5] And no English poet or established critic has ever made any serious attempt to gainsay that impression of a work whose reputation in Europe still stands high. On the whole, apart from Shelley and Carlyle, *Faust* has been ignored or dismissed by English men of letters.

By comparison with Coleridge, Carlyle was an enthusiastic champion not only of Goethe but of everything German: Kant, Novalis, J.-P. Richter, Frederick II, and many writers almost forgotten now in their own country. It was through Carlyle's translations, particularly of *Wilhelm Meister*, that German literature became known as much as it did in Prince Albert's time. Yet for all Carlyle's enthusiasm, his letters show how bored he was with Goethe's novel, and his introductory remarks do not lead readers to expect great things.

Of romance there is next to none in *Meister*; the characters are samples to judge of, rather than persons to love or hate; the incidents are contrived for other objects than moving or affrighting us; the hero is a milksop, whom, with all his gifts, it takes an effort to avoid despising. The author himself, far from 'doing it in a passion', wears a face of the most still indifference throughout the whole affair; often it is even wrinkled by a slight sardonic grin. For the friends of the sublime, then, for those who cannot do without heroical sentiments, and 'moving accidents by flood and field', there is nothing here that can be of any service.[6]

Carlyle's argument is of course devious: the suggestion that the reader who expects real people in real situations is identical with the one who wants heroics and excitement slips past him unnoticed. But so is his whole presentation devious; we find him speaking on the next page of 'the minute and skilful delineation of men', 'the lively genuine exhibition of the scenes they move in', of the author's 'eloquence, tenderness', and of a style so rich in 'general felicities'.[7] This contradictory ambiguity is everywhere in Carlyle's criticism: it is a part of that generosity which made him attempt to understand what his contemporaries readily laughed off as German mysticism; he sought to allow for what his readers might say and yet put forward the claims of the unfamiliar. The same generosity led him also, however, into the world of paradox and ambivalence in which Goethe lived, and it did not help him in his criticism. Matthew Arnold was right to say 'On looking back at Carlyle, one sees how much of *engouement* there was in his criticism of Goethe, and how little of it will stand'.[8] Samuel Butler, on the other hand, furious at having been persuaded to get through 'perhaps the very worst book I ever read', wanted to know whether it was all a practical joke, and whether the translation he had used could really be that of Goethe's *Meister*. 'What a wretch Carlyle must be to run Goethe as he has done....'[9] Ruskin was equally indignant: 'The *Wilhelm Meister* is of all stories that ever human being of brains wrote, the intolerablest for dullness and weak romance, mashed up with a precious spice of wisdom—but who has learned anything of it?—except Carlyle.'[10] De Quincey found the novel 'in some capital circumstances... absolutely repulsive'—to the countrymen of 'Mrs Inchbald, Mrs Harriet Lee, Miss Edgeworth and Sir Walter Scott'.[11] Wild as some of these accusations are, they are symptoms of a general feeling strangely at variance with that of Friedrich Schlegel, who ranked the *Meister* with Fichte's philosophy and the French Revolution as one of the most significant developments of his own times—a view which is still current in the German-speaking world.

A more balanced view is to be had from Matthew Arnold, for whom Goethe was a great and powerful spirit, one of the modern writers he most cared for, and supreme among all poets of the Continent in the hundred years before his own day. Arnold admired Goethe's thorough sincerity, his intellectual power, his striving for clarity and firmness. Yet as he himself said, 'Considering how much I have read of Goethe, I have said in my life very little about him'.[12] Apart from references in letters, mostly very brief, Arnold wrote only one critical account of Goethe, and that not so much an exposition of his own views as a running commentary on those of the French critic Edmond Schérer. His purpose seems to have been to deflate the pretensions of Hermann Grimm, who, in calling Goethe the greatest poet of all times and of all peoples, was in Arnold's view 'looking at the necessities, as to literary glory, of the new German empire'[13]—that is, of Bismarck's Reich. In Arnold's eyes, the value of Schérer's criticism, adverse though it often was, lay in its discriminations. In the end, however, with all the reservations Arnold was able to make, his praise for *Faust* and the lyric poems, he still felt impelled to assert plainly, 'It is by no means as the greatest of poets that Goethe deserves the pride and praise of his German countrymen. It is as the clearest, the largest, the most helpful thinker of modern times.'[14] And again, with more precision,

Goethe is the greatest poet of modern times, not because he is one of the half-dozen human beings who in the history of our race have shown the most signal gift for poetry, but because, having a very considerable gift for poetry, he was at the same time, in the width, depth, and richness of his criticism of life, by far our greatest modern man. He may be precious and important to us on this account above men of other and more alien times, who as poets rank higher. Nay, his preciousness and importance as a clear and profound modern spirit, as a master-critic of modern life, must communicate a worth of their own to his poetry, and may well make it erroneously seem to have a positive value and perfectness as poetry, more than it has. It is most pardonable for a student of Goethe, and may even for a time be serviceable, to fall into this error. Nevertheless, poetical defects, where they are present, subsist, and are what they are.[15]

It was, in short, as a sincere thinker that Arnold prized Goethe most, and in this he was close to Carlyle, even though he was not disposed to smile away imperfections as Carlyle had done. In his denial of universal rank to Goethe, Arnold is also echoed by T. S. Eliot, at least in his earlier writings. Of Goethe's poetry Eliot once wrote

...because of its partiality, of the impermanence of some of its content, and the Germanism of the sensibility; because Goethe appears, to a foreign eye, limited by his age, by his language, and by his culture, so that he is unrepresentative of the whole European tradition, and, like our own nineteenth-century authors, a little provincial, we cannot call him a *universal* classic. He is a universal author, in the sense that he is an author with whose works every European ought to be acquainted: but that is a different thing.[16]

In Eliot's more extensive exposition, delivered at Hamburg on being awarded a Goethe Prize, this view is revised only in a sense almost coincident with Arnold's. As his title, 'Goethe as the Sage',[17] implies, it is not primarily in his poetry that Eliot sees Goethe's pre-eminence, but rather in his wisdom, and in this, he would seem to say, Goethe is more than provincial. Yet despite this larger welcome, it asserts far less than would be claimed on Goethe's behalf in most European countries.

Of the need to respect that claim, no one was more aware than Henry James, whose opinion of Goethe's work was high, though rarely explained.[18] James's review of Carlyle's version of the *Meister*, written at the age of 24, is thus especially valuable. In it, he reveals a generosity and enthusiasm more evidently genuine than Carlyle's had been, a readiness to offer a welcome quite free from irony or deviousness. In defending the novel against the reputation it apparently already had, in 1867, of belonging to 'the class of the great unreadables', he was willing, it is true, to speak of wearisome *minutiae*, flatness, inexpressible dullness, at least as impressions which would be received by a reader unable, for whatever reason, to discover 'behind the offensive details a steadily shining generality'. 'It would not, therefore, be difficult to demonstrate', he added, 'that the great worth of *Wilhelm Meister* is a vast and hollow delusion, upheld by a host of interested dupes.'[19] That James felt the impact of Goethe's wisdom, and valued the novel largely on that account, seems certain—like Carlyle, he could be well content with that, and was inclined to speak in terms of the highest possible praise. Only the occasional remark suggests any doubt on that score, as when he speaks of Wilhelm's ideal of 'perfect harmony with himself'. 'This is certainly a noble idea', James writes. 'Whatever pernicious conclusions may be begotten upon it, let us freely admit that at the outset, in its virginity, it is beautiful.'[20] He does not tell us in more detail what was in his mind, or how the idea seemed to him in its final realization. Was there a hesitation? If there was, it seems to have become a little stronger when he adds, a little later, 'it will be seen that, taken as a whole, *Wilhelm Meister* is anything but a novel, as we have grown to understand the word. As a whole, it has, in fact, no very definite character;

and, were we not vaguely convinced that its greatness as a work of art resides in this very absence of form, we should say that, as a work of art, it is lamentably defective.'[21] It may be, then, that even James, defending a work which he knew to be unpopular, was frankly aware of the difficulties of his case, and a trifle inclined to force the issue, an impression which his conclusion, part diffident, part challenging, seems to confirm.

For most English readers until recently, acquaintance with Goethe has been the chief link with German literature, and there has been opposition from the start. Lamb, Hazlitt and Leigh Hunt were among the censurers of an author who was held to advocate bigamy—in *Stella*, and suicide—in *Werther*. (These were the works by which Goethe first became known.) Wordsworth is said to have expressed his revulsion at Goethe's 'profligacy' and 'inhuman sensuality',[22] and to have thought him 'greatly overrated' as a poet.[23] In fact popular belief about all German authors in the nineteenth century supposed some immorality—Kant was a subtle atheist, and the daring nature of all German speculation was felt to be menacing. Nor was this belief wholly unjustified, for all its crudeness. From Goethe to Nietzsche and on to Thomas Mann, there has been an antinomian trend in German letters which the moral concern of English writers finds hard to accommodate. Gerard Manley Hopkins puts the point with rather more regard for poetic values than Hazlitt showed, when he speaks in one breath of Goethe and Burns, 'scoundrel as the first was, not to say the second'. 'But then', Hopkins adds, 'they spoke out of the real human rakishness of their hearts and everybody recognized the really beating, though rascal, vein.'[24] He makes a point related to this when he charges *Faust* not only with lack of unity—a criticism made frequently by English poets—but also 'want of earnestness'.[25] What Goethe freely admitted on more than one occasion to be a series of 'very seriously intended jokes' is by the same token defective in Hopkins's eyes. The weight of the paradox, if indeed it has any, escapes him. The flippant tone of many of the most serious passages in the *West-Eastern Divan* would probably have

offended Hopkins in the same way. For the particular spirit of
irony found in Goethe as in Mann is, in English literature, to be
found almost nowhere but in Shaw. It is not the irony which
appeals to a recognized standard, so that the intended reverse
impression is fairly readily read off. It is rather the irony which
comes from embracing a comprehensive 'Weltanschauung' which
one knows to be in reality less than comprehensive and which one
nevertheless affirms: a 'Weltanschauung' which is thought not
merely good enough as a rule of thumb, but also essentially true,
and yet, since experience widens every day, not true. In this way,
whatever is affirmed is certainly seriously meant, and yet also
mocked by the author, often in the same breath.[26] It is the
principle of Heine's 'Stimmungsbruch', the sudden reversals in
his poems from gushing Romanticism to cynical contempt, both
moods meant and not meant, which one finds also in Mann's
novels and in *Faust*. This ambivalence has never taken root in
English literature; similarly the oscillations between appearance
and reality, the detachment from all questions of good and evil
which German critics have found in Shakespeare, have never been
so generally noted in English criticism. Thus Arnold's final
comment in his essay on Heine, solemn as it is, is understandable
as part of the puritan strain. Heine was for Arnold, of course, the
direct descendant of Goethe, 'a brilliant soldier in the War of
liberation of humanity', and yet not an adequate interpreter of the
modern world. 'Heine had all the culture of Germany; in his
head fermented all the ideas of modern Europe. And what have
we got from Heine? A half-result for want of moral balance, and
of nobleness of soul and character.' No doubt Heine's possession
of the German cultural inheritance is disputable. All the same,
Arnold is picking here on the one point, Heine's antinomian
fecklessness, which has most struck English writers about such
German authors as they chanced to read:

> Traum der Sommernacht! Phantastisch
> Zwecklos ist mein Lied. Ja, zwecklos
> Wie die Liebe, wie das Leben,
> Wie der Schöpfer sammt der Schöpfung![27]

Aimlessness, though it is inherent in *Finnegans Wake* and *Waiting for Godot*, has till recently been accounted boring, and its synonym 'pointless' is adverse criticism as a rule. A world in which, as in the basic sets of atonal music, there is 'no absolute down, no right or left, forward or backward',[28] is not the world we are accustomed to find in English literature, though the scientific discoveries of this century urge it on us more and more strongly.

Moral concern, so far as it does exist, is no doubt responsible for the unanimity of English writers in praise of Lessing, in whose day the ambivalent systems were still relegated to the world of pietism and Jacob Boehme. When William Taylor, the first English historian of German literature, came to deal with Lessing's *Minna*, he omitted to give the plot, as he had done for most other works, since the play had succeeded on the London stage and was 'too well known to require analysis here'.[29] It is doubtful whether that could have been said of any other German work in the nineteenth century, except Goethe's *Faust* and perhaps Grillparzer's *Die Ahnfrau*, which had some fame as pure melodrama. Lessing was favoured not only by Coleridge, for his theological views,[30] and by Carlyle, but also by De Quincey whose attitude to most German writers was hostile, and by George Saintsbury, who had little regard for the bulk of German literary criticism, but ranked Lessing considerably higher than 'most of his contemporaries and successors'.[31] But Lessing, as Hugo von Hofmannsthal said, represented a possible trend in German literature which never developed after his day. He is a rare representative of a mode of writing not rigidly governed by a systematic world-view. He has no 'Weltanschauung' in the sense that Nietzsche and Mann have one, and it was precisely the sweepingly ideological element in German thought which disturbed some English critics, whether Acton in his study of German historians, or even Bradley in his attempt at enlarging Hegel's theory of tragedy—although few poets or critics of literature seem to have been aware of the dominant role played by ideology in the German works they, for their part, had read.

The ideas current in the main stream of German literature since

Goethe's beginnings are potent enough, and have a long neo-Platonist and mystical tradition behind them. The notion of a world imbued with complementary opposites, and of the need to combine these in a single unity, goes back to Plotinus and beyond him at least as far as the *Symposium*. While the restriction of the categories to a mere dualism rather than to a multiplicity almost always seems arbitrary, the very ambitiousness of the speculations has a certain impressiveness. Faced with such a weighty line of poets and philosophers, concerned for generation after generation with the problem of achieving a godlike unity out of these polar contradictions, Germans have been ready to take the intention for the deed. To solve the 'problem of the theodicy', to demonstrate a reconcilement of the simultaneous existence of good and evil in the world, has properly seemed a more important task for novelists, dramatists and poets than what looks like an unambitious contentment in recording isolated series of events, seen with the eyes of a mere individual. As a German undergraduate said, explaining his own lack of interest, English literature has 'no problems'; he meant that it does not as a rule deal in cosmologies. A German writer (speaking broadly) must first feel that he has gained a more than individual standpoint, just as a German critic must first feel that he has achieved a comprehensive aesthetic, or at least a definition of the 'Zeitgeist', before either is justified in offering his work to the world at large. Thus what sometimes looks like supreme egoism in an apparent self-identification with the Absolute at least begins in humility. The systems are arrived at from a sense that anything less than all-embracing must be presumptuous. The danger of the systems is their suggestion that anything could be all-embracing. At one point or another, the system is seen to be inadequate, and the famous irony slips in, or else the shortcomings themselves are given absolute value, as seems to be done in the line from the Chorus mysticus in the Second Part of *Faust*.[32] Or if neither of these attitudes is present, the alternative is a naïve confidence in the system, whichever it may be, as a key to all reality. To quote an English critic of Rilke's interpreters, 'If there is any widespread German weakness to counterbalance the English weakness which has led to the term "happy ending" being adopted in more than one foreign language, it is perhaps the limitless faith in what can be achieved by "Synthese" '.33 Where the happy ending has been the main value attached to any of these systems, they have led towards the acceptance of that all-embracing philosophy which claimed, not wholly unjustly, to represent the German tradition in 1933.34

Few of the writers in Great Britain with whom we are concerned have been aware of the precise nature and importance of these speculations. Yeats, however, was well aware of the issues involved, and his comments thus have a special interest. When Yeats said that he belonged to a species of man in whom 'nothing so much matters as Unity of Being', he had in mind the same kind of unity, synthesis, as the one Germans more than any others have striven after in recent times. Yet he puts his finger on a point that has been essential in many of the English criticisms when he adds,

but if I seek it [Unity of Being] as Goethe sought, who was not of that species, I but combine in myself and perhaps as it now seems, looking backward, in others also, incompatibles. Goethe, in whom objectivity and subjectivity were intermixed, I hold, as the dark is mixed with the light in the eighteenth Lunar Phase, could but seek it as Wilhelm Meister seeks it, intellectually, critically, and through a multitude of deliberately chosen experiences; events and forms of skill gathered as if for a collector's cabinet; whereas true Unity of Being, where all the nature murmurs in response if but a single note be touched, is found emotionally, instinctively, by the rejection of all experience not of the right quality, and by the limitation of its quantity. Of all this I knew nothing.... Nor did I understand as yet how little that Unity, however wisely sought, is possible without a Unity of Culture in class or people that is no longer possible at all.35

This is the old criticisms in a new guise. Where Yeats speaks of a 'collector's cabinet', Coleridge spoke of 'mere magic-lantern pictures', Hopkins of a lack of unity, and Arnold said of *Faust* that it was a work of episodes and detached scenes, 'not a work where the whole material has been fused together in the author's mind by strong and deep feeling, and then poured out in a single jet'.[36] The distinction implied is the one Coleridge made between fancy and the 'esemplastic' imagination, a distinction which he probably learned from German sources, and which Goethe knew of well enough. (Fancy corresponds to what he calls in his scientific work 'Mischung' as opposed to 'Steigerung', the mingling of many elements rather than their transcending and illuminating fusion.) What Yeats adds to the earlier criticisms is an interpretation of their meaning within the framework of the ambivalent systems itself. It is, fundamentally, that all self-conscious, intellectual apprehension of these systems is self-destroying: it allows the left hand to know too well what the right hand is doing. As he put it at another time: 'It seems to me that I have found what I wanted. When I try to put it all into a phrase I say "Man can embody truth but he cannot know it". I must embody it in the completion of my life. The abstract is not life and everywhere drags out its contradictions. You can refute Hegel but not the Saint or the Song of Sixpence.'[37] Even this may be thought over-conscious, and perhaps that is inevitable in the social conditions of which Yeats speaks. Still he makes a point here about Hegel which he might have extended to Goethe (of whom William James said that Hegel was his philosophical interpreter), namely that abstract thought clothed in literary form results not in the paradox which may very well be the final mystery, but in distinct contradictions, flat and easily refutable. In so far as such clothing of abstractions is characteristic of Goethe's work—and it is so of nearly all his plays and novels, as of his scientific work—it is clear why so many critics have preferred his wisdom to his artistry. In aphorisms and epigrams, as in the general intentions of his works, abstractions can sound and rightly be imposing. On the other hand, this eating of the fruit of the tree of knowledge, with its promise of becoming as the gods are, can be the supreme deception, fairy-money. The abstraction sounds ultimate, it seems to be the expression of a super-individual, but in the process of turning into reality it crumbles and vanishes.

It is significant for the strength of this feeling in England that E. M. Forster, who uses the German systematization unobtrusively both in *Howards End*, and to a lesser extent in *A Passage to India*, always stops short of the synthesis which crowns (though ironically) most of the novels of Thomas Mann, his contemporary. *Howards End*, with its motto 'Only connect'. . . is in theme the exact counterpart of Mann's many 'artist-novels', with their polar opposites of 'burgher' and 'artist'. Only connect the intellectual world of Margaret Schlegel with the practical, business-like world of Henry Wilcox, and the great achievement is made. But the attempt is unsuccessful: where Mann's *Tonio Kröger* ends with a contradictory and incredible fusion of the two sides in Tonio himself, just as Goethe's *Tasso* does, Margaret Schlegel is never wholly one with her husband, despite her loyalty. 'It is part of the battle against sameness', she explains to Helen. 'Differences— eternal differences, planted by God in a single family, so that there may always be colour; sorrow perhaps, but colour in the daily grey.' The concepts are the familiar ones from German novels, but the conclusion is different. Later, in *A Passage to India*, Mr Forster developed the point after the collapse of the effort at understanding and union between Indian and Englishmen. . .'No, not yet. . .No, not there.' Any such unity was not for here and now.

But if Mr Forster ends on a note of gentle pessimism, D. H. Lawrence both enters more fully into the ambivalent systems and makes use of them in a way characteristic of an English tradition, perhaps even assimilating them in a quite new way. Lawrence's relationship to Germany was both more intimate and more critical than that of any other English writer—he was perhaps the first of these to marry a German wife—and yet his opinions of German writers were hostile when they were not contemptuous, as they were of Goethe[38] and Thomas Mann.[39] More than this, he instinctively recoiled both from the German nation and from the very atmosphere of Germany: 'Out of the very air', he wrote of a post-war visit, 'comes a sense of danger, a queer, *bristling* feeling of uncanny danger.' It was not that the people were actually planning or plotting or preparing; there was nothing conscious in what Lawrence saw already in 1924 as the ancient spirit of prehistoric Germany coming back, 'at the end of history'. Nor, needless to say, was he thinking in terms of rival nationalisms, having opposed the war of 1914–18. Rather, it was that 'the northern Germanic impulse is recoiling towards Tartary, the destructive vortex of Tartary'. And, in a German mood himself, 'it is a fate; nobody now can alter it. It is a fate.'[40]

Lawrence's sense of this fatal course in German and thereby in European history is reflected nowhere better in his work than in *Women in Love*, a novel which must strike every reader familiar with German literature as almost cast in a German mould. It is not in fact cast—Lawrence does no more than make use of the ambivalent systems in giving his work structure; he does not write from out of a settled 'Weltanschauung', as Thomas Mann or Hermann Hesse do. He remains essentially an explorer. Yet a discussion of *Women in Love* in its more German aspects may be useful not only in drawing attention to features that may be ignored, but also in indicating the contribution the novel may make to the European culture of the future.

One thing likely to be noticed by anyone with a mainly German background is the number of German words the novel contains—'Wille zur Macht', 'Blutbrüderschaft', the 'Glücksritter' desired by Gudrun—and the fact that, unlike most of the other foreign words in it, these refer to essential concepts in the novel. More important, however, is the role played in the whole structure by the concept of 'polarity', one rarely found in English literature but a commonplace in German. Structurally, although in no other respects, no novel corresponds so closely with *Women in Love* as does Goethe's *Elective Affinities*. Here there is the same pattern of two pairs of lovers, Eduard and Ottilie, Charlotte and the Captain, the same occult affinity bringing the one pair together and towards a spiritual union, the other towards a lower and less rewarding one, as there is, although with different implications, in Rupert Birkin and Ursula, Gerald Crich and Gudrun Brangwen.

It is not merely that Lawrence chooses to write of two pairs—that in itself is undistinctive. It is rather that, like Goethe, he is writing of the attraction and repulsion within the pairs and between them, in terms of what he explicitly calls 'polarity', a hidden magnetism. Again, it is not that the two novels point to a similar conclusion. Goethe's is concerned with 'resignation': the awareness that the impulse to love can have no real fulfilment until after death. It also treats of love as making the lovers unconsciously reach towards closer and closer identity with one another, in the spirit of that 'synthesis' which was always one of Goethe's preoccupations. Ottilie's handwriting comes to resemble Eduard's more and more, her whole personality grows like his, so that the ultimate union beyond the grave, spoken of in the final lines, must seem meant as a final and complete transubstantiation of the woman in the man. Moreover, the man himself, Eduard, is so passive and dull a character (for whom Goethe himself had little regard) that the prospect of fulfilment remains bleak. For Rupert Birkin on the other hand, the desire for assimilation in the other lover is a way to catastrophe. The differences between the two selves are not to be overcome or whittled away. On the contrary, they are to be heightened, intensified; the woman to become more herself as a woman and the man more himself as a man; only then may they come together, not in fusion but in distinct selfhood, the man keeping the woman 'single within himself, like a star in its orbit'.[41] It is not identity with the mystery of the other's presence that matters, but apartness in the awareness of mystery, the 'palpable revelation of living other-ness'.[42] In this formulation, which Lawrence was evidently attached to more passionately than to many others in his novel, he was, whether he knew it intellectually or not, reiterating a tradition of considerable antiquity.[43] He was also affirming the essential difference he felt between himself and Goethe, for whom, as he believed, there was never any capacity for '*development* of contact with other human beings'. 'Goethe *began* millions of intimacies, and never got beyond the how-do-you-do stage, then fell off into his own boundless ego.'[44] That incapacity, on Lawrence's interpretation, was the counterpart of the desire for identity, the inability to respect otherness. He might have quoted Faust's desire to enjoy all the joys and sufferings of all mankind, and thus to extend his selfhood to embrace all self-hood:45 this has the same boundless egoism and the same barren-ness of contact, for Faust as a rule feels no joys or sorrows but his own, and when he does feel *for* someone else (Gretchen is the only instance) he at once ascribes universal importance to the fact.

The insistence on diversity within unity is one characteristic of *Women in Love*, but the novel is not solely concerned with the struggle of Rupert and Ursula towards fulfilment—a fulfilment which is in any case only felt intensely for a moment, to become after that a source of life, a sense of having the pulse 'beating direct from the mystery'.46 The story also contains the struggle of Gerald and Gudrun towards their own fulfilment, their perfection, as Lawrence calls it, and this is to Rupert's and Ursula's fulfilment as negative to positive. The love of Gerald and Gudrun is a purely self-annihilating one, without immediate relationship to the mystery beyond or in the lovers. And being self-annihilating in this sense it is also self-assertive, perhaps because when the self is dead without recourse to any fertility beyond it, it is faced with sheer nothingness, an intolerable void from which it recoils on itself with even greater avidity. This is how it is with Gerald, the 'Dionysus' of the story (whereas Rupert is more often compared with Jesus, and spoken of deprecatingly as a would-be 'Salvator Mundi'). It is Gerald whom we most often see assertive, domi-nating his mare, digging his spurs into her at the level-crossing to force her to obey his will as the frightening locomotive rumbles past.47 It is he who cows the struggling rabbit with a vicious blow on the back, and he who runs his factory with a ruthless disregard for the old and infirm. But it is also Gerald who, ulti-mately, is terror-struck at the awareness of death, and who goes to Gudrun as a suppliant, to be perfected not in distinctness from her but in complete self-yielding to her. The love between Gerald and Gudrun is always one of self-assertion on the one hand and self-surrender on the other, now the man, now the woman being dominant. There is never fulfilment for both together, but always for one only, while the other lies awake and conscious, hatred growing within. And as Lawrence shows it, this attempted violation of the other's mystery is destructive, nihilistic, ultimately disastrous. Gudrun begins the destructive progression when she hits Gerald in the face, saying with little awareness of her own meaning that she has struck the first blow. Gerald ends it when, unable any longer to assert his will over Gudrun, he first tries to strangle her and then, realizing that he has not enough truly positive will to accomplish even that, goes off up the mountain to fall unconscious and freeze to death.

These are the two pairs, corresponding, but very distantly corresponding, to the two in Goethe's novel. Lawrence does not, however, take sides, he does not condemn Gerald as though he thought him capable of choosing another course. Rupert continues to love Gerald in death, he even conceives of himself as on the same path to destruction. The fulfilment of Gerald and Gudrun is spoken of as their perfection, and perfect it must seem from that 'inhuman' plane where Rupert meets Ursula—'there can be no calling to book, in any form whatsoever', he tells her, 'because one is outside the pale of all that is accepted, and nothing known applies. One can only follow the impulse, taking that which lies in front, and responsible for nothing, asked for nothing, giving nothing, only each taking according to the primal desire.'[48] This is a kind of fatalism which sees the two courses, the two forms of perfection, the creative and the destructive, and follows them through to their goals, each in its way a fulfilment of the mysterious purpose in creation which embraces them both. There are times when the book seems to be written on that inhuman plane, as though the savage descriptions of the mountains and the tender evocations of flowers were issuing from a superhuman creator. But that is not the whole story. Lawrence is tempted towards the superhuman, and yet remains essentially human and sane.

It is at this point that the name of Nietzsche most readily springs to mind, and it is indeed only a few pages after the passage I have just quoted that the 'Wille zur Macht', the 'will-to-power' is mentioned. Lawrence ranges up and down Nietzsche's ideas, the Dionysian and the Apolline; Dionysus and Christ; the 'master-morality' of Gerald Crich displayed in the organizing of his industry; the need for man to be surpassed in the course of evolutionary creation; the achievement of a state beyond good and evil; the dominance of the male over the female; the aristocratic temper contrasted with the slave-temper; the need for self-annihilation in order to transcend the self. He is as paradoxical as Nietzsche, as full of contradictory beliefs and ideals; when he writes of Gerald's brutalities one is inclined to see in him just such an admirer of the 'blond beast' as Nietzsche has often been held to be. Yet there are two essential distinguishing features. First, Nietzsche's thought is entirely aphoristic. One aphorism will often contradict another, and there are times when contradictions follow one another within the compass of a short passage. There is no comprehensive pattern, no exposition, development, climax, catastrophe, and taking stock, as there is in the novel. 'I am not a man' Nietzsche wrote, 'I am dynamite', and the truth of that can be seen in the form of his writing. The thoughts explode into the air with the force of an eruption, the individual blocks soar out and sink down, and one looks in vain for a coherent aim or purpose. It is on this account, I believe, that Nietzsche has been held responsible for the disaster which overtook Germany thirty years after his death. Whether or not Nietzsche would have welcomed the Nazi seizure of power, the destructive impact of his thought, its incoherence and lack of creative direction did, as I think, insidiously undermine humane thinking in Germany, and thus seriously weakened resistance to the Nazi movement. Lawrence on the other hand, while treating of just the same ideas, places them within the framework of a novel where their particular juxtapositions are significant. In the chapter curiously entitled 'Excurse' we see the union of Rupert and Ursula; in the immediately following chapter 'Death and Love' we see that of Gerald and Gudrun, and from then on their progressive hatred and unwilling isolation. We are not asked to 'call to book' any of these characters, and yet as we take the impulse, take 'that which lies in front', we see the full nature of their loving. It is not a choice, not a decision, but a horrible awareness of the implications of the ideal, of all that has led up to it and is likely to stem from it. This Lawrence achieves, where Nietzsche does not achieve it, by virtue of the impulse which brings him to place this event after that one, the Gerald and Gudrun chapter after the Rupert and Ursula chapter, to balance one against another and let the scales rise or fall as they will. There is a humane morality in Lawrence which takes cognizance of Nietzsche's inhuman or superhuman morality and the morality of master and slave, and which does not condemn it, any more than Rupert condemns Gerald, but yet *shows* a contrast so plainly as to resolve our hearts and minds.

Moreover, and this is the second point I referred to, Lawrence is able as a novelist to introduce that detachment which is so lacking in Nietzsche. One is aware that Nietzsche is self-critical, intensely self-critical. Yet how seldom does a note of humour enter: the note is solemnly intense, apart from such dull flashes of Voltairean wit as those in the 'Lieder des Prinzen Vogelfrei'. Nietzsche admired Aristophanes and Petronius, yet his own prose runs on burdened feet of seriousness. He is too intent on impressing us with the awful terror of his message to strike the more light-hearted note of indifference which his doctrine sometimes implies. Lawrence, on the other hand, while he certainly uses Rupert Birkin as a mouthpiece, is not identified with him. Rupert is properly contrasted with other characters who find him priggish and sanctimonious, over-concerned to put his ideals into words; he is worsted in arguments and his lapses are seized on and defined by others in a way that shows how much Lawrence himself was aware of them.

This kind of detachment is not in Nietzsche, nor is Rupert Birkin's tenderness with flowers and animals and women. Nietzsche remains abstract; Lawrence would have said that he was all intellect, despite his Dionysianism, and he seldom writes of the natural scene or of individual human beings. Thoughts are his real concern; myths and generalizations, not minute particulars, are his means of communication. He could not spare time to spend a chapter near the climax of a work to describe the buying of an old chair.49

With Rilke it is a different matter. In Rilke there is, especially in his middle period, much time to spare for the detail of things— flamingoes, a panther, a hydrangea, a cathedral, a statue. And Rilke shares with Lawrence an antipathy to Christianity, a concern with love between men and women, a determination to love in a world in which there is no God, and indeed most of the Nietzschean preoccupations. In many ways they are quite surprisingly alike, and I find it a hard task to put in a small compass the distinctions I still find between them. It can perhaps be put like this. There is a quite remarkable similarity between the final image of Rilke's *Duino Elegies*, of a man setting out to walk further and further into the increasing darkness of total death, up into the mountains of Primal Pain, and the final image of Gerald Crich moving away from the half-strangled Gudrun to climb higher and higher to his death among frozen rocks. The *Elegies* and the novel were written at about the same time,50 and it is as though each writer saw and knew the reality of the destructive way in his age. Lawrence, as I noted earlier, saw both this way and a way represented in Rupert and Ursula, although he had sympathy with, knew himself close to, both ways. And Rilke also saw two ways. He saw the way which led to the never-ending *impasse* of the *Elegies*, and he saw the way to which he gave expression in the companion-piece to the *Elegies*, the *Sonnets to Orpheus*. In the *Sonnets* there is a gaiety, a refreshed enjoyment which is only announced, scarcely ever realized in the *Elegies*, and I am tempted strongly to say that, just as Lawrence knew himself to be in both Rupert and Gerald, so Rilke knew himself both as the desperate lamenter of the *Elegies* and as the rejoicing singer of the *Sonnets*. But I cannot feel that is quite the case. For Rilke does not present the final image of the *Elegies* as a tragic ending, as Lawrence presents the death of Gerald. It is rather an end desirable in itself: true happiness is to know this

347

increasing destruction of oneself, to realize more and more fully the death that is bearing in. And the Orphic image is equally a realization of 'true' happiness, the refreshment and the acceptance in the *Sonnets* is as much true as the decomposition and the pain and lament. The *Elegies* and the *Sonnets* seem to me to stand over against each other in pure contradiction, just as so many of the lines they contain are contradictory even down to adjoining words and phrases. One is left at the last rather with the sense of contradiction, of an unresolved polarity, rather than with the pattern within a single work, the clear impulse towards one end, which there is in *Women in Love*.

Rilke's and Lawrence's way of feeling about love is similarly close and yet distant. Rilke's ideal of love without reciprocity, love that does not ask for love to be returned, is remarkably close to Lawrence's twin stars, 'asked for nothing, giving nothing'.[51] Like Lawrence, Rilke despised the give and take of love which was no more than mutual support over a void; lovers, he said, 'hide from each other their lot'. Yet Rilke's lovers are totally isolated, set over against one another as the *Elegies* are set over against the *Sonnets*, each complete in himself or herself—Narcissistically complete, like Gudrun near the lowest point in her course. 'It seemed to [Gerald]', Lawrence writes, 'that Gudrun was sufficient unto herself, closed round and completed, like a thing in a case. In the calm, static reason of his soul, he recognized this, and admitted it was her right, to be closed round upon herself, self-complete, without desire.... He knew that it only needed one convulsion of his will for him to be able to turn upon himself also, to close upon himself as a stone fixes upon itself, and is impervious, self-completed, a thing isolated.'[52] And such a condition is surely that of Eurydice in Rilke's poem, who has no need of Orpheus but turns back into the livid paths of Hades: 'sie war in sich, und ihr Gestorbensein erfüllte sie wie Fülle'. 'She was within herself, her having-died fulfilled her like full harvest'—a condition dreadful and yet in its way perfected. But there is in Rilke's conception of love no way out from this total isolation. There is no awareness of otherness, the 'immemorial magnificence of mystic, palpable, real otherness'.[53] There is nothing that could lead to such a dialogue as that at the end of Lawrence's novel, after Gerald's death.

> 'It's a bitter thing to me', [Rupert] said.
> 'What—that he's dead?' she said.
> His eyes just met hers. He did not answer.
> 'You've got me', she said.
> He smiled and kissed her.
> 'If I die', he said, 'you'll know I haven't left you.'
> 'And me?' she cried.
> 'And you won't have left me', he said. 'We shan't have any need to despair, in death.'[54]

Rilke's lovers have no such knowledge, for they have only the isolation, not the living contact of realized selves. They are 'constellations' ('Sternbild' is a key-word in Rilke), not stars together in orbit. Ultimately, they are all one within the transcendent order of Rilke's Angels, yet each one separate and alone in its consciousness, incapable of reaching out to others except by the way of the Angels, that is, by themselves embracing all in one totality. Thus it is that in Rilke's life there were many lovers; he is like Gerald in that, and unlike Rupert, or Lawrence for that matter, for whom marriage was a relation between chosen man and chosen woman. The all-embracing love, seeing the many as one, denying to the one its individual distinctness, leads to that isolation where there is only the one self and, as Lawrence so clearly saw, to ultimate destruction not only for the individual but for the civilization in which that mode of loving prevails.

This concern of Lawrence's both for a union and for distinctness is one of the features that marks him off from many of his predecessors in the main German tradition of thought and literature. In this he resembles Hölderlin—at least in one of his moods—the Hölderlin who wrote the distich entitled 'Root of all Evil':

> Einig zu sein, ist göttlich und gut; woher ist die Sucht denn
> Unter den Menschen, daß nur Eines und Einer nur sei?

'To be at one is divine and good, whence comes then the yearning of men that only the One, only Oneness should be?' This yearning has been marked in Germany for two centuries; it appears in a variety of forms. It can be expressed in Faust's attempt at embracing all human experience—'and so extend my self to cover all their selves'—as well as in Fichte's vision of the world created by the self—in each case there is a Oneness which does not permit and does not want the existence of anything outside the self. It can be expressed in Hegel's 'world-historical man' who is held to be the very embodiment of the age in which he lives, and is thus entitled to draw along with him even his opponents. It is in all the attempts at fashioning a 'Weltanschauung', establishing a final truth about the world, valid for all men, all the attempts at establishing a point of vantage outside history, from which the writer speaks with a quasi-divine authority. It is not in Kant, who remained conscious of the otherness of the 'thing-in-itself'. But then Kant, as Stefan Zweig observed, is the 'arch-enemy of all German poets'. It is in Schopenhauer, who tried to bridge the gap between the inner and the outer world by declaring 'we *are* the thing-in-itself'. It is not in Hölderlin when he writes 'einsam / Unter dem Himmel wie immer bin ich'—to be *beneath* the sky, yet in touch with its mystery, is essential to his way of feeling. On the other hand, the yearning is in Kleist, Kleist who was so shattered by Kant's insistence on otherness that he portrayed the Amazon lover Penthesilea literally tearing at the breast of Achilles with her teeth, almost devouring him in her need to consume him wholly within herself, as Gerald later seeks to consume Gudrun. And it is not unjust to associate *that* form of the yearning with the striving for political unity in Germany in the last century and a half. In politics also there has been on the one hand the desire for autarky, for a Narcissistic isolation shorn of all contact with the outside world, and on the other a determination to obliterate the distinctiveness of the outside world, to consume it and assert the essential 'Deutschtum' of everything it contains. That has not been the whole story, it is perhaps needless to say. There have

been Germans, less able to make their voice heard, for whom the
Faustian image is completely inappropriate, and recent developments in the Bundesrepublik encourage the hope that the whole
spirit of the all-inclusive 'Weltanschauung' is diminishing.55 But
Kleist's Penthesilea, coupled with Kleist's insane and brutal
nationalism, is an apt image of the link between the yearning for
oneness in sexual love and in social organization.

Lawrence must have been aware of the implications his novel
had for Germany. It is unlikely to be mere chance that the novel
moves from England in the final chapters towards Germany—to
the Austrian Tyrol, in fact, to a place near Innsbruck. Nor does
it seem insignificant that Gudrun, becoming incapable of enduring Gerald's love any longer, falls in love with the sculptor
Loerke from Düsseldorf. By now Gudrun's repleteness in herself has reached the point of almost complete indifference to the
outside world. She cannot bear to experience Gerald's need for
her, and indeed his desire has now become a voluptuous ecstasy
in the thought of destroying her. In Loerke, the satirical gnome-
like figure, diabolically free in his own indifference to everything,
she finds a new lease of life—'she was happy like a child, very
attractive and beautiful to everybody, with her soft, luxurious
figure, and her happiness. Yet underneath was death itself.'56
With Loerke she can enjoy a pure game, neither giving, neither
taking, each engaged in an intellectual delectation of himself
through the other. Gudrun's indifference is so great that her
fulfilment with Loerke seems perfect. 'You are going away
tomorrow?' he asks her. '"Wohin?"' That was the question—
wohin? Whither? Wohin? What a lovely word! She never wanted
it answered. Let it chime for ever.'57 It is as though Lawrence
had read Rilke's words in the Sonnets to Orpheus (I, xxiii): 'Erst
wenn ein reines Wohin'—only when some 'pure whither' is
learned will fulfilment come. Impatience, the desire to dictate one's
own path, leads astray. The wind blows where it lists, and for
Gudrun, as Loerke tells her, the wind 'goes towards Germany'.58
After Gerald's death she leaves for Dresden, and we hear no more
of her. It is as though Lawrence had perceived that her deathly

wish for isolation and domination would find a natural environment there.

Lawrence does not write detachedly of Gudrun, any more than he does of Gerald: he does not point a warning finger. On the contrary, Gudrun's feelings and thoughts are as persuasively set down as though they were Lawrence's own. The sense of a disaster in her life that is still to come arises rather from its juxtaposition with that of Rupert and Ursula, pure juxtaposition. Gudrun is given over to Loerke, of whom she knows that 'he admitted no allegiance, he gave no adherence anywhere. He was single and, by abstraction from the rest, absolute in himself.'59 He has the same self-repleteness as there is in Gudrun, as there is in Rilke's Eurydike, he is just as satisfied as she is with a 'reines Wohin'. And yet—isn't there something in this very similar to Rupert Birkin's passage about having one's pulse beating direct from the mystery? Isn't that the same kind of dependence on the wind that blows where it wants to? It *is* dependence, it is the same in the sense that it yields up personal control. It is different, in that what Loerke and Gudrun yield to is nothing, pure arbitrariness, and what Rupert speaks of is 'having the faith to yield to the mystery'.60 Gudrun, like one of Rilke's lovers, runs on past the other, 'auf Nichts zu'. Rupert, remembering the other, gains faith in the mystery, grows warmer with a new trust in living. There is this essential difference.

But this is not a tract about Germany, it is a novel. If I have drawn attention to German aspects of it, it has been at best in the hope that I might draw attention to particular features of Lawrence's work, make clearer what they are by pointing out how they differ from others that resemble them in a general way. I said earlier on that to define a pattern, a skeletal form, might seem inappropriate in talking about so spontaneous a writer as Lawrence, and that still holds true. For *Women in Love* is not a novel with a message, it is not instructing us to adopt one course rather than another. It can only present us with an imitation of life, and it will be more or less of a fine work as it gives more or less of a balanced picture. Had Lawrence written about Rupert and Ursula alone, or Gerald and Gudrun alone, without including the other pair, his picture would not be balanced, he would have written a tract. In fact, he has written a tragedy. The mood at the end of the book is not one of condemnation but of bitter sorrow for the death of Gerald, and there cannot be sorrow or tragedy where a message is being imparted or a lesson taught. There is neither message nor system nor 'Weltanschauung' here— Lawrence uses the mechanism of systems and 'Weltanschauungen' to build the structure of his novel, but he surrenders himself as he writes to the spontaneity of the moment, and that means surrendering as much to the spirit of one pair of lovers as to that of the other. There is, of course, what Ursula calls the 'Salvator Mundi touch' about Lawrence himself, there *is* a would-be redeemer in him, who keeps putting forward what looks like a message. But Lawrence is aware of that, he puts it in its place within the novel by means of Ursula's scepticism; the picture remains balanced.

All the same, by virtue of his juxtapositions Lawrence does provide us with insights we might well not have, if the novel had remained entirely within the 'German' tradition as I have outlined it. *Women in Love* is deeply indebted to German ideas, but it is also, that goes without saying, a particularly English novel; it marries something from the English world, especially an insistence on individuality and morality, with something from the German world that had better just be called mysticism, whatever the misunderstandings that may arise: antinomianism, the sense of all-embracingness, are two of its features. The 'Blutbrüderschaft' which Rupert looks for between himself and Gerald is also the kind of relationship Lawrence must, I think, have looked for between himself and Germany: a combination of empiricism and 'mystical' beliefs. In his Englishness, moreover, Lawrence does often closely resemble 'English' Blake,[61] in whom a similar preoccupation with ultimately German ideas (Boehme) was apparent, and nowhere more closely than in relation to the lines from *Jerusalem*, in which the 'Only General and Universal Form' is identified with benevolence 'Who protects minute particulars, every one in their own identity'.[62] It is the combination of mystical union with enduring separateness here which places both Blake and Lawrence in a line of English writers who have made use of German ideas to produce something peculiarly their own. Apart from anything else, in the present political state of Europe this has a special value.

NOTES

INTRODUCTION

1 H. G. Atkins writes, 'Before 1933 he [Thomas Mann] was generally regarded, at home as well as abroad, as being the greatest living German novelist, and (with Gerhart Hauptmann) one of the two most representative German writers' (*German Literature Through Nazi Eyes*, London, 1941, p. 73). For Käte Hamburger Mann was 'the universally acknowledged representative of German writing in this century' (*Thomas Manns Roman*, '*Joseph und seine Brüder*', Stockholm, 1945, p. 9). Similarly, Roy Pascal speaks of Mann as 'the most representative German of this century' (*The German Novel*, Manchester, 1956, p. 291).

2 See T. Mann, *The Genesis of a Novel* (London, 1961), p. 9.

3 Erich Heller, *The Ironic German* (London, 1958), p. 285.

4 *The Genesis of a Novel*, p. 51.

5 H.-E. Holthusen, *Die Welt ohne Transcendenz* (Hamburg, 1949), and W. Muschg, *Tragische Literaturgeschichte* (Berne, 1948), pp. 254–6.

6 I have written at greater length on this theme in *Kafka's Castle* and *The Twentieth Century Views Kafka*.

7 H. von Hofmannsthal, *Buch der Freunde, Tagebuch-Aufzeichnungen* (Leipzig, 1929), p. 93: 'An Goethe kann man sich bilden, wofern man sich an ihm nicht verwirrt; an der deutschen Literatur kann man sich nicht bilden, nur verwirren.'

8 *Op. cit.* p. 61: 'Geistige Deutsche werden schwer und spät zum eigentlichen Leben geboren: sie machen dann eine zweite Geburt durch, an der viele sterben.'

9 *Op. cit.* p. 75: 'Wir haben keine neuere Literatur. Wir haben Goethe und Ansätze.'

10 F. von Biedermann, *Goethes Gespräche* (Leipzig, 1910), vol. III, p. 388 (Eckermann, 3 May 1827).

CHAPTER I

1 'Desireless, illusionless, most sacred realm of choice' (R. Wagner, *Gesammelte Dichtungen*, ed. Julius Kapp, Leipzig, n.d., II, 286). Wagner deleted these words from the final version of the libretto of *Götterdämmerung*, saying that the music expressed the ideas contained in them with far greater precision.

2 *Loc. cit.*

3 Rilke, however, treated of the new cities in his early work, the *Book of Hours*, and in *Malte Laurids Brigge*, though not in the spirit of the Naturalists.

4 Nietzsche, *Menschliches, Allzumenschliches*, vol. II, para. 187.

5 *Op. cit.* vol. I, para. 477.

6 Quoted in Erich Eyck, *Bismarck and the German Empire*, 2nd edn. (London, 1958), p. 68.

7 For instances, see Ludwig Dehio, 'Ranke and German Imperialism', in *Germany and World Politics in the Twentieth Century* (London, 1959; German edn., 1955).

8 E.g. the last poem of *Der Stern des Bundes*.

9 *Deutsche Literatur in Entwicklungsreihen*, 'Vom Naturalismus zur neuen Volksdichtung', vol. 1 (*Naturalismus*), ed. W. Linden (Leipzig, 1936), p. 83.

10 *Op. cit.* p. 66.

11 'unsere menschliche Tier-göttlichkeit'. R. Dehmel, *Aber die Liebe* (Fischer, Berlin, n.d.), p. 180.

12 One of Sorge's unpublished plays, for a sight of which I am indebted to Mr R. Hinton Thomas, reveals something of the uncertainty in which Nietzsche left young men at this time. A group is seen discussing Nietzsche's views in the reading-room of a public library, and particularly the question whether Nietzsche intended to preach the killing of the infirm. One of the group leaves, and returns to announce that he has just killed a cripple. Thereupon Nietzsche or his spirit enters the room and turns off the light, declaring that those who really understand him can read him in the dark.

13 Cf. the early chapters in Ernst Toller, *Eine Jugend in Deutschland*.

14 Quoted in J. P. Mayer, *Max Weber and German Politics* (London, 1944), p. 57.

15 Quotations from Rilke's *Fünf Gesänge* are from his *Ausgewählte Werke* (Insel, 1948), vol. 1, pp. 335–41.

16 A. Moeller van den Bruck, *Das dritte Reich*, 3rd edn. (Hamburg, 1931), p. 303.

17 Thomas Mann, *Friedrich und die große Koalition* (Berlin, 1915), p. 15.

18 *Op. cit.* p. 123.

19 The 'Third Reich' had not at this stage its later implications. Mann may have had in mind its use by Ibsen in *Emperor and Galilean*, where it means a kind of Kingdom of Heaven on earth, a synthesis of body and spirit.

20 Thomas Mann, *Betrachtungen eines Unpolitischen* (Berlin, 1922), p. 458.

21 *Op. cit.* p. 477.

22 See Hofmannsthal's legend-creating essays on national heroes: Prince Eugène, Grillparzer, and Maria Theresa; also the study of these in *Hofmannsthal's Festival Dramas*, by Brian Coghlan (Cambridge, 1964).

23 E.g. Günther Anders, *Kafka pro und contra*, and E. Burgum in *The Kafka Problem*, ed. A. Flores.

24 This would appear to be untrue of *The Trial* and of *America*, of which the final chapters exist, though the chapters immediately preceding them do not.

25 See further my 'The Structure of Kafka's Works: A reply to Professor Uyttersprot' in *German Life and Letters* (October, 1959). My own attempt at such a unitive interpretation in the appendix to *Kafka's Castle* (Cambridge, 1956), I now think, was mistaken, although I would not say the same of the argument in the main body of the book.

26 E.g. Maurice Blanchot and Samuel Beckett. Cp. Maja Goth, *Franz Kafka et les lettres françaises, 1928–1955* (Paris, 1956).

27 E.g. Martin Buber, *Two Types of Faith* (London, 1951), also in *The Twentieth Century Views Kafka*, ed. Ronald Gray (Englewood Cliffs, N.J., 1962).

NOTES

CHAPTER II

1 See J. W. Wheeler-Bennett, *The Nemesis of Power; the German Army in Politics, 1918–1945* (London, 1953), and Rudolf Coper, *The Failure of a Revolution* (Cambridge, 1955).
2 See Harry Domela, *Der falsche Prinz* (Berlin, 1927).
3 R. M. Rilke, *Briefe an eine junge Frau* (Inselverlag, Leipzig, p. 43).
4 Kasimir Edschmid, *Über den Expressionismus in der Kunst und Literatur* (Berlin, 1920)
5 E. Vermeil, *The German Scene* (London, 1956), p. 142.
6 S. Kracauer, *From Caligari to Hitler* (London, 1947).
7 See Paul Rotha, *The Film Till Now* (London, 1949), supplement by Richard Griffiths, pp. 582–5.
8 B. Brecht, *Hauspostille* (Berlin, 1927; reprint of 1952), p. 151.
9 Gottfried Benn, *Trunkene Flut* (Wiesbaden, 1952), p. 9.
10 A. Moeller van den Bruck, *Das dritte Reich*, ed. cit. p. 301.
11 Mann, *Friedrich und die große Koalition*, p. 11.
12 E.g. those by Romano Guardini and Jacob Steiner.
13 See pp. 227–98 below.   14 See p. 47 above.
15 Fritz Dehn, quoted in E. C. Mason, *Rilke's Apotheosis* (Oxford, 1938), p. 21.
16 R. Strauss and H. v. Hofmannsthal, *Briefwechsel*, p. 468.
17 Hofmannsthal, 'Gotthold Ephraim Lessing', in *Ausgewählte Werke*, ed. R. Hirsch (Frankfurt, 1957), vol. II, p. 775.
18 See pp. 157–72 below.
19 See the section 'Die neue Sachlichkeit' in E. Schumacher, *Die dramatischen Versuche Bertolt Brechts, 1918–1933* (Berlin, 1955), pp. 140–56, for an account of the Communist aspects of the movement.
20 E. Jünger, *Der Arbeiter* (Hamburg, 1932), p. 44.
21 *Op. cit.* p. 254.
22 Jünger's relation with the Nazis is treated on pp. 90–1 below.
23 See the criticisms of Hesse's prose and poetry in Karlheinz Deschner, *Kitsch, Konvention und Kunst* (Munich, 1957).
24 Jethro Bithell, *Modern German Literature, 1880–1938*, 2nd edn. (London, 1946), p. 318.
25 See pp. 164–9 below.
26 See the version in B. Brecht, *Gesammelte Werke* (Malikverlag, 1938), and compare the version in *Stücke*, vol. IV (scene vii).
27 See A. Soergel, *Dichtung und Dichter der Zeit*, vol. III for accounts of the leading figures of literature remaining in Germany after 1933.
28 Mann, *The Genesis of a Novel*, p. 131.
29 *Hitler's Speeches*, ed. N. H. Baynes (Oxford, 1942), vol. I, p. 226.
30 *Op. cit.* vol. II, p. 1385.   31 *Op. cit.* vol. I, p. 373.
32 See *Das Braunbuch über Reichstagsbrand und Hitlerterror*, Vorwort von Lord Marley (Basle, 1933), especially pp. 332–54.
33 F. Meinecke, *The German Catastrophe* (Cambridge, Mass., 1950), pp. 85–6.
34 Vermeil, *The German Scene*, p. 181.
35 R. d'O. Butler, *The Roots of National Socialism, 1783–1933* (London, 1941), p. 294.

NOTES

CHAPTER III

1 S. Kierkegaard, *Fear and Trembling*, transl. W. Lowrie (Princeton, 1941), pp. 53–4.

2 Quoted in *Primal Vision, selected writings of Gottfried Benn*, ed. E. B. Ashton (London, 1961), p. xiv.

3 *Op. cit.* pp. 52–3. 4 *Op. cit.* p. 48.

5 In her autobiography Katharine Trevelyan writes of leading members of the German (non-Nazi) Youth Movements in 1933 that their attitude was: 'If Hitler has come to power, it proves that it must be Germany's destiny' (*Fool in Love*, London, 1962, p. 86).

6 Cf. the essay 'Ranke and German Imperialism' in Dehio, *Germany and World Politics in the Twentieth Century*.

7 M. Heidegger, *Die Selbstbehauptung der deutschen Universität*. Rede gehalten bei der feierlichen Übernahme des Rektorats der Universität Freiburg i. Br. am 27. 5. 1933 (W. G. Korn Verlag, Breslau), p. 21.

8 *Ibid.* p. 14.

9 Paul Ernst, *Erdachte Gespräche*, ed. W. Walker Chambers (London and Edinburgh, 1958), p. xix.

10 E. M. Forster, *Two Cheers for Democracy* (London, 1951), p. 235.

11 Atkins, *German Literature Through Nazi Eyes*, p. 74.

12 For extracts from the Nazi critics of Mann, see Atkins, *op. cit.* pp. 73–80.

13 Mann, *Achtung, Europa!*, p. 106.

14 All quotations in this section are from Mann's preface to his *Achtung, Europa!*

15 'sie wird der Notwendigkeit gerecht, höchst illoyale Vorteile der Gegenseite aufzuheben': at a guess, this obscurely phrased passage might mean that the Nazis would no longer have the exclusive right to claim to represent 'Deutschtum', if their opponents joined them.

16 On 5 July 1963 a serial-story in the *Deutsche National-Zeitung und Soldaten-Zeitung* (the nearest thing to a Nazi paper in post-war Germany) concerned two soldiers running away from the front during the collapse of the German army: 'Wir haben als Soldaten unsere Pflicht getan, obwohl wir klare politische Gegner Hitlers sind....'

17 R. Musil, *Der Mann ohne Eigenschaften* (Berlin, 1931), p. 50.

18 *Gerhart Hauptmann*, by Kurt Lothar Tank (Hamburg, 1959), pp. 136 and 137.

19 See p. 62 above.

20 *Ernst Jünger*, by Karl O. Paetel (Hamburg, 1962), pp. 104–5.

21 *Primal Vision*, ed. cit. p. 207.

22 See p. 47 above.

23 Isaiah Berlin, *Karl Marx, his life and environment*, 2nd edn. (London, 1948), p. 207.

24 Marx, it may be recalled, approved the terrorism of the Paris Commune which had sickened other working-class representatives.

25 See further Ruth Fischer, *Stalin and German Communism* (Harvard University Press, Cambridge, 1948), pp. 643 ff.

26 *Sinn und Form*, Zweites Sonderheft Bertolt Brecht, p. 23.

NOTES

27 *Kriegsbriefe gefallener Studenten 1939–1945*, ed. W. and H. W. Bähr
   (Tübingen, 1952), p. 19.
28 *Op. cit.* p. 305. 29 *Op. cit.* p. 86.
30 *Op. cit.* pp. 156–7. My italics.
31 *Op. cit.* p. 255. 32 *Op. cit.* p. 241.
33 *Op. cit.* p. 361. 34 *Op. cit.* p. 250.

CHAPTER IV

1 *Buddenbrooks*, Book XI, chap. 1.
2 The mention of both 'praktische' and 'ideelle' advantages is a little obscure,
   owing to the ambiguousness of 'ideell': the sense can hardly be taken to be
   'ideal' (i.e. 'perfect') and is presumably more like 'notional' or 'imaginary'—the wife perhaps continues to enjoy in her thoughts the fact that she
   is still a married woman.
3 As Erich Heller says, *Buddenbrooks* 'ironically oscillates in its critique of life
   between Nietzsche's affirmation of the Will and Schopenhauer's moral
   denial of it' (*The Ironic German*, p. 53).
4 *Lotte in Weimar*, E.T. pp. 63–4. Quoted in H. Eichner, *Thomas Mann.
   Eine Einführung in sein Werk* (Berne, 1953), p. 86. Eichner seems to accept
   Riemer's argument here, saying that the Goethe of the novel 'bridges over
   the gap' between good and evil. (I do not understand this metaphor.)
   Note, however, the loose associations by which the argument advances,
   a feature of Mann's style which remained till the end. 'Destructiveness'
   ('Vernichtung') is in effect equated with 'indifference', a negative action
   with a neutral mood, and the latter is abruptly associated with the 'diabolical'. (It might sometimes of course be reprehensible, which is not the
   same thing at all.)
5 *Buddenbrooks*, X, 4. 6 See note 3 above.
7 *Die Welt als Wille und Vorstellung*, para. 54. My italics.
8 *Ausgewählte Erzählungen*, Stockholmer Ausgabe (= SA), p. 451.

CHAPTER V

1 E. Wilkinson (ed.), *Thomas Mann: Tonio Kröger* (Oxford, 1945), p. xii.
2 *The Ironic German*, p. 39. 3 *Buddenbrooks*, I, 1.
4 *The Ironic German*, pp. 39 and 41.
5 *Buddenbrooks*, II, 1. 6 *Buddenbrooks*, VIII, 4.
7 *Loc. cit.* 8 *Loc. cit.*
9 *Betrachtungen eines Unpolitischen* (Berlin, 1918), pp. 34–5.
10 Pascal, *The German Novel*, p. 281.
11 If the reader should demur at 'preferred', it is enough for my purpose at the
   moment if he will accept that Mann treats these alternative attitudes as at
   least equally justifiable, and tends to show self-doubting in a bad light,
   while glossing over some objections to self-assertion (e.g. in speaking of
   Weinschenk's fraud).
12 *Loc. cit.* 13 See p. 114 above.

14 *Buddenbrooks*, x, 5 (italics in the original).
15 *Loc. cit.* (my italics).
16 Pascal, *loc. cit.*   17 *Buddenbrooks*, x, 5.
18 *Betrachtungen eines Unpolitischen, loc. cit.*
19 *Loc. cit.*   20 *Loc. cit.*
21 *Loc. cit.*   22 *Loc. cit.*
23 In much the same way, the self-identification with Thomas in the *Betrachtungen* (*loc. cit.*) is choked with an approving intensity—'dem Leidenden, der tapfer standgehalten', etc.
24 *Ausgewählte Erzählungen*, SA, p. 452 ('das Wunder der wiedergeborenen Unbefangenheit').
25 *Buddenbrooks*, xi, 2.   26 *Loc. cit.* (my italics).
27 *Ausgewählte Erzählungen*, SA, p. 150.
28 *Buddenbrooks*, xi, 2.   29 *Loc. cit.*
30 Compare the episode of Hanno's self-gratification with Mann's story, *Wälsungenblut*, in which incestuous love—another form of Narcissism, at least in this particular case—is greeted by one of the characters as the means to greater creativity. Compare also Adrian Leverkühn's apparently false confession (p. 216 below) that he has committed incest, Felix Krull's seeming approval of it, and the fruitful incest of Gregor in *Der Erwählte*. Gustav von Aschenbach's homosexual love, in *Der Tod in Venedig*, seen as an inward-turning relationship to one of his own sex, is related to this: it is another form of self-love.
31 *Buddenbrooks*, xi, 3.
32 Viktor Mann, *Wir waren fünf.* I have no record of the page reference.

CHAPTER VI

1 See p. 54 above.
2 *Ausgewählte Erzählungen*, SA, pp. 173–4.
3 *Op. cit.* p. 151. 'Ein Herr der Welt' is translated in the standard English edition as 'a man of the world', and an English reader has expressed a doubt whether my version is correct. Cf., however, the Duden Stilwörterbuch, 1934, p. 237, where the phrase occurs in the following list of synonyms: '[der] H. Jesus; der H. der Schöpfung (iron.: der Mann); der H. der Welt; der H. der Erde'. 'Man of the world' would have been 'Weltmann'.
4 *Op. cit.* p. 142.   5 *Op. cit.* p. 144.
6 *Op. cit.* p. 147.
7 E.g. the reference to Hamlet, *op. cit.* p. 147, and the imputation of certain feelings to him.
8 *Op. cit.* p. 149. 'mit den Augen des Geistes' does not mean 'in the mind's eye', as the standard version has it.
9 The reference on p. 149 to Cesare Borgia, whom Tonio does not wish to imitate, must be meant to suggest Nietzsche's admiration for this superman of the Renaissance, expressed in the last paragraph of *Der Antichrist*.
10 *Ausgewählte Erzählungen*, p. 150.
11 *Op. cit.* p. 189.

NOTES

12 Cf. I Corinthians xiii.

13 Cf. Nietzsche, *Menschliches Allzumenschliches*, vol. II, para. 301: 'Jemand sagte: Über zwei Personen habe ich nie gründlich nachgedacht: es ist das Zeichen meiner Liebe für sie.' ('Someone said, "there are two people I have never thought about deeply—that is the sign of my love for them".')

14 E.g. by E. M. Wilkinson (*Thomas Mann: Tonio Kröger*) and by Hans Eichner, *Thomas Mann. Eine Einführung in sein Werk.*

15 *Ausgewählte Erzählungen*, p. 190.

16 Quoted in the advertisement of *Tristan* in the 39th edition of *Buddenbrooks* (Berlin, 1908).

17 *Ausgewählte Erzählungen*, p. 446.

18 *Op. cit.* p. 447. The standard translation loosely renders 'verwalten' (administrate) by 'sustain'. (The immediately following reference to Aschenbach's mail, 'die *Wertzeichen* [stamps] aus aller Herren Länder trug' is translated as 'a daily post heavy with *tributes* from his own and foreign countries'.)

19 *Op. cit.* p. 450. I use here D. H. Lawrence's translation in his review of this story (since published in *Phoenix* and in *Selected Literary Criticism*).

20 *Op. cit.* p. 450.   21 *Op. cit.* p. 447.

22 *Op. cit.* p. 528.   23 *Op. cit.* p. 452.

24 *Op. cit.* pp. 497–8.   25 *Op. cit.* p. 453.

26 *Op. cit.* p. 468.   27 *Loc. cit.*   28 *Op. cit.* p. 491.

29 A study of the use of rhetorical questions in this story would show that much of what seems to be asserted is really only asked, although asked in such a way that to give a negative answer would be to remove interest in the story. (It is only by giving the answer 'yes' that a reader can maintain coherence.)

30 *Op. cit.* p. 520.

31 *Op. cit.* p. 475. The incident is probably symbolic of part of Tadzio's role, which is not only that of the beauty created by the Will, but also of the Will's cruelty.

32 *Op. cit.* p. 501.   33 *Loc. cit.*

34 *Op. cit.* p. 531. The German includes a word here which recurs in the account of Thomas Buddenbrook's vision (he is 'berauscht von irgend etwas Neuem, Lockendem und Verheißungsvollem') and of Hanno's music (whose main theme is said to be like 'eine unbegreiflich selige Verheißung').

35 *Op. cit.* p. 475.

36 *Loc. cit.* Note the rhetorical question, and cf. note 29 above.

37 Cf. p. 122 above.

38 Even Schopenhauer, in his denial of the Will, does not escape this ambiguity. At the conclusion of his argument in the fourth book of *Die Welt als Wille und Vorstellung* his language leads him into it. Thus, having affirmed that there is, after the Will has been denied, nothing left to be faced but the Naught, he asserts that for him the whole cosmos is Naught. This can be taken to mean 'worthless', and is certainly so meant in the earlier part of this section. Yet the later meaning is that 'Naught' is an ideal state, to be attained. Thus the final phrase 'this so very real world of ours...is Naught' can mean both that the world is worthless and that it is an ideal place.

39 *Die Welt als Wille und Vorstellung*, end of para. 35.

361

NOTES

CHAPTER VII

1 H. Weigand, *The Magic Mountain: a study of Thomas Mann's novel 'Der Zauberberg'*. Chapel Hill, N.C., 1964 (formerly called *Thomas Mann's novel 'Der Zauberberg'*).
2 Pascal, *The German Novel*, p. 269.
3 H. Hatfield, *Thomas Mann* (London, 1952), p. 11 and p. 9.
4 See p. 58 above.
5 *Der Zauberberg*, SA, vol. I, p. xxii.
6 See articles by Hans Eichner and J. A. Asher ('Thomas Mann and Goethe'), in *Publications of the English Goethe Society*, vol. XXVI, N.S. (1957), pp. 81–98.
7 *Der Zauberberg*, I, xxvi (in the lecture delivered by Mann at Princeton).
8 *Ibid.*
9 *Op. cit.* I, xxv.   10 See p. 120 above.
11 *Der Zauberberg*, II, 187.   12 *Op. cit.* II, 188.
13 *Op. cit.* II, 207. The ensuing quotations are from the next few pages of the novel.
14 *Op. cit.* II, 218.   15 *Op. cit.* II, 227.
16 *Op. cit.* II, 230.   17 *Op. cit.* II, 229.
18 For completeness' sake, it should be mentioned that the temple also contains a statue of a mother and child, presumably the kindlier counterpart, the polar opposite, of the horrible scene within: in other words, the temple is itself a unity containing a duality.
19 *Op. cit.* II, 228.
20 *Op. cit.* II, 572 (all remaining quotations *loc. cit.*).
21 See p. 12 above.

CHAPTER VIII

1 Many of the sentences in this story, as in others, in which the words 'der Mann' occur, seem to show a curious toying with Mann's own name, such as he thought typical of men of genius. (See the remarks on this in the essay, 'Tolstoi und Goethe'.) The words mean not only 'the man', but, in the German usage which puts the definite article before the personal name, simply 'Mann' ('Ein Mann' also occurs). The great majority of such instances here refer to Cipolla, e.g. 'I am a man of some self-love, put that in your pipes and smoke it!'; 'The man had as yet achieved nothing, but his speaking alone was esteemed as an achievement, and he had managed to make an impression with it....Elegance and mastery produce human respect, which is why even the little man ("der kleine Mann"), once he is concerned with making an effect, tries out choice turns of phrase and fashions them with care'; 'There was a cleavage between the interest in seeing something miraculous succeed and the wish that the pretentious man ("der anspruchsvolle Mann") might suffer a defeat'. Compare the joke in the Joseph novels about Abraham as the man from Ur of the Chaldees ('der Ur-Mann', or 'the original Mann').

NOTES

CHAPTER IX

1 *Der junge Joseph* (Berlin, 1934), p. 54.
2 *Op. cit.* p. 59.
3 *Joseph der Ernährer* (Stockholm, 1948), p. 152.
4 See p. 24 above.   5 *Der junge Joseph*, p. 238.
6 See Genesis xxxviii.   7 *Joseph der Ernährer*, p. 402.
8 *Op. cit.* p. 458.   9 *Op. cit.* p. 464.
10 *Loc. cit.*
11 We have already noted the phrase 'ein Mann wie ich'; at this point we may also refer to the curious claim made a little later on behalf of the author of the Joseph novels; 'Der Verfasser dieser Geschichte, unter welchem wir den zu begreifen haben, der alles Geschehen verfaßt...' (*Joseph der Ernährer*, pp. 471–2). Mann could have said of himself, as he did of Joseph, 'daß dies Höhere träumerisch-verführerisch ineinanderlief mit seiner Person'.
12 *Op. cit.* pp. 465–6.   13 *Op. cit.* p. 466.
14 Genesis xlv.   15 *Op. cit.* p. 596.
16 Heller, *The Ironic German*, p. 257.   17 See p. 163 above.

CHAPTER X

1 In *Der Erwählte* (*The Holy Sinner*) Mann becomes very conscious of the existence of the narrator and draws special attention to the fact that it is the narrator, not himself, who tells the story.
2 *Doktor Faustus* (Stockholm, 1947), p. 687.
3 This is a parallel to the twenty-four years of the pact made by Faust in the Renaissance 'Volksbuch'. For further details see E. M. Butler, 'The Traditional Elements in Thomas Mann's *Doktor Faustus*', in *Publications of the English Goethe Society*, vol. XVIII (1949).
4 *Doktor Faustus*, p. 382.
5 *Loc. cit.* 'Eine Sündhaftigkeit, so heillos, daß sie ihren Mann (*sic*; cf. note to chap. VIII) von Grund aus am Heile verzweifeln läßt, ist der wahrhaft theologische Weg zum Heil.'
6 After the devil has outlined the hell that is in storefor Leverkühn, and has concluded 'Das Extreme daran muß dir gefallen', Leverkühn replies 'Es gefällt mir', which, though not a pact, is a kind of acceptance.
7 Quoted by E. Cassirer in *The Platonic Renaissance in England*, p. 81.
8 S. Weil, *Waiting on God* (London, 1951), p. 4.
9 R. Knox, *Enthusiasm* (Oxford, 1950), p. 255.
10 The events leading to the murder may be recalled. Leverkühn and Schwerdtfeger are both in love with Marie Godeau, but Leverkühn is too much of a recluse to ask her hand in person. Schwerdtfeger has also been in love with Ines Roddes, and there is a homosexual relationship between the two men. Leverkühn sends Schwerdtfeger to woo Marie on his behalf; she declines him and grows attached to Schwerdtfeger instead. Ines Roddes, on hearing this, shoots Schwerdtfeger out of jealousy. In narrating this, Zeitblom suggests darkly that Leverkühn has foreseen and even planned this ending:

in sending Schwerdtfeger to Marie Godeau, Zeitblom hints, he was implicitly inviting Ines Roddes to murder him. But a plan so dependent on the unpredictable responses of three people, if it existed at all, reads like the dream of a madman, and the alternative explanation, that Leverkühn sent Schwerdtfeger in all *naïveté*, is never contradicted by the story. This is one more instance of an action outlined by Mann appearing both innocent and guilty, because no definite information is given about it.

11 *Doktor Faustus*, p. 577.   12 *Op. cit.* p. 578.

13 As, for instance, in these lines by Aragon:

> Gal, amant de la reine, alla, tour magnanime,
> Galamment de l'arène à la Tour Magne, à Nîmes.

14 I am not competent to deal with the question whether Arnold Schönberg's atonal music corresponds to the music of Leverkühn. Schönberg has written in *Style and Idea* that the twelve-tone set has 'no absolute down, no right or left, forward or backward', which at any rate suggests a kind of unity 'beyond the opposites' philosophically similar to Leverkühn's.

15 *Doktor Faustus*, p. 738.   16 *Loc. cit.*
17 *Op. cit.* p. 739.   18 *Op. cit.* p. 744.
19 *Op. cit.* p. 745.   20 *Op. cit.* p. 733.
21 *Op. cit.* p. 773.   22 *Op. cit.* p. 71.

CHAPTER XI

1 For the dates at which the different parts of the *Elegies* were written (the earliest in 1912), see E. C. Mason, *Lebenshaltung und Symbolik bei Rainer Maria Rilke* (Weimar, 1939).

2 The mood is very familiar to German readers, from association with the final scene in Schiller's *Don Carlos*, in which the passionate lover takes a restrained leave of the Queen.

3 The senses of the words 'rein' and 'Reinheit' may be appreciated from these paraphrases in Jacob Steiner, *Rilkes Duineser Elegien* (Berne and Munich, 1962): 'Ungestörtheit' (p. 196), 'frei vom Besitzergreifenwollen' (p. 148), 'von keiner Absicht gelenkt' (p. 194), 'von keinen Rücksichten auf Vorläufiges getrübt' (p. 96), 'von allen Zufällen frei' (p. 273).

4 Letter to Clara Rilke of 13 October 1907.

5 Rilke, *Ausgewählte Werke*, vol. II, p. 310.

6 S. S. Prawer, *German Lyric Poetry* (London, 1952), p. 222.

7 Rilke, 'Sonett auf Elizabeth Barrett Browning'.

8 *Ausgewählte Werke*, vol. II, p. 210.

9 The difficulty has been noted by one of the most conscientious and enlightening of Rilke's commentators, Romano Guardini: 'Here we resist, for a mirror behaves in the opposite fashion, first receiving, then reflecting. The mirror of the image must therefore be understood in a particular way, in the form of that movement of outgoing and return that has been mentioned above' (*Zu Rainer Maria Rilkes Deutung des Daseins*, Berne, 1946, p. 40). This is as much as to say, however, that the word 'mirrors' adds nothing to the thought, which is self-contained and has to be known already, from other

parts of the poem, if the passage is to make reasonable sense. (Jacob Steiner, who also compares the mirror image in Sonnet II, 3, does not find a difficulty here: 'Die Engel...strömen Schönheit aus. *Indem sie aber zugleich auch Spiegel sind, fangen sie sie* in den ihnen allein gemäßen, unbetretbaren Raum der reinen Bezüge...' (*Rilkes Duineser Elegien*, p. 45) (my italics).)

10 *Tractatus Logico-Philosophicus*, para. 6. 522. Wittgenstein, who contributed money to assist Rilke when they were both young men, is said to have found his later verse superficial. See Norman Malcolm's Memoir.

CHAPTER XII

1 *Der cherubinische Wandersmann*, 8. Spruch.
2 R. C. Zaehner, *Mysticism Sacred and Profane* (Oxford, 1957), p. 109.
3 Zaehner, *op. cit.* pp. 51–2.
4 'Burnt Norton.' My italics, except in the case of the German word.
5 Zaehner, *op. cit.* p. 204.
6 Quoted from the translation by J. B. Leishman in *Duino Elegies*, 3rd edn. (London, 1948), pp. 153–5.
7 The two pieces are printed consecutively under the title 'Erlebnis' in *Ausgewählte Werke*, vol. II, pp. 264–9.
8 *Selected Essays*, 3rd edn. (London, 1951), p. 258.
9 E.g. 'Der Ölbaumgarten', 'Pietà', 'Der Auferstandene', 'Christi Höllenfahrt', 'Auferweckung des Lazarus', 'Emmaus'.
10 Luke xxii. 43.
11 Compare Kafka's story, 'Der Jäger Gracchus', in this respect.
12 This is the only occasion in the Elegies where Rilke speaks of 'Gott', without the definite article that suggests a lesser deity.

CHAPTER XIII

1 Letter to his wife, 4 September 1908.
2 Letter to Clara Westhoff, 13 October 1907.
3 Letter to Kippenberg, Good Friday 1910.
4 Letter of 11 April 1910.
5 Letter of 13 May 1906 and of 8 September 1908.
6 Letter of 2 June 1909. 7 Letter of 30 August 1910.
8 Letter of 7 September 1910.
9 *Briefe aus Muzot*, no. 2 (undated). 10 See p. 266 above.
11 See *Dichtung und Volkstum* (1936), vol. I, facing p. 96, for a facsimile of the opening lines as originally written, with 34 more lines which were ultimately omitted.
12 Mr Leishman translates here 'inconsolable', which is also within the meaning of 'untröstlich'.
13 It was pointed out to me at a late stage in the composition of this book that the 'last line' referred to can sound settled, assured, even serene, and this I must admit to be true. The full truth is, perhaps, that the line is ambiguous and may be read either way with full justification, rather than that one reading is less justified than the other.

CHAPTER XIV

1 Quoted by Jane Harrison in *Prolegomena to the Study of Greek Religion*, 3rd edn. (1922), p. 471. E. M. Butler observes the 'remarkable resemblance' between the impression made by Orpheus (in Miss Harrison's account) and that made by Rilke (*Rainer Maria Rilke*, Cambridge, 1946, p. 343).

2 Harrison, *op. cit.* p. 464.

3 *Op. cit.* p. 473.

4 Quoted and translated by J. B. Leishman, *Sonnets to Orpheus*, 2nd edn. (1946), pp. 20–1.

5 Leishman, *op. cit.* p. 18.

6 With the exception of the first six lines of the Ninth, written in 1912.

CHAPTER XV

1 C. J. Burckhardt, *Erinnerungen an Hofmannsthal* (Basle, 1944), pp. 28–9.

2 R. Alewyn, *Über Hugo von Hofmannsthal* (Göttingen, 1958), p. 6.

3 Hofmannsthal, 'Gotthold Ephraim Lessing', in *Ausgewählte Werke*, ed. R. Hirsch (Frankfurt, 1957), vol. II, p. 775. (Hereafter referred to as *A.W.*)

4 Hofmannsthal, *Gesammelte Werke, Aufzeichnungen* (1959), p. 213.

5 *Ibid.* 6 *A.W.* I, 14.

7 *Aufzeichnungen*, p. 213.

8 Hofmannsthal, *Gedichte und Lyrische Dramen* (Stockholm, 1946), p. 291.

9 *A.W.* I, 37. 10 *Ibid.*

11 The surname of the central character, Bühl, has suggestive overtones of 'der Buhle', the lover.

12 E. Staiger, *Meisterwerke deutscher Sprache* (Zürich, 1957), p. 223.

13 *A.W.* I, 405. 14 *A.W.* I, 457.

15 *A.W.* I, 39; 'Dichtkunst':
Fürchterlich ist diese Kunst! Ich spinn aus dem Leib mir den Faden,
Und dieser Faden zugleich ist auch mein Weg durch die Luft.

16 *A.W.* I, 461. 17 *A.W.* I, 462.

18 F. N. Mennemeier in *Das Deutsche Drama*, ed. B. von Wiese (Düsseldorf, 1958), vol. II, p. 246.

19 *A.W.* I, 467. 20 *A.W.* I, 458.

21 *A.W.* I, 480. 22 *A.W.* I, 482.

23 *Andreas* (Berlin, 1932), p. 141.

24 *A.W.* I, 493. 25 *A.W.* I, 494. 26 *A.W.* I, 451.

27 *A.W.* I, 495. 28 *A.W.* I, 440. 29 *A.W.* I, 442.

30 *A.W.* I, 511. 31 *A.W.* I, 524. 32 *A.W.* I, 488.

33 *Ibid.* 34 *A.W.* I, 528. 35 *A.W.* II, 174.

36 *A.W.* I, 440. 37 *A.W.* I, 536. 38 *A.W.* I, 489.

39 *A.W.* I, 538.

CHAPTER XVI

1 D. H. Lawrence, *Phoenix* (London, reprinted 1961), p. 473.
2 See above, Introduction.
3 Letter of 10 April 1822, in Shelley's *Prose Works* (London, 1888), vol. II, p. 353.
4 Coleridge, *Table-Talk*, ed. C. Patmore (Oxford, 1917), p. 207 (16 February 1833).
5 *Loc. cit.*
6 *Wilhelm Meister* (London, 1899), Translator's Preface, p. 6.
7 *Op. cit.* p. 7.
8 M. Arnold, *Letters*, ed. G. W. E. Russell (London, 1895), letter dated December 1877.
9 *Samuel Butler*, by H. F. Jones (1919), vol. I, p. 216.
10 J. Ruskin, *Works* (London, 1903–12), vol. XXXVII, p. 277, letter of 17 March 1879.
11 De Quincey, *Collected Works*, ed. D. Masson (Edinburgh, 1890), vol. IV, p. 417.
12 M. Arnold, *Letters, op. cit.*
13 M. Arnold, *Mixed Essays* (London, 1880), p. 279.
14 *Op. cit.* p. 311.   15 *Loc. cit.*
16 T. S. Eliot, *On Poetry and Poets* (London, 1957), p. 67.
17 *Op. cit.* pp. 207–27.
18 See *Literary Reviews and Essays by Henry James*, ed. Albert Mordell (New York, 1957), pp. 110–18 and 118–22.
19 *Op. cit.* p. 268.   20 *Op. cit.* p. 269.
21 *Op. cit.* p. 270.
22 Wordsworth, *Prose Works* (1876), vol. III, p. 465. (Reminiscence by Lady Richardson, 26 August 1841.)
23 *Op. cit.* p. 435.
24 *Correspondence of G. M. Hopkins and R. W. Dixon*, ed. C. C. Abbott (London, 1935), p. 25 (letter of 27 February 1879).
25 *Letters of G. M. Hopkins* (London, 1938), p. 212 (letter of 4 April 1885).
26 For the plainest statement of this attitude, see the words put in the mouth of Karl Kraus by Erich Heller (unjustifiably, one hopes, in view of their illogicality) in his essay on the Austrian satirist. 'I mean what I say; yet what I say means the opposite of what you understand it to mean. Therefore I mean what I say *and* its opposite. Nevertheless, I mean something more exact than your sense of exactitude is likely to grasp. For the world of the word is round, and language is Delphi.' (E. Heller, *The Disinherited Mind*, Cambridge, 1952, p. 189.)
27 Heine, *Atta Troll*, first stanza of 'Kaput III'. ('Dream of midsummer night, fantastically aimless is my song. Yes, aimless as Love, as Life, as the Creator and Creation!')
28 A. Schönberg, *Style and Idea* (London, 1951), p. 113.
29 *Historic Survey of German Poetry*, by W. Taylor, of Norwich (London, 1830), vol. I, p. 385.
30 Cf. H. Chadwick, *Lessing's Theological Writings* (London, 1956).

31 George Saintsbury, *A History of Criticism*, vol. III, book VIII, chap. III (on 'Goethe and his Contemporaries').

32 'Das Unzulängliche, hier wird's Ereignis'—does it mean, as it appears to do, that in heaven 'the inadequate' becomes not transformed but in some way actualized, recognized as the providentially intended, true status of all human striving? That would not contradict the tenor of the rest of the work.

33 E. C. Mason, *Rilke's Apotheosis* (Oxford, 1938), p. 32.

34 See R. D'O. Butler, *The Roots of National Socialism 1783–1933* (London, 1941).

35 W. B. Yeats, *Autobiographies* (London, 1956), pp. 354–5.

36 M. Arnold, *Mixed Essays*, p. 309.

37 Quoted in R. Ellmann, *Yeats, the Man and the Masks* (London, 1949), p. 289.

38 See Letter to A. Huxley, 27 March 1928.

39 *Phoenix*, pp. 308–13.

40 *Phoenix*, p. 110.

41 *Women in Love*, Phoenix edition, p. 142.

42 *Op. cit.* p. 312.

43 Heinrich Suso, the medieval mystic, writing of the man who is 'entirely lost in God', adds the paradox that the same man's being 'remains, though in a different form, in a different glory, and in a different power' (quoted in R. C. Zaehner, *Mysticism, Sacred and Profane*, p. 21). Lawrence's 'human' mysticism, in which the male lover often seems close to the God of Suso, retains this old tradition of a distinctiveness in identity.

44 Letter to A. Huxley, 27 March 1928.

45 'Und so mein eigen Selbst zu ihrem [der Menschheit] Selbst erweitern.'

46 *Women in Love*, p. 470.

47 Gudrun thinks 'Gerald would be freer, more dauntless than Bismarck'.

48 *Women in Love*, p. 138.

49 I had not, at the time of writing, read R. L. Drain's dissertation (Cambridge, 1962), *Formative Influences on the work of D. H. Lawrence*. I am glad to find myself agreeing with Dr Drain on the idea that Nietzsche was for Lawrence a point of departure, but that Lawrence at his best put aside the egotist for the sake of taking 'our decent place' in the whole (*op. cit.* p. 233).

50 *Women in Love* in 1916, the *Elegies* between 1912 and 1922.

51 *Women in Love*, p. 138.

52 *Op. cit.* p. 436.

53 *Op. cit.* p. 312.

54 *Op. cit.* p. 472.

55 Cp. Uwe Kitzinger, 'The Death of Ideology', in *The Listener*, 18 January 1962.

56 *Women in Love*, p. 459.

57 *Op. cit.* p. 461.   58 *Op. cit.* p. 462.

59 *Op. cit.* p. 443.   60 *Op. cit.* p. 471.

61 Contrary to Dr Leavis's disclaimer, *D. H. Lawrence, Novelist*, p. 12, although I am generally in agreement with his views on *Women in Love*.

62 Quoted in Joseph H. Wicksteed, *Blake's Vision of the Book of Job* (London, 1910), p. 116.

SELECT BIBLIOGRAPHY

This list is meant to give indications of where more may be learned about the topics treated in this book; it therefore concentrates on introductory surveys of periods, themes or authors, especially those containing further bibliographies. Occasionally, however, more specialized works are included, when they are particularly worth recommending.

HISTORY AND POLITICS

For the general history of the period 1871–1945, see the bibliography in E. J. Passant and others, *A Short History of Germany 1815–1945* (Cambridge, 1959), which is divided into shorter periods and graded. For more detailed bibliographies on the shorter periods see H. Quigley and R. T. Clark, *Republican Germany* (London, 1928) and A. Bullock, *Hitler. A Study in Tyranny* (revised edn, London, 1962). The list of books consulted in W. M. Knight-Patterson, *Germany from Defeat to Conquest 1913–1933* (London, 1945) is long and contains some unusual items.

WRITERS AND POLITICS

Atkins, H. G. *German Literature Through Nazi Eyes*, London, 1941.

Berendsohn, W. A., *Die humanistische Front. Einführung in die deutsche Emigrantenliteratur.* Teil I. *Von 1933 bis zum Kriegsausbruch 1939*, Zürich, 1946.
Commentary interspersed with numerous bibliographies.

Bruford, W. H., *Culture and Society in Classical Weimar 1775–1806*, Cambridge, 1962.
See chapter VI, 'The Later History of the Weimar Ideals', which inquires about 'the fatal flaw in the philosophy of Goethe's Germany'.

Butler, E. M., *The Direct Method in German Poetry. An Inaugural Lecture*, Cambridge, 1946.
The 'direct method in poetry', when used in life, 'exterminates it on the grand scale'.

Butler, R. d'O., *The Roots of National Socialism, 1783–1933*, London, 1941.

Demetz, P., *Marx, Engels und die Dichter. Zur Grundlagenforschung des Marxismus*, Stuttgart, 1959.
Traces Marxist criticism of literature up to Lukács.

Esslin, M., *Brecht. A Choice of Evils*, London, 1959.

McGovern, W. M., *From Luther to Hitler. The History of Fascist-Nazi Political Philosophy*, Boston, New York, Chicago, 1941.

Marx–Engels–Lenin, *Über Kunst und Literatur. Aus ihren Schriften* (ed. M. Jakubietz and H. Koch), Leipzig, n.d. (Reclam series).

Masaryk, T. G., *Modern Man and Religion*, London, 1938.
By the President of Czechoslovakia. See chapters on 'Goethe's *Faust*' and 'German Faustism'.

Mayer, J. P., *Max Weber and German Politics*, London, 1944.

Rehfisch, H. J. (ed.), *In Tyrannos. Four Centuries of Struggle against Tyranny in Germany. A Symposium*, London, 1944.
Contains essays on Lessing, Hegel, Marx, Nietzsche, Kraus, etc.

Ritscher, H., *Fontane. Seine politische Gedankenwelt*, Göttingen, 1953.
Contains bibliography.

Rühle, J., *Literatur und Revolution. Die Schriftsteller und der Kommunismus*, 1960.

Santayana, G. *Egotism in German Philosophy*, London, 1916 and 1939.
'The German philosophers...shared and justified prophetically that spirit of uncompromising self-assertion and metaphysical conceit which the German nation is now reducing to action.'

Schonauer, E., *Deutsche Literatur im Dritten Reich. Versuch einer Darstellung in polemisch-didaktischer Hinsicht*, Olten and Freiburg im Breisgau, 1961.

Snyder, L. L., *German Nationalism. The Tragedy of a People*, Harrisburg, 1952.

Soergel, A., *Dichtung und Dichter der Zeit. Dritte Folge*, Leipzig, 1934.
Chapters on writers officially favoured after 1933. Less compendious than earlier volumes, see p. 371 below.

Sontheimer, K., *Thomas Mann und die Deutschen*, Munich, 1961.
Traces Mann's political development.

Stirk, S. D., *The Prussian Spirit. A Survey of German Literature and Politics, 1914–1940*. London, 1941.

——*German Universities—Through English Eyes*, London, 1946.

The Third Reich (U.N.E.S.C.O. publication), London, 1955.
On the intellectual origins of National Socialism.

Wulf, J., *Die bildenden Künste im Dritten Reich. Eine Dokumentation*, Gütersloh, 1963.
Concerns painting and sculpture, not literature.

WORKS OF REFERENCE

Kindermann, H. (ed.), *Wegweiser durch die moderne Literatur in Österreich*, Innsbruck, n.d. (1954?).
Dictionary entries in chronological order, beginning in the 1890's. Exhaustive.

Körner, J., *Bibliographisches Handbuch des deutschen Schrifttums*, 3rd edn, Berne, 1949.
Concise, authoritative bibliographies for all German literature.

Kosch, W., *Deutsches Literatur-Lexikon* (revised by B. Berger), Berne and Munich, 1963.

Lennartz, F., *Dichter und Schriftsteller unserer Zeit*, 7th edn, Stuttgart, 1957.
Dictionary entries.

Schmitt, F. and Fricke, G., *Deutsche Literaturgeschichte in Tabellen*. Teil III. *1770 bis zur Gegenwart*, Bonn, 1952.
Original typographical layout of facts. Conservative tendency in allocation of space to authors.

Smith, H., *A Dictionary of Modern European Literature*, Oxford, 1947.
Brief articles on European authors since Baudelaire.

Soergel, A., *Dichtung und Dichter der Zeit*, vol. 1, Leipzig, 1911; vol. 2, Leipzig, 1925. Vol. 1 revised by Curt Hohoff, Düsseldorf, 1961.
Compendious and exhaustive accounts of writers of Naturalist and Expressionist periods, with numerous portraits, photographs of book-illustrations, stage décors, manuscripts, etc.

Wiegler, P., *Geschichte der neuen deutschen Literatur*. 2. Band. *Von der Romantik bis zur Gegenwart*, Berlin, 1930.
Connected accounts of individual authors and plots of works, with no overall plan.

Wilpert, G. von, *Lexikon der Welt-Literatur*, Stuttgart, 1963.
Very full details of dates of publications, brief biographies, with wide coverage of German authors.

HISTORIES OF LITERATURE

Bithell, J., *Modern German Literature 1880–1938*, 2nd edn, London, 1946.
Contains bibliography.

Friedmann, H. and Mann, O., *Deutsche Literatur im Zwanzigsten Jahrhundert*, 2 vols., 4th edn, Heidelberg, 1961.
The principal authors treated by leading 'Literaturwissenschaftler'.

Mahrholz, W., *Deutsche Literatur der Gegenwart,* revised by M. Wieser, Berlin, 1930.
>   Of particular interest for its large bibliography, mainly of primary works.
Naumann, H., *Die deutsche Dichtung der Gegenwart,* 5th edn, Stuttgart, 1931.
>   The edition of 1933 was coloured by political events.
Robertson, J. G., *A History of German Literature,* 3rd edn, revised by E. Purdie and others, Edinburgh and London, 1959.
>   Contains bibliography.
Stammler, W., *Deutsche Literatur vom Naturalismus bis ʒur Gegenwart,* 2nd edn, Breslau, 1927.

Bennett, E. K., *A History of the German 'Novelle',* 2nd edn, revised by H. M. Waidson, Cambridge, 1961.
Pascal R. *The German Novel,* Manchester, 1956.
>   Contains chapters on Fontane, Mann, Kafka, etc.

NATURALISM AND EXPRESSIONISM

Linden, W., *Naturalismus,* Leipzig, 1936.
>   Vol. 1 in the uncompleted series 'Vom Naturalismus zur neuen Volksdichtung' in *Deutsche Literatur in Entwicklungsreihen* contains theoretical pronouncements by Naturalists, but is influenced in choice by political events.
Ruprecht, E., *Literarische Manifeste des Naturalismus 1880–1892,* Stuttgart, 1962.
>   Reprints manifestoes.
Edschmid, K., *Frühe Manifeste. Epochen des Expressionismus,* Hamburg, 1957.
>   Reprints manifestoes.
Martini, F., *Was war Expressionismus? Deutung und Auswahl seiner Lyrik,* Urach, 1948.
Raabe, P., *Die Zeitschriften des literarischen Expressionismus. Repertorium der Zeitschriften, Jahrbücher, Anthologien, Sammelwerke, Schriftenreihen und Almanache 1910–1921,* Stuttgart, 1964.
Samuel, R. and Hinton Thomas, R., *Expressionism in German Life, Literature and the Theatre 1910–24,* Cambridge, 1939.
Sokel, W. H., *The Writer in Extremis. Expressionism in Twentieth-Century German Literature,* Stanford, California, 1959.

INDIVIDUAL WRITERS

Ashton, E. B., *Primal Vision. Selected Writings of Gottfried Benn*, London, 1961.
Mainly translations. Contains a short bibliography.
Lennig, W., *Gottfried Benn in Selbstzeugnissen und Bilddokumenten*, Hamburg, 1962.
Documentary survey with bibliography.
Lohner, E., *Gottfried Benn. Bibliographie 1912–1956*, 2nd edn, Wiesbaden, 1960.

Demetz, P. (ed.), *Brecht*, Englewood Cliffs, New Jersey, 1962.
Anthology of criticisms.
Esslin, M., *Brecht. A Choice of Evils*, London, 1959.
Contains bibliography.
Gray, R. D. *Brecht*, Edinburgh and London, 1961.
Contains bibliography.
Kesting, M., *Bertolt Brecht in Selbstzeugnissen und Bilddokumenten*, Hamburg, 1959.
Documentary survey with bibliography.
Schumacher, E., *Die dramatischen Versuche Bertolt Brechts 1918–1933*, Berlin, 1955.
Willett, J., *The Theatre of Bertolt Brecht*, London, 1959.
Contains extensive bibliography.

Bennett, E. K., *Stefan George*, Cambridge, 1954.
Contains short bibliography.
Gundolf, F., *George*, Berlin, 1920.
By a close friend.
Klussmann, P. G., *Stefan George...mit einer George-Bibliographie*, Bonn, 1961.
Morwitz, E. and Valhope, C., *Poems by Stefan George*, London, 1944.
Originals and translations with an introduction by Ernst Morwitz, a close friend of the poet.
Schonauer, F., *Stefan George in Selbstzeugnissen und Bilddokumenten*, Hamburg, 1960.
Documentary survey with bibliography.

Alexander, N. E., *Studien zum Stilwandel im dramatischen Werk Gerhart Hauptmanns*, Stuttgart, 1964.
Garten, H. F., *Gerhart Hauptmann*, Cambridge, 1954.
Short bibliography.

Tank, K. L., *Gerhart Hauptmann in Selbstzeugnissen und Bilddokumenten*, Hamburg, 1959.
Documentary survey with bibliography.
Alewyn, R., *Über Hugo von Hofmannsthal*, 3rd edn, Göttingen, 1963.
Coghlan, B., *Hofmannsthal's Festival Dramas*, Cambridge and Melbourne, 1964.
Contains extensive bibliography.
Staiger, E., *Meisterwerke deutscher Sprache*, Zürich, 1957.
Contains chapter on *Der Schwierige*.

Paetel, K. O., *Ernst Jünger. Eine Bibliographie*, Stuttgart, 1953.
—— *Ernst Jünger in Selbstzeugnissen und Bilddokumenten*. Hamburg, 1962.
Documentary survey with bibliography.
Stern, J. P., *Ernst Jünger. A Writer of Our Time*, Cambridge, 1953.

Flores, A. and Swander, H. (edd.), *Franz Kafka Today*, Madison, 1958.
Anthology of criticisms with bibliography.
Gray, R. D. (ed.), *Kafka*, Englewood Cliffs, New Jersey, 1962.
Anthology of criticisms with bibliographical survey by H. S. Reiss.
Hemmerle, R., *Franz Kafka. Eine Bibliographie*, Munich, 1958.
Järv, H., *Die Kafka-Literatur. Eine Bibliographie*, Malmö and Lund, 1961.

Kerry, O., *Karl Kraus. Bibliographie*, Vienna, 1954.
Revised edition in preparation.
Kraft, W., *Karl Kraus. Beiträge zum Verständnis seines Werkes*, Salzburg, 1956
Wild, H. and Pfäfflin, F., *Nachrichten aus dem Kösel-Verlag. Sonderheft zum 90. Geburtstag von Karl Kraus*, Munich (Kösel), 1964.
Contains bibliography of Kraus's works and related material.

Bürgin, H., *Das Werk Thomas Manns. Eine Bibliographie*, Frankfurt, 1959.
Lists only primary literature.
Hatfield, H., *Thomas Mann. An Introduction to his Fiction*, London, 1952.
—— (ed.), *Thomas Mann*, Englewood Cliffs, New Jersey, 1964.
Anthology of criticisms.
Heller, E., *The Ironic German*, London, 1958.

Holthusen, H.-E., *Die Welt ohne Transcendenz. Eine Studie zu Thomas Manns 'Doktor Faustus' und seinen Nebenschriften*, Hamburg, 1949.

Jonas, K. W., *Fifty Years of Thomas Mann Studies: a Bibliography of Criticism*, Minneapolis, 1955.

Lukács, G., *Thomas Mann*, Berlin, 1949.
Study by the well-known Marxist critic.

—— *Wider den mißverstandenen Realismus*, Hamburg, 1958.
Contains essay 'Franz Kafka oder Thomas Mann?'

Mayer, H., *Thomas Mann. Werk und Entwicklung*, Berlin, 1950.
Study by East German critic who has since emigrated to the West.

Berghahn, W., *Robert Musil in Selbstzeugnissen und Bilddokumenten*, Hamburg, 1963.
Documentary study with bibliography.

Kaiser, E. and Wilkins, E., *Robert Musil. Eine Einführung in das Werk*, Stuttgart, 1962.

Bertram, E., *Friedrich Nietzsche*, 7th edn, 1929.

Jaspers, K., *Nietzsche. Eine Einführung in das Verständnis seines Philosophierens*, 2nd edn, 1947.

Lea, F. A., *The Tragic Philosopher. A Study of Friedrich Nietzsche*, London, 1957.

Oehler, M., *Die Deutsche Nietzsche-Literatur seit 1890*, 1938.

Guardini, R., *Rainer Maria Rilkes Deutung des Daseins. Eine Interpretation der Duineser Elegien*, Munich, 1953.
Translated as *Rilke's Duino Elegies*, London, 1961.

Holthusen, H.-E., *Rilke in Selbstzeugnissen und Bilddokumenten*, Hamburg, 1958.
Documentary survey with bibliography.

Mason, E. C., *Rilke*, Edinburgh and London, 1963.
Contains bibliography.

—— *Rilke's Apotheosis. A Survey of Representative Recent Publications on the Work and Life of R. M. Rilke*, Oxford, 1938.
A narration forming a critical bibliography.

Ritzer, W., *Rilke-Bibliographie*, Vienna, 1951.

Killy, W., *Über Georg Trakl*, Göttingen, 1960.

Mayer, H., *Richard Wagner in Selbstzeugnissen und Bilddokumenten*, Hamburg, 1959.
Critical survey with illustrations and bibliography.

Newman, E., *The Life of Wagner*, 4 vols., London, 1933–47.

SELECT BIBLIOGRAPHY

COMMENT AND CRITICISM

Deschner, K.-H., *Kitsch, Konvention und Kunst. Eine literarische Streitschrift*, Munich, 1957.
    Mainly on Hesse, Broch and Trakl.

Emrich, W., *Protest und Verheißung. Studien zur klassischen und modernen Dichtung*, Frankfurt a. M. and Bonn, 1960.
    Contains essays on Hauptmann, Hofmannsthal's *Der Schwierige*, Kafka, etc.

Hohoff, C., *Geist und Ursprung. Zur modernen Literatur*, Munich, 1954.
    Essays on Kafka, Benn, Jünger, etc.

Holthusen, H.-E., *Kritisches Verstehen. Neue Aufsätze zur Literatur*, Munich, 1961.
    Essay on Brecht, etc.

Jens, W., *Statt einer Literaturgeschichte*, Pfullingen, 1962.
    Essays on Brecht, Mann, Rilke, Hofmannsthal, Kafka, etc.

Kayser, W., and others, *Deutsche Literatur in unserer Zeit*, Göttingen, 1959.
    Essays on lyric, drama, novel, etc.

Martini, F., *Das Wagnis der Sprache. Interpretationen deutscher Prosa von Nietzsche bis Benn*, Stuttgart, 1954.

Muschg, W., *Von Trakl zu Brecht. Dichter des Expressionismus*, Munich, 1961.

Pfeiffer, J., *Wege zur Erzählkunst. Über den Umgang mit dichterischer Prosa*, Hamburg, 1953.
    Criticism of Mann, Hofmannsthal, Kafka, etc., as well as earlier writers.

Szondi, P., *Theorie des modernen Dramas*, Frankfurt, 1959.
    An influential study.

INDEX

INDEX